Reframing 1968

Reframing 1968

American Politics, Protest and Identity

Edited by
MARTIN HALLIWELL AND
NICK WITHAM

EDINBURGH
University Press

Edinburgh University Press is one of the leading university presses in the UK. We publish academic books and journals in our selected subject areas across the humanities and social sciences, combining cutting-edge scholarship with high editorial and production values to produce academic works of lasting importance. For more information visit our website: edinburghuniversitypress.com

Edinburgh University Press Ltd
The Tun – Holyrood Road, 12(2f) Jackson's Entry, Edinburgh EH8 8PJ

Typeset in 10/13 Giovanni by
Servis Filmsetting Ltd, Stockport, Cheshire
and printed and bound in Great Britain by
CPI Group (UK) Ltd, Croydon CR0 4YY

A CIP record for this book is available from the British Library

ISBN 978 0 7486 9893 6 (hardback)
ISBN 978 0 7486 9895 0 (paperback)
ISBN 978 0 7486 9894 3 (webready PDF)
ISBN 978 0 7486 9896 7 (epub)

CONTENTS

FIGURES

Stefan M. Bradley is Associate Professor and Chair in the Department of African American Studies at Loyola Marymont University. He is author of *Harlem vs. Columbia University: Black Student Power in the Late 1960s* (2009) and co-editor of *Alpha Phi Alpha: A Legacy of Greatness, The Demands of Transcendence* (2011). His work has featured in the *New York Times, Chronicle of Higher Education* and *Washington Post* and he is currently working on a new monograph, *Blackened Ivy: Civil Rights, Black Power and the Ivy League in Postwar America*.

Simon Hall studied history at Sheffield and Cambridge, and held a Fox International Fellowship at Yale University, before moving to the University of Leeds, where he is currently Professor of Modern History. He has published extensively on the civil rights and anti-war movements of the 1960s, the gay rights movement and the relationship between political protest and American patriotism. His monographs include *American Patriotism, American Protest: Social Movements since the Sixties* (2011) and *Rethinking the American Anti-War Movement* (2012), and his most recent book is *1956: The World in Revolt* (2016).

Martin Halliwell is Professor of American Studies at the University of Leicester. He is the author of ten books, including *The Constant Dialogue: Reinhold Niebuhr and American Intellectual Culture* (2005), *Therapeutic Revolutions: Medicine, Psychiatry, and American Culture,*

1945–1970 (2013) and *Voices of Mental Health: Medicine, Politics, and American Culture, 1970–2000* (2017), and he is the co-editor of *American Thought and Culture in the 21st Century* (2008) and *William James and the Transatlantic Conversation* (2014). He was the 18th chair of the British Association for American Studies.

Penny Lewis is Associate Professor of Labor Studies at the Joseph S. Murphy Institute for Worker Education and Labor Studies at the City University of New York. She writes about labour, class and social movements, and is the author of *Hardhats, Hippies and Hawks: The Vietnam Antiwar Movement as Myth and Memory* (2013) and co-editor of *The City is the Factory: New Solidarities and Spatial Strategies in an Urban Age* (2017). She is currently working on a public history project and tour guide, *A Peoples Guide to New York City*, and a study of the mass popular uprisings following the Arab Spring and Occupy.

Daniel Matlin is Senior Lecturer in the History of the United States since 1865 at King's College London. He is the author of *On the Corner: African American Intellectuals and the Urban Crisis* (2013), which was co-winner of the Arthur Miller Centre First Book Prize and of the Benjamin Hooks National Book Award for Outstanding Scholarly Work on the American Civil Rights Movement and Its Legacy. He has also published articles in the *Journal of American History* and *Journal of American Studies* and is currently researching the intellectual history of Harlem.

Sharon Monteith is Professor of American Literature and Cultural History at Nottingham Trent University and holder of a Leverhulme Major Research Fellowship. Her publications include *Gender and the Civil Rights Movement* (1999; 2004; 2017), *South to a New Place: Region, Literature, Culture* (2002), *Film Histories* (2006), *American Culture in the 1960s* (2008), *The New Encyclopedia of Southern Culture: Media* (2011), *The Transatlantic Sixties* (2013) and *The Cambridge Companion to the Literature of the American South* (2013). Her forthcoming book is *SNCC's Stories: Narrative Culture and the African American Freedom Struggle in the US South*.

Andrew Preston is Professor of American History at the University of Cambridge, where he is also a Fellow of Clare College. He is the author of *The War Council: McGeorge Bundy, the NSC, and Vietnam* (2006) and *Sword of the Spirit, Shield of Faith: Religion in American War and Diplomacy* (2012), and co-editor of four other books on various aspects of American diplomatic, political and transnational history, including *Nixon in the World* (2008) and, with Doug Rossinow, *Outside In: The Transnational Circuitry of US History* (2017).

Doug Rossinow is Professor of History at the University of Oslo. He is the author of *The Politics of Authenticity: Liberalism, Christianity, and the New Left in America* (1998) and *The Reagan Era: A History of the 1980s* (2015), among other works, and he is co-editor, with Andrew Preston, of *Outside In: The Transnational Circuitry of US History* (2017). He is currently writing a history of US Zionism since 1948.

Elizabeth Tandy Shermer is Assistant Professor of History at Loyola University Chicago. She has published widely on American politics and economic development. Her publications include opinion pieces, scholarly articles, edited collections and the monograph *Sunbelt Capitalism: Phoenix and the Transformation of American Politics* (2013). She is currently working on the political economy of higher education, first through a short book on the student-loan industry, *Indentured Students*, and a broader study of the trajectory of American public universities, provisionally titled 'The Business of Education'.

Stephen Tuck is Professor of Modern History at Pembroke College, University of Oxford. His research focuses on the history of racial oppression and resistance in the United States and its links abroad. He is a former Director of the Oxford Research Centre in the Humanities and his books include *Beyond Atlanta: The Struggle for Racial Equality in Georgia, 1940–1980* (2003), *We Ain't What We Ought To Be: The Black Freedom Struggle from Emancipation to Obama* (2010) and *The Night Malcolm X Spoke at the Oxford Union: A Transatlantic Story of Antiracist Protest* (2014).

Anne M. Valk serves as the Associate Director for Public Humanities at Williams College, Massachusetts. Since receiving her PhD from Duke University, she has published on topics related to feminism, oral history and public history, including *Radical Sisters: Second-Wave Feminism and Black Liberation in Washington, DC, 1963–1980*, a recipient of the Richard L. Wentworth Illinois Award in American History. Her second book, written with Leslie Brown, *Living with Jim Crow: African American Women and Memories of the Segregated South*, won the 2011 book award of the Oral History Association.

Stephen J. Whitfield holds the Max Richter Chair in American Civilization at Brandeis University, Massachusetts, where he has taught since 1972. He is the author of eight books, including *A Death in the Delta: The Story of Emmett Till* (1988), *The Culture of the Cold War* (1991; expanded edition 1996) and *In Search of American Jewish Culture* (1999). He has taught as Fulbright visiting professor at the Hebrew University of Jerusalem and at the Catholic University of Leuven and Louvain-la-Neuve in Belgium. Whitfield has taught American Studies twice at the Sorbonne and has served as Allianz visiting professor at the Ludwig–Maximilian University in Munich.

Nick Witham is Lecturer in US Political History at the Institute of the Americas, University College London. His first book, *The Cultural Left and the Reagan Era: US Protest and Central American Revolution* (2015), won the British Association for American Studies Arthur Miller Centre First Book Prize. He is currently working on a project titled 'The Popular Historians: American Historical Writing and the Politics of the Past, 1945–present'.

ACKNOWLEDGEMENTS

We first and foremost want to thank the talented authors included in this volume for their exceptional contributions to this reappraisal of the causes, consequences and legacy of 1968. When we began working on *Reframing 1968* in autumn 2013 we thought that as an act of historical remembrance we were on fairly stable ground. However, as we write these words, history has caught up with us, given the wave of protests in response to the surprise outcome of the 2016 US presidential election. Some of these chapters assess the links between 1968 and two contemporary protest movements – Occupy and Black Lives Matter – but we have not addressed the 'Not My President' demonstrations that criss-crossed campuses and cities during the winter of 2016–17 or the marches and rallies against the Trump administration that continued through 2017. Nor do we attempt to second-guess the potency or shape of future activist movements, except to say that we anticipate that anti-capitalist, civil rights and environmental protests are likely to intensify in the coming years, as an embodiment of what the New Year 2017 issue of the *New Yorker* calls the 'return of civil disobedience'.

For feedback on various aspects of this book we are grateful to colleagues and participants at a number of talks, including those given at the Modern Language Association Conference, Austin, Texas (January 2016); the British Association for American Studies annual conference at Queen's University Belfast (April 2016); the University of Cambridge American History

Seminar (October 2016); the US Studies Programme at King's College London (October 2016); and the Peter Whitehead and the Long 1960s conference at De Montfort University, Leicester (March 2017).

We would like to thank our two hugely supportive editors at Edinburgh University Press, Jenny Daly and Michelle Houston, as well as the two anonymous peer reviewers who provided vital comments and criticism. Martin would like to express gratitude to the following for direction and advice on a whole range of matters during the development and writing of this volume: Zalfa Feghali, Corinne Fowler, Jo Gill, Andrew Johnstone, Will Kaufman, George Lewis, Philip McGowan, Catherine Morley, Andy Mousley, Joel Rasmussen, Annette Saddik, Phil Shaw, Joe Street, Brian Ward, Harry Whitehead and Alex Zagaria. In terms of the longer arc of this project, he would like to acknowledge the influence of the ground-breaking 68/98 event, organized by Laraine Porter and Steve Chibnall at Phoenix Arts, Leicester, in March 1998. Nick would like to show his gratitude to the colleagues and friends who gave him important feedback on chapter drafts and talks as the volume developed: Jonathan Bell, Gary Gerstle, Josh Hollands, Zoe Hyman, Ruth Lawlor, Kevin Middlebrook, Maxine Molyneux, Iwan Morgan, Kate Quinn and Kate Saunders-Hastings. As ever, Lydia Plath provided vital support at all the right moments. Nick also wants to thank Roger Fagge, whose undergraduate module on twentieth-century US political and social history at the University of Warwick ignited an interest in the 1960s that has now lasted more than a decade.

For enabling us to publish the images in this volume we are very grateful to Gerald Adler; the Beinecke Rare Book and Manuscripts Library, Yale University (both archivist Susan Brady and Thomas Walker of the Living Theatre); the Rare Book & Manuscript Library, Columbia University (particularly archivist Jocelyn Wilk); PA Images; Rex Features; the David M. Rubenstein Rare Book & Manuscript Library, Duke University (and the collection librarian Kelly Wooton); the Victoria and Albert Museum, London; the Peter Whitehead Archive, De Montfort University, Leicester (both to Harry Whitehead and Steve Chibnall); and the Woody Guthrie Center, Tulsa (especially Michael Ochs).

Every effort has been made to find and contact copyright holders but if any have been inadvertently overlooked the publisher will be happy to make the necessary adjustments at the first opportunity.

Martin Halliwell and Nick Witham
Leicester and London (April 2017)

1968: A Year of Protest

Martin Halliwell and Nick Witham

Speaking at a civil rights conference in London in May 2016, Jon Else, activist and co-producer of the landmark documentary *Eyes on the Prize*, pictured 1968 as a 'year of tremendous chaos and heartache'.[1] Given Else's work in helping to protect voter rights in Mississippi during the mid-1960s, he was thinking particularly of the death of the civil rights leader Martin Luther King, Jr. in Memphis on 4 April 1968 and the race riots that engulfed the cities of Washington DC, Chicago, Cincinatti, Trenton and Baltimore in the ensuing days. This evocative phrase 'tremendous chaos and heartache' stretches in two directions. It speaks to the obvious tragedies of the year – the assassinations of King and New York Senator Robert F. Kennedy two months later, and the rising body count of the Vietnam War – but also to the intensifying schisms between successive generations, political persuasions and social groups that in 1968 led to more directly confrontational action than in previous years. Although insurgencies were nothing new in the history of the United States, a culture of rebellion marked a year that saw critiques of authority yoked to the conviction that institutions of power should be held immediately accountable for their divisive policies. In this respect, Else's words are delicately balanced between social analysis and emotional engagement. However, although the phrase may prompt us to think about the year's key events in terms of death, destruction and loss, as the thirteen essays in this volume explore, 1968 also witnessed the birth of new political directions and alliances.

The importance of the year is beyond dispute, not just as a flash-point in the twentieth-century United States, but across the Americas and Europe too. It is equally clear that there is no consensus about what '1968' means, either as an intensely experienced twelve-month period or as a symbol of radical protest. Generations of critics, scholars and public figures have wrestled with this question of meaning and have arrived at different conclusions. These conclusions are largely determined by the level of personal involvement in the events of that year, the evaluation of less confrontational forms of protest, and in terms of how later moments colour the historical lens.[2] For these reasons 1968 is a complex signifier and one that warrants reappraisal in the form of this fifty-year anniversary volume.

1968 in Decennial Focus

The power of 1968 has resounded especially at ten-year intervals. It is there, for example, in the opening pages of Charles Kaiser's twenty-year retrospective *1968 in America*, in which the thirty-eight-year-old Kaiser remembers a year that 'marked the end of hope' for many young Americans like himself, but also brought to the surface 'the power of idealism, the power of music, the power of the bullet, and the power of the press'.[3] The year clearly had a hold on Kaiser thirty years later, signifying what Doug Rossinow in the first chapter of this volume calls a 'watershed of mobilization, confrontation and global youth consciousness'. However, the tendency to exaggerate 1968 as a watershed has often led to a formulaic rehashing of its most newsworthy events. A June 1978 ABC documentary, *1968: A Crack in Time*, for example, called it a 'monstrously dangerous year', and two months later a CBS news special took stock of a 'year we're still paying for'.[4] The tendency to recycle hyperbolic phrases is evident in the title of a *Time* magazine twenty-year retrospective, '1968: The Year that Shaped a Generation', and the forty-year *Guardian* piece '1968: The Year that Changed Everything', as well as the subtitle of Mark Kurlansky's 2005 book *1968: The Year that Rocked the World*.[5] This sensationalism speaks to what Kurlansky, who offers a month-by-month global account, sees as the unique status of 1968 among other years that could be claimed as major turning points.[6]

Such a hyperbolic impulse often overshadows other, more nuanced reinterpretations. One example of this is the twenty-year retrospective *Chicago 68/88: Visions of Dissent* run by the Chicago Filmmakers group in August 1988. This exhibition sought to 'dig deeper into the surface of 1968 than what was shown on television at the time' by mixing archive film and photography from 1968 (some of which revisited the violent demonstrations that surrounded that September's Democratic National Convention) with later cultural takes on the ripple-effects of the year.[7] These later texts included the hard-hitting 1971 documentary *The Murder of Fred Hampton* (focusing on the assassination of the Illinois Black Panther leader in December 1969) and Jon Jost's 1988 film essay *Uncommon Senses* (which grapples with the ways in which technology and media changed the country in the 1970s and 1980s).

Often accounts of 1968 take a parallax view in which writers and critics struggle to recapture the raw experiences of the year, even as they recognize the difficulty of doing so. An instructive example of this is novelist Paul Auster's 2008 *New York Times* piece 'The Accidental Rebel'. This column returns to the Columbia University student protests of April 1968 from a forty-year vantage point, which paradoxically gives Auster both clarity on and a disconnection from those events. He begins the piece with the line: 'It was the year of years, the year of craziness, the year of fire, blood and death . . . the world seemed headed for an apocalyptic breakdown.'[8] Despite the revolutionary language, as a literature student at Columbia, Auster only reluctantly joined the cause, not as he says to protest the building of a segregated gymnasium in the neighbouring African American community of Morningside Park (see Chapters 4, 6 and 7), but because he had 'the poison of Vietnam in my lungs' and like his fellow Columbia students, he surmises, he needed to 'lash out at something, anything'.

The young Auster was carried along by the culture of dissent, but forty years later he believed that the occupation of five university buildings did not accomplish 'much of anything'. He concludes that the student sit-ins were effective in preventing the building of the gymnasium, but they had little tangible influence on the Vietnam War or on curbing the bullish exercise of police powers. He thinks, ultimately, that attacking the power base of a private university was only a symbolic gesture and less meaningful than the class-based insurgency of French students in Paris in early May, only a week after New York City Police broke up the Columbia occupation. A column that begins with great drama and activist potential ends with an image of the solitary author, now in his sixties, contemplating the long drawn-out war in Iraq – a war which was in contravention of President Reagan's and Bush's promises in the 1980s and early 1990s to beat the 'Vietnam syndrome' by avoiding extended overseas conflicts (as discussed in Chapter 3).

The fact that Auster wrote the essay following a wave of grassroots and campus protests against what many Americans thought was an unnecessary, if not illegal, war led him to suggest that activism, at least in this form, is futile. Auster's column certainly raised the hackles of three Columbia alumni who were motivated to write to the *New York Times* editor to complain. The first correspondent argued that Auster underestimated the importance of the campus protests, claiming that they 'instilled passion in many of the participants' and were life-changing for many in both deed and imagination.[9] The second believed that this wave of student activism illuminated the dangers of overseas combat, stating that the Columbia demonstrations were 'a small step' in the right direction of forging a democratic polity. And the third correspondent pointed to the 'enormous energy and momentum' that he believed stemmed from the protests, although he ends with a sigh, wishing that such accomplishments were still possible. The second and third correspondents kept alive the hope that social movements could emerge or gain momentum from dramatic events, but they also returned nostalgically to a moment when some activist groups were coming together while others were splintering. The three letters resonate with Else's phrase 'tremendous chaos and heartbreak', even though they differ from his view that 'everything went wrong in 1968'.[10] More importantly, the dialogue provoked by Auster's *New York Times* piece suggests that no single take on one of the major protest events of 1968 can do justice to the year or explain its historical reach.[11]

To address the question of what this singular year means a half century later, when many of its participants are now in their seventies (among the student generation) or have passed away (among institutional leaders of the time), *Reframing 1968* offers a series of intersecting readings that revisit the events, ideas, processes and texts that account for the significance of the year, as well as what Kristin Ross calls its 'afterlives'.[12] The thirteen authors in this volume not only approach 1968 from different perspectives, but they trace the arc of the year in distinctive ways, focusing particularly on clashes between divergent agendas, opinions and persuasions. Sometimes the year is read as the culmination of a sequence of events; other essays see the year as a working through of a complex and sometimes occluded historical process; others interpret it as an emergent phase for movements that became more obviously visible during the 1970s. In this respect, *Reframing 1968* shares with the 2013 volume *The Long 1968* the commitment to avoid simply chronicling the headline events of the year in favour of exploring 'connections, diachronic as well as synchronic' that explain what 1968 meant in its own moment and what it means now, half a century later.[13]

It is easy, as Auster discerned in 'The Accidental Rebel', to pile too much significance into a single year or to invest heightened symbolism in certain public figures and events. It is easy, too, to fall into the trap of polarizing the year along ideological lines: either valorizing rebellion as morally right whatever its cause or condemning dissent as unpatriotic and even un-American. Despite the symbolism that often marks anniversaries and commemorations, 1968 is, as Michael A. Cohen discerns in *American Maelstrom: The 1968 Election and the Politics of Division* (2016), undeniably a year which now serves 'as an inflection point on the language and tenor of American politics' – even if Richard Nixon's election as the nation's thirty-seventh president in November of that year looked like a lurch back to the 1950s rather than a shift forward.[14] By exploring these 'inflection points' across a spectrum of political, cultural and social activities, these thirteen essays, from diverse angles and at varying speeds, each attempt to move beyond historical fetishization and ideological polarization to investigate the trajectory and legacy of modern protest movements in the United States – which, as the images included in this volume illustrate, cannot be reduced to a particular kind or paradigmatic mode.

Key Themes in The American 1968

In order to pursue these directions, *Reframing 1968* is organized into three parts, each of which aims to rethink the political, cultural, intellectual and social contexts that framed American protest and activism in the late 1960s. The first part of the book, 'Politics of Protest', examines the ideological and political underpinnings of the upheaval that characterized 1968 in the United States, discussing the New Left, the New Right, the legacy of the Vietnam War and the political idea of 1968. Part Two, 'Spaces of Protest', considers how activism was shaped by the physical, cultural and institutional spaces in which it was located, from the city to the university campus, and from musical and theatrical performances to cinema and television screens. And the third part, 'Identities and Protest', extends the frame to examine the significance of 1968 for a range of previously marginalized communities: African Americans, gays and lesbians, women and the working class, to assess to what extent the legacy of 1968 has impacted upon the rights and citizenship of these groups.

Drawing together these areas of politics, space and identity are four major themes that run through all the chapters. The first concerns memories of protest: how has individual and collective memory shaped the historiography of 1968? How has our understanding of 1960s protest changed as the voices of historians with no direct memory or personal experience of the period have begun to predominate? The second centres on the precise forms that protest took: how did the definition of what constituted protest change during the 1960s? What made for effective protest and why did many protest movements fail or morph into different forms of action? What did it mean to begin to think of protest as a cultural as well as a social and political act? The third interrogates the discordant ideologies that motivated sixties protestors: What were the ideological commonalities and disparities undergirding the forms of protest that shaped the upheavals of 1968? To what extent can the 1960s be thought of as a decade of the 'left' or the 'right' and how has this ideological divide played out in the fifty years since? Finally, the authors consider the geographies of protest in 1968: to what extent have recent conceptualizations of the 'global 1960s' altered understandings of 1968 in the United States? To what extent did a combination of local, national and international factors influence the nature of protest in the period? In addressing these overlapping themes, the authors demonstrate the intersectionality of the activist moment represented by 1968. As Penny Lewis so aptly states in Chapter 12, 'the social movements of the 1960s, taken together, foregrounded the interpenetration of capitalism, multi-faceted oppressions and war'.

By reframing the US experience of 1968, we hope to show how a series of global, national, regional and local conflicts overlapped to draw Americans' attention to the deep fissures in their nation's politics. In the two decades since 1998, a considerable body of scholarship has developed seeking to re-conceptualize our understanding of the 1960s by decentring the position of the nation state in narratives of the decade and its activism. In some cases, such as Arthur Marwick's *The Sixties* (1998) and Gerd-Rainer Horn's *The Spirit of '68* (2008), this has involved comparative research focusing on the commonalities between experiences of the decade in the United States and Western Europe.[15] Indeed, the success of popular histories by Mark Kurlansky and Gerard DeGroot have shown how comparative global histories of the 1960s can reach audiences outside of the academy.[16] Other scholars, such as Jeremi Suri in his book *Power and Protest* (2003), have charted the history of the decade's social movements and their relationship to international political developments, thus demonstrating the interpenetration of foreign and domestic politics across the globe.[17] However, perhaps the most productive vein of historical writing on the global sixties has developed out of a central concern with the overlapping webs and interpenetrating networks of activists themselves. For example, Martin Klimke has highlighted the intersections between West German and American student protests, Daniel Geary has shown how the ideas of C. Wright Mills circulated amongst activists involved in the global political culture of the student New Left, and Sara M. Evans has argued that gender played a fundamental role in structuring young people's understandings of the transnational 1968.[18] Internationalism was also a significant factor shaping the way the 1960s were experienced by people of colour, especially those involved in anti-racist activism. Cynthia Young, Judy Wu and

Lorena Oropeza have argued that international travel and transnational communication contributed significantly to the protest cultures of African American, Asian American and Chicana/o activists respectively throughout the decade.[19] In all of these cases, protest has remained a central motif, but with an emphasis since 1998 on its transnational implications for an inherently globalized world.

In returning to think about the specifically *national* meanings of 1968 in the United States, we do not seek to resist this 'transnational turn' in the study of the 1960s. Instead, we argue that the historiographical innovations of transnationalism only become fully visible once they are brought to bear on the national and regional specificities of grassroots politics and protest. In other words, whilst the process of decentring the nation state has been vital to the recent study of the 1960s, and of 1968 in particular, it is important not to lose sight of how particular national experiences can be better understood with the help of international, transnational and global insights. Another way in which the collection aims to 'reframe' 1968, then, is by bringing these various approaches into constructive dialogue.

1968's Reverberations

A further motive for bringing together the themes of the three sections – politics, spaces and identities of protest – is to assess how the events and ideas of 1968 resonate through its afterlives. The reverberations were felt strongly in the following decade, but over the fifty years since then their meaning and significance have become ever-more contested, as Chapters 9 and 10 exemplify. Stephen Tuck questions whether the 1970s actually saw the end of the civil rights movement, as is commonly interpreted, or whether it provided both a springboard 'for unprecedented confrontational protest' and a platform to 'extend the rights of African Americans rather than simply defend previous gains'. In contrast, Simon Hall shows how the 'spirit of '68' played out for gay rights activists beyond the Stonewall moment of 1969, by tracing the complex relationship between the Gay Liberation Front and radical protest.

For other authors, it is two recent movements that strike chords with the protests of 1968. The first of these is the Occupy movement that emerged in 2011 but can be traced to the disruption of the Seattle World Trade Organization convention by anti-capitalists in winter 1999. The global movement with its slogan 'occupy everywhere' found its activist impetus in the wake of worldwide recession, as recognized by Todd Gitlin, leader of the Students for a Democratic Society in the mid-1960s – although Gitlin's interest in Occupy is more for its differences than its similarities to sixties-style protest.[20] The second of these is Black Lives Matter, which has confronted systemic racial violence triggered by a wave of police shootings since 2013. On an intellectual level, the Black Lives Matter movement can be seen to reflect the indictment of white racism in the Kerner Report of February 1968 (prepared for President Johnson by the National Advisory Committee on Civil Disorders) and, on an activist level, it reprises collective resistance to the brutal tactics of law enforcement officers to disperse the Columbia University sit-ins of April 1968 and outside the Chicago Democratic Convention that September. As Daniel Matlin discusses in Chapter 5, violent policing remains one of 'the most explosive issue[s] in American race relations'.[21]

It is too soon to provide a full historical appraisal of these two movements, but the communication networks that underpin them (albeit now organized via social media and with a more dispersed leadership) are reminiscent of the grassroots and underground information channels by which protestors connected in the late 1960s. Each of these movements has set its sights high to tackle systems of power and to make democracy accountable. This might suggest the revival of a unified counterculture with a common cause – injustice framed economically and racially – in contrast to the factions associated with a fraying of revolutionary potential in the 1970s. The specific demands of Occupy and Black Lives Matter may not be as clear as they were for 1960s protesters, but the two agendas make visible the ideological and social pressures rooted in locality and place at the same time that they point to transnational questions of inequality, violence and oppression. These geographies return us to our primary focus on protest within the United States – both at and below the federal level – but with an eye on broader processes that resonate across temporal, spatial and conceptual borders.

If, as the intellectual historian Richard King asserts, the mid-1960s can be read as a shift from the universalizing humanist values that shaped the post-World War II period to the particularism that spoke to the identity politics of the decade's emerging social movements, so 1968 brought these two impulses to a head.[22] And if, as Stephen Whitfield discusses in this volume's conclusion, 1968 can be read as the apotheosis or 'coming apart', then these essays tackle both this national fraying and the varieties of protest that have emerged in the decades since. The year 1968 was undoubtedly one of 'tremendous heartache and chaos', to recall Jon Else's phrase, but it also raises profound questions about historical change, group dynamics, institutional power, the ethics of foreign policy, political contestation and cultural interconnection. There is a broad sweep to some of these topics – to their global resonances and historical echoes – but also a fascinating particularity that returns us to the indissoluble aspects of 1968. These thirteen essays do not speak to all the specificities of those twelve months. Nor do we claim that it was the year that changed everything. But what we try to capture within these pages are the many compelling stories that emerged in 1968 and that continue to pulse through the second decade of the twenty-first century.

Notes

1. 'Civil Rights, Documentary Cinema and the 1960s: Transatlantic Conversations on History, Race and Rights', British Academy, London, 24–26 May 2016. See Jon Else, *True South: Henry Hampton and 'Eyes on the Prize,' the Landmark Television Series that Reframed the Civil Rights Movement* (New York: Viking, 2017).
2. Some of these conflicting views are captured in a thirty-year *Washington Post* piece that links the tumult of the late 1960s to the culture wars of the 1990s: 'One Nation, Torn Apart: The '60s Culture Clash Underlies a New Crisis', *Washington Post* (19 December 1998).
3. Charles Kaiser, *1968 in America* (New York: Weidenfeld and Nicolson, 1988), x.
4. *1968: A Crack in Time*, ABC (11 June 1978), and *1968: A Year That Changed America*, CBS (27 August 1978).
5. '1968: The Year that Shaped a Generation', *Time* (11 January 1988); '1968: The Year that Changed Everything', *The Guardian* (17 January 2008); Mark Kurlansky, *1968: The Year that Rocked the World* (New York: Random House, 2005).

6. For example, Fred Kaplan argues that 1959 was actually the year that 'every-thing changed': Fred Kaplan, *1959: The Year Everything Changed* (London: Wiley, 2009).

7. The Director of the Chicago Filmmakers, Linda Balek, as quoted in 'Film, Photo Exhibit Replays What '68's World Was Watching', *Chicago Tribune* (12 August 1988).

8. Paul Auster, 'The Accidental Rebel', *New York Times* (23 April 2008). For broader context see the University Protest and Activism Collection, 1958–1999 in the Columbia University Archives. A photographic exhibition of the April 1968 occupation is available at the 1968: Columbia in Crisis website: exhibitions.cul.columbia.edu/exhibits/show/1968

9. 'In '68, Our Protest Made a Difference', *New York Times* (30 April 2008). Auster also discusses his time as a Columbia student in *Hand to Mouth: A Chronicle of Failure* (New York: Picador, [1997] 2003).

10. Else, *True South*, 28.

11. April is a popular month for protests at Columbia University. This includes occupations of Low Library when students pressured the university administration to open an ethnic studies department (in April 1996) and to divest from fossil fuel companies (in April 2016).

12. See Kristin Ross, *May '68 and its Afterlives* (Chicago: University of Chicago Press, 2002).

13. Daniel Sherman et al. (eds), *The Long 1968: Revisions and New Perspectives* (Bloomington: Indiana University Press, 2013), 1.

14. Michael A. Cohen, *American Maelstrom: The 1968 Election and the Politics of Division* (Oxford: Oxford University Press, 2016), 8.

15. Arthur Marwick, *The Sixties: Cultural Revolution in Britain, France, Italy, and the United States, c.1958–c.1974* (New York: Oxford University Press, 1998); Gerd-Rainer Horn, *The Spirit of '68: Rebellion in Western Europe and North America, 1956–1976* (New York: Oxford University Press, 2008). See also Grzegorz Kosc et al. (eds), *The Transatlantic Sixties: Europe and the United States in the Counterculture Decade* (Bielefeld: Transcript-Verlag, 2013).

16. Kurlansky, *1968*; Gerard DeGroot, *The Sixties Unplugged: A Kaleidoscopic History of a Disorderly Decade* (Basingstoke: Macmillan, 2008).

17. Jeremi Suri, *Power and Protest: Global Revolution and the Rise of Détente* (Cambridge, MA: Harvard University Press, 2003).

18. Martin Klimke, *The Other Alliance: Student Protest in West Germany and the United States During the Global 1960s* (Princeton: Princeton University Press, 2010); Daniel Geary, '"Becoming International Again": C. Wright Mills and the Emergence of a Global New Left, 1956–1962', *Journal of American History* 95 (December 2008), 710–36; Sara M. Evans, 'Sons, Daughters and Patriarchy: Gender and the 1968 Generation', *American Historical Review* 114(2) (April 2009), 331–47.

19. Cynthia Young, *Soul Power: Culture, Radicalism, and the Making of a U.S. Third World Left* (Durham, NC: Duke University Press, 2006); Judy Tzu-Chun Wu, *Radicals on the Road: Internationalism, Orientalism, and Feminism during the Vietnam Era* (Ithaca, NY: Cornell University Press, 2013); Lorena Oropoeza,

¡Raza Sí! ¡Guerra No! Chicano Protest and Patriotism During the Viet Nam War Era (Berkeley: University of California Press, 2005).

20. See Todd Gitlin, *Occupy Nation: The Roots, the Spirit, and the Promise of Occupy Wall Street* (New York: HarperCollins, 2012). On the horizontal organization of Occupy and its communication channels, see Stuart Price and Ruth Sanz Sabido (eds), *Contemporary Protest and the Legacy of Dissent* (London: Rowman & Littlefield, 2015), 61–110.

21. For a comparison of the 1968 and 2015 race riots in Baltimore (the latter following the death of twenty-five-year-old Freddie Grey whilst in police custody), see 'Lessons for Baltimore from 1968', *Time* (29 April 2015). See also Christopher J. Lebron, *The Making of Black Lives Matter: A Brief History of an Idea* (New York: Oxford University Press, 2017).

22. See Richard H. King, *Civil Rights and the Idea of Freedom* (Baltimore: Johns Hopkins University Press, 1992).

Part One

Politics of Protest

ONE

The New Left: The American Impress

Doug Rossinow

The New Left was all about reinvention. Any leftist movement wishes to remake society. But beneath this drive for large-scale change, many radical insurgencies also entail dreams of transformation for the individuals who throw in with them. This was certainly true of the New Left, and its members were very conscious and open about that personal goal. A protest wave that embraced slogans such as 'We are the vanguard of fantasy', 'All power to the imagination!' and 'I am a Marxist, of the Groucho tendency' – the latter two graffiti associated more with French New Leftists than with the United States, but celebrated across national boundaries – was one that declined to sacrifice inner yearnings at the altar of social-structural change.[1] In New Left thought, individuals committed to their own rebirth would be those willing to embrace the status of political outsiders, even revolutionaries. But the connection between personal and social change worked both ways. The very experience of risk and struggle would assist in the pursuit of a life more intense, meaningful and intact than the divided and isolated state of 'alienation' that radicals decried as the fate of humans within a capitalist, racist and imperialist society.

These visions of transformation form an established part of the New Left's record, but this movement's profile etched two additional styles of reinvention that also should be described clearly. First, the New Left's history embodied a paradoxical reality of transnational protest and North American primacy. The US war against the Vietnamese revolution drove a global surge of leftist protest, often taking an anti-American form that began to remake the world's left into a political formation whose concerns centered on Washington DC. The New Left made a distinct North American impress on the global left – a figure with longevity to match that of US power itself – even as it was merely a segment of a worldwide youth rebellion. The New Left inside the United States was globalized in the years leading up to the political explosions of 1968. But US radicals also did much to Americanize the global left.

Second, the New Left announced with its very name, which was first spoken between 1956 and 1960, its intention to transform the tradition of the modern left within the United States itself. Just as the New Testament reorganized Jewish scripture as the Old Testament, the coinage 'New Left' invented the idea of the 'Old Left'. The New Left succeeded in making long-term changes within American radicalism. The New Left's anti-systemic protest stance retained its legitimacy long after the broad political circumstances that had produced the sharply anti-systemic ambience of 1968 vanished. 'Leaderlessness' and even 'structurelessness' became features, not bugs, in the Left's operating system of protest. Some of the modes and methods of the New Left proved remarkably durable in fixing the horizon for North American rebellion.

Incorporating these transformations, 1968 became not just a date but also a myth for the world's left, a prolonged moment understood as a watershed of mobilization, confrontation and global youth consciousness. It marked, in the true, lived experience of the New Left, not the movement's demise, as some – disillusioned with New Left neo-Marxism and anti-imperialism – once lamented. Nor, on the other hand, did it signal the triumph of an exhilarating new politics that fused pleasure with revolt. Instead, 1968 is better understood as a fork in the road. From this juncture, several paths forward diverged for the New Left. Tracing each of these paths reveals the fate of the New Left's efforts at transformation.

This essay now proceeds in three parts. First, it recounts crucial themes and transitions in the history of the New Left in the United States, explaining how 1968 was a splitting-off point that opened onto several ways of radicalism. Second, it explores the imperial Americanization of the global left. And, third, it explains how the New Left changed North American radicalism for the long term.

Together, these matters compose much of the lasting legacy of the New Left.

The New Left through 1968

The New Left in the United States appeared around 1960, with the formation of Students for a Democratic Society (SDS), the insurgency of the Student Nonviolent Coordinating Committee (SNCC) – which focused on mobilizing African Americans to struggle against white supremacy, and which, if it was not truly a part of the New Left, was certainly a major catalyst for it – and the militant activism of other youth-based groups around the country. The term 'New Left' had emerged earlier in France and Britain, specifically to announce the disaffection of young Communist intellectuals from Moscow's leadership following the Soviet Union's 1956 invasion of Hungary.[2] The role of former Communists in the origin of the New Left was comparatively minor in the United States. The more important US precursors to the New Left were nonviolent protesters, many of them from a definite Christian background and typically very impressed with the thought of Mohandas Gandhi. From the 1940s onward they tilted their lances at 'the warfare state', nuclear weapons testing and US racial apartheid, with what they called 'direct action'. Their most important forum for discussion was the journal *Liberation*, founded in 1956. Figures in the *Liberation* circle like David Dellinger and Staughton Lynd, and most of all the storied leaders of SNCC such as Robert Moses, Ruby Doris Smith and John Lewis, accrued unmatched moral authority among young idealists in the 1960s. They furnished examples of personal integrity and commitment.

As reflected in such new role models, the hope of salvaging moral authenticity from a degenerate world, so redolent of religious revivalism, was soldered to the pursuit of social change at the New Left's inception. New Left radicals perceived the Old Left as debased by tactical cynicism and compromise with large systems that stifled human freedom, including state communism. This moral separation of ends from means was something the young radicals of the 1960s wished to avoid. The New Left also drew heavily on the post-scarcity views expressed by many young people in the world's wealthiest societies starting in the 1950s. Post-scarcity youth agreed with their countries' elites that the macro-economic problems of an earlier generation had been solved. The British socialist Anthony Crosland wrote, in a typical comment, 'capitalism [has] been reformed out of all recognition'.[3] The new challenge, it seemed, was to enrich the quality of life, not to stock-pile more consumer goods, which came to seem like so much trash. Finding meaningful work – and leisure – rather than merely finding work, were the cutting-edge problems now. The simple life appealed to young radicals, as it had to mendicants for centuries before them, but its opposition to a repellent mass consumerism was entirely contemporary, and its subtle connection to political agitation, through the ideas and exemplars of authenticity and direct action, was new.

Although most US New Leftists had abandoned nonviolence by 1968, the primacy of direct action – a legacy, to repeat, of militant nonviolence – endured. The commitments to moral authenticity and direct action – as well as the downgrading of economic concerns, and with them of the trade union movement, from the special status these had enjoyed in the world of the Old Left – were what young North Americans in the 1960s meant primarily when they said they were a *New* Left. While the Old Left had focused on agitation among those at the heart of the industrial capitalist social structure, the New Left directed their encouragements at people who were outsiders and thus would be uninhibited in seeking to destabilize society. New Left radicals saw the centres of power as well shielded from truly democratic influences, and therefore they resolved to shake the power structure from without, and recon-ceived of civic participation, in a bureaucratic age, as direct action.

The New Left was, almost exclusively, a movement of white people who viewed white supremacy as the leading tangible defect of their society. They have been subject to criticism from within radical ranks that they were insufficiently committed to African American empowerment.[4] Nevertheless, to other white Americans the New Left likely appeared preoccupied with that very goal. They tended to view imperialism, their other major specific political concern, through the lens of race, as a global version of the institutionalized racism they saw everywhere within US borders. Fundamental to their sympathies with Cuban, Chinese and Vietnamese communism was the status of these versions of Leninist revolution as vehicles for national liberation by peoples of colour, historically oppressed by the Global North, whether from Washington DC, London, Paris or Moscow.[5]

Some historians have sought to redefine the New Left to include the African American movement, the Chicano movement of the 1960s, the second wave of feminism and the gay liberation movement.[6] This effort echoes the flawed universalism of the New Left in its heyday, in which this movement's members assumed that they spoke a language and enacted a method that held the keys to freedom for all people. Of the other social movements mentioned here, only the radical wing of the feminist movement – and possibly the gay movement, in its early days – overlapped significantly with the New Left. Participants in the others (and most radical feminists as well) stated clearly that the New Left did not speak for them. By 1966, the African American movement's leading youth cadres made clear that white radicals should leave them alone and attempt the difficult task of organizing white Americans against racism. In the following years, life in the United States was filled with radical activism on the part of African Americans, Latinos and other people of colour, a good deal of which was plainly shaped by Marxism and other leftist traditions. The Black Panther Party was the best known example, but it was far from alone. However, the demands for autonomy and recognition of cultural difference among radicals of colour in the late 1960s ensured that they generally refrained from association with the category of the New Left, which was perceived all around as a white movement. Indeed, for anyone in the United States who was not white to affiliate herself or himself with the idea of the New Left at any point in time was extraordinarily rare.[7] The Black Studies scholar Grant Farred reflects this virtual consensus among activists of colour in the late 1960s when he describes 'the New Left . . . as an ideological formation against which the new social movements (implicitly) defined themselves: the New Left had to be rejected in order for gay, ethnic, and women's organizations to produce their public voices and visages'.[8]

The New Left's strategy for creating change shifted a number of times in the 1960–8 period, with the Vietnam War increasingly overtaking other concerns after 1965. Until the end of John F. Kennedy's presidency in 1963, some in SDS hoped to help catalyse a realignment of partisan politics, in which the Democrats would become an avowedly social democratic party. But that idea quickly faded in favour of an effort to rouse the poorest Americans, white and black, into an outsider movement that would demand far-reaching social and political changes from those with power. New Left radicals formed urban organizer communes around the country, but the results were disappointing and this effort faltered by 1965. In that year, President Lyndon Johnson's dramatic expansion of the US war in Vietnam brought a new focus to the New Left, which from its start had opposed the heavy hand of US power in the Third World. The swift appearance of antiwar sentiment among university students (incidentally, usually not threatened with conscription) now made the campus the site of New Left political opportunity.

Despite all these changes in focus, the anti-systemic orientation of the New Left stayed true. The war issue proved an accelerant for the outsider political firestorm of the 1960s. The Vietnam conflict was the Democrats' war first and foremost, with the opposition Republicans also giving strong support to the Kennedy–Johnson policy. In these circumstances, the New Left saw no option of working within the party system to stop the war and change US foreign policy. The war, at least through 1968, was tailor-made for a radical movement predisposed to anti-systemic protest. More broadly, the liberal ascendancy of the pre-1968 period strengthened the perception that a 'liberal establishment' was running the country – in Washington DC, as in the universities and the churches. The notion that liberals were the ruling elite, and thus deeply invested in maintaining the existing order – a perception that received analytical expression in radical critiques of 'corporate liberalism' – made the New Left's anti-systemic posture seem quite sensible to almost all radicals in the United States.[9]

The politically explosive events of 1968 ratified the basic course of the New Left, while generating contradictory prospects for successful insurgency. In late January and February, Communist forces in Vietnam, in the Tet Offensive, shook the nation's confidence in victory, and effectively pushed Johnson into announcing he would retire rather than attempt re-election. During the spring, SDS and African American students at Columbia University in New York took over university buildings to protest war-related research on campus and insensitivity by the university toward the largely poor, black community in the Harlem neighbourhood where Columbia was located. In April, Martin Luther King, Jr. – whose nonviolence was embattled among young insurgents of all races, but who retained a unique moral standing nonetheless in their eyes – was murdered in Memphis, Tennessee, as he strove to support the cause of the black working class. African Americans rose in violent protest in many cities, prompting intensive violent repression by police and National Guard troops. Amid such scenes of domestic military rule, young militants rallied to protest in Chicago that August, where the Democrats were certain to nominate Vice President Hubert Humphrey (perceived as faithful to Johnson's disastrous Vietnam policy) for the presidency. The Chicago police gave better than they got in the ensuing August street clashes with protesters, as filmed for national television broadcast. Meanwhile, reports of seemingly parallel repression of youth protest in Prague (through the first eight months of 1968), as well as in other global cities, filtered through to North American radicals. A distinctive mood, combining excitement and despair, enveloped the US New Left.

The climactic confrontations of 1968 forced New Left radicals to choose which road they would take. In the remaining seven-odd years that the New Left retained cohesion as a social movement, three basic paths opened forward. The first was a course of escalating confrontation with the power structure, a path that led to insurrection, even terrorism, and underground existence. The second was a path back toward the student (and, increasingly, ex-student) constituency that had seemed fruitful previously; this option took the form of peaceful community-building as a way of creating an alternative society within the larger unreformed one. The third was a path of commitment to the dogged work of organizing constituencies to demand discrete reforms from the political system – constituencies that included labor, the poor, church folk and peace and anti-imperialist activists. As these three paths diverged, those on each of them felt diminishing connections to those on the others, although some recognition of mutual origins and shared social analysis lingered. At the same time, women in the New Left organ-ized and agitated powerfully for the cause of women's equality, arguing that basic social and cultural changes were required to achieve it. Some of these radical feminists parted company with the New Left because of the latter's domination by men, some of them very sexist. But many radical feminists effectively maintained dual membership in leftist and feminist movements.[10] One can view feminism as a kind of part-way fourth path onward for the New Left after 1968, although I view it here, rather, as a tendency broadly dispersed, although not equally, in all three basic post-1968 sectors of the New Left.

The insurrectionary path, closely linked to the Weatherman or Weather Underground faction of SDS (which broke apart as an organization in 1969), reflected a striking combination of hope and pessimism about the prospects for radical change. These des-peradoes saw little to be lost by making themselves enemies of their countrymen at large; an appeal only to a saving remnant, from within a corrupt society, was conceivable to them. They saw the US political regime amid its Vietnam debacle vulnerable to destruction by the onslaught of a revolutionary Global South, and they planned to be the fifth column of the assault, along with racially defined groups inside the United States, such as the Black Panthers, the Young Lords and the American Indian Movement, who seemed willing to 'pick up the gun'. This fantasy led the white advocates of violence to a lonely outlaw life, after they perpe-trated a wave of bombings targeting government offices and other establishment facilities. Unlike the openly terrorist groups in other countries with whom they felt a kinship, like the Red Army Faction in West Germany or the Red Brigades in Italy, the North Americans generally refrained from trying to kill people, although some of them turned to violent crime to sustain themselves.[11] They never numbered more than several hundred – out of a New Left that probably had hundreds of thousands of adherents after 1968 – but the insurrectionists attracted enormous attention. Decades later, they were the subjects of novel and film and a rather comic pro-fusion of memoir.[12] The uninformed took them as exemplary of a radical movement whose broader tendencies were not so vividly recalled.

The path of alternative community-building among white college-educated youth was probably the biggest distinctive effort of New Left radicals after 1968. Enclaves of hip life, as the argot of the day called it, expanded rapidly. Neighbourhoods in Burlington, Ithaca, Madison, Ann Arbor, Lawrence, Austin, Chapel Hill, Missoula, Eugene and other college towns, along with larger areas in Berkeley and Brooklyn, formed a nationwide island chain of geographic zones where young people, including New Left activists, could feel they were making a new, less alienated and more moral subculture. In the end, these communities formed not a world apart but a leavening presence within the larger society, increasingly appreciated as sources of cultural innovation that could be consumed and enjoyed by all. Businesses, often run on a cooperative basis, grew successful, while home values rose. Social democracy, including stalwart anti-imperialism, also became respectable and often, in local politics, successful, whether through the Democrats or some alternative party. In a way, the New Left's investment in hip communities fulfilled the imperative taken from the African American movement that white radicals should organize their own social peers. However, they organized not a radical anti-racist vanguard, but a post-scarcity white liberalism – or, as Régis Debray framed the legacy of 1968 in France, 'the cradle of a new bourgeois society'.[13]

The last of the major post-1968 paths for the New Left – easily compatible with the project of building alternative communities, but nonetheless distinct – was a reconciliation with the organizing tradition. Some embraced Marxism–Leninism in a peaceful form, in a 'New Communist Movement', and joined trade unions to agitate for worker-based socialism, sometimes linking arms with African American and Latino labor radicals.[14] Others quietly turned toward a less ambitious labor liberalism. Protestant and Catholic churches, meanwhile, experienced an infusion of young people shaped by the New Left but never drawn to violent confrontation. In the early to mid-1960s, the initial religious inspirations of the New Left were swamped by vast numbers of young radicals disaffected from religion. But a steady stream of believers, generally committed to a synthesis of peace and justice in the United States and abroad, had worked among church people, witnessing against poverty, racism and war and sometimes taking highly militant action against 'the war machine'.[15] The anti-imperialist organizing of the 1970s, directed at US policy in Latin America as well as Southeast Asia, became a venue for renewed cooperation between the religious and atheist components of the New Left. Quite on their own, radicalized evangelical Protestants also, by the early 1970s, aligned themselves with New Left thought, arguing that Jesus was a revolutionary and that, as one said, 'Rome has begun to burn. The time has run out.' But soon many of them retreated from apocalypticism and began working to ameliorate contemporary evils.[16] For religious and atheist activists alike, this path required a revision of the neat distinction the New Left earlier had made between those working inside and outside the political system, as leftists colonized major institutions they and their comrades once had disdained.

The Americanization of The Left

Activists in the US pacifist and antinuclear movements had nurtured their international connections for decades before the 1960s, and the young people of the New Left followed in this tradition, establishing links with counterparts in Cuba, West Germany, Vietnam and elsewhere by 1968.[17] The remarkably widespread appearance of youth radicalism around the world in 1968, in rich and poor countries alike, has prompted some to describe structural explanations of this phenomenon (explanations whose most apparent hazard is the risk of too easily lumping First World and Third World rebellions together).[18] Most significant are the efforts of Jeremi Suri and Tor Egil Førland. Suri locates the inspiration for the 'international counterculture' in a set of heightened expectations for a meaningful life and for a responsive politics that the Cold War conditions of ideological intensity and newfound affluence produced.[19] Førland, in a bracingly contrarian view, sees the scale of protest activity in this era as a reflection of the sheer size of the generation coming into adulthood, and minimizes the substantive innovations in insurgent thought and politics.[20] Overall, scholars of the New Left have worked to establish that young North Americans did not operate in a political world bounded by national borders.

Instead, the New Left in the United States was a part and, in some ways, a product of global upheaval.

To lay stress upon transnational influences on North American radicalism from 'outside in' is a welcome development in light of the privileged position the US New Left occupied in global context, and the potential for insensitivity to the external forces shaping US residents. However, to neglect the force of the United States in shaping the rebellions of 1968 elsewhere – 'inside out', as it were – is a serious error. Scholars too often have failed to emphasize the decisive US impact on much of the global youth protest of 1968. The central place that the United States – its military power first of all – occupied in international affairs in 1968 all but ensured that America would become an object of protest around the world, as it did. This meant that the US New Left, in essential ways, set the pace and established the agenda for leftist mobilizations elsewhere in this pivotal year. Local issues were sometimes neglected in favour of the imported American agenda, particularly in Western Europe. This was a form of imperial influence that merits attention.

Everywhere in the NATO countries, it seemed, the driving issue was Vietnam. The International Vietnam Congress, held in West Berlin on 17–18 February 1968, brought events to fever pitch there. In Britain (where 1968 was not a year of such confrontation as elsewhere), the Vietnam Solidarity Campaign, led by the Pakistani émigré Tariq Ali, was 'the single most important British 1968 organization'.[21] In Italy, 'a deeply rooted Communist tradition that condemned American imperialism from the early postwar years offered students a useful argumentative support' when they took after the Vietnam enterprise starting in 1965.[22] In France, the Algerian War of 1954–62 was an important precursor to French anti-US imperialism, but it was Vietnam that sparked the rising of youth in 1968. Indeed, Kristin Ross, for one, calls the US war against Vietnam 'the one international dimension that could be said to have played the most important role in the French uprisings and that united those uprisings to the insurrections occurring in Germany, Japan, the United States, Italy, and elsewhere'.[23] When one turns to one of the earliest US New Left first-hand accounts of the European 1968, *Long March, Short Spring*, by Barbara and John Ehrenreich (published in 1969), one finds the Vietnam issue to have been ubiquitous. In the words of the Ehrenreichs, in the Federal Republic:

> students had been following the growth of an increasingly militant anti-war movement in the United States. They had read about the direct action techniques of the civil rights movement in the American South. Now, the urgency of the war in Vietnam seemed to demand direct action in Germany.[24]

The visit of the Shah of Iran in June 1967 is routinely noted as a take-off point for the German New Left, but the Ehrenreichs recount that the initial stimulus was Vice President Hubert Humphrey's arrival two months earlier, which inspired anti-US protests and a police crackdown. In Italy, where 'Vietnam demonstrations attracted far more students than might have been expected for a country so little involved in the war . . . Left students found nothing to agree on . . . outside the Vietnam issue'. In France, with the memory of the Algerian agony quickly receding, 'it wasn't until 1965–66 that students found a clear focus for political activity again: the American war in Vietnam'; the British were 'not only indebted to us for the issue, but for many of the tactics and analyses it engendered'; and in 'Italy, France, and Germany, university problems' – which were a matter of widespread complaints from students – 'ran headlong into the fact of Vietnam'.[25]

Certainly in some cases, other matters of urgent concern moved students in Western Europe, but the US–Vietnam War became the occasion for acting on those concerns with new passion and force. As is well known, young leftists in the Federal Republic protested in anguish the lingering unrepentant ex-Nazi element in West German institutions. In Italy, overcrowded and unresponsive universities prompted student discontent. In France, younger students and workers alike chafed against the continuing social dominance of their elders. And, in many countries – definitely in France and West Germany – official intolerance of dissent and sharp police repression of protest sent that very protest skyrocketing upward. But without the Vietnam issue, the initial mobilizations that led to the cycle of repression and heightened protest might never have taken hold at all. In France, the local grievances of protesters were manifold and shifting; many French citizens, evidently finding the complaints insubstantial, ended the crisis by giving the Gaullists a new conservative election mandate.

As the centre of imperial power had shifted from Western Europe to the United States, international anti-imperial protest shifted its focus accordingly. Worldwide leftist sympathy with the Vietnamese was very powerful, but in a real sense, the issue in the protests was not Vietnam but the United States, especially its foreign policy. The clear primacy of US power as an issue was confined to the countries within the US security alliance. European radicals now directed their well-worn anti-imperialist critiques westward toward Washington DC. The only Asian country where the US–Vietnam War was central to the protest thrust of 1968 was, tellingly, Japan, where the Zengakuren had protested US militarism since at least 1960 and focused sharply on Vietnam by 1968.[26]

The shift in focus of First World protest to the United States inhered not only in the European echoes of the US New Left's anti-Vietnam War protest and of its anti-systemic protest stance. This shift also was evident in the lacunae within Western European protest in 1968. A critical awareness of the postcolonial legacies of Europe – such as discrimination, exploitation or racism directed against Muslims or Africans inside Britain, France or Germany – was all but nonexistent in the European 1968. Britain saw the beginnings of civil rights organizing by Afro-Caribbeans in the early 1960s, and some discussion of racism occurred in France around 1965.[27] But this dawning consciousness of racism close to hand largely failed to infiltrate the uprisings of 1968. Tyler Stovall notes, in his study of African American expatriates in Paris, 'the massive student revolt that erupted spontaneously in Paris during the spring of 1968 did not for the most part address issues of racial discrimination' against any persons of colour, no matter their point of origin.[28] The French activist Patrick Lozès notes that 'in fact, amazing as it seems when viewed from abroad, the fight against discrimination' in France 'was largely absent from French political debate before the creation of the CRAN [Conseil Représentatif des Associations Noires]' in 2005.[29] Allison Blakely writes in a 2012 publication that 'respect for a French Republican tradition that rejects the acknowledgment of ethnic categories based on colour prevented until now open discussion of what is being called *"la question noire"*.[30] It was as if the generation of 1968 in Europe felt their own countries' imperial histories had no living legacies or consequences yet to confront. Some Europeans were conscious of racism toward African Americans in the United States, but they did not mobilize to support the struggles of low-caste ethnic groups in Europe such as the Roma. The young radicals of Western Europe did not simply imitate the US New Left method, they adopted its North American agenda as well.

Outside the US-led alliance, in the 1968 of the Second and Third Worlds more authoritarian regimes repressed youth protest in sometimes violent frays, and in many cases conflicts internal to particular countries remained salient throughout. Recent scholarship shows that US power was less prominent a point of mobilization here than in Western Europe. Youth living under Communist regimes in the Warsaw Pact nations had pressing concerns at home, in the form of political dictatorship and Russian military domination. New Left radicals in the West expressed feelings of kinship with their counterparts in Prague; protesters at the Democratic National Convention in 1968 held up banners reading 'Czechago', to establish the unity of all who stood up to violent authorities. This feeling may have been reciprocated across the Iron Curtain. Nonetheless, the East European protest agenda was too crowded to take on the misdeeds of the US empire as well as those of Soviet power. Tellingly, each empire's rebellious youth focused on its own regime's evils.

Youth protest shook Third World countries like Mexico, India, Jamaica and Zimbabwe, among others, in 1968, but national conflicts defined those protests, even if the willingness to defy state power was contagious across world regions in this year. The best-known case is probably Mexico, where the Summer Olympics were held 12–27 October 1968 and where, mere days beforehand, the government murdered hundreds in the Plaza de las Tres Culturas at Tlatelolco in Mexico City, crushing a powerful protest movement. Julia Sloan concludes that the protesters' 'most forceful and ultimately effective attacks on the legitimacy of the Mexican state . . . came not from foreign ideology, but rather from a critique of the core tenets of the dominant Mexican political narrative of revolutionary nationalism'. The protesters did express outrage over the US war in Vietnam. However, 'while the rank and file members of the student movement integrated such international issues into their demonstrations and rhetoric, they never made them their focus'.[31] To take the most titanic example of internal conflict in the Global South during 1968, China was wracked by the efforts of Mao Zedong and other rulers to check the fearsome power that they previously had unleashed in the Great Proletarian Cultural Revolution. Virtual civil war raged.[32] The Chinese Red Guards surely denounced Western imperialism, but 'rightist' revisionism at home was the enemy against which they really struggled.

As these instances make clear, the limits of the imperial influence of US New Left protest were defined in 1968 by the fault-lines of the geopolitical system. In later years, after the end of the Cold War and the fall of communism, the United States would become the prime issue for antimilitarist protesters in all world regions. When there is only one empire left, it will be *the* focus of anti-imperial politics. This would be perfectly clear by the time of the US invasion of Iraq in 2003, and to a significant degree even during the Persian Gulf War of 1990–1. Anti-imperialist and peace activists inside the United States would hear a truly global echo of their own outcries when they found themselves in the heart of the whole planet's dominant state. In 1968, that arrangement was only partly in place. But the North Americanization of the world's left had begun.

Conclusion: Remaking The US Left

While the US New Left began to reshape the world's left in its image in 1968, the New Left also reshaped the left tradition within the United States. The prior history of the North American left had been one of repeated symbolic parricide, in which young radicals defiantly rejected an earlier generation's methods and priorities as bankrupt, either tactically or morally or both. Such dramas always had exaggerated the sharpness of the breaks between different radical generations, and each cohort had tended to caricature its elders. Regardless, the point is that the absence of any true re-enactment of such intergenerational conflict in the New Left's aftermath – now a half-century after 1968 – marks a sea change in the contours of US radicalism.[33] One reason for this change is that state power failed to repress the New Left, in contrast to the very effective repression of the left during 1917–20 and in the severe anti-communist period of the 1940s and 1950s. Unlike with the African American militants of the 1970s, political surveillance and manipulation of the white left after 1968, while outrageous, was not particularly effective.[34] It sometimes damaged worthy efforts, but overall it extinguished little that was vital or promising. Many who had been active in the New Left built impressive careers, acquiring status and protégés. Post-1968 radicals have had to contend with the power and position of New Left veterans, and have not seen the need to reinvent radicalism the way that earlier generations did in the aftermath of political repression. Many histories of the New Left have been defensive, even sentimental. One has to look outside the ranks of historians to find the critical view offered by the artist and scholar Paige Sarlin, who argues that commemorations of the New Left in the United States 'support a kind of political inertia in which history is represented as an ineffectual loop of repetition and circulation'.[35]

The New Left's values of direct action and authenticity, like its desire to resist system and structure, have maintained their authority within the left since 1968, although a sequence of important critiques from within the left have emerged over the years. The earliest rethinking of central features of the New Left came while the movement still existed. The political scientist Jo Freeman, herself a 1960s insurgent, first named 'the tyranny of structurelessness' in the early 1970s as a problem in the women's liberation movement.[36] But anyone active in the New Left would have found Freeman's description familiar. Freeman criticized 'leaderless' activist groups for concealing and denying the power that informal leaders exercised. Leaders existed in the New Left, but only local and temporary ones, their legitimacy always precarious. The movement as a whole really was led by no one; this was as its members wished. Critics never persuaded new cohorts of protesters to abandon the informal 'leaderless' and 'structureless' style. Instead, in the 1970s and after, radicals used 'affinity groups' and other methods to disperse power within movements.

The conservative climate of the 1980s and 1990s eventually yielded new critiques on the left. The historian Thomas Frank helped to start *The Baffler* in 1988–90, training university-bred analysis and gleeful mockery on the pretensions of neoliberal free-market dogma. Frank argued that rebellion was not simply exhausted within American culture but had been corrupted long ago and had become a mere mode of consumerism, an engine for capitalism. His thesis of neoliberalism's warm annihilation of dissent had no ready answer from the left. *The Baffler* and Frank found a less ambivalent response among sympathetic readers with their call to return to the Old Left battle against capitalist exploitation, a struggle neglected as passé by the New Left but, now, all too plainly in order. In the new motion toward the ground of exploitation, the neglect of the economic by the post-scarcity radicals of the New Left was rarely noted.[37]

The US left reappeared with new vitality as it pitched into battle against triumphant capital, first in the protests against the World Trade Organization in Seattle, Washington, in 1999, and then, winning wide sympathy after the banking crisis of the new century, in the Occupy Wall Street mobilization of 2011.[38] These protests departed sharply from the New Left in their substantive focus on exploitation. But their methods and atmospherics continued to recall the generation of 1968. Lamentations over the devotion of Occupy to its own ambience, one that gave a taste of a possible anarchist utopia, fell largely on deaf ears inside the protest space. Occupy Wall Street had its detractors within the left, but they often lapsed into unimaginative, recycled criticisms of the later New Left, rather than articulating more basic critiques of the values and modes into which the tendencies of Occupy were hard-wired.[39] The world of 2011 and the world of 1968 were very different. But for this reason, one might have expected to see an insurgent method far more innovative in 2011, one far less indebted to 1968.

As *The Baffler* was the expression of lonely dissent and devil-may-care humorous contempt befitting a world without rebellion, *Jacobin*, which began publishing as an online venture in 2010, styled itself the house journal of the new anti-capitalist boom. *Jacobin*'s socialism and Marxism were freshly packaged, designed for a new youth market (and largely humour-free). Initially it wavered between the roles of critic and cheerleader, and quickly made the only sensible market-based choice, the latter one.[40] Any critique of the 1968 legacy rapidly attenuated to a muted, almost inaudible note.

An expression of a new radical generational identity in the form of a major challenge to the continuing value of direct action, to the posture of anti-system resistance, or to the imperative of authenticity within radicalism seems literally almost unthinkable. The fact that the elevation of these sympathies within the US left resulted from the specific conditions of the twentieth century, and in some cases from the briefer early Cold War era of the 1950s and 1960s, matters little. The New Left's impress within US radicalism, while compromised by the new concerns so urgently on the minds of the whole world fifty years after 1968, remains clear. It would be a supreme irony of the New Left, with its burning desire to make radicalism – and America – new, should mark the end of the American left's noble history of renovation.

Notes

1. For the first and last of these slogans (appearing, respectively, in New York and Paris), see Barbara and John Ehrenreich, *Long March, Short Spring: The Student Uprising at Home and Abroad* (New York: Monthly Review Press, 1969), 21, 73.

2. Madeleine Davis, 'The Origins of the British New Left', in Martin Klimke and Joachim Schlaroth (eds), *1968 in Europe* (New York: Palgrave Macmillan, 2008), 47–48. See also Ingrid Gilcher-Holtey, 'France', in the same volume: 113–14.

3. This was in 1957. Quoted in Eric Hobsbawm, *The Age of Extremes: A History of the World, 1914–1991* (New York: Vintage, 1996), 269.

4. David Barber advances this curious view in *A Hard Rain Fell: SDS and Why It Failed* (Jackson: University Press of Mississippi, 2008).

5. The fundamental work is Van Gosse, *Where the Boys Are: Cuba, Cold War America, and the Making of a New Left* (London: Verso, 1993). Also see Judy Tzu-Chun Wu, *Radicals on the Road: Internationalism, Orientalism, and Feminism during the Vietnam Era* (Ithaca, NY: Cornell University Press, 2013).

6. Van Gosse has advanced this view energetically, in works including *The Movements of the New Left, 1950–1975: A History with Documents* (Boston, MA: Bedford/St Martin's, 2005) and *Rethinking the New Left: An Interpretative History* (New York: Palgrave Macmillan, 2005).

7. Other historians who wish to take the insurgent movements of the era as a whole have abandoned New Left as their master category in favour of less problematic ones such as the 'Third World Left'. See Max Elbaum, 'What Legacy the Radical Internationalism of 1968?', *Radical History Review* 82 (Winter 2002),

37–64; Cynthia Young, *Soul Power: Culture, Radicalism, and the Making of a U.S. Third World Left* (Durham, NC: Duke University Press, 2006).

8. Grant Farred, 'Endgame Identity? Mapping the New Left Roots of Identity Politics', *New Literary History* 31(4) (Autumn 2000), 628. Farred bases his view more on the British than the US New Left, but in a basic way his scheme applies to the North American scene as well.

9. Leftist historians offered important versions of this critique, including Martin J. Sklar, 'Woodrow Wilson and the Political Economy of Modern United States Liberalism', *Studies on the Left* 1(3) (Fall 1960), 7–47, and James Weinstein, *The Corporate Ideal in the Liberal State, 1900–1918* (Boston, MA: Beacon Press, 1968).

10. See Alice Echols, *Daring to Be Bad: Radical Feminism in America, 1967–1975* (Minneapolis: University of Minnesota Press, 1989), and Doug Rossinow, *The Politics of Authenticity: Liberalism, Christianity, and the New Left in America* (New York: Columbia University Press, 1998), 297–333. Recent works including Kimberly Springer, *Living for the Revolution: Black Feminist Organizations, 1968–1980* (Durham, NC: Duke University Press, 2005), and Maylei Blackwell, *¡Chicana Power! Contested Histories of Feminism in the Chicano Movement* (Austin: University of Texas Press, 2011), have expanded the scope and definition of radical feminism in this era.

11. See Jeremy Varon, *Bringing the War Home: The Weather Underground, the Red Army Faction, and Revolutionary Violence in the Sixties and Seventies* (Berkeley: University of California Press, 2004), and Ron Jacobs, *The Way the Wind Blew: A History of the Weather Underground* (London: Verso Books, 1997).

12. These novels include Marge Piercy, *Vida* (Oakland, CA: PM Press, [1979] 2012); Susan Choi, *American Woman* (New York: HarperCollins, 2003); Dana Spiotta, *Eat the Document* (New York: Scribner, 2006). *Weather Underground*, directed by Sam Green and Bill Spiegel, DVD (New Video Group, 2003). Memoirs include: Susan Stern, *With the Weathermen: The Personal Journey of a Revolutionary Woman* (New Brunswick, NJ: Rutgers University Press, [1975] 2007); Bill Ayers, *Fugitive Days: Memoirs of an Antiwar Activist* (Boston, MA: Beacon Press, 2001); Cathy Wilkerson, *Flying Close to the Sun: My Life and Times as a Weatherman* (New York: Seven Stories Press, 2007); Mark Rudd, *Underground: My Life with SDS and the Weathermen* (New York: William Morrow, 2009); David Gilbert, *Love and Struggle: My Life in SDS, Weatherman, and Beyond* (Oakland, CA: PM Press, 2011).

13. Quoted in Gilcher-Holtey, 'France', 121, and also in Kristin Ross, *May '68 and Its Afterlives* (Chicago: University of Chicago Press, 2002), 185. Ross forcefully rebuts Debray's interpretation regarding the French protests. I use his comment here as a convenient description of one legacy of the US New Left.

14. See Elbaum, *Revolution in the Air*, and Heather Ann Thompson, *Whose Detroit? Politics, Labor, and Race in a Modern American City* (Ithaca, NY: Cornell University Press, 2001).

15. See Penelope Adams Moon, '"Peace on Earth – Peace in Vietnam": The Catholic Peace Fellowship and Antiwar Witness, 1964–1976', *Journal of Social History* 36(4) (Summer 2003), 1033–57; Michael S. Foley, *Confronting the War*

Machine: Draft Resistance during the Vietnam War (Chapel Hill: University of North Carolina Press, 2003); Patricia F. McNeal, *Harder than War: Catholic Peacemaking in Twentieth-Century America* (New Brunswick, NJ: Rutgers University Press, 1992).

16. Quoted in David R. Swartz, 'The New Left and Evangelical Radicalism', *Journal for the Study of Radicalism* 3(2) (Fall 2009), 56.

17. In addition to those already cited, major works in this field are Arthur Marwick, *The Sixties: Cultural Revolution in Britain, France, Italy, and the United States, c.1958–c.1974* (Oxford: Oxford University Press, 1998); Jeremi Suri, *Power and Protest: Global Revolution and the Rise of Détente* (Cambridge, MA: Harvard University Press, 2003); and Martin Klimke, *The Other Alliance: Student Protest in West Germany and the United States in the Global Sixties* (Princeton, NJ: Princeton University Press, 2010).

18. See the polite dissent registered in Arif Dirlik, 'The Third World', in Carole Fink et al. (eds), *1968: The World Transformed* (Cambridge: Cambridge University Press, 1998), 295–317.

19. Jeremi Suri, 'The Rise and Fall of an International Counterculture, 1960–1975', *American Historical Review* 114(1) (February 2009), 45–68.

20. Tor Egil Førland, 'Cutting the Sixties Down to Size: Conceptualizing, Historicizing, Explaining', *Journal for the Study of Radicalism* 9(2) (Fall 2015), 125–48.

21. Davis, 'Origins of the British New Left', 54.

22. Jan Kura and Marica Tolomelli, 'Italy', in Klimke and Schlaroth (eds), *1968 in Europe*, 87.

23. Claus Leggewie, 'A Laboratory of Postindustrial Society: Reassessing the 1960s in Germany', in Carole Fink et al. (eds), *1968: The World Transformed*, 288. Ross, *May '68 and Its Afterlives*, 10.

24. Ehrenreich and Ehrenreich, *Long March, Short Spring*, 32–3.

25. Ibid. 53, 56, 74, 106, 117. For Humphrey's visit to West Berlin see Suri, *Power and Protest*, 176.

26. Mark Kurlansky, *1968: The Year that Rocked the World* (New York: Ballantine, 2004), 83; David Caute, *The Year of the Barricades: A Journey through 1968* (New York: HarperCollins, 1988), 28–30.

27. Marwick, *Sixties*, 229–44. See also Stephen Tuck, *The Night Malcolm X Spoke at the Oxford Union: A Transatlantic Story of Antiracist Protest* (Berkeley: University of California Press, 2014).

28. Tyler Stovall, *Paris Noir: African Americans in the City of Light* (Boston, MA: Houghton Mifflin, 1996), 273.

29. Patrick Lozès, 'The Invention of Blacks in France', in Trica Danielle Keaton, T. Denean Sharpley-Whiting and Tyler Stovall (eds), *Black France/France Noire: The History and Politics of Blackness* (Durham, NC: Duke University Press, 2012), 106.

30. Allison Blakeley, 'Coda: Black Identity in France in a European Perspective', in Keaton et al. (eds), *Black France/France Noire*, 289.

31. Julia Sloan, 'Revolution on the National Stage: Mexico, the PRI, and the Student Movement in 1968', in Samantha Christiansen and Zachary A. Scarlett

(eds), *The Third World in the Global 1960s* (New York: Berghahn, 2013), 171–2, 174–5.

32. See Zachary A. Scarlett, 'China's Great Proletarian Cultural Revolution and the Imagination of the Third World', in Christiansen and Scarlett (eds), *Third World in the Global 1960s*, 39–56.

33. For a superb, often thrilling, history see Howard Brick and Christopher Phelps, *Radicals in America: The U.S. Left since the Second World War* (Cambridge: Cambridge University Press, 2015).

34. For a more detailed discussion see Doug Rossinow, 'Letting Go: Revisiting the New Left's Demise', in John McMillian and Paul Buhle (eds), *The New Left Revisited* (Philadelphia: Temple University Press, 2003), 247–52.

35. Paige Sarlin, 'New Left-Wing Melancholy: Mark Tribe's "The Port Huron Project" and the Politics of Reenactment', *Framework* 50(1–2) (Spring–Fall 2009), 144. Sarlin discusses literal re-enactments of key New Left speeches and protest gatherings, but her critique also has wider implications.

36. Jo Freeman, 'The Tyranny of Structurelessness', *Berkeley Journal of Sociology* 17 (1972–3), 151–65.

37. Thomas Frank and Matt Weiland (eds), *Commodify Your Dissent: Salvos from The Baffler* (New York: Norton, 1997); Thomas Frank, *The Conquest of Cool: Business Culture, Counterculture, and the Rise of Hip Consumerism* (Chicago: University of Chicago Press, 1997).

38. Economic concerns were not the sole preoccupation of the US left in these years. US wars in Afghanistan and Iraq, following the 9/11 attacks on America, invited a return to anti-imperialist mobilization. Massive protests against the Iraq invasion occurred around the world. This antiwar movement was not a leftist movement on the whole, but did include a leftist element.

39. For a defence of OWS, see nplusonemag.com/online-only/occupy . I place Occupy Wall Street in broader perspective in Doug Rossinow, 'What Happened to Occupy? The Divided Left and the Demise of a Movement', *Christian Century* (10 July 2013), 22–3, 26–7.

40. For *Jacobin* see www.jacobinmag.com/issue

TWO

1968 and The Fractured Right

Elizabeth Tandy Shermer

Pundits and scholars reflexively think of 1968 as a pivotal year in American politics. Violence framed the Democratic Party's convention where higher-ups brokered the backroom deals naming unpopular Vice President Hubert Humphrey the party's presidential nominee. Republicans defeated their opponents in a veritable landslide. Richard Nixon captured thirty-two states, 301 electoral votes, and roughly 43 per cent of the popular vote. Historians have subsequently cited his win as ushering in the 1970s, when economic, international and domestic crises nurtured a New Right. That contingent's white blue-collar workers, suburbanites and churchgoers opposed secularization, feminism, integration, federal authority and welfare spending. These voters have subsequently been credited with giving Ronald Reagan the political mandate to oversee the 1980s dismantling of the New Deal order.[1]

Yet neither Nixon, Reagan, nor their Republican successors have won or governed easily. They were plagued by left-wing radicals, liberals and moderates but also other self-proclaimed conservatives, like George Wallace, the American Independent Party's nominee in 1968. The Alabama governor had a folksy, salty but also devout air to his politics. He had always campaigned as an everyman but boldly asked voters in 1968: 'Can a former truck driver married to a dime-store clerk and son of a dirt farmer be elected President?' The answer that year – and again in 1964, 1972 and 1976 – was 'no'. He nevertheless thrilled many Americans in 1968 when he declared 'there isn't a dime's worth of difference' between parties in the nation's 'Tweedledee and Tweedledum system'. Almost 10 million voted for him in 1968, roughly 13.5 per cent of the electorate and enough to secure 46 electoral votes from five states in the Deep South, a region that Nixon has long been credited for winning over with the GOP's infamous Southern strategy.[2]

Yet the disaffected conservatives who rallied behind Wallace and other protest candidates before and after 1968 rarely received focused attention from the press or scholars. Doug Rossinow notes that young people consciously christened themselves the 'New Left' in the 1960s, but journalists initially tended to label all critics of liberalism and the left as a part of an amorphous ill-defined 'New Right'. That moniker presumed their complaints were unprecedented and somehow different than the old white, Anglo-Saxon, Protestant conservatives defined by their elitism, racism and anti-Semitism, as well as their preference for free markets and local control.[3]

In some respects, the frustrations of insurgents in the 1960s and 1970s were immediate reactions to the 1960s advancement of civil rights, feminist and anti-poverty causes. However, historians have uncovered that the complaints on the right after 1968 echoed the concerns of the many Americans involved in forging the movement in the early postwar years. Three decades of serious scholarship have indicated that the conservative movement had deeply entrenched divisions. Disagreements during the Depression, World War II and early Cold War actually slowed the development of the coalition amongst the intellectuals who first defined and named this ideology, the anti-communist policy-makers who disagreed over whether Soviets or liberals were more nefarious, the high-ranking executives who debated economic policy, the local business interests who furiously competed with each other for investments and political offices, and the top Republicans who clashed over how to reconquer Washington. They eventually coalesced behind putting long-term Arizona Senator Barry Goldwater at the head of the 1964 Republican ticket. He lost that year, but won over a largely white, suburban bloc that was the movement's electoral base in succeeding elections. Indeed, he did well in three of the five Southern states that Wallace captured just four years later.[4]

The GOP's base of support still proved fractious and undecipherable. Voters often embraced protest candidates like Wallace, but also rebelled at the local level against taxation, welfare, integration, affirmative action and secularization (whether in the form of mass protests, suburban exoduses or ballot initiatives). Many of these revolts did not necessarily seem conservative, either then or now, but rather 'vigorously left, right, and center', the phrase Michael Harrington used in the 1970s to describe that tumultuous decade.[5] By the mid-1990s, historians traced this dissension back to spirited contests before 1968. Scholars accordingly chafed at labelling 1960s and 1970s suburban warriors as a part of a New Right, which also steadily dropped out of non-academic discussions of the country's conservative impulses.

Some researchers and journalists embraced 'populist' to describe everyday Americans whose politics and demands defied simple categorization as either liberal, conservative, racist, reactionary or evangelical. The knee-jerk political impulse to protect the many weak against the few powerful is now considered a powerful, longstanding political trope, which never belonged to a single party, sliver of the political spectrum or religious tradition. That latest work on postwar populism also rejects claims that elite Republicans illegitimately captured this David and Goliath rhetoric after 1968. Neighbourhood rancour was often genuine, particularly local education, housing and employment conflicts that escalated into dramatic late twentieth-century protests and political campaigns that Democrats and Republicans struggled to parse, ignore or defeat.[6]

Such bottom-up, potent, persistent challenges to the men and women who had founded the early movement accordingly challenge longstanding presumptions that 1968 was a pivotal moment for American conservatism. That year did not foretell the emergence of a new right-wing contingent in lockstep with the movement's founders. Wallace's candidacy instead brought more than a decade's worth of divisive intra-movement warfare into the upper echelon of American politics for the first, but certainly not the last, time.

Even the right's most celebrated statesmen found themselves bedevilled throughout their careers by their presumed grassroots supporters. Insurrections before and after 1968, for example, plagued the career and state GOP that Goldwater had helped fashion. Renegades continually frustrated the senator and other movement leaders, who found their postwar language of freedom, democracy and free enterprise used against them on Election Days. Lay protestors became more insistent in their demands for genuinely direct democracy in the early 1960s, which reflected new expectations for democratic representation found across the political spectrum and throughout activist circles. The grassroots, regardless of party affiliation, began to enjoy a stronger voice at the polls and in primaries in these years because the Supreme Court started to slowly attack malapportionment. Reallocating seats at the state and federal level helped those white grassroots candidates who proclaimed themselves the true defenders of democracy, conservatism and, for the devoted, God. Renegades garnered votes in sprawling cities and decaying metropolises, sometimes winning on platforms that established liberal and conservative politicians across the country considered extreme and contradictory.

Sprawl's Discontented Origins

Goldwater's generation of conservatives had been the mutineers of the GOP in the 1930s, 1940s and 1950s. Militant anti-communists (such as Wisconsin Senator Joseph McCarthy), intellectuals (such as Michigan State's Russell Kirk), top executives (including General Electric's Lemuel Ricketts Boulware), influential radio announcers (like the former Dean of Notre Dame Law School Clarence Manion) and well-known publishers (especially the devout William F. Buckley, Jr.) had often described themselves as such in the early postwar period. All had profound objections to the New Deal and the liberal order it seemed to have established in the 1930s and that expanded its appeal during the 1940s.[7]

This elite, top-down counter-revolution depended on local efforts across the country led by conservatives, such as department store owner Goldwater. The early movement's entrepreneurs and professionals were not grassroots figures. Sociologists at the time instead considered them to be the 'grasstops', since successful businessmen at the local and regional level were situated between the working and middle classes and the political, corporate and social powerbrokers who already made headlines nationally. This contingent, for example, may have lived in whistle-stops like Phoenix but they often had degrees from elite colleges, memberships in national professional organizations, and direct business dealings with large corporations. These hometown high rollers hence had entrée into elite circles nationally, as well as cachet among the grassroots back home. This vantage point helped them defend 'free enterprise' – an anti-statist, anti-communist, generally secular rallying cry against liberalism also used by the top strata of the nation's postwar conservatives.[8]

Conservative small-town retailers, bankers, newspaper publishers, lawyers and other professionals also used that phrase in their efforts to attract industry by building benign-sounding 'business climates'. Their simplistic business first rhetoric belied the policies and methods that conservative policy-makers used to obtain office as well pass tax, zoning and regulatory easements that together made plant relocations profitable. New operations brought more job opportunities, which drew Americans to southern cities such as Atlanta, Charlotte, Dallas, Houston and Las Vegas. Growth did not just aid the executives eagerly shifting operations out of the nation's Democratic strongholds (the Steel Belt and coastal California). Rather, sprawl turned homespun politicians and boosters of the town's investment potential into leading figures in the conservative movement.[9]

Goldwater's political fortunes, for example, increased alongside outside investment in Phoenix, Arizona, one of the cities that Nixon aide Kevin Phillips singled out as vital to *The Emerging Republican Majority*, which he wrote following the 1968 election.[10] This desert whistle-stop had much in common with other small towns that became Sunbelt metropolises but also stood out for being home to leading conservatives, Richard Kleindienst, William Rehnquist and Sandra Day O'Connor. Goldwater in fact paved the way for their national notoriety after starting his own career in one of the many southern and southwestern grasstops political machines. In the 1930s and 1940s trade groups, like the Phoenix Chamber of Commerce, spearheaded municipal reforms through nonpartisan slating groups in the name of good governance and economic potential. Business-run efforts decried ward voting and praised at-large elections as well as a host of other charter revisions that served to stop poor, working-class or minorities communities from sending representatives to city hall. Business-run machines, such as Dallas's Citizens Charter Association and Albuquerque's Citizens Committee, dominated city politics in the postwar South and Southwest.

Phoenix's Charter Government Committee (CGC) was one of the most entrenched machines after coming into power in 1949 and including Goldwater on its inaugural slate. The CGC hardly represented the electorate during its twenty-five year reign. Slates included candidates from different religious backgrounds, known Democrats, at least one woman, and, by the early 1950s, one person of colour (usually Latino). Every candidate always championed free enterprise and thus sympathized with, if they were not already a part of, the building conservative movement. The CGC's Selection Committee was even more exclusive: it put together the ticket every two years and only grew to twenty-two members toward the end of the CGC's reign. 'In the smoke-filled room', a member remembered, 'we would go after [candidates] and . . . persuade them to run'. The Phoenix business elite used their power to slash taxes on manufacturing, shift the burden of paying for roads and schools onto homeowners and shoppers through higher personal property and sales taxes, and enforce anti-union legislation that limited the power of trade unions. Such anti-labor laws lessened the voice and power of workers on the job but also made them hard to mobilize on Election Day.[11]

The council rarely explained how they ran or funded Phoenix's business climate. Businessmen-politicians, like their counterparts elsewhere, favoured anti-statist, at times overtly anti-communist, secular language to explain their broad defence of free enterprise. Stumping left out their actual plans to use state power to promote industry by building roads, giving away acres, rezoning neighbourhoods or expanding schools. For example, Paul Fannin, who served Arizona as both governor and senator during his career, publically dedicated himself to 'tak[ing] Government out of business by putting business into government' because 'if businessmen do not take a part in government, government will take business apart'. He and other boosters seldom explained how they paid for attracting and building the infrastructure for industry: tax cuts for businesses made up on higher levies for personal income, property and consumption.[12]

The CGC, like other political machines at that time, also prioritized administrative governance, not representative democracy. Councillors left the nuts and bolts of policymaking to an unelected city manager, who did not reduce the government's size but in fact enlarged it by hiring the staff to directly oversee permits, contracts, zoning changes and many other aspects of day-to-day governance. Growth only exacerbated voters' disenfranchisement. Across the South and Southwest, policymakers eagerly annexed the independent suburbs growing around prospering central cities, something that was harder to do in the Northeast and Midwest where the commuter belt had been established much longer and usurpation laws tended to be stricter. But city planners could easily target brand-new bedroom communities in the emergent Sunbelt; Arizona laws even allowed the CGC to do so without the majority of homeowners' consent.[13]

Long before property owners were deemed a part of a New Right, these voters continually elected the CGC as well as the members who started running for state-level office. 'Charter Government', as one member explained, 'was the nucleus of what turned out to be the Republican Party'. Goldwater was just one of many postwar crusaders who detested both Arizona's Democrats and its Republicans. Phoenix's top retailers, lawyers, bankers and newspaper publishers systematically rebuilt the GOP into a powerful organization. The devout Baptists, Catholics and Jews joined Goldwater in dedicating their party to a secular, free-enterprise conservatism incongruous with Roosevelt's and Truman's liberalism as well as the modern Republicanism practised in the 1950s by President Eisenhower and Vice President Nixon. Like the CGC, Arizona's young, upstart Republicans damned moderates, liberals, trade unionists, business taxes and workplace regulations as affronts to American entrepreneurialism and economic growth. Their wives and neighbours helped spread this message in old-fashioned registration drives that got the vote out for these ambitious, young, white, Republican men, who faced an uphill battle. Arizona's legislature was severely malapportioned: sparsely populated, Democrat-heavy rural areas were over-represented in the legislature. Hard work reaped rewards. When Goldwater secured his second Senate term in 1958, leading pundits declared the state GOP a potent force in Arizona politics. Just six years later he clinched the party's nomination for president.[14]

'Don't Intend to Be a Sucker'

Postwar insurgents across the country, not just in Phoenix, built the movement behind Goldwater's 1964 run but also unwittingly nurtured the next generation of self-described renegades. Most of the literature on post-1964 suburban uprisings, as well as their support for George Wallace's 1968 third-party presidential bid, have focused on working- and middle-class whites' attacks on liberal politicians and values. However, these suburbanites had also been tormenting local business elites, who struggled to quell populist rebellions against integration, zoning and taxation policies.[15]

In Phoenix, for example, discontent simmered during the 1950s when residents increasingly bore the burden of paying for Phoenix's business climate. Arizona actually ranked seventeenth in per capita levies ($208.35) in 1960 but eleventh in regards to taxes as a percentage of personal income (10.36% to sixteenth-placed California's 10.14%). White homeowners felt the pinch the most: they shared the sales tax burden with working-class minorities but still bore much of the property tax load because they were also the target of city annexation programmes. City planners had also come to rely on these newly annexed Phoenicians' property taxes in order to fund city investment initiatives but also to make up for the revenue shortfalls that accompanied slashing business levies.[16]

The frustrated did complain, most often attacking boosters, investors and recruitment policies in the Chamber's language of efficient, corruption-free, free-enterprise governance. 'My taxes were increased', a resident fumed to the editors of the *Arizona Republic* in 1953: 'I am willing to pay my fair share, but don't intend being a sucker'. Some drew attention to spotty and inefficient public services for residential areas, exasperation that questioned the fruits of free-enterprise rule. Others decried annexation. Leonard Grube, for example, damned councillors who usurped a tract in which GE owned the majority of the land. The city had only to persuade executives to sign off on the deal in order to appropriate the entire parcel, his subdivision included. He reasoned that residents 'may not want the city Police cars giving minor traffic citations in their bailiwick. They may not want to pay city taxes. They may not want the city building inspectors sticking their noses in their room addition.'[17]

The Chamber faced serious electoral challenges by the early 1960s. Earlier oppositional slates had tended to campaign on reduced individual taxes and more public services, failed to mount an effective challenge, and had not generated voter interest. Phoenicians also did not rally behind the Stay America Committee (SAC). That 1961 ticket nonetheless generated national interest after Chalmers Roberts covered SAC in the *Washington Post*. He reported Phoenix dailies 'jammed with the words of the ultra right' and California donors. This broad 'reactionary right' helped Goldwater to transform 'Phoenix's claim to be "the valley of the sun" into . . . "the valley of fear"'.[18]

SAC really reflected how divided the right was. No one was a member of the grasstops. This genuinely diffuse, grassroots campaign relied on housewives ringing doorbells and making phone calls. 'We don't really have an organization', a candidate enthused. CGC governance and the business climate united candidates and supporters, who considered the status quo a plot against their populist definition of democratic capitalism. An outspoken Baptist minister represented the faithful alongside Reverend Wesley Darby, a thirty-three-year-old Valley native, who balanced his ecclesiastical duties with work as Greenlee County's deputy assessor. They shared the slate with Ted MacDonald, a college-educated forty-seven-year-old insurance agency owner originally from Texas. MacDonald moved to Arizona to establish his own firm, just like thirty-two-year-old SAC candidate Thomas Davis, who applied his economics coursework to manage his accounting practice. Mayoral candidate W. Buckner Hanner was a veteran from Seattle who had used the GI Bill to pay for his University of Southern California business administration degree.[19]

SAC's platform reflected the growing multifaceted critiques of and solutions to business first governance. SAC supported direct elections for the police chief and city finance director, championed ward voting, advocated firing the city manager in order to give elected officials (not appointed bureaucrats) more power over day-to-day affairs, and urged a ballot referendum to repeal and revise the charter. SAC candidates mixed their general fight for representative, responsive government with individual concerns. Darby passed around 'girlie magazines', which, he explained to an audience, were easily obtained and thus evidence of 'a growing moral decay'. But MacDonald decried road conditions because narrow gauges and missing left-turn arrows endangered the citizenry. Hanner demanded pay increases for police officers and firefighters, which reflected SAC complaints that CGC policies were irresponsible and burdensome. Candidates also found booster rhetoric and politics incongruous, particularly increasing property taxes and doubling water rates.[20]

SAC considered higher costs evidence of a communist conspiracy, not a government-built business climate designed to protect investors. Hanner deemed CGC members, including Goldwater, dupes who did not realize that the housing code had been an attempt to give the International City Managers Association's control over Phoenix. Hanner held that the National Municipal League, an organization that had given Phoenix multiple All-American city awards, controlled municipal governance through 'itinerant experts', such as the city manager the CGC had hired from Kansas City. 'Experts are planning to plan us out of our freedom', a candidate cautioned. Hanner shared this fear. He alleged that the city manager could unseat elected representatives, which indicated an imminent, national 'Metro plot' by 'Socialistic planners' 'to erase all city, county and state boundaries for easier political control' in order to commandeer American power sources (such as Colorado River dams) and destroy state capitals.[21]

Far-fetched accusations reflected the extent to which booster rhetoric and governance had constrained politics. Free-enterprise conservatism never utilized a nuanced vocabulary to explain the critical role of governance to national and local business conservatism. Those who were uncertain or opposed to these trends only had labels such as 'liberalism', 'socialism' or 'Communism' to describe the state's expansion, articulate how annexation disenfranchised homeowners, and complain that unelected bureaucrats oversaw day-to-day governance. These loaded words were meaningful to many suburbanites, who considered their definition of local, democratic control a bulwark against the kind of authoritarianism that radicalism, liberalism and even postwar conservatism represented.

CGC enthusiasts struggled to deflect these accusations in the political lexicon that they had set. 'I am not a dupe of the Communist conspiracy', Mardian declared, 'I do not approve of vice or pornography. I am not dedicated to the elimination of our traditional political subdivisions or to the creation of a municipal dictatorship.' 'The opponents of Charter Government', a former CGC councilman fumed, 'are making irresponsible and malicious statements under the guise of superpatriotism [sic], which does violence to the anti-Communist cause'. Others complained that the 'militant group' ran a 'quiet type of whispering campaign' because members lacked 'the intestinal fortitude to tell us to our faces the blubberings we've been hearing'. These frustrations reflected how good-government, investment-first conservative governance was at odds with the mass democracy ideals that were fuelling 1960s civil rights and massive resistance campaigns.[22]

SAC menaced the Phoenix elite. National attention to 'ultra-conservatives' (as *New York Times* staffers labelled upstarts) or 'ultra groups' that 'scare the suspender buttons right off such veteran anti-Communists as myself' (as conservative syndicated columnist Victor Riesel described them) threatened the Chamber's carefully constructed business climate. This investment framework had always depended on evidence of a supportive citizenry. Candidates also sparked debate among the electorate. Some residents regarded them as dangerous and delusional. Methodist clergyman Paul Alexander told churchgoers that East Coast, far right extremists had founded SAC. 'At least one', he recounted, 'is reliably reported to be a member of the John Birch Society. Two of them are openly anti-Semitic . . . [and] offer nothing but hate and suspicion and innuendo as their stock in trade'. Others fretted that leaders would later court 'these "fire in the belly" radical rightists', 'the drudgery that wins elections'. Yet some, who had observed quick, quiet suburban annexations, shouldered tax increases and paid higher utility bills, looked at the undeniable expansion of local, state and national governments and also considered it to be un-American: 'An extreme right-wing type of government is what was created for us by our founding fathers, not the New Frontier monstrosity of today which is strangling freedom to an ever increasing degree.'[23]

A SAC victory proved a pipedream, not a nightmare. Only 29 per cent of eligible voters bothered to go to the polls in 1964; 32,000 out of 45,000 endorsed the CGC in the primary, results that pre-empted a general election. SAC did make some inroads into neighbourhoods. Candidates carried five southside and two northside precincts.[24]

Renegades mounted another effort two years later, in a three-way contest that reflected the ways in which white and minority liberals and civil rights activists helped end business rule across the South and Southwest. In Phoenix, as in other Sunbelt metropolises, suburban white discontent coexisted with minority unrest because industrial investment had not yielded substantive dividends in working-class neighbourhoods, regardless of their racial make-up. Few, for example, found lucrative work in manufacturing or a home in Phoenix's wealthy, predominately white northside. But postwar campaigns for racial progress did not directly challenge the CGC until the early 1960s. For example, the multiracial alliance that nominally desegregated Phoenix schools in 1954 had relied on support from the white business elite who helped pressure legislators to pass a bill that allowed individual school boards to desegregate voluntarily, a strategy used to quell investors' fears of violent massive resistance. Action displaced manoeuvring in the early 1960s. Mexican Americans' boycotts of downtown bargain department stores, such as Sears, helped to improve hiring practices. Well-planned campaigns also gave African Americans a foothold in the city's largest, most prominent firms. NAACP members, for example, organized hundreds to apply for work at GE and other large manufacturers.

A year later, leading activists in these campaigns fought for seats on the council. The Action Citizens' Ticket represented both politically re-engaged civil rights activists and a shift within the business elite. Black mortician Lincoln Ragsdale, white liberal Democrat Richard Harless, teacher Madelene Van Arsdell, businessman Manuel Peña, and educator Charles J. Farrell included Ed Korrick on their slate. He was the son of Chamber man and local retailer Charles Korrick. His son did not have a real foothold in the Chamber, which corporate executives and branch-plant managers had come to dominate as Phoenix had sprawled. 'I did not have any argument of principle with Charter Committee in the past', he later explained, 'but felt that it should democratize and broaden its base'. 'What has started as dedication to the reform movement', he emphasized, 'has ended in dedication to "the establishment"'. ACT's platform did challenge the status quo. Candidates attacked the CGC for spending money on golf courses, not pools, parks or youth centres. They promised to fight discrimination, raise city employee salaries, subsidize residential water bills, pave southside neighbourhood roads, and apply for federal aid. 'Many millions', one candidate asserted, 'have been lost through inaction and lack of leadership'. Their politics impressed the Phoenix Central Labor Council, who gave support after a long absence from local politics.[25]

Honesty, Economy, and Representation (HEAR) candidates, in contrast, jettisoned SAC's anti-communist warnings and Christian moralism, not its basic criticisms of CGC rule and desires for residential services and empowerment. 'We don't know what's going on in City Hall is our platform', the mayoral candidate explained. Neither the 'liberal' ACT and 'conservative liberal' CGC, he added, 'has the capacity to adequately represent the best interests of all the people'. 'Non-partisan and conservative' HEAR advocated increased spending, reduced taxes and better representation through a reduction of the tax on food and medicine, reinstating the office of tax assessor to equalize assessments and improving public neighbourhood infrastructure. Candidates opposed a 3 per cent room tax to pay for a civic auditorium, wanted to limit annexations, and denounced 'dictatorial' planning and zoning, elements of free-enterprise statecraft.[26]

The two fronts forced the CGC to hire a full-time public relations agency in autumn 1963, which managed a campaign anchored in promises of expansion, efficiency and thrift and old attacks on the labour movement, liberalism and ward voting. CGC defenders called the HEAR slate 'ultra-conservatives' whose opposition to expansion would yield independent satellite communities that would choke the city with unplanned, revenue-draining, environmentally damaging suburbs. Reporters called ACT candidates 'a combination of liberal politicians (who see the Phoenix

City Hall as a way station to the state capital building) and well-heeled labor leaders (who have tried unsuccessfully to organize city hall with union members)'. 'Liberal-labor bosses', a council contender remarked, 'want to take over the entire city, returning to the patronage-ridden system'. Charter candidates argued that ACT's platform and policies were also an unnecessary extension of government power. 'You simply can't do what these people propose', a candidate warned, 'without doubling taxes, relying on federal aid and spending the taxpayers into oblivion'.[27]

The CGC still triumphed. More than 53 per cent of registered voters participated in the November primary, more than in any city election since 1949. Participants only overwhelmingly endorsed the CGC's mayoral pick. HEAR council candidates did well in northwest suburbs and ACT nominees received at least 25,000 votes. Results guaranteed a general election. Turnout remained high that December: 43.4 per cent of the registered voters returned to their polling places, still higher than any contest since 1951. ACT endorsees each received between 26,000 and 35,000 votes (as well as HEAR's endorsement because they preferred anyone over the CGC). 'We didn't win', an ACT candidate proclaimed, 'but we did shake up city hall!'[28]

ACT and HEAR tickets had provoked the electorate. 'In the beginning of the Charter Government, I worked for them', James DeWitt explained, 'they have been in office too long. They are thinking in the past and doing nothing to solve the problems of today.' Some mixed their irritation with the CGC with a desire for better representation. One *Republic* reader even denounced newsmen for ignoring this democratic ideal. 'You further erred in reporting as fact that 'the Charter Government represents all elements and groups', the Phoenician fumed, 'in truth, no six people could'. Yet critics did not necessarily profess faith in rival slates. 'ACT candidates have shown me nothing in the way of a definite program', DeWitt asserted, 'HEAR guys . . . are worse'. 'I can find only one thing that they stand for', he lamented, 'tax equalization . . . But this is only appealing to the ignorance of voters. Only a fool would think that the city council has anything to do with equalization.'[29]

The Frankenstein's Monster

Yet Phoenicians, like Americans across the country, increasingly put their trust in populist candidates. Radical journalist Andrew Kopkind was one of the few who recognized that this version of the right was hardly new, nor was it actually united. In 1965, just a year after Wallace's bid for the Democratic Party's presidential nomination and Goldwater's ill-fated presidential run, Kopkind travelled to Phoenix, where desert Republicans closest to Goldwater feared what the reporter called, 'a Frankenstein's monster which no longer does their bidding'. 'Our state and our city are suffering from an excessive orientation toward conservatism', an unnamed banker confided. Even mayor Graham lamented: 'we've been blindly conservative (and I consider myself a conservative)'. This 'sad qualification was necessary', Kopkind opined, because '"conservatism" is so much a part of the credo that anyone who dares criticize must do so in its name'.[30]

Successful candidates did not always proclaim themselves conservative. Korrick did when he won a seat on the council in 1969, the first independent candidate elected in twenty years. The CGC backed his re-election two years later but never supported Gary Peter Klahr, who pulled off an electoral upset in 1973. The Bronx-born lawyer defined himself as a rebel who did not easily fit within the New Left or postwar right. He had registered as a Republican to spurn his New Deal Democrat parents, sued the Arizona Board of Regents to stop mandatory ROTC training, filed the 1964 suit that triggered Arizona's reapportionment, and switched his party affiliation after he started taking high-profile American Civil Liberties Union cases. During his campaign, Klahr deemed the charter undemocratic. He remained a critic in office: advocating an end to at-large elections, lambasting CGC 'rent a minority' policy as illusionary representation, and assailing the *Arizona Republic* for brainwashing voters into thinking that only the CGC can 'keep us from having rats in the street and prostitution'. This renegade worried the machine's stalwarts: 'Nobody in town knows who Charter is.' 'We really don't know what the people want', the mayor fretted just a few years before the CGC was finally unable to seat a majority of its chosen delegation.[31]

Goldwater's generation of Republicans, which now constituted the party and movement's establishment, also struggled to appeal to Arizonans after electoral districts were redrawn. Across the country, court challenges to malapportioned legislatures steadily enfranchised metropolitan voters who, before the rise of gerrymandering, had better guarantees of representation and therefore more influence over party platforms. Reapportionment initially thrilled Goldwater's generation of Phoenix Republicans. A federal district court had dictated that the legislature have sixty representatives and thirty senators; half of each went to sprawling Maricopa County. The GOP subsequently took control of both legislative houses in the November 1965 election.[32]

But freshman legislators, especially John Conlan, alarmed the party's ageing guard. He was not a part of an emergent New Right. His zealotry had actually alarmed Fannin staffers in the late 1950s; they had fired him because he had seemed more interested in 'selling Bibles instead of the work he was supposed to be doing'. But his fervour spoke to the Scottsdale voters who elected him to a newly created state senate in 1965. During his seven years in office, he supported lower taxes, mandatory free-enterprise high school courses, but also tougher drug laws. His political and religious perseverance was fully paid off once population growth created Arizona's fourth district. Both the Arizona Christian Conference on Adult and Youth Programs and the Executive Committee of Billy Graham's Arizona Crusade supported his 1972 campaign to bring 'constitutional government' and 'individual freedom' to the House. Once in Washington, Conlan won the favour of top Christian conservatives, many of whom had been involved in American politics and its right wing for decades. Evangelicals' growing power in the GOP led strategist Richard Viguerie and Nixon aide Charles Colson to float Conlan's name as a future presidential contender in the years when many other members of the religious right freely condemned Goldwater for insisting on a separation between church and state as well as a woman's right to choose to have an abortion. Goldwater and Fannin, now Arizona's other senator, could no longer sideline Conlan nor make wholly secular appeals to his supporters any more. 'Conlan has a personal relationship with Jesus Christ', a voter noted in a letter asking Goldwater if he had been saved, 'Why don't you get [Conlan] to tell you about it? Ask him what Christ means to him. You'll be glad you did.'[33]

Insurgent candidates like Conlan also appealed to voters outside the Christian right, such as those who joined religious Arizonans in furthering Evan Mecham's political career. Mecham had been a fixture in state politics since the early 1960s, when the Utah-born Mormon identified with the libertarian Americans for Constitutional Action. This car dealer's particular brand of conservatism had been sewn by boosters, nurtured by business-climate governance, and proven ripe for insurgent campaigns. But he defined himself against ageing Republicans, including a Goldwater confidant who initially cottoned to Mecham's warnings of a 'Creeping Socialism . . . in the minds of those who want to take all the struggle and pain out of living, who will trade freedom for what appears to be security, who gladly eat the fruits of another's labor'. Mecham's 1962 victory over Stephen Shadegg, Goldwater's devout former campaign manager, in the Senate primary alarmed the Phoenix business elite. They looked askance at Mecham's 'Let's Get Arizona for the People' programme, which favoured the sale of 11 per cent of federal lands in order to reduce individual property taxes so as to 'give many people an opportunity to strike out on their own' and put the land to better use than 'privileged interests who obtain Federal land leases for a few cents and acre . . . and sub-lease the land for profits up to 1000 per cent'.[34]

Arizona GOP leaders continued to loathe this perennial candidate after this defeat. Mecham mounted six incendiary failed bids for the GOP's gubernatorial nomination. Another loss seemed imminent in the 1986 contest between Burton Barr and Mecham. The influential state senate majority leader represented everything Mecham 'despised about Arizona politics. He had wielded his authority in the state legislature to enrich himself and his friends, while giving lip service to the needs of the state'. Mecham promised to limit spending, pledged to reduce the sales tax, and vowed to revoke state observance of the federal Martin Luther King, Jr. holiday. Polls predicted this self-described 'Constiutionalist' would receive 5 per cent of the vote, but he won the primary by 54 per cent. 'It's not socially acceptable in some circles to admit you're voting for Evan Mecham', an aide explained. The nominee then triumphed in the three-way general election against a Democrat (the former state superintendent of public instruction) and a third-party candidate (a wealthy real estate developer).[35]

Mecham prevailed because he appealed to conservative voters who embraced free enterprise and democracy as defined by populist insurgents, like Wallace, over the previous two decades. The coordinator of his southern Arizona campaign opined that the 'working classes saw Mecham as the enemy of BMW owners who exploit them'. 'Mecham had everything against him except that he opposed the higher taxes all of his establishment rivals favored', an independent Flagstaff city councilwoman explained. This grassroots conservatism appealed to many concerned about the economy and basic governance. 'The Mechamites', a staffer explained, 'include many non-religious blue-collar workers, farmers and small business owners', 'raucous, anti-establishment beer bar crowds', and those who 'accept that the Bible is the literal word of God and that the United States Constitution was divinely inspired'.[36]

Arizonans largely considered his short tenure disastrous. Like other anti-establishment insurgents, tax policy preoccupied him. 'Our income tax rates are near the national average', he noted in a 1988 address, 'our sales tax ranks among the top ten in the nation, and Arizona was fourteenth in the nation in state taxes as a percentage of personal income'. Yet Mecham, like many grassroots rebels, also invoked the free-enterprise rhetoric behind the mid-century business tax revolt: 'to attract new industries and create new jobs for Arizonans, we must hold the line on taxes'. His expenditure proposals reflected this reinterpretation of booster growth politics: he wanted to slash university budgets and dedicate an additional $1 million for a rural job and investment initiative.[37]

Mecham's racial politics generated even more controversy. Nationally ranked journalists took note of him when he ended state recognition of Martin Luther King, Jr. Day. Some 10,000 people protested in Phoenix on 20 January 1987. U2 and Stevie Wonder boycotted the state, and the National Football League cancelled plans to hold the 1993 Super Bowl in Arizona. State officials calculated that the decision had cost $500 million in tourism revenue. National and local disgust and mockery increased after Mecham complained about too many African American NBA athletes, objected to civil rights for gays and lesbians, asserted working women were responsible for rising divorce rates, told a Jewish audience that they lived in a 'Christian nation', made racist remarks against Asian visitors, and defended creationism in the classroom.[38]

Conclusion: The Legacy of The Fractured Right

Mecham's tenure as the seventeenth Governor of Arizona lasted just under sixteen months, from January 1987 to April 1988. Recall demands turned into an actual movement 180 days after his inauguration, the legal time requirement for such an effort. 'This state has had enough', a GOP state representative told reporters. A Phoenix developer complained, 'he's had a really adverse effect on the business climate'. A gay Phoenix businessman collected 350,000 signatures, twice the support needed, in just a few months. Noted Arizona Democrats signed the petitions and Goldwater publicly asked for Mecham's resignation. The governor lampooned the effort in the salty tongue Wallace and other populist candidates favoured: 'if a band of homosexuals and a few dissident Democrats can get me out of office, why heavens, the state deserves what else they can get'. Citizens never went to the polls to decide the matter. Arizona Supreme Court jurists cancelled the May 1988 recall election after Mecham was impeached on charges of concealing a $350,000 campaign contribution, loaning $80,000 in public funds to support his car dealership, and obstructing justice. Mecham was ultimately acquitted on all counts.[39]

The Mecham debacle nonetheless proved Andrew Kopkind's 1965 pronouncement correct: Goldwater's generation of elite Republicans had created a suburban 'Frankenstein's monster' that they could not sideline, comprehend or control. Few in the mainstream press understood the conservative movement's history or dynamics, but the right that they had identified in the years after the three-way 1968 presidential election was hardly new. Conservative boosters across the South and West had considered white homeowners, whether religious or secular, their natural base of support and cultivated their postwar allegiance by promoting a generally secular business conservatism as the key to metropolitan growth, individual opportunity and general prosperity. And boosters, even the most devout, largely sold the business climate to voters in an areligious language of freedom, democracy, good governance and capitalism in the 1940s, 1950s and 1960s, when such arguments appealed to many Americans fearful of liberalism, communism and another Great Depression but also protective of their new-found affluence, regardless of whether they dedicated their wealth to religious, civic or personal causes.

Yet governance under this first generation of postwar conservatives had relied on policies fundamentally at odds with secular and spiritual grassroots definitions of local control and personal prosperity. The fifty years following 1968 saw political tensions escalate as taxes soared, government agencies grew, courts redrew districts, and working- and middle-class wages stagnated while the gap between rich and poor increased. But self-described renegades like George Wallace and Evan Mecham did not besmirch conservatism. They and subsequent generations of right-wing populists instead prioritized issues that had not been the primary concern of movement founders, like religion, or matters that had only recently made national headlines, like integration and feminism. But renegade campaigns almost always questioned the power and therefore the legitimacy of the movement's architects, many of whom shared Goldwater's 1980 lament that 'I can't really make out what [voters] want'.[40] Indeed, in the new millennium, liberals, as well as the heirs to the elite business executives, intellectuals and publishers who had organized the postwar conservative movement from the top down, have continued to find the Republican base and their preferred candidates bedevilling, unpredictable and uncontrollable.

Notes

1. See Bruce Schulman, *The Seventies: The Great Shift in American Culture, Society, and Politics* (New York: Da Capo Press, 2002).
2. Michael Kazin, *The Populist Persuasion: An American History* (Ithaca, NY: Cornell University Press, 1998), 234, 240.
3. Leo P. Ribuffo, 'Conservatism and American Politics', *Journal of the Historical Society* 3(2) (Spring 2003), 163–75.
4. Julian Zelizer, 'Rethinking the History of American Conservatism', *Reviews in American History* 38(2) (June 2010), 367–92; 'Conservatism: A Roundtable', *Journal of American History* 98(3) (December 2011), 723–73.
5. Quoted in Jefferson Cowie, *Stayin' Alive: The 1970s and the Last Days of the*

Working Class (New York: The New Press, 2010), 3. See also Michael Kazin, 'The Grass-Roots Right: New Histories of U.S. Conservatism in the Twentieth Century', *American Historical Review* 97(1) (February 1992), 136–55.

6. Michael Kazin, *The Populist Persuasion: An American History* (Ithaca, NY: Cornell University Press, 1995); Elizabeth Tandy Shermer, 'Who is Wagging Whom? Power and the New History of American Populism', *Historical Journal* 57(3) (September 2014), 1–29; David A. Horowitz, *Beyond Left and Right: Insurgency and the Establishment* (Urbana: University of Illinois Press, 1997).

7. Kim Phillips-Fein, *Invisible Hands: The Making of the Conservative Movement from the New Deal to Reagan* (New York: Norton, 2009), 26–114.

8. Elizabeth Tandy Shermer, *Sunbelt Capitalism: Phoenix and the Transformation of American Politics* (Philadelphia: University of Pennsylvania Press, 2013), 1–16.

9. Ibid. 93–146.

10. Kevin P. Phillips, *The Emerging Republican Majority* (New York: Arlington House, 1969).

11. Shermer, *Sunbelt Capitalism*, 158.

12. Ibid. 147–224, 259.

13. Ibid. 116–46.

14. Ibid. 158.

15. Shermer, 'Who is Wagging Whom?'; Kazin, *Populist Persuasion*; Kevin M. Kruse, *White Flight: Atlanta and the Making of Modern Conservatism* (Princeton, NJ: Princeton University Press, 2005).

16. Shermer, *Sunbelt Capitalism*, 302–34.

17. California State Chamber of Commerce, 'Interstate Tax Differentials As a Factor in Industrial Development (California Compared to Other States)' (19 October 1961), 1, 4, 7, Box 91, Folder 1, San Diego Chamber of Commerce Records, Special Collections and University Archives, San Diego State University, San Diego [hereafter SD]; Subscriber, 'Driven Out By Taxes', *Arizona Republic* (2 November 1953), 6; 'Four-Year Record of Charter Council Speaks for Itself!', *Arizona Republic* (2 November 1953), 10 [hereafter AR]; Wenum, 'Spatial Growth and the Central City', 157–59.

18. Brent Whiting Brown, 'An Analysis of the Phoenix Charter Government Committee as a Political Entity', unpublished MA thesis, Arizona State University, 1968, 50–8; 'Ex-Chief Justice of Arizona "High Priest" of Ultra Group', *Washington Post* (20 December 1961); 'Ultras Drawing Impressive Financial Backing', *Washington Post* (21 December 1961); 'Support in the Press Provides "Ultras" With Respectability', *Washington Post* (22 December 1961).

19. 'Who's Who on Stay American Committee's Ticket', *AR* (5 November 1961); 'One Too Many Talks Led to Candidacy, Hanner Says', *AR* (4 November 1961).

20. 'Pastor's Editorial Blasts SAC Group', *AR* (2 November 1961); 'The Voter's Choice', *AR* (2 November 1961); 'Misquoted, SAC Says on TV', *AR* (4 November 1961).

21. 'Pastor's Editorial Blasts SAC Group', *AR* (2 November 1961); 'The Voter's Choice', *AR* (2 November 1961); 'Misquoted, SAC Says on TV', *AR* (4 November 1961); 'Phoenix Red Target, Candidates Say', *AR* (4 November 1961); 'Williams Decries SAC's Statements', *AR* (2 November 1961); 'SAC

Candidate Says Reds Plot Power Coup, *AR* (5 November 1961); 'Phoenix Red Target, Candidates Say', *AR* (4 November 1961); 'Inside Labor: Extremist Label Pinned On SAC', *AR* (4 November 1961).

22. 'The Voter's Choice'; 'Udall Tags Opposition "Irrational"', *AR* (4 November 1961).

23. 'Right-Wing Slate on Phoenix Ballot'; 'Pastor's Editorial Blasts SAC Group', *AR* (November 1961); 'Fascists Belong on Extreme Left', *AR* (2 November 1961); 'Inside Labor: Extremist Label Pinned On SAC', *AR* (4 November 1961).

24. Shermer, *Sunbelt Capitalism*, 302–35.

25. Ibid.

26. William S. Collins, *The Emerging Metropolis: Phoenix 1944–1973* (Phoenix: Arizona State Parks Board, 2005), 66; 'CG Blasts Basis of ACT Plea', *AR* (1 November 1963); Robert J. Early, 'ACT Program Questioned', *AR* (4 November 1963); 'Hill Urges Tax Assessor For Phoenix', *AR* (8 November 1963); 'ACT Forges Major Opposition Slate', *AR* (10 November 1963); 'HEAR Ticket Entered Race Late; Places Stress on Conservatism', *AR* (10 November 1963); 'U.S. Aid Promised by ACT', *AR* (10 November 1963).

27. Matthew C. Whitaker, *Race Work: The Rise of Civil Rights in the Urban West* (Lincoln: University of Nebraska Press, 2005), 167–8; Amy Bridges, *Morning Glories: Municipal Reform in the Southwest* (Princeton, NJ: Princeton University Press, 1997), 177; Brown, 'An Analysis', 58–62; Joanne Smoot Patton, Press Release (4 November 1963), Box: unassigned, Folder 'Rosenzweig: Government & Public Policy, Charter Government Committee, 1963' (2 of 3), Newton Rosenzweig Collection, Arizona Historical Foundation, Tempe [hereafter Rosenzweig]; [Joanne Smoot Patton], 'In a Nutshell' memo to all [CGC] candidates, Box: unassigned, Folder 'Rosenzweig: Government & Public Policy, Charter Government Committee, 1963' (1 of 3), , Rosenzweig; Patton, 'Highlights of 1962–6' (24 October 1963), Rosenzweig; Patton, 'Phoenix Growth History', (24 October 1963), Rosenzweig; Robert J. Early, 'Graham Raps ACT', *AR* (5 November 1963); 'Charter Government', *AR* (3 November 1963).

28. Shermer, *Sunbelt Capitalism*, 302–35.

29. Mrs. Joan Patrick, 'Reader Criticizes Republic Editorial', *AR* (2 November 1963); James V. DeWitt, 'ACT Candidates Offer No Program', *AR* (9 November 1963).

30. Andrew Kopkind, 'Modern Times in Phoenix: A City at the Mercy of its Myths', *The New Republic* (6 November 1965), 14–15.

31. Frosty Taylor, 'Klahr zaps Charter Government in Speech', *Paradise Valley News* (19 January 1974), n.p., Box 1, Folder 14, Lewis; 'Review of C.G.C. Campaign Publicity & P. R. Agencies' (29 July 1965), Box: unassigned, Folder: 'Rosenzweig: Government & Public Policy, Charter Government Committee', 1963 (1 of 3), Rosenzweig; 'Report by 1963 Chairman Charter Government Committee & Election (8 April–31 December), undated, Rosenzweig; Whitaker, *Race Work*, 167–69; Collins, *Emerging Metropolis*, 68; Philip VanderMeer, *Desert Visions and the Making of Modern Phoenix, 1860–2009* (Albuquerque: University of New Mexico Press, 2010), 240–2; Marvin Andrews interview by Dean Smith,

typescript (11 May 1990), 9–10, Oral History Collection, Department of Archives and Special Collections, Arizona State University, Tempe; John Driggs interview by Karen Smith (13 July 1978), transcript, 1–8, Phoenix History Project, Arizona Historical Society, Tempe; Amy Silverman, 'Old Glory', *Phoenix New Times* (4 July 2002).

32. Shermer, *Sunbelt Capitalism*, 302–35.

33. Jason Cranbtree LaBau, 'Phoenix Rising: Arizona and the Origins of Modern Conservative Politics', unpublished PhD thesis, University of Southern California, Los Angeles, 2010, 142, 145.

34. Data for League of Women Voters, Box 9, Folder 17, Evan Mecham Collection, Arizona State University Archives and Special Collections, Tempe [hereafter Mecham]; Speech Notes, [1962], 1–2, Box 9, Folder 17, Mecham; untitled speech, [1962], 1, Box 9, Folder 23, Mecham; draft statement for *Small Business Review*, [1962], Box 9, Folder 23, Mecham; 'Mecham talk to Phoenix Kiwanis Club' (14 August 1962), 1, Box 9, Folder 23, Mecham; untitled speech, [1962], 1, Box 9, Folder 23, Mecham; untitled press release, [1962], Box 9, Folder 23, Mecham.

35. Stephen C. Shadegg, *Arizona Politics: The Struggle to End One-Party Rule* (Tempe: Arizona State University Press, 1986), 125–6; James W. Johnson, *Arizona Politicians: The Noble and the Notorious* (Tucson: University of Arizona Press, 2002), 40.

36. 'Jury Acquits Governor', *Wall Street Journal* (21 June 1988), 38; quoted in Johnson, *Arizona Politicians*, 41; 'Up in Arms in Arizona', *New York Times* (1 November 1987), 59; 'The Resurrection of Evan Mecham', *National Review* 41 (May 1989), 42–3.

37. Johnson, *Arizona Politicians*, 38–42; Ronald J. Bellus, 'Evan Mecham: Governing Arizona', *Washington Post* (17 July 1987); T. R. Reid, 'Arizona's GOP Governor Ridiculed by the Voters', *Washington Post* (21 June 1987); Evan Mecham, 'State of the State Address' (11 January 1988): www.kensmith.us/2009/05/state-of-state-1988.html

38. Paula D. McClain, '"High Noon": The Recall and Impeachment of Evan Mecham', *PS: Political Science and Politics* 21(3) (Summer 1988), 623–38; Weisman, 'Up in Arms in Arizona'; 'Arizona Torn by Governor-Elect's Plan to Drop King Holiday', *New York Times* (23 December 1986).

39. Associated Press, 'Evan Mecham, Ousted Governor, Dies at 83', *New York Times* (23 February 2008); Smith, 'Resurrection of Evan Mecham'; Lindsey Gruson, 'A Family Gathering Shows Split Over Mecham Goes Deeper Than Politics', *New York Times* (19 March 1988); William E. Schmidt, 'Republicans Join the Roster of Arizona Governor's Foes' (15 October 1987); 'Evan Mecham, Please Go Home', *Time* (9 November 1987): quoted in Johnson, *Arizona Politicians*, 42.

40. LaBau, 'Phoenix Rising', 149.

THREE

The Irony of Protest:
Vietnam and The Path to Permanent War

Andrew Preston

1968: it is difficult to think of a more consequential year during the American war in Vietnam. The series of cascading events triggered by the Tet Offensive – Lyndon Johnson's decision not to run for re-election, the beginning of the first-ever direct negotiations between the US and North Vietnam, the removal of General William Westmoreland, the antiwar riots in Chicago, and the election of Richard Nixon on a vague promise to end the war – helped form the major pivot point of the entire conflict. Before Tet, the United States was determined to preserve the independence of South Vietnam through the use of military power; after Tet, it was committed to finding a way out of Indochina. Before Tet, the president was a Democrat who Americanized the war by deploying a peak ground force of over half a million troops; after Tet, the president was a Republican who introduced 'Vietnamization' – that is, withdrawing American troops and turning the ground war over to the augmented forces of the South Vietnamese army – as his primary strategy for America's military withdrawal from Vietnam. Until 1968, then, the major military trend had been the escalation and Americanization of the conflict; after 1968, it was marked by withdrawal and Vietnamization. If there was a beginning of the end to America's war in Vietnam, Tet provided it.[1]

The tumultuous events in Vietnam had wider ramifications, as well. Without the relative decline in American power inflicted by the war, it is unlikely that Nixon would have opened relations with the People's Republic of China or embarked on detente and arms control with the Soviet Union. Not only were Nixon and Henry Kissinger, the president's chief foreign policy adviser, hoping to manage the spiralling costs of waging the Cold War, they were sure that Moscow and Beijing could apply pressure on Hanoi to settle the war.[2] US negotiations on three separate but interlocking fronts unfolded simultaneously, with the Soviet Union, China and North Vietnam. While the great-power talks with Moscow and Beijing yielded breathtaking results, namely nuclear arms control with the Soviets and the recognition of Communist China that ended its twenty-year international isolation, the Paris-based negotiations with the North Vietnamese proved more intractable. The agreement eventually reached in January 1973, the Paris Peace Accords, papered over key differences rather than solving them.[3] Just over two years later, in April 1975, North Vietnamese tanks rolled into Saigon and ended forever the experiment in South Vietnamese sovereignty. A year later, the two Vietnams were officially reunified as the Socialist Republic of Vietnam.

There is still a lively debate over the extent to which the antiwar movement successfully pressured the US government to end the fighting in Vietnam.[4] There is little doubt, however, that antiwar activism played a large role in creating the conditions that made 1968 appear to be such a pivotal year in the war. As early as the summer of 1967, it was clear that the war had stalemated, both in the air over North Vietnam and on the ground in South Vietnam. Although we now realize that Westmoreland did have an appreciation for counterinsurgency and pacification, his overall strategy was based upon a war of attrition.[5] By 'killing anything that moves', the US military hoped to wear down the National Liberation Front (NLF) in South Vietnam, and by raining down an unprecedented amount of ordinance from the sky it would force North Vietnam to sue for peace on American terms. Neither of these objectives turned out to be effective, or even realistic.[6] Indeed, US military strategy helped provoke unrest at home as a growing number of Americans became uncomfortable with their nation's actions in Indochina. In response, Johnson recalled General Westmoreland to Washington for a series of congressional briefings and public appearances, all designed to shore up flagging support for the war. Westmoreland, a true believer, was unwavering in his optimism. In his autumn 1967 'progress campaign' back in the United States, which culminated in a speech before a special joint session of Congress, he claimed that the United States and South Vietnam were winning the war and that the end of the insurgency was simply a matter of time.[7] Thus when the Tet Offensive hit a few months later, on 30 January 1968, it belied all of Westmoreland's optimistic claims. It mattered little that the Tet Offensive actually resulted in heavy losses for the NLF without any corresponding gains, and that South Vietnamese and American forces recaptured all their lost ground fairly quickly. The damage to Westmoreland's credibility – and Lyndon Johnson's – was irreparable.[8]

Paradoxically, it was excessive concerns with credibility that dragged the United States into Vietnam in the first place. As Fredrik Logevall has pointed out, policymakers were obsessed with three, often overlapping and mutually reinforcing, types of credibility.[9] First, policymakers in the Kennedy, Johnson and Nixon administrations worried that America's international credibility, particularly with its adversaries but also with its allies, would suffer if the United States withdrew from Indochina and South Vietnam fell to communism. Second, they feared the domestic political consequences of appearing soft on communism. Third, policymakers sought to preserve their own personal credibility; this was particularly acute for Johnson administration officials, who had been devising Vietnam policy under Kennedy and felt it difficult, if not impossible, to repudiate their own handiwork and walk away from an ally, South Vietnam, they had been struggling to protect. With cruelly sharp irony, Tet destroyed all of these assumptions: the United States' international standing as a military leviathan had been severely undermined by a surprise attack orchestrated by poorly equipped guerrilla forces; Johnson's domestic credibility was so shattered that he immediately sought once-unpalatable direct negotiations with North Vietnam; and the confidence Americans may have once had in the 'best and the brightest', to use David Halberstam's sardonic reference to the Kennedy and Johnson administration officials who led the nation into Vietnam, evaporated.[10]

Johnson put all this into motion in a momentous televised address to the nation on 31 March 1968. In it he unveiled three surprise moves, each a direct consequence of the Tet Offensive.

He announced that he was 'taking the first step to deescalate the conflict . . . unilaterally, and at once', by halting the bombing of North Vietnam (a continuous operation, ominously codenamed ROLLING THUNDER, that had begun three years earlier, in March 1965) and entering into direct talks with Hanoi. But the biggest surprise came in the closing words at the very end of the speech, when Johnson announced that he would not run for re-election in November.[11] LBJ claimed that it was now time to find a lasting peace in Vietnam and that a re-election campaign would distract him from this task. And while there is no reason to doubt his sincerity, it was also increasingly clear that he would struggle to win the presidential nomination of his own party, let alone the general election. Tet revealed the poverty of US military strategy in Vietnam, which in turn raised questions about the very purpose of American intervention. Doubts about the war in Vietnam, coupled with gnawing but widespread concerns about Johnson's integrity and competence, led to a surprisingly successful challenge by Eugene McCarthy, a little-known US senator from Minnesota who ran against Johnson in the New Hampshire primary in February. While he did not win, McCarthy defied even his own expectations by coming close, losing by only 7 per cent to an incumbent who had been one of the most powerful political figures for the past two decades.[12] This was unprecedented. With Johnson weakened, McCarthy's unexpectedly strong showing encouraged a more serious rival, Senator Robert F. Kennedy, to enter the race, also on a platform that was largely antiwar. Facing such humiliation over Vietnam at the hands of his own party, Johnson decided to quit.

Accordingly, the presidential election campaign of 1968 was dominated by the issue of Vietnam. McCarthy's challenge lost momentum once Kennedy was in the race, but Kennedy's candidacy was cut short by an assassin's bullet in June. Johnson's vice president, Hubert Humphrey, once a private sceptic on escalation, secured the nomination, but not without protest: at the Democratic National Convention in Chicago, police attacked antiwar demonstrators, causing a riot and severe disruption to the proceedings. The intensity of the antiwar protests in Chicago, alongside the even more violently intense response by the Chicago police, symbolized a nation that had come apart over Vietnam.[13] Once nominated,

Humphrey continued Johnson's new policy of seeking peace in Vietnam but not at any price. The Republican nominee, Richard Nixon, also pledged to find a way out of Indochina. He implied (but never explicitly stated) that he had a secret plan to do so without humiliating the United States. When Americans entered the voting booth on 5 November, then, they were presented with the narrowest of choices between two candidates who both promised to extricate the nation from Vietnam. Antiwar sentiment, still a fringe element only a year before, had captured the political centre.[14]

Richard Nixon and 'Peace with Honor'

Beneath the surface, however, the tumultuous events of 1968 did not change all that much. Underlying structural forces, be they the pressures of Cold War credibility or American domestic politics, shifted only very slightly, so that the appearance of dramatic change was much greater than the actual change effected by Tet and the surge of antiwar activism.

Most notably, once he won the White House and assumed the presidency, Nixon pursued a strikingly similar objective to Johnson's, despite superficial differences. Worried that the South Vietnamese were no longer capable of suppressing the communist-nationalist insurgency waged by the Vietcong and supported by North Vietnam, Johnson had Americanized the war in 1965 – that is, he took over the waging of war from the South Vietnamese. Under pressure from Congress and the public to withdraw from Indochina, Nixon did so under a rubric of 'peace with honor' and based on a strategy of 'Vietnamization'. Yet, while both slogans implied significant policy change, they actually pursued something closer to the status quo because Nixon's ultimate goal – the maintenance of an independent, non-communist state in South Vietnam – was identical to Johnson's (and indeed, to Kennedy's and Eisenhower's before). Properly deconstructed, 'peace with honor' was no different from previous US policy; it could very well have been Johnson's slogan before it was Nixon's. 'Peace' did not mean the absence of war – far from it. Instead, in Nixon's vision, it meant the absence of US troops in Vietnam, which, not coincidentally, seemed to be the root cause of much antiwar dissent among young people in the United States. Accordingly, between 1969 and 1972, Nixon withdrew ground forces at a rate similar to Johnson's deployment of them between 1965 and 1968; by April 1973, no regular combat soldiers remained anywhere in South Vietnam aside from a handful to guard the US Embassy in Saigon. 'Honor', an even more powerfully emotive word, meant that Nixon would not withdraw troops in a precipitous manner that could trigger the collapse of South Vietnam. It was 'honor', in other words, that signalled Nixon's intention to preserve an independent South Vietnam.

How did Nixon intend to attain a goal that had eluded Lyndon Johnson and destroyed his presidency? And how would Nixon achieve it without the hundreds of thousands of American ground forces Johnson had deployed? Nixon may have begun the de-escalation of America's ground war, but his strategy for 'peace with honor' was based on two escalatory measures Johnson had steadfastly resisted. One, Nixon drastically increased the US air war. He approved the bombing of targets previously considered off-limits, either because they risked provoking tensions with the Soviets or Chinese (such as Haiphong harbour, where the ships of North Vietnam's communist allies docked) or because they were predominantly civilian targets (such as urban centres like Hanoi, or the system of dykes that controlled flooding in the Red River Delta). Two, Nixon expanded the war geographically to the rest of Indochina. Cambodia and Laos were now considered legitimate targets, on the ground and from the air. Both suffered a major ground attack: US and South Vietnamese troops jointly invaded Cambodia in 1970, while South Vietnamese troops invaded Laos by themselves in 1971. Both were also subjected to relentless bombing campaigns by the US Air Force.

The escalation of the war, geographically and in the air, was complemented by two other policies that were meant to buttress America's commitment to South Vietnam without the need to commit ground troops. The first, of course, was the process of Vietnamization, which was managed by Secretary of Defense Melvin Laird and would in theory transfer fighting from the Americans to the South Vietnamese. In order to do so, South Vietnam's armed forces would have to be augmented in terms of size and firepower.

To backstop Vietnamization, and give South Vietnam time and breathing space to develop its new military, Nixon deployed US air power to provide close support for South Vietnamese troops. In South Vietnam's failed Operation Lam Son, in 1971, and during North Vietnam's successful Easter Offensive, in 1972, American bombing prevented a full-scale rout of the South Vietnamese army. In 1973, as the US military was planning to depart Vietnam, Nixon secretly pledged economic and military aid, and indefinite US air support, to South Vietnamese president Nguyen Van Thieu.

The second policy, orchestrated by National Security Adviser Henry Kissinger in tandem with Nixon himself, was an intricate diplomatic strategy pursued along two separate but linked tracks. In Paris, at first in secret and then very much in public, Kissinger negotiated peace terms directly with the North Vietnamese. Simultaneously, in Washington, Moscow and Beijing he negotiated new cooperative relationships with the Soviets and the Chinese. In exchange for America's recognition of their legitimacy, as well as capital credits and surplus foodstuffs, the Soviets and Chinese would apply pressure on Hanoi to settle the war on terms that were acceptable to the United States.[15]

In theory, both Vietnamization and Kissinger's grand diplomacy were brilliant manoeuvres designed to maximize America's political, economic and technological leverage while avoiding the disastrous military policies pursued by Johnson and Westmoreland. In reality, neither worked. Vietnamization could not instantly transform the South Vietnamese military into a world-class fighting force that could withstand one of the most effective insurgencies in modern history.[16] Diplomacy, once it moved beyond Kissinger's control, faced similar limitations. Having been betrayed by Soviet and Chinese pressure in 1954, when the Geneva Conference on Indochina agreed to divide Vietnam in half in what was supposed to be temporary but soon became indefinite, the North Vietnamese were not about to be pressured into any more settlements that would compromise their dream of national reunification under communist rule.[17]

Whatever the effectiveness of Nixon's overall strategy for Vietnam, it hardly marked a new departure. The expansion of US bombing operations, the spread of war to Cambodia and Laos, the secret promises to Thieu, and Vietnamization created the conditions for indefinite warfare in Vietnam rather than any semblance of 'peace with honor'.[18] This was not all that different from Johnson's commitment to the long-term survival of South Vietnam, which resulted in the Americanization of the conflict not because LBJ wanted war – he actually did everything he could to avoid going to war – but because he felt he had no other option.[19]

Under Nixon, and with the assistance of Kissinger, the American phase of the Second Indochina War officially ended with the Paris Peace Accords of January 1973 and the withdrawal of the remaining US forces by April that same year. But the war continued, until April 1975, when North Vietnamese tanks entered Saigon and overthrew the US-backed South Vietnamese regime. Thieu went into exile in London, his secret promises from Nixon ruined by the Watergate scandal and the tenacity of his communist adversaries in Vietnam. Yet by demonstrating an unwavering willingness to deploy massive firepower, and by using Vietnamization to shift culpability for a future collapse onto the Saigon regime, Kissinger (and President Gerald Ford after Watergate forced Nixon's resignation) had insured American credibility against the collapse of South Vietnam.[20] Whether this aim for a 'decent interval' – that is, a sufficient gap of time between the American military withdrawal and the inevitable fall of South Vietnam – was deliberate policy or unwitting consequence is a matter of intense historiographical debate.[21] What is certain, however, is that warfare continued to devastate Indochina a full seven years after Johnson announced, in March 1968, that the United States was looking for an end to the conflict.

Muting Dissent

If the overall strategic objectives in Vietnam did not change all that much due to 1968, nor did the antiwar movement and its relationship to the broader political culture undergo much in the way of significant transformation. The mass peace movement, which began in earnest in the spring of 1965 and peaked with the March on the Pentagon in October 1967, continued through the entire Nixon era right to the end of American involvement in 1975.

Figure 3.1 Anti-Vietnam war protesters march down Fifth Avenue, Manhattan, in protest against US involvement in the Vietnam War, 27 April 1968. Courtesy of AP/Press Association Images.

After gathering pace through 1966 and into 1967, the antiwar movement probably reached its zenith in October 1967, with a large demonstration of 100,000 people at the Lincoln Memorial in Washington followed by a smaller but still substantial and much more radical crowd who marched to the Pentagon, surrounded it, and demanded an end to the war. In response to a wider sense that the war had stalemated but also to the growing crescendo of radical antiwar activism, the Johnson administration mounted a public relations campaign to convey its confidence and cautious optimism. Johnson recalled General Westmoreland from Saigon to give a series of speeches in the United States which culminated in a rare address to a special joint session of Congress. As Westmoreland told the deputy US commander in Vietnam, General Creighton Abrams, in November, there was 'some light at the end of the tunnel' in the war effort.[22] While perhaps not imminent, victory was in sight.

Little did Westmoreland know, the light he perceived was not sunshine but an oncoming train. As he himself later conceded, his assessment of the American war effort was overly optimistic and wildly off the mark.[23] This became all too clear at the end of January, when the Tet Offensive struck with more ferocity than Westmoreland, or almost any other American war planner, either in Saigon or in Washington, anticipated.[24]

The antiwar movement peaked under Johnson and Westmoreland, but some of the largest spasms of antiwar opposition occurred because of Nixon's escalatory policies. After promising to end the war but not moving with all that much alacrity to do so, in October 1969 the Vietnam Moratorium launched a protest against the war by millions of people nationwide; a month later, the Moratorium leaders organized a march in Washington of a half-million demonstrators. The Moratorium protests were notable for their middle-class respectability and nationwide simultaneity. In late April and early May the following year, Nixon's invasion of Cambodia, which included 30,000 US troops at a time when the war was supposedly being 'Vietnamized', provoked the most widespread student demonstrations of the entire era. Hundreds of college campuses shut down, and several were occupied by student activists. The demonstrations against the Cambodian invasion ended in tragedy when the National Guard shot students at Kent State University in Ohio, killing four and wounding nine; ten days later, at Jackson State University in Mississippi, two more students died in clashes with police.

Yet on the whole, the movement slowly lost momentum each year after 1968. The incidents surrounding the Moratorium and Cambodia represented dramatic exceptions in an otherwise downward trajectory. To be sure, antiwar protest did continue until 1975, much of it highly public and probably somewhat influential on broader popular attitudes about Vietnam. In fact, with the emergence of violent organizations such as the Weather Underground and powerful acts of civil disobedience by former war planners such as Daniel Ellsberg, who leaked the Pentagon Papers to the *New York Times* and the *Washington Post* in 1971, the antiwar movement entered a decidedly more radical phase after 1968.[25] But antiwar activism dwindled in numbers and effectiveness, its increasing radicalism reflective of frustrations that the war continued despite the desire of a clear majority of Americans that it come to an end.

Here, once again, Nixon defied the circumstances that had imprisoned Johnson in a mutually reinforcing cycle of military escalation and domestic unrest. In doing so, Nixon was able to continue the war and maintain the nation's commitment to South Vietnam, and one could argue that if it had not been for Watergate he would have been able to sustain his delicate balancing act between American withdrawal and South Vietnamese survival. Instead, scandal forced him from office and emboldened Congress to end the war by terminating the appropriations that funded South Vietnam. But how could he balance such violently polarized forces? Several factors were important, but two stand out in particular: the withdrawal of ground troops; and the reframing of the war as a test of America's very identity rather than simply as a test of America's international credibility.

As we have seen, the 'peace' in Nixon's 'peace with honor' simply meant the removal of US troops. This was not simply a measure of strategic necessity or a way to address military ineffectiveness: Nixon realized that American boots on the ground in Vietnam was a primary cause of antiwar dissent. Vietnamization was driven in part by a need to transfer the burden of fighting away from Americans for military reasons, but another key impetus was the unrest roiling the nation's students and young people. Not long after taking office, Nixon announced a review of the draft system; his desire to end conscription was widely known, and the review marked the beginning of its end.[26] To be sure, the transition to an all-volunteer military took several years to implement, but the withdrawal of troops from Vietnam, alongside the announcement that the draft would soon come to an end, meant that young Americans had less reason to fear being sent to fight foreign wars against their conscience. The antiwar movement sputtered as a result. For example, when Nixon authorized the invasion of Laos in 1971, South Vietnamese forces did the fighting; while the US Air Force provided substantial air cover, especially when the South Vietnamese attack was swiftly repulsed, no American troops took part.[27] Unlike a year earlier, when the invasion of Cambodia provoked a spate of antiwar demonstrations and student occupations that brought campuses across the country to a standstill, and led members of Congress to introduce resolutions aiming to limit the deployment of US forces in Indochina, the invasion of Laos generated comparatively little opposition.

Even more important was Nixon's revision of the war's ultimate purpose. America's geopolitical credibility had always been the nation's underlying purpose in Vietnam. In 1954, on the flimsy premise of the 'domino theory', Eisenhower committed the United States as South Vietnam's guardian, and Kennedy and Johnson continued that commitment lest the United States appear weak to its allies and enemies. But by negotiating directly with North Vietnam, the Soviet Union and the People's Republic of China, Nixon did not have to worry as much, or in quite the same way, about shoring up American credibility. He of course sought an exit from Indochina that would not make the United States look weak, but he also saw the contest in Vietnam as a battle for the soul of America. In Nixon's telling, outlined in a major speech after the Moratorium protests of October 1969, opposition to the war, which had never enjoyed broad popular support even as a majority of Americans turned against the war itself, became synonymous with opposition to the purpose and promise of America. This was behind Nixon's political masterstroke of pitting a 'silent majority' of patriotic Americans against a minority of antiwar activists. If the United States suddenly withdrew from Indochina and left South Vietnam to its fate, America's allies would lose confidence in its ability to uphold international peace. But the consequences were graver still. 'Far more dangerous', Nixon warned, 'we would lose confidence in ourselves' and 'scar our spirit as a people'. It was not simply the future of South Vietnam that was at stake; so too was the future of the United States: 'If a vocal minority, however fervent its cause, prevails over reason and the will of the majority, this Nation has no future as a free society.' Nixon would thus not accept a peace at any price; he would instead pursue 'peace with honor', for America's sake as well as South Vietnam's. 'Let us be united for peace', he concluded. 'Let us also be united against defeat. Because let us understand: North Vietnam cannot defeat or humiliate the United States. Only Americans can do that.'[28] He encouraged prowar sympathizers, such as the infamous 'hard-hats', and tried with little success to stimulate a broad-based prowar movement to counter antiwar activism.[29] The effect was to divide Americans between unpatriotic opponents of the war and faithful supporters of the nation.

The Legacies of Vietnam

By making the war a populist cause in an era of conservative grass-roots politics, and by pivoting the fundamentals of American military strategy from the ground to the air, Nixon not only continued Johnson's commitment to South Vietnam – he also paved the way for an era of permanent war in US foreign policy. And while Nixon himself was not able to tame the populist forces he unleashed, he made it easier for his successors in the Oval Office to deploy military force in the service of diplomatic and geopolitical goals.[30] The irony of Vietnam is that America's most ignominious military failure made it more likely, not less, that warfare would be an acceptable option in the nation's dealings with the wider world. What makes this irony even sharper still is the antiwar movement's unwitting role in bringing it about.

The path to permanent war did not happen immediately. After the fall of Saigon in April 1975, US foreign policy succumbed to a condition generally known as 'Vietnam syndrome'. Scarred by the waging of a difficult limited war for opaque political ends, which in turn divided Americans against each other more deeply than they had been for a century, policymakers avoided intervening in foreign conflicts and the public placed little pressure on them to do so. Washington did not exactly abandon anti-communism as its grand strategy, but no longer would it uphold containment through indefinite military intervention in distant civil wars, as it had done first in Korea and then in Vietnam. Strategically, Nixon signalled this shift in an eponymous 'doctrine' announced in July 1969: while the United States would support its allies in their resistance to communism, it would do so politically, diplomatically, financially, and ultimately with the backing of the US nuclear arsenal, but the United States would not itself intervene directly in the wars of others.[31] While the Nixon Doctrine did not mention the deployment of conventional air power, Nixon's Vietnam policies effectively added it to the foundations of America's new security framework. When South Vietnamese forces faltered in Laos in February 1971 and against North Vietnam's Easter offensive in April 1972, sustained massive US bombing prevented their total collapse. Air power proved to be an attractive alternative to the deployment of hundreds of thousands of ground troops and was thus an easy, if unofficial, addendum to the Nixon Doctrine.

The Vietnam syndrome flourished for the decade and a half after the war ended. Despite the eruption of major crises in Central America and the Middle East, Presidents Gerald Ford, Jimmy Carter and Ronald Reagan authorized the deployment of only a small number of troops in only a handful of situations. Each one of those situations, moreover, turned into either a fiasco or a disaster, or both, thus reinforcing the premises and power of the syndrome. In April 1980, nearly five years to the day after the fall of Saigon, Carter authorized a mission to rescue over fifty Americans being held hostage in Iran. While aborted before it was even launched, the mission ended in humiliation when an accidental collision of two American aircraft resulted in the deaths of eight servicemen. In October 1983, a Hezbollah suicide bomber destroyed the barracks housing US forces in Beirut as part of an international peacekeeping mission; 241 US Marines died and all remaining military personnel were withdrawn without engaging in retaliatory action. And in 1986, following mounting tensions between the United States and Libya, Reagan authorized the bombing of targets connected to the regime of Muammar Gaddafi; no ground troops were involved.

When US forces were sent into action between 1975 and 1990, it was most often in disproportionately overwhelming numbers in a proximate region of obvious strategic interest. Thus US troops invaded the Caribbean island of Grenada, in 1983, to prevent a communist takeover, and invaded the Central American republic of Panama, in 1989, to arrest its leader, Manuel Noriega. Both invasions, designed to forestall prolonged fighting or a lengthy occupation, resulted in relatively quick victories for the United States, followed by a swift departure. In more intractable hemispheric conflicts that did not offer such easy solutions, such as the civil wars raging in El Salvador and Nicaragua, the United States adhered to the Nixon Doctrine and provided material and political aid but no direct military participation itself. Even that proved too much: with the shadow of Vietnam still looming, Congress explicitly forbade any direct US involvement and eventually cut off all funding for America's anti-communist allies.[32]

The two main ideological blueprints for US foreign policy in the post-Vietnam years reflected, in their very different ways, a grand strategy of limits. The first was the Reagan Doctrine, which promised aid to resistance groups and governments fighting communism around the world.[33] Like most presidential foreign policy 'doctrines', Reagan's aimed to provide a general theory to justify action taken in specific circumstances. The 1947 Truman Doctrine, for instance, called for the global containment of communism even though it emerged from particular events in Greece and Turkey. The Nixon Doctrine, which applied to all US allies, of course emerged from the need to withdraw from Vietnam. In similar fashion, the Reagan Doctrine promised a global offensive against communism based upon the immediate problem of Central America. Superficially, by promising offensive action against communism and offering a more robust version of containment, it resembled the Truman Doctrine. But by promising aid and support, but explicitly not the involvement of US forces, the Reagan Doctrine also betrayed the more cautionary effects of Vietnam; in this sense, it was more akin to Nixon's doctrine than Truman's.

The second programmatic statement of America's grand strategic principles in the post-Vietnam world was the 1984 Weinberger Doctrine. Named after a major speech delivered by Secretary of Defense Caspar Weinberger, this doctrine carefully stipulated the precise terms under which US ground troops would be deployed into action. In going to war, Weinberger explained, presidents must use overwhelming force in pursuit of clear objectives and with an exit strategy articulated even before the initial intervention; ideally, the president should also proceed only when backed by congressional and popular support. It was articulated as a response to the Beirut bombing – in which the US Marines, participating in an ill-defined political mission of indefinite duration, were a soft and easy target – and as a way to head off pressure to deploy American troops to Nicaragua.[34] The Weinberger Doctrine was, in other words, clearly designed to avoid another Vietnam War, as policymakers strove to avoid waging difficult wars that would almost inevitably provoke strong antiwar resistance and stoke partisan and social divisions at home.

Yet the Vietnam syndrome was remarkably short-lived. After the end of the Cold War in 1989–90, the United States found itself in a state of perpetual military intervention. In 1991, President George H. W. Bush committed well over half a million troops to war against Iraq after it had invaded and occupied Kuwait, a US ally and key oil producer. The Gulf War resulted in a heavy bombing campaign against Iraq and a successful ground offensive to oust its army from Kuwait. Flush with victory, Bush exulted, 'by God, we've kicked the Vietnam syndrome once and for all'.[35] And so it seemed. In 1992, US troops deployed to Somalia to assist United Nations humanitarian operations. In 1995, US warplanes provided massive air support in a war against Bosnian Serbs; four years later, they reprised their role against Serbia over the fate of Kosovo. In response to the 9/11 attacks, US forces invaded Afghanistan in 2001 and Iraq in 2003. In 2011, US airships were integral in the campaign to remove Gaddafi from power in Libya. And from the early 1990s right up to the present, US warplanes have been deployed against targets in Afghanistan, Pakistan, Sudan, Syria, Yemen and elsewhere.[36]

Conclusion: 1968 and The Path to Permanent War

To optimists, the end of the Cold War promised to mark 'the end of history' and the triumph of liberal internationalism across the planet.[38] This 'new world order', as Bush called it in 1990, would hopefully be peaceful and cooperative, but if challengers emerged – such as Saddam Hussein's Iraq – it would ultimately be underwritten by US military power in partnership with allies.[38] But instead of a cooperative new world order, the United States found itself mired in a 'forever war' for the Middle East and confronting rising tensions with Russia in Europe and China in Asia.[39]

How did this happen? In pronouncing a 'new world order', Bush had spoken too soon, mainly because his other key declaration, that the Vietnam syndrome had been 'kicked', was misplaced. Bush was correct that the nation had overcome the Vietnam syndrome's reluctance to use military force. But he was wrong to suggest that it marked a return to an older way of warfare, such as the model everyone wanted to emulate: World War II.[40] After Vietnam, policy-makers desperately wanted to avoid waging stalemated wars, which would not only be a drain on the Pentagon's resources and capability to intervene but also aggravate domestic unrest. Memories of the domestic turmoil that came to a crescendo in 1968 remained vivid and painful. The Nixon Doctrine, the all-volunteer military and the reluctance to commit ground troops overseas all stemmed from this overriding goal. But nor did policymakers envision a world without war, or even a world without the use of American military power. So they devised a series of caveats, such as those articulated in the Weinberger Doctrine, to make the use of force more palatable, not less. Weinberger's rules, which his protégé Colin Powell later adapted when he was chairman of Joint Chiefs of Staff during the Gulf War, were not designed to prevent war, but to make it easier to wage in a post-Vietnam world of public scrutiny and antiwar dissent.[41]

Weinberger and Powell's vision was enabled by the advent of a 'revolution in military affairs' (RMA), specifically the refinement of air power, which transformed the way of warfare from the early 1980s onwards. Throughout history, RMAs have been transform-ative thresholds that shifted the very basis of how wars are fought and won.[42] The post-Vietnam RMA was little different. Stung by failure in Vietnam but determined to persevere in a more chal-lenging political and normative environment, the Pentagon placed much greater emphasis – and financial resources – on technological innovation. Emerging in symbiosis with the information and dig-ital revolutions, the post-Vietnam RMA enabled the US military to strategize wars that could be waged in a more precise and less indis-criminate manner, requiring fewer American boots on the ground and causing fewer civilian casualties abroad. Military technologies in the air and at sea – traditionally the leading edge of technologi-cal innovation – became highly computerized and technologically sophisticated.[43] In World War II, bombs that fell within a few miles of hitting their target were considered accurate; by the Kosovo War in 1999, bombs that fell more than a few yards away from their target were considered inaccurate. It was no coincidence that the Vietnam War occurred in the breach and provided the catalyst for change between these two eras of industrial and post-industrial warfare.[44]

The 1991 Gulf War with Iraq was the first American conflict to show the effects of the post-Vietnam RMA, both in the air and on the ground. Essentially, the United States deployed to devastating effect a post-industrial, computer-age military against a much more cumbersome, heavily industrialized Iraqi enemy. This latest RMA, however, has proven much less effective in fighting asymmetrical, anti-terror or counterinsurgent warfare, as the shocking failures of the second American campaign in Iraq, launched in 2003, illustrated.[45] In the wake of another losing campaign against a technologically inferior enemy, the ghosts of Vietnam returned once more.[46]

Presidents since Nixon have followed his lead in linking US national security policies to the soul of American nationalism. This included the waging of war. Whether it has been to defend freedom or punish adversaries, Americans celebrated the military even when its foreign wars went badly. At home, the result has been the militarization of American life; abroad, the result has been permanent war.[47] The irony of protest, which culminated with unprecedented success in 1968, is painfully clear: war would be made clean and quick, rather than be avoided altogether. Rather than bring about an end to the American way of war, 1968 simply marked a new beginning.

Notes

1. The literature on the 1968 Tet is enormous, but for an excellent recent overview, see James H. Willbanks, *The Tet Offensive: A Concise History* (New York: Columbia University Press, 2007).

2. On relative decline, in large part induced by the stalemate in Vietnam and its attendant economic, cultural and political effects, as the instigator of detente and the opening to China, see Fredrik Logevall and Andrew Preston (eds), *Nixon in the World: American Foreign Relations, 1969–1977* (New York: Oxford University Press, 2008).

3. Pierre Asselin, *A Bitter Peace: Washington, Hanoi, and the Making of the Paris Agreement* (Chapel Hill: University of North Carolina Press, 2002). On the collapse of the Paris accords, see Johannes Kadura, *The War after the War: The Struggle for Credibility during America's Exit from Vietnam* (Ithaca, NY: Cornell University Press, 2016).

4. On balance, a majority of historians argue that the antiwar movement limited the Johnson and Nixon administrations' ability to escalate the conflict

and wage war and induced an early end to the fighting. For the most notable examples, see Melvin Small, *Johnson, Nixon, and the Doves* (New Brunswick, NJ: Rutgers University Press, 1988); Tom Wells, *The War Within: America's Battle Over Vietnam* (Berkeley: University of California Press, 1994); and Rhodri Jeffreys-Jones, *Peace Now! American Society and the Ending of the Vietnam War* (New Haven: Yale University Press, 1999). For a contrasting view, which argues that the antiwar movement's impact on the conduct of the war was limited and if anything helped prolong the war, see Adam Garfinkle, *Telltale Hearts: The Origins and Impact of the Vietnam Anti-War Movement* (New York: St. Martin's Press, 1995). For an insightful and concise overview of the debate, which deftly evaluates these two contrasting views, see Simon Hall, *Rethinking the American Anti-War Movement* (New York: Routledge, 2012), 137–42.

5. Gregory A. Daddis, *Westmoreland's War: Reassessing American Strategy in Vietnam* (New York: Oxford University Press, 2014).

6. On the limitations of US strategy in the air, see Mark Clodfelter, *The Limits of Air Power: The American Bombing of North Vietnam* (New York: Free Press, 1989), and Robert A. Pape, *Bombing to Win: Air Power and Coercion in War* (Ithaca, NY: Cornell University Press, 1996), 174–210. On the ground, see George C. Herring, *LBJ and Vietnam: A Different Kind of War* (Austin: University of Texas Press, 1994), and Nick Turse, *Kill Anything That Moves: The Real American War in Vietnam* (New York: Metropolitan Books, 2013). For a nuanced overview and reassessment, see Gregory A. Daddis, *No Sure Victory: Measuring U.S. Army Effectiveness and Progress in the Vietnam War* (New York: Oxford University Press, 2011).

7. David F. Schmitz, *The Tet Offensive: Politics, War, and Public Opinion* (Lanham, MD: Rowman & Littlefield, 2005), 43–82.

8. There is a large and contentious literature on these developments, but for balanced overviews see Schmitz, *Tet Offensive*, and Willbanks, *Tet Offensive*.

9. Fredrik Logevall, *Choosing War: The Lost Chance for Peace and the Escalation of War in Vietnam* (Berkeley: University of California Press, 1999).

10. David Halberstam, *The Best and the Brightest* (New York: Random House, 1972).

11. 'The President's Address to the Nation Announcing Steps To Limit the War in Vietnam and Reporting His Decision Not To Seek Reelection' (31 March 1968), *The American Presidency Project*: www.presidency.ucsb.edu/ws/?pid=28772

12. Dominic Sandbrook, *Eugene McCarthy: The Rise and Fall of Postwar American Liberalism* (New York: Knopf, 2004), 163–86.

13. The best account is still David Farber, *Chicago '68* (Chicago: University of Chicago Press, 1988).

14. Andrew Preston, 'Beyond the Water's Edge: Foreign Policy and Electoral Politics', in Gareth Davies and Julian E. Zelizer (eds), *America at the Ballot Box: Elections and Political History* (Philadelphia: University of Pennsylvania Press, 2015), 219–37. It should be noted, however, that there is a key difference between antiwar sentiment as discussed here (a sense that the war effort was failing and that it should be brought to an end) and antiwar activism (protests and civil disobedience designed to force the government to bring the war to an

end). While the former was widespread, there remain doubts as to the latter's effectiveness.

15. On Kissinger's elaborate grand strategy, see Jussi M. Hanhimäki, *The Flawed Architect: Henry Kissinger and American Foreign Policy* (New York: Oxford University Press, 2004), and John Lewis Gaddis, *Strategies of Containment: A Critical Appraisal of American National Security Policy during the Cold War* (New York: Oxford University Press, 2005), 272–341.

16. For a cogent analysis of Vietnamization's failings, see James H. Willbanks, *Abandoning Vietnam: How America Left and South Vietnam Lost Its War* (Lawrence: University Press of Kansas, 2004).

17. Asselin, *Bitter Peace*, and Lien-Hang T. Nguyen, *Hanoi's War: An International History of the War for Peace in Vietnam* (Chapel Hill: University of North Carolina Press, 2012), 194–230.

18. On 'permanent war' as a deliberate strategy see Larry Berman, *No Peace, No Honor: Nixon, Kissinger, and Betrayal in Vietnam* (New York: Free Press, 2001).

19. Andrew Preston, *The War Council: McGeorge Bundy, the NSC, and Vietnam* (Cambridge, MA: Harvard University Press, 2006).

20. See Kadura, *The War after the War*.

21. The most prominent, and forceful, advocate for the 'decent interval' thesis is Jeffrey P. Kimball's *Nixon's Vietnam War* (Lawrence: University Press of Kansas, 1998) and Kimball's *The Vietnam War Files: Uncovering the Secret History of Nixon-Era Strategy* (Lawrence: University Press of Kansas, 2004). The clearest counterargument, which stresses Nixon's indefinite commitment to South Vietnam, is found in Berman, *No Peace, No Honor*. For a middle path, characterized as a kind of insurance policy, see Kadura, *The War after the War*.

22. Telegram, William Westmoreland (Honolulu) to Creighton Abrams (Saigon), 25 November 1967, Document 416, *Foreign Relations of the United States, 1964–1968*, vol. V: *Vietnam, 1967*: history.state.gov/historicaldocuments/frus1964-68v05/d416

23. 'General Disputes Quote in CBS Trial', *New York Times* (30 November 1984).

24. For a good analysis why, see Daddis, *Westmoreland's War*, 138–44. More broadly, see James J. Wirtz, *The Tet Offensive: Intelligence Failure in War* (Ithaca, NY: Cornell University Press, 1994).

25. Jeremy Varon, *Bringing the War Home: The Weather Underground, the Red Army Faction, and Revolutionary Violence in the Sixties and Seventies* (Berkeley: University of California Press, 2004).

26. Beth Bailey, *America's Army: Making the All-Volunteer Force* (Cambridge, MA: Harvard University Press, 2009).

27. James H. Willbanks, *A Raid Too Far: Operation Lam Son 719 and Vietnamization in Laos* (College Station: Texas A&M University Press, 2014).

28. 'Address to the Nation on the War in Vietnam' (3 November 1969), *The American Presidency Project*, www.presidency.ucsb.edu/ws/?pid=2303

29. Sandra Scanlon, *The Pro-War Movement: Domestic Support for the Vietnam War and the Making of Modern American Conservatism* (Amherst, MA: University of Massachusetts Press, 2013).

30. See, for example, Michael J. Allen, *Until the Last Man Comes Home: POWs, MIAs, and the Unending Vietnam War* (Chapel Hill: University of North Carolina Press, 2009).

31. On the Nixon Doctrine, see the classic account in Robert S. Litwak, *Détente and the Nixon Doctrine: American Foreign Policy and the Pursuit of Stability, 1969–1976* (Cambridge: Cambridge University Press, 1986).

32. For an insightful summary of these events, see Doug Rossinow, *The Reagan Era: A History of the 1980s* (New York: Columbia University Press, 2015).

33. James M. Scott, *Deciding to Intervene: The Reagan Doctrine and American Foreign Policy* (Durham, NC: Duke University Press, 1996).

34. Andrew Preston, 'A Foreign Policy Divided Against Itself: George Shultz vs. Caspar Weinberger', in *A Companion to Ronald Reagan*, ed. Andrew L. Johns (Malden, MA: Wiley-Blackwell, 2014), 546–64.

35. 'Remarks to the American Legislative Exchange Council' (1 March 1991), *The American Presidency Project*: www.presidency.ucsb.edu/ws/?pid=19351

36. On US foreign policy in the post-Cold War era, see Derek Chollet and James Goldgeier, *America Between the Wars: From 11/9 to 9/11* (New York: PublicAffairs, 2008).

37. Francis Fukuyama, *The End of History and the Last Man* (New York: Free Press, 1992).

38. 'Address Before a Joint Session of the Congress on the Persian Gulf Crisis and the Federal Budget Deficit' (11 September 1990), *The American Presidency Project*: www.presidency.ucsb.edu/ws/?pid=18820

39. Dexter Filkins, *The Forever War* (New York: Knopf, 2008).

40. On the emergence World War II nostalgia in 1990s America, see Gary L. Gerstle, 'In the Shadow of Vietnam: Liberal Nationalism and the Problem of War', in Michael Kazin and Joseph McCartin (eds), *Americanism: New Perspectives on the History of an Ideal* (Chapel Hill: University of North Carolina Press, 2006), 128–52.

41. On this point, see Gail E. S. Yoshitani, *Reagan on War: A Reappraisal of the Weinberger Doctrine, 1980–1984* (College Station: Texas A&M University Press, 2011).

42. The classic account is William H. McNeill, *The Pursuit of Power: Technology, Armed Force, and Society since A.D. 1000* (Chicago: University of Chicago Press, 1982), although it appeared before the post-Vietnam RMA. For historical perspectives which do take account of more recent RMA theory, see Geoffrey Parker, *The Military Revolution: Military Innovation and the Rise of the West, 1500–1800*, 2nd edn (Cambridge: Cambridge University Press, 1996); MacGregor Knox and Williamson Murray (eds), *The Dynamics of Military Revolution, 1300–2050* (Cambridge: Cambridge University Press, 2001); Max Boot, *War Made New: Technology, Warfare, and the Course of History, 1500 to Today* (New York: Gotham, 2006); and, more sceptically, Colin Gray, *Strategy for Chaos: Revolutions in Military Affairs and the Evidence of History* (London: Frank Cass, 2002).

43. For example, the US Navy was at the forefront in creating the first military-industrial complex at the turn of the twentieth century. See Katherine C. Epstein,

Torpedo: Inventing the Military-Industrial Complex in the United States and Great Britain (Cambridge, MA: Harvard University Press, 2014).

44. Benjamin S. Lambeth, *The Transformation of American Air Power* (Ithaca, NY: Cornell University Press, 2000), 12–53.

45. See especially Keith L. Shimko, *The Iraq Wars and America's Military Revolution* (Cambridge: Cambridge University Press, 2010).

46. Lloyd C. Gardner and Marilyn B. Young (eds), *Iraq and the Lessons of Vietnam: Or, How Not to Learn from the Past* (New York: New Press, 2007); David Ryan and John Dumbrell (eds), *Vietnam in Iraq: Tactics, Lessons, Legacies and Ghosts* (New York: Routledge, 2007); Robert K. Brigham, *Iraq, Vietnam, and the Limits of American Power* (New York: PublicAffairs, 2008).

47. Andrew J. Bacevich, *The New American Militarism: How Americans Are Seduced by War*, 2nd edn (New York: Oxford University Press, 2013).

FOUR

Life Writing, Protest and The Idea of 1968

Nick Witham

In 2007, Robert Stone published *Prime Green*, a memoir of life in 1960s America. The novelist, who had had been an active participant in the Californian counterculture during the decade, concluded his book with a reflection on the nature of generational memory:

> My generation left the country better in some ways, not least by destroying the letter of the laws of racial and sexual discrimination . . . We learned what we had to, and we did what we could. In some ways the world profited and will continue to profit by what we succeeded in doing. We were the chief victims of our own mistakes. Measuring ourselves against the masters of the present, we regret nothing except our failure to prevail.[1]

In making this case, Stone defended the political and cultural perspectives of 1960s radicals, and sought to demonstrate the continuing relevance of the decade's politics by drawing a comparison between the long-term achievements of civil rights and feminist activists on the one hand, and the policy blunders made during the George W. Bush presidency on the other.

Stone's fusion of personal and generational reflections highlights both the slipperiness and the significance of life writing – an umbrella term used here to refer to memoir, autobiography and participant history – for historians of the 1960s. In the fifty years since 1968, a variety of historical narratives have emerged about what 'the sixties' were, and how the period's contentious historical experiences have shaped contemporary US politics, society and culture. Those involved in the social upheavals of the 1960s, and of 1968 in particular, have used memories of the year to provide accounts of their actions, to supplement and correct the historical record, and, perhaps most importantly, to explain both changes and continuities in their political thinking, as well as that of their generation. The opening words of the Port Huron Statement set the precedent that so many have followed. 'We are people of this generation, bred in at least modest comfort, housed now in universities, looking uncomfortably to the world we inherit', declared the 1962 manifesto published by Students for a Democratic Society (SDS).[2] The Statement would go on to define the ideas of the US student New Left, thereby drawing attention to the movement's desire to speak not just for its participants, but for all Americans now referred to as 'baby boomers'. In this process, the genre of life writing has been particularly influential, and the idea of speaking for 'a generation' has shown remarkable persistence.[3]

To develop a better understanding of the importance of sixties life writing in shaping both academic and popular understandings of the idea of 1968, this chapter seeks to historicize examples of the genre published in three distinct periods: the immediate aftermath of 1968, as exemplified in memoirs by Abbie Hoffman and Jerry Rubin, together with the autobiography of Angela Davis; the 1980s, via Todd Gitlin's participant history and Tom Hayden's memoir; and the 1990s and early 2000s, in Paul Berman's generational history and memoirs by Susan Brownmiller and Bill Ayers. By demonstrating how each phase reconfigured the idea of 1968, I highlight both the significance and the ambiguity of the year's events for contemporaneous political thinking, and also complicate a now commonplace observation in historical writing on the global sixties. It has been argued that as the voices of historians with no living memory of the decade have come to dominate the field, its historiography has changed, to a large extent for the better, with some scholars talking of a move away from 'memory' towards 'history'.[4] This shift has undoubtedly taken place, even if an essentialized distinction between memory and history should be met with scepticism. However, the current chapter shows how the study of sixties memory as it is represented in life writing can contribute to an understanding of the decade's historical malleability, and of the many political valences it has developed in American political thinking. A detailed and nuanced understanding of sixties life writing is therefore vital, not only for the opportunities this rich genre provides historians of the 1960s, but also for the insights it provides into the changing meanings of the idea of 1968 over the subsequent fifty years.

'Children Were Born': Life Writing in The Immediate Aftermath of 1968

Three of the first memoirs and autobiographies to deal explicitly with the repercussions of 1968 were written by Abbie Hoffman, Jerry Rubin and Angela Davis. Hoffman's *Revolution for the Hell of It* (1970) and Rubin's *Do It! Scenarios of the Revolution* (1970) recounted their authors' roles as founders of the Youth International Party (or Yippies), whilst Davis's *An Autobiography* (1974) focused on her deepening involvement with Black Power and communist politics. In each case, these notable participants in the protest culture of 1968 grappled with the problem of generational conflict, and used personal experiences to illustrate the necessity of a radical approach to what they perceived as the breakdown of the American political system. In Rubin's words, these early memoirs fleshed out their authors' contrasting experiences of a process through which revolutionary 'children were born', a youthful cohort who were unafraid of, and unapologetic about, the idea of revolution.[5]

Both Hoffman and Rubin framed their life writing in the context of generational struggle. The introduction to Hoffman's surrealist memoir consisted entirely of a letter from 'Mom' dated 1 November 1967, which recounted an imaginary parent's response to learning about her children's participation in antiwar protests via *Time* magazine. 'I used to be so proud of all that you kids did', the letter read,

> But now I just don't know. If you didn't have such potential, it would be different, but how can you waste what you have on such trash????? I can't understand it at all . . . It is the action of children, not supposedly grown, mature, intelligent adults.[6]

In framing his memoir in this way, Hoffman sarcastically pointed to the generational divide and rejected the notion of adulthood expounded by his fictional parent. Similarly, Rubin opened his memoir by describing himself as 'a child of America. If I'm ever sent to Death Row for my revolutionary "crimes," I'll order as my last meal: a hamburger, French fries and a Coke.'[7] However, the author quickly shifted tack to suggest, 'I dropped out. I dropped out of the White Race and the Amerikan nation . . . I live for the revolution . . . I'm an orphan of Amerika.'[8] The two authors therefore framed their narratives in the terms of generational conflict, both with their notional parents, and with the dominant culture of the nation at large, expressed in the image of Rubin's mass-produced diet. Indeed, his use of the term 'Amerika' heightened this contrast, by using the well-known sixties designation that drew comparisons between the Cold War American state and that of Nazi Germany.

In narrating how this process of generational disavowal had taken place, the central events of 1968 for both Hoffman and Rubin were the converging antiwar and countercultural protests at the Democratic National Convention between 26 and 29 August, organized by SDS, the Yippies and various other activist groups, and famously termed the 'siege of Chicago' by novelist Norman Mailer.[9] There were four goals of the Yippie's presence in Chicago, as Hoffman summarized them. The first was to blend 'pot into politics' and therefore initiate a 'cross-fertilization of hippie and New Left philosophies'. The second was to create a 'gigantic national get together' for activists of all stripes. Third, and more ambitiously, was to develop 'a model for an alternative society'. Finally, Hoffman argued that the Yippies wanted to make a 'revolutionary-action-theater' statement 'about LBJ, the Democratic Party, electoral politics, and the state of the nation'.[10] Rubin concurred, arguing that the mission of the protests was 'to freak out the Democrats so much that they disrupt their own convention. And meanwhile demonstrate to the world the alternative: our own revolutionary youth culture.'[11]

The protests brought thousands of demonstrators into the city's streets, and led to a violent response from the Chicago police force, which had been instructed by the city's mayor, Richard Daley, to 'shoot to kill' at arsonists, and to 'shoot to maim' at looters.[12]

Figure 4.1 A Chicago police officer squirts mace at anti-Vietnam War demonstrators outside the Conrad Hilton Hotel during the 1968 Democratic National Convention, 29 August 1968. Courtesy CSU Archives/Everett Collection. REX/Shutterstock.

Nonetheless, after three days of demonstration and confrontation, both authors deemed the Yippies' actions in Chicago to have been a success. 'We had won the battle of Chicago', Hoffman suggested, continuing, 'as I watched the acceptance speech of Hump-Free I knew we had smashed the Democrats' chances and destroyed the two-party system in this country and perhaps with it electoral politics'.[13] As he described the national television coverage of the protests, Rubin's narrative was also triumphant: 'scenes of brave youth battling back flashed over and over again on every TV channel: infinite replay of the fall of Amerika'.[14] The narcissism and bombast of these reflections is self-evident, and has subsequently been called into question in the life writing of other participants in the protests. In his account *The Wedding Within the War* (1971), which was published only months after Hoffman's and Rubin's memoirs, Yippie ally Michael Rossman recalled that he had warned Rubin in a letter dated 16 March 1968 that he should avoid publicizing Chicago as a revolutionary festival and instead emphasize both the danger and the explicitly political nature of the protests:

If we're mythmaking, let's build our symbols with deliberate care . . . A multitude of kids with false expectations will at best dilute the symbol, and may render it unworkable, or, at worst, help transmute it helplessly into quite a different symbol, dark with despair and passion.[15]

On balance, Rossman's prediction that the Chicago protests would be remembered in despairing rather than celebratory terms was more realistic than the exultant recollections of Hoffman and Rubin. Nonetheless, the glorification of the Yippie approach evident in *Revolution for the Hell of It* and *Do It!* helps to demonstrate their authors' desire to represent the protest generation of the 1960s as clearly and decisively alienated from their parents, and, at the same time, dedicated to a radical and confrontational mode of political engagement.

Angela Davis, also an advocate of revolutionary political change, wrote the bulk of her autobiography from a jail cell, as she awaited charges associated with a 1970 courthouse siege in Marin County, California, that had failed to free George Jackson, Fleeta Drumgoole and John Clutchette: three African American prisoners commonly referred to as the 'Soledad Brothers'. In this sense, her book bore the hallmarks of such significant examples of African American life writing as *The Autobiography of Malcolm X* (1965), Eldridge Cleaver's *Soul on Ice* (1968) and Huey P. Newton's *Revolutionary Suicide* (1973), all of which contained significant reflections on time in prison, and represented conversion narratives documenting the process by which their authors had developed radical critiques of US racial and class oppression that ran against the grain of the non-violent civil rights movement. The book therefore fits into the genre of 'political autobiography' as outlined by literary historian Margo V. Perkins, to the extent that it represented an attempt by Davis to 'use her own story both to document a history of struggle and to further its political agenda'.[16] At the same time, it also intervened in debates about intergenerational radicalism in a manner that contrasted in important ways with the interpretations offered by Hoffman and Rubin two years earlier.

By the time of publication, Davis was a member of the Communist Party of the United States (CPUSA), and, when she explained her radicalization, 1968 was deemed to be a pivotal year. Her recollections opened with a discussion of the challenges she faced in finding opportunities to undertake 'serious revolutionary work' and to put into practice the Marxist ideas she had developed as a student of Herbert Marcuse.[17] She had involved herself with the nationwide effort to free Black Panther activist Huey Newton, but soon became exasperated at declarations that the state should 'Free Huey!' that were not followed by serious political strategizing. 'In response to the appeal', she asked, 'the applause was ample enough, but where were we to go from there?'[18] Davis found some satisfaction from her work with the Student Nonviolent Coordinating Committee (SNCC) in Los Angeles, and described her experiences as a community organizer with the group, which had promoted an ideology of 'black power' since Stokely Carmichael's tenure as its chair between 1965 and 1966.[19] Davis described the period of her involvement with SNCC both romantically, as a moment when 'we experienced the heights of brotherhood and sisterhood', and in strategic terms, as an opportunity to build 'a mass movement among Black people in LA'.[20] However, SNCC also gave Davis the opportunity to witness at first hand what she and many other female participants perceived as the misogyny of certain Black Power activists:

> All the myths of Black women surfaced. [We] were too domineering; we were trying to control everything, including the men – we wanted to rob them of their manhood. By playing such a leading role in the organization, some of them insisted, we were aiding and abetting the enemy, who wanted to see Black men weak and unable to hold their own.[21]

This experience led Davis to consider constructive engagement with the CPUSA via the Che-Lumumba Club, a youth wing of the party in Los Angeles dedicated to engaging with African American students.

In making the decision to join the CPUSA in July 1968, she described herself as needing to 'become a part of a serious revolutionary *party*' that would serve more of a purpose than 'ephemeral ad-hoc groups that fell apart when faced with the slightest difficulty'.[22] Narrated as a pivotal moment in her movement away from Black Power politics and towards the CPUSA, Davis's 1968 therefore contained a very different set of reference points to those of

Hoffman and Rubin. She hardly mentioned the white New Left and the protests in Chicago, nor many of the other events that would come to characterize the popular memory of the year. Whilst the two Yippies turned their experiences into affirmations of the politics of the 1960s counterculture and its penchant for guerrilla theatre, Davis's experiences pushed her away from the Black Power movement and towards the CPUSA with its explicitly Old Left political preoccupations. In making this move, Davis participated in what Jonathan Bell has described as California's culture of 'insurgency politics', which 'had far deeper roots than the explosion of New Left and student protest in the early 1960s'.[23] Her example demonstrates that in the year's immediate aftermath, 1968 could serve not only as a radical moment of rupture, as it had for Hoffman and Rubin, but also as a moment of reflection, thus providing the inspiration for a return to more traditional left-wing political affiliations. If life writers such as Hoffman, Rubin and Davis all contributed to idea that revolutionary 'children were born' during 1968, then, they conceptualized the mechanics of radical politics in very different ways.

A 'Succession of Exclamation Points': The 1968s of Todd Gitlin and Tom Hayden

As the 1970s and 1980s wore on, the radicalism of this early group of life writers came to be viewed with considerable scepticism. Many former activists began to focus not on what set them apart from their elders, but on replaying the arguments that developed between the various factions of the New Left, and by arguing for themselves as, in the words of literary historian John D. Hazlett, 'survivors of a generational diaspora' who could mark themselves out from those of their peers who had, in one way or another, turned away from the spirit of the sixties.[24] Todd Gitlin's participant history *The Sixties: Years of Hope, Days of Rage* (1987) and Tom Hayden's memoir *Reunion* (1988) exemplify this turn. The books discussed their authors' respective transitions from roles as key SDS activists to members of mainstream society, with Gitlin becoming a Sociology professor at the University of California Berkeley, and Hayden a California State assemblyman. For both authors, the experience of 1968 was one of declension: much of the patient work they had done to lay the groundwork for student and anti-war protests ground to a halt as the late sixties became, in Gitlin's words, 'a succession of exclamation points' that drew the New Left towards ultra-radicalism and violence.[25]

In these accounts, the key events of 1968, along with the Democratic Convention in Chicago, were the student occupation of Columbia University in April and May, and the assassination of Robert F. Kennedy in June. The occupation of several key Columbia buildings developed as a response to plans to expand the campus into the predominantly African American Morningside Heights neighbourhood of New York City, the absence of student participation in disciplinary procedures, and the university's broader complicity in the Vietnam War and military industrial complex via the Institute for Defense Analysis. Several hundred students participated in the occupation, which lasted for over a month and drew attention from mainstream media sources until it was violently broken up by the New York City Police. The occupation represented a fleeting but nonetheless significant activist coalition between student New Leftists, African Americans and the counter-culture. At the same time, it demonstrated the potential for 1960s protest to develop, in the words of historian Blake Slonecker, 'an intimate relationship between local protest and national and international issues', thereby attracting a variety of activists to contribute to a common cause.[26]

For Gitlin and Hayden, however, the Columbia protests left an ambiguous legacy, especially when viewed from the vantage point of the 1980s. Both authors arrived in New York to observe and participate in the protests as outsiders, and whilst they were still significant figures within SDS, they were also several years older than the student activists they encountered at Columbia, and by that point held a less radical view of the political situation than those in the organization's leadership. Gitlin, for example, described the birth of the 'action faction' of SDS led by Mark Rudd, which would soon evolve into the Weather Underground, as a problematic shift to a theory of 'disruptive action' based around the unrealistic idea that 'the university was a bastion of reaction' and that students would only be radicalized through confrontation with violence 'at the point of a billy club'.[27] Hayden's recollection of the occupation chimed with Gitlin's to the extent that he claimed Rudd and his faction to have been 'absolutely committed to an impossible yet galvanizing dream: that of transforming the entire student movement . . . into a successful effort to bring down the system'.[28] In making these arguments with the benefit of almost twenty years' hindsight, both authors were keen to point to themselves as, in Gitlin's phrase, 'old New Leftists' who were 'anathema' to the radical factions that developed in the late sixties. The Columbia occupation was a transformational moment in the history of 1968, then, but as a 'rehearsal for a coming apocalypse', rather than a productive moment of intersectional alliance.[29]

This sense of impending doom was quickly reinforced by the assassination of Robert F. Kennedy on the night of 5 June 1968. Kennedy, who had announced his candidacy for the Democratic presidential nomination earlier in the year, was shot at the Ambassador Hotel in Los Angeles shortly after winning the California primary. In their memoirs, the event provided Gitlin and Hayden with the opportunity to reflect on their changing attitudes towards the relationship between electoral politics and activism. Hayden, for example, discussed an evolution in his thinking in 1968, during which he came to see Kennedy as the 'rational alternative to war and tumult' who would prove the radical wing of SDS wrong by demonstrating that the American political system 'might work'.[30] In the aftermath of the assassination, Gitlin similarly remembers asking, 'Who us, mourn a liberal? We could not see a thread of hope or a spark of consolation in any politician or celebrity . . . but we still wanted the system to work, and hated it for failing us.'[31] Neither author remembered holding out hope for the success of peace candidate Eugene McCarthy. Instead, they saw Kennedy's death as a victory for the Democratic establishment, who would have a free path to nominate Lyndon Johnson's preferred successor, the pro-war Hubert Humphrey.[32] To explain the significance of these developments, Gitlin looked back to earlier watersheds in the history of the 1960s:

To think about the enormous repercussions of the assassinations of 1968, we need to backtrack to the imagery and mood of a more general

Armageddon, for which the triggering moment is the assassination of 1963. Kennedy, King, Kennedy: they sometimes felt like stations in one protracted murder of hope.[33]

Indeed, Hayden struck a remarkably similar chord in suggesting of these three figures: 'my personal future would have been different had these men lived; so would the lives of most Americans'.[34] Once again, then, Gitlin and Hayden presented their readers with a cataclysmic turning point in the history of 1968, in which the bankruptcy of electoral politics left little room for manoeuvre for those opposed to both the status quo and a descent into hedonism or political violence. The language of 'Armageddon' and 'apocalypse' used to describe the Columbia protests and Robert Kennedy's assassination led the authors to view the Democratic Convention in Chicago as a violent end point for their vision of participatory democracy and protest. After the violence that erupted between protestors and Mayor Daley's police force, the New Left was in disarray: 'available channels having apparently failed, much of the New Left set to dig its own . . . grave', argued Gitlin, with Hayden concluding that 'after 1968, living on as a ruptured and dislocated generation became our fate'.[35]

Nonetheless, both authors also used their books to provide detailed balance sheets of the successes and failures of the 1960s, and to conclude that more was gained by the patient activism of the decade's early years than was lost by the infantile leftism they witnessed in 1968. Hayden's analysis betrays this sensibility most clearly: 'despite outer repression and inner absurdity, we of the sixties accomplished more than most generations in American history'.[36] In providing this declensionist yet defiant account of the idea of 1968, the two authors anticipated the historian Arthur Marwick's 2005 contrast between 'fruitful' and 'futile' 1960s protest, in which the former was non-violent and led to a 'permanent transformation' in the societies of North America and Western Europe, whilst the latter, usually aiming towards revolutionary violence, was dramatic and exciting to participate in, but ultimately 'closed' to long-term political, social or cultural influence.[37]

One way of historicizing this attempt by Gitlin and Hayden to position themselves as 'fruitful' participants in the upheavals of the

1960s is to consider the manner in which they were influenced in their life writing by the politics of the 1980s. Both authors framed their accounts in explicit relation to the rightward turn of that decade, as represented by the two presidential terms of Ronald Reagan and their attendant financial deregulation, decreased taxation, militarism, and a marked decline in trade union militancy.[38] Hayden, for example, described his position as such:

> It is twenty years since I battled on the streets of Chicago ... I am a California State assemblyman, preparing to seek a fourth term. The state's Republicans attack me as if the Chicago conspiracy trial [in which Hayden was indicted] had never ended.[39]

In this way, then, Hayden framed his memoir by presenting a direct connection between his days as a New Left activist and his experiences as a Democratic politician in an era of increasing partisanship.

Perhaps even more revealing is the anecdotal discussion of the aftermath of the 1968 presidential election that concluded Gitlin's chapter on the upheavals of the year. He described participating in an event at San Francisco State College (SFSC) shortly after election day, and witnessing a strike by students calling for the establishment of ethnic studies programmes, open admissions for minority students, and the retention of an instructor who was a Black Panther activist and therefore risked being fired. Whilst enthused by the levels of student agitation, Gitlin reflected:

> I was struck by the fact that not one speaker found the election of Richard Nixon worthy of mention ... The silence about Nixon reflected more than the normal geographical-cum-cultural distance: it displayed the distance between the movement's side shows and the place where power was actually deployed.[40]

As subsequent research by Martha Biondi has shown, the outcomes of the SFSC strike were paradoxical: whilst in the short term it was crushed by a conservative college administration, in the longer term striking students were able to win 'the tools to create a multicultural university' via the establishment of Black Studies curricula.[41] In 1987, though, Gitlin's analysis of the strike demonstrates how his memories of 1968 helped him to formulate the critique of post-sixties campus politics that he would develop in his 1995 book *The Twilight of Common Dreams*: that academics and students were becoming obsessed with the control of college English departments, but remained indifferent to the control of the White House.[42]

In framing their memoirs against the backdrop of Reagan-era political culture, both Gitlin and Hayden demonstrated the period's ongoing controversies surrounding the idea of 1968. This is hardly surprising, given that Reagan had forged his political credentials in response to the New Left as the Republican Governor of California between 1967 and 1975.[43] But at the same time, their attempts to highlight what they viewed as the rights and wrongs of the decade developed a highly partisan approach to sixties memory. If, as Gitlin's subtitle suggested, 1968 saw 'years of hope' descend into 'days of rage', early New Leftists like him and Hayden were not at fault, and had the fulfilment of their dreams blocked not only by those in the political establishment, but also by those to their left who had insisted on taking the New Left in a more radical direction.

Invisible Aftermaths: Sixties Life Writing and The Culture Wars

The persistence of sixties memory in American political and cultural conflict developed a new prominence in the aftermath of the Cold War, as participants in the upheavals of 1968 sought to understand the experiences of their generation against the backdrop of a changing international landscape and the deepening of the political divide between right and left. Paul Berman's *A Tale of Two Utopias: The Political Journey of the Generation of 1968* (1996) provides one example of this trend. Born in 1949, Berman became involved with the New Left during the course of an undergraduate degree at Columbia University, where he arrived shortly after the 1968 protests.[44] Berman shifted his attention to anarchism in the early 1970s, motivated by that movement's critique of Soviet Communism and of the Cuban Revolution, which fitted with, in his own words, a growing 'revulsion against the Leninist passions that were claiming so much of the New Left' as personified by the violent bombing campaign launched by the Weather Underground faction of SDS.[45]

This declensionist theme in Berman's account strikes a chord with the arguments made by Gitlin and Hayden. But Berman's analysis in *A Tale of Two Utopias* moved beyond these examples of sixties life writing by embracing an international and post-Cold War frame of analysis. The book examined what Berman described as the two ideological utopias that dictated the course of left-wing politics in the US and Western Europe during the second half of the Cold War: first, the worldwide political upheavals of 1968 and, second, the fall of communism in Russia and Eastern Europe between 1989 and 1994. The 'invisible aftermath' of the 1960s, he argued, created a shift in thinking amongst the majority of '68ers', who turned their backs on direct democracy and revolutionary socialism in order to embrace political liberalism, either in its social-democratic or free market forms.

In most cases, Berman argued, leftists reconciled themselves to Western-style political institutions: the 'imaginary' revolutions of 1968 were rejected in favour of the 'real' revolutions of 1989.[46] Buried within this macroscopic analysis was a more specific critique of the 'anti-anticommunism' of the US New Left, as represented in its opposition to Cold War ideology and the war in Vietnam. In Berman's reading, the New Left's failure to embrace a robust anti-Stalinism meant that it inevitably tended towards the 'culture of criminal leftism' embraced by the Weather Underground and various other Maoist and Marxist–Leninist sects.[47] In this analysis, the true significance of 1968 could only be viewed through the lens of the post-Cold War triumph of liberal democracy in Eastern Europe: the childishness of US New Left aspirations to overthrow capitalism in the name of revolutionary socialism were eventually and necessarily outgrown, leading to a more mature, less ambitious view of history that, in Berman's closing words, was 'humble, skeptical, anxious, afraid, shaken'.[48]

In her 1999 book *In Our Time: Memoir of a Revolution*, Susan Brownmiller also argued for a reformulation of the significance of 1968, but drew markedly different conclusions to Berman. For Brownmiller, who participated in the civil rights movement with the Congress on Racial Equality (CORE) and SNCC during the early 1960s before settling in New York City and becoming a key figure in the development of the city's radical feminist movement, 1968 marked not a moment of declension, but instead an important starting point for American women's critique of patriarchy. In doing so, Brownmiller clearly articulated an alternative memory of 1968 that was primarily focused on women's activism. For example, in telling the story of the split that took place between women's liberation and the New Left after 1968, Brownmiller emphasized the significance of the Miss America protests undertaken by New York Radical Women in Atlantic City in September of that year, when 400 feminist activists descended on the pageant and protested the commercialization of sexuality it represented, lying as it did at the intersections of, in Brownmiller's words, 'capitalism, militarism, racism and sexism, all in one fell swoop'. She went on to quote an interview she had conducted with radical feminist activist and thinker Robin Morgan, in which the veteran activist recalled debates that took place between feminists and the New Left in the summer of 1968 about where 'the revolution was going to start': Chicago or Atlantic City.[49] This reference highlights the weight of attention paid to the Chicago protests in comparison to the relative neglect of the Miss America protests, which Brownmiller used to highlight the positive legacies of 1968 when viewed as a moment of regeneration for radical feminism as it developed independently of the New Left. This was a moment, then, in which 'passions were released, the overlooked found their voices, and new ideas floated into the culture'.[50]

Brownmiller's discussion of the Miss America protests also highlights an important dimension of her book's methodology: the extensive use of conversations with contemporaries to help develop her narrative. The endnotes of *In Our Time* cite the dozens of interviews with feminist activists Brownmiller had undertaken: as well as Robin Morgan, these figures included the historians Rosalyn Baxandall, Roxanne Dunbar, Gerda Lerner, Linda Gordon and Ellen DuBois, the activist Betsy Warrior, and the music critic Ellen Willis. As such, Brownmiller's book was marked by its author's desire to speak for the group of radical feminists who felt that they could call the period from the late 1960s through the early

1980s 'our time'. One major limitation of the book, however, is the lack of recognition given to what Benita Roth has referred to as 'the multiple and plural nature of the era's feminist resurgence', which saw the tense coexistence of numerous movements characterized by racial and ethnic distinctiveness, rather than a coherent, singular US feminism.[51] If Brownmiller cut herself apart from the generational narratives of Hoffman and Rubin by telling a collective rather than an individualistic story, then, she also highlighted her complicity in the 'whitewashing' of feminist history by activists unwilling to recognize the asymmetrical power relations between white feminists and feminists of colour.

By contrast, Bill Ayers's 2001 book *Fugitive Days: Memoirs of an Antiwar Activist* articulated an interpretation of the political upheavals of 1968 that aimed to serve a project of explicitly personal redemption. Ayers was a key figure in the establishment of the Weather Underground and spent five years as a fugitive from justice after the accidental explosion of a bomb in a Greenwich Village townhouse that killed three members of the group. *Fugitive Days* attempted both to account for the process of radicalization that drew him and others towards revolutionary politics and to mitigate the criticisms levelled at the Weather Underground by a great number of sixties participants in the intervening years. In Ayers's telling, 1968 was a 'year of wonder and miracle', during which,

> the Vietnam War and the idea of freedom defined me, propelled me out of bed every morning, powered my hopes and fears, troubled my sleep, and, for better or for worse, consumed me . . . We were bent on revolution right here on earth, right here in America.[52]

This breathless description of 1968 as a revolutionary moment for both Ayers and those around him provided the author with a justification for his involvement in violent political activity. The year was, in his words, 'a time of transgression' that itself demanded more and more transgressive acts.[53] Indeed, much later in the book, Ayers compared the turn towards political violence of the Weather Underground to the actions of Hugh Thompson, Lawrence Colburn and Glen Andreotta, three US soldiers who 'happened upon the My Lai massacre on March 16, 1968', confronted its perpetrators, and were able to 'prevent further atrocities'. In order to draw the link between these actions and those of the Weather Underground, Ayers suggested that 'it took more than twenty-five years to imagine their actions as heroic, to remember something moral in doing the unthinkable right thing in war, even when it seemed like the wrong thing'. How much longer, Ayers asked, until the Weather Underground were thought of in the same terms?[54]

In this and other ways, Ayers used *Fugitive Days* to draw attention to the vicissitudes of sixties remembrance. A considerable proportion of the book consisted of reflections on the unreliability of Ayers's own memory, but also that of his generation: the book's first chapter, for example, opens with the reflection that 'memory is a motherfucker'.[55] In his discussion of the events of 1968, Ayers made this point even more forcefully: 'malignant memory', he argued, 'twists and turns, flatters and begs, often torments. But everything gets garbled in the end, everything burns to ash, and I can't remember it.'[56] He consequently framed 1968 as a moment of radicalization and of the acceleration of a political situation, but also as a moment that, upon reflection, draws the unreliability of memory into sharp focus, thus rendering accurate recollection and precise meaning-making impossible.

The memories of Berman, Brownmiller and Ayers offer a perspective not only into the individual memories of their authors, then, but also into the ways sixties memory was refracted though the lens of 1990s American political culture. All three books were written during the decade, a period in which the memory of the 1960s played a prominent role in national political discourse. When he came into office in January 1993, Bill Clinton was the first US president from the baby boomer generation. Both the political and personal controversies of his presidency were viewed by many Americans as, in the words of political scientist Philip Abbott, 'a metonymy of the Sixties-after-the-Sixties, less as a result of [Clinton's] endorsement of the decade than from his studied ambivalence' towards it.[57] At the same time, the decade's 'culture wars' raged over issues relating to gender, sexuality, race and religion in ways that repeatedly pitted the ideas of sixties liberals and leftists against those of their conservative opponents on issues such as abortion, gay marriage, affirmative action and school prayer.[58]

All three examples of Clinton-era sixties life writing can be instructively understood as participants in these debates. Berman, a sixties radical turned post-Cold War liberal, sought to demonstrate that the animating political desires of his generation had been modified to accommodate the democratic capitalism that he saw as the defining feature of world politics after 1989. For Brownmiller, memories of 1968 helped to explain the 'explosive rise', but also the 'slow seepage, symbolic defeats, and petty divisions' that attended the decline of the radical feminist agenda in the 1980s and 1990s. Finally, in the case of Ayers, the pliability of sixties memory was demonstrated by the impact of the terrorist attacks of 11 September 2001 on the reception of *Fugitive Days*. The book was published before the attacks, but in one particularly notable review written in their aftermath, Brent Staples commented in the *New York Times Book Review* that, in Ayers's account of his life, a career in terrorism had become 'a harmless episode out of a John le Carré novel', and that 'in the aftermath of the terrorist attacks that killed thousands of people in Lower Manhattan and the Pentagon', readers would find Ayers's 'playacting with violence very difficult to forgive'.[59] In this sense, then, if the ideas contained within Ayers's memoir represented the debates of the Clinton era, its reception in the post-9/11 milieu directed readers' attention to a completely different set of reference points, concerned not with generational transgressions, but with the consequences of political violence as a tool of extremism.

Conclusion: The Contemporary Idea of 1968

Sixties life writing has undergone a series of mutations since the early 1970s, when participants in the protest culture of the decade began to publish their autobiographies, memoirs and other personal histories. The genre has ranged widely in its conceptual scope, oscillating between the highly personalized narratives of figures such as Hoffman, Rubin and Ayers, the polished political memoirs of Hayden, and the more academic approaches taken by Gitlin and Berman. And whilst the genre has been dominated by white male authors, prominent women and writers of colour such as Susan Brownmiller and Angela Davis have intervened to revise the parameters of life writing in significant ways. What draws these disparate examples together, though, is the manner in which the idea of 1968 provided a focal point for discussions of 1960s protest. In each case, to remember the 1960s was to grapple unavoidably with the legacies of the decade's most violent and controversial year.

What is the significance of the idea of 1968 and of 1960s memory more generally for contemporary US protest? In recent years, the two most prominent left-wing movements have been Occupy Wall Street and Black Lives Matter, both of which have wrestled with their own memories of sixties-era activism. For example, in an influential essay on the development of the Occupy protests published in 2011, the radical journalist Rebecca Solnit described how, in aiming to speak for the '99 percent', the movement had won 'a huge victory' by focusing attention on the question of economic inequality in the aftermath of the 2008 financial crisis, and had created a tangible sense of 'fear' amongst those in seats of political power.[60] In doing so, Solnit recognized that the Occupy protests had the potential to establish what Eithne Quinn has termed 'a new discursive collectivity . . . of poor, working-class, and middle-class peoples' opposed to rampant levels of economic inequality.[61] However, Solnit also identified a key fissure in the movement's culture, one that reflected divisions within the 1960s left. She argued that 'the majority in our movement would never consent to violent actions', but that Occupy protests in various US cities had been hijacked by anarchists intent on damaging private property and confronting the police with violence. Solnit likened these protestors to the 'bumbling Weather Underground', who had given American leftists 'a bad name we've worked hard to escape'. In making this case, she drew directly on memories of 1968 by discussing the Weather Underground's 'days of rage' in Chicago:

> A handful of delusions-of-grandeur young white radicals thought they'd do battle with the Chicago police and thus inspire the working class to rise up. The police clobbered them; the working class was so not impressed. If you want to address a larger issue, getting overly entangled with local police is a great way to lose focus and support.[62]

In Solnit's understanding, then, clear-sighted knowledge of the history of 1968 would provide the Occupy movement with an awareness of the pitfalls of political protest in 2011, by providing a clear example of the superiority of non-violence protest strategies.

In the case of Black Lives Matter, the question of intergenerational memory has also played a key role in the development of the movement. Since its origins in the Ferguson, Missouri protests against racialized police brutality, Black Lives activists have contended that the current wave of protest is, in the words of a popular slogan, 'not your grand-mamma's civil rights movement'.[63] As a consequence, they have rejected the politics of respectability expressed by Jesse Jackson, Al Sharpton and other leaders with roots in the black freedom struggle of the 1960s.[64] In this sense, Black Lives activists have used memories of the decade to challenge the methods that have come to symbolize its approach to racial justice. However, in drawing attention to the violence done to black bodies by agents of the state, Black Lives Matter has also highlighted the physical and existential threats posed by racial violence. As historian Robin D. G. Kelley expressed in a 2015 roundtable on the movement, 'the killing of black people' has been a constant theme in US history, and is therefore an experience that defies clear generational categorization.[65] As such, the movement draws connections between generations at the same time as it emphasizes intergenerational friction.

Both Occupy Wall Street and Black Lives Matter have therefore been shaped by the remembrance of sixties-era protest enacted by their participants. As this chapter has shown, a focus on the widespread and influential genre of sixties life writing helps to develop an understanding of how these recollections have been formed. From the memories of Hoffman, Rubin and Davis in the early 1970s, via the Reagan-era reconfigurations of Gitlin and Hayden, to the culture wars narratives of Berman, Brownmiller and Ayers, sixties remembrance as articulated in participants' life writing was profoundly shaped by contemporaneous political discourse. If taken too literally, then, these examples have the potential to distort the historical record. However, when read with a view to the malleability of memory, particularly memory of this controversial decade, they also show us how significant the idea of 1968 can be in understanding the present state of American politics and protest movements.

Notes

1. Robert Stone, *Prime Green: Remembering the Sixties* (New York: Harper Collins, 2007), 228–9.

2. 'The Port Huron Statement' (1962), in Richard Flacks and Nelson Lichtenstein (eds), *The Port Huron Statement: Sources and Legacies of the New Left's Founding Manifesto* (Philadelphia: University of Pennsylvania Press, 2015), 239.

3. John D. Hazlett, *My Generation: Collective Autobiography and Identity Politics* (Madison: University of Wisconsin Press, 1998), 41–9.

4. For historiographical overviews that make this point explicitly see Andrew Hunt, 'When Did the Sixties Happen? Searching for New Directions', *Journal of Social History* 33(1) (Autumn 1999), 147–61; M. J. Heale, 'The Sixties as History: A Review of the Political Historiography', *Reviews in American History* 33(1) (March 2005), 133–52.

5. Jerry Rubin, *Do It! Scenarios of the Revolution* (London: Jonathan Cape, 1970), 186–8.

6. Abbie Hoffman, *Revolution for the Hell of It* (New York: Dial Press, 1970), 4.

7. Rubin, *Do It!*, 12.

8. Ibid. 13.

9. See Norman Mailer, *Miami and the Siege of Chicago: An Informal History of the Republican and Democratic Conventions of 1968* (New York: World Publishing, 1968).

10. Hoffman, *Revolution for the Hell of It*, 102.

11. Rubin, *Do It!*, 161.

12. David Farber, *Chicago '68* (Chicago: University of Chicago Press, 1988), 94. See also Frank Kusch, *Battleground Chicago: The Police and the 1968 Democratic National Convention* (Chicago: Chicago University Press, 2008).

13. Hoffman, *Revolution for the Hell of It*, 105.

14. Rubin, *Do It!*, 173.

15. Michael Rossman, *The Wedding Within the War* (New York: Doubleday, 1971), 265.

16. Margo V. Perkins, *Autobiography as Activism: Three Black Women of the Sixties* (Jackson: University Press of Mississippi, 2000), 7.

17. Angela Davis, *Angela Davis: An Autobiography* (New York: Random House, 1974), 162.

18. Ibid. 168.

19. For more on SNCC, see Claybourne Carson, *In Struggle: SNCC and the Black Awakening of the 1960s* (Cambridge, MA: Harvard University Press, 1981); Peniel Joseph, *Waiting 'til the Midnight Hour: A Narrative History of Black Power in America* (New York: Henry Holt, 2006); Wesley C. Hogan, *Many Minds, One Heart: SNCC's Dream for a New America* (Chapel Hill: University of North Carolina Press, 2007).

20. Davis, *An Autobiography*, 170.

21. Ibid. 181.

22. Ibid. 189.

23. Jonathan Bell, 'Building a Left Coast: The Legacy of the Popular Front and the

Challenge to Cold War Liberalism in the Post World War II Era', *Journal of American Studies* 46(1) (February 2012), 71.

24. John D. Hazlett, 'Generational Theory and Collective Autobiography', *American Literary History* 4(1) (Spring 1992), 88.

25. Todd Gitlin, *The Sixties: Years of Hope, Days of Rage* (New York: Bantam Books, 1987), 286.

26. Blake Slonecker, 'The Columbia Coalition: African Americans, New Leftists, and Counterculture at the Columbia University Protest of 1968', *Journal of Social History* 41(4) (Summer 2008), 987. For other useful discussions of the Columbia occupation see Stefan M. Bradley, '"Gym Crow Must Go!" Black Student Activism at Columbia University, 1967–1968', *Journal of African American History* 88(2) (Spring 2003), 163–81; Theodore Patrick Abraham Sweeting, '"Many Columbias": Remembering the New Left', unpublished PhD dissertation, University of Nottingham, 2013.

27. Gitlin, *The Sixties*, 307–8.

28. Tom Hayden, *Reunion: A Memoir* (New York: Random House, 1988), 275.

29. Ibid. 272.

30. Ibid. 263, 268.

31. Gitlin, *The Sixties*, 310.

32. For useful discussions of the electoral politics of 1968 see Rick Perlstein, *Nixonland: The Rise of a President and the Fracturing of America* (New York: Scribner, 2008); Michael Nelson, *Resilient America: Electing Nixon in 1968, Channeling Dissent, and Dividing Government* (Lawrence: University Press of Kansas, 2014); Margaret O'Mara, *Pivotal Tuesdays: Four Elections that Shaped the Twentieth Century* (Philadelphia: University of Pennsylvania Press, 2015).

33. Ibid. 311.

34. Hayden, *Reunion*, xviii.

35. Gitlin, *The Sixties*, 285; Hayden, *Reunion*, 326.

36. Hayden, *Reunion*, xix.

37. Arthur Marwick, 'The Cultural Revolution of the Long Sixties: Voices of Reaction, Protest, and Permeation', *International History Review* 27(4) (December 2005), 782.

38. The best overarching accounts of these political and social processes are Michael Schaller, *Right Turn: American Life in the Reagan-Bush Era, 1980–1992* (Oxford: Oxford University Press, 2007) and Doug Rossinow, *The Reagan Era: A History of the 1980s* (New York: Columbia University Press, 2015).

39. Hayden, *Reunion*, xv–xvi.

40. Gitlin, *The Sixties*, 340.

41. Martha Biondi, *The Black Revolution on Campus* (Berkeley: University of California Press, 2012), 43–4.

42. See Todd Gitlin, *The Twilight of Common Dreams: Why America is Wracked by Culture Wars* (New York: Metropolitan Books, 1995).

43. An excellent overview of this phase of Reagan's career is provided in Gerard De Groot, *Selling Ronald Reagan: The Emergence of a President* (London: I. B. Tauris, 2015). See also Seth Rosenfeld, *Subversives: The FBI's War on Student Radicals, and Reagan's Rise to Power* (New York: Farrar, Straus, and Giroux, 2012).

44. For biographical details of Berman, see Alan Johnson, 'Interrogating Terror and Liberalism: An Interview with Paul Berman', *Democratiya* 5 (Summer 2006), 111–13.
45. Ibid. 113.
46. Paul Berman, *A Tale of Two Utopias: The Political Journey of the Generation of 1968* (New York: Norton, 1996), 14–16.
47. Ibid. 92–3. For discussions of the Weather Underground, see Jeremy Varon, *Bringing the War Home: The Weather Underground, The Red Army Faction, and Revolutionary Violence in the Sixties and Seventies* (Berkeley: University of California Press, 2004), and Dan Berger, *Outlaws of America: The Weather Underground and the Politics of Solidarity* (Cleveland, OH: AK Press, 2005). For the splintering of the New Left into far left factions, see Max Elbaum, *Revolution in the Air: Sixties Radicals Turn to Lenin, Mao and Che* (New York: Verso, 2002).
48. Berman, *A Tale of Two Utopias*, 339.
49. Susan Brownmiller, *In Our Time: Memoir of a Revolution* (New York: Dial Press, 1999), 36.
50. Ibid. 59.
51. Benita Roth, *Separate Roads to Feminism: Black, Chicana and White Feminist Movements in America's Second Wave* (New York: Cambridge University Press, 2003), 2.
52. Bill Ayers, *Fugitive Days: Memoirs of an Antiwar Activist* (Boston, MA: Beacon Press, 2001), 122.
53. Ibid. 136.
54. Ibid. 287.
55. Ibid. 7.
56. Ibid. 141.
57. Philip Abbott, 'A Long and Winding Road: Bill Clinton and the 1960s', *Rhetoric and Public Affairs* 9(1) (Spring 2006), 2.
58. For a recent account of the culture wars that views them as a continuation of the intellectual and cultural battles of the 1960s, see Andrew Hartman, *A War for the Soul of America: A History of the Culture Wars* (Chicago: Chicago University Press, 2015).
59. Brent Staples, 'The Oldest Rad', *New York Times* Book Review (30 September 2001), 11.
60. Rebecca Solnit, 'Throwing Out the Master's Tools and Building a Better House', in Astra Taylor and Keith Gessen (eds), *Occupy! Scenes from Occupied America* (New York: Verso, 2011), 149.
61. Eithne Quinn, 'Occupy Wall Street, Racial Neoliberalism, and New York's Hip-Hop Moguls', *American Quarterly* 68(1) (March 2016), 75.
62. Solnit, 'Throwing Out the Master's Tools', 155.
63. Frederick C. Harris, 'The Next Civil Rights Movement?', *Dissent* 63(3) (Summer 2015), 35.
64. Stefan M. Bradley, 'The Rise of #blacklivesmatter', *American Book Review* 37(3) (March/April 2016), 5.
65. Robin D. G. Kelley, quoted in Percy Green II et al., 'Generations of Struggle', *Transition* 119 (April 2016), 14.

Part Two

Spaces of Protest

.

FIVE

On Fire:
The City and American Protest in 1968

Daniel Matlin

'Has This Country Gone Mad?' The question was put to readers of the *Saturday Evening Post* in May 1968 by Daniel Patrick Moynihan, the Harvard academic and former Kennedy and Johnson aide who, by the year's end, would be named as urban affairs adviser to President-Elect Richard Nixon. In 1968, urban America was, often literally, on fire. The assassination of Martin Luther King, Jr. in Memphis prompted uprisings in 125 cities in April: in Washington DC, buildings burned just a few streets from the White House; flames devoured more than twenty city blocks on the West Side of Chicago, whose mayor instructed police to 'shoot to kill' any arsonist. Violence – which, Moynihan noted, had 'rarely been altogether absent from American life' – seemed now to consume the nation. From 'the violence of the military overseas' to the sight of looters, arsonists and tanks on the streets of 'the cities at home', violence was becoming a 'way of life', Moynihan believed, for a 'nation that exhibits the qualities of an individual going through a nervous breakdown'.[1]

If the Vietnam War was the global mirror in which Americans confronted the violent, coercive nature of their nation's power, the city was the point at which America's violence was seen to be reflected back on itself. Increasingly abandoned to the poor and people of colour throughout the post-World War II era, the nation's cities had become, for many, a repository of groups whose criminality, grievances and difference were to be feared and avoided. In diagnosing an 'urban crisis', commentators by the early 1960s

Figure 5.1 The West Side of Chicago burns during riots triggered by the assassination of Martin Luther King, Jr. on 4 April 1968. Courtesy of Underwood Photo Archives. REX/Shutterstock.

had acquired a shorthand for the effect on cities – especially in the Northeast and Midwest – of a cluster of interlinked postwar phenomena: the exodus of much of American industry and the white middle class to racially exclusive suburbs; the in-migration of millions of impoverished African Americans, Puerto Ricans and Appalachian whites; the strain on city finances from depleted tax bases; and the poverty and frustration entrenched by discriminatory institutions and hypersegregated urban space. By mid-decade, press coverage of muggers, murderers and addicts was joined by fraught discussion of the riots that convulsed black urban neighbourhoods across the country, crystallizing a widespread view of the city as the kernel of America's growing lawlessness, divisions and moral decay.[2]

Yet, for an array of American social movements and countercultural groups, the city held promise as a vital terrain of protest, of struggles for visibility and empowerment, and of hope. If cities were sites of oppression and exploitation, they were also potential sites of self-determination and liberation that loomed large in the imaginaries and strategies of 1960s radicals. Despite a persistent strain of American anti-urbanism, cities have featured prominently in the American utopian imagination at least since John Winthrop's 'Citty vpon a Hill' sermon of 1630. Some 300 years after a group of Puritans had named their settlement by the Passaic River as 'New-Ark', the poet, playwright and activist Amiri Baraka (LeRoi Jones) in 1968 imagined his postindustrial New Jersey hometown rising from the ashes of its recent uprising, again as a 'New-Ark', this time signifying a Black Power covenant of the city's African American majority.[3]

In this chapter, I look to capture the importance of the American city in 1968 as both a *site* of protest (a place in which to demonstrate against the Vietnam War, for instance) and a *focus* of protest (a place whose own dynamics of oppression and deprivation were cause for mobilization and insurgency). I argue that ideas about the nature and possibilities of urban space shaped the character of many of that year's iconic protests. For many 1960s activists and counterculturalists, the city held a powerful appeal as the principal realm of the 'real' and 'authentic', the antidote to the complacency of the suburbs and the privilege and seclusion of the campus. The city was where 'the community' could be found, and where 'the streets' offered a stage for performing dissent, challenging authority, and constituting new forms of political power and identity. Street theatre (also discussed in Chapter 7) was indeed integral to many 1960s protests, from the 'guerrilla theatre' unleashed by the Yippies in Chicago during the 1968 Democratic National Convention to the armed street patrols mounted by the Black Panther Party in Oakland, California. Contestation of urban space was critical not only as a symbolic practice – as when antiwar activists sought to expose the fragility of the prevailing order by denying Mayor Richard Daley control over Chicago's streets – but also as a means for communities to resist oppressive policing or displacement by urban renewal.

Urban protest during the 1960s, as in other eras, assumed forms that mirrored the idea of the city itself: an idea of human congregation of a scale and density that had evoked, for Charles Baudelaire a century earlier, the prospect of a 'universal communion', and that signalled to generations of radicals the possibility of strength through unity.[4] The urban march, rally and riot all make visible the communal power of the crowd, whether organized or disorganized, and do so within the type of human settlement that instances human collectivity more than any other. The city's public spaces of circulation and interaction – its streets, squares and parks – become the arena in which a challenge to authority is visualized and enacted: a notion of the city *as its people* manifests itself as a force capable of disrupting the established authority that calls itself, in the United States, 'the City'. This notion was especially vivid during the 1960s, when the New Left's ideal of 'participatory democracy' challenged the validity of America's institutions of representative government, and when protesters declared that 'democracy is in the streets'.

As the events of 1968 would make clear, however, such unity more often than not proves elusive. A majority of Chicagoans backed 'the City' in its vehement crackdown on protesters during Convention week, as did a majority of Americans. This section of the people did not want power wielded in the streets, except by police and National Guards. Keenly aware of this, Richard Nixon held a 'triumphal procession through the streets' of Chicago just days after the city had witnessed a 'police riot' against protesters. The image of the city on fire would redound to Nixon's advantage at the presidential election in November.[5]

The City as a Site of Protest

Memories of 1968 as a year of global protest invoke a litany of names of cities – Prague, Paris, West Berlin, Warsaw, Chicago, Kingston, Mexico City – and the distinctly urban imagery of 'marching in the streets'. Capital cities suggested themselves as especially resonant sites for protesting government actions, but cities more generally had long attracted political radicals and subcultural groups, their size and diversity seeming to offer relative safety for dissidents and the opportunity to switch between anonymity and visibility at will. For many young Americans, notwithstanding the urban crisis, cities held even greater appeal during the 1960s as places to live, experiment and protest than in earlier periods. Suburbanization and the dramatic postwar expansion of higher education had produced a generation of white American youth who, in many cases, perceived in cities the variety, dynamism and excitement they had been denied by their cosseted upbringings. Ellen Sander, a rock music journalist during these years, recalls in her memoir:

> There was a migration from homes and campuses to the street. Whatever it was that was making us so unhappy pulled us toward the street. It was the only way out and it was completely open. The street was the place to meet kindred souls of every physical description, the place to score dope, the place to hang out and find out what was happening . . . It was where we lived, learned, worked, played, taught, and survived.[6]

San Francisco's Haight-Ashbury, Chicago's Old Town and New York's East Village – as well as neighbourhoods in smaller cities and college towns such as Minneapolis, Austin, Athens and Gainesville – coalesced as spaces shared, sometimes uneasily, by counterculturalists and New Left politicos. The right to occupy these spaces became, in itself, a matter for protest. In Los Angeles, hippies joined politicos in 1968 to resist the City's attempts to use loitering laws and police harassment to clear them out of Venice Beach and redevelop their enclave as luxury housing.[7]

Artists during the 1960s displayed a similar enchantment with the urban as the realm of the 'real'. Marshall Berman notes a heightened intimacy between the arts and the 'real life' of 'the streets', evident in the use of objects found amid the detritus of the urban scene, and in 'happenings' staged in the spaces of the city. In Claes Oldenburg's *The Street: A Metamorphic Mural* (1960), the veneer and artificiality of a suburbanized, affluent society were punctured by what the artist called the 'depth and beauty' of 'dirt'. Exhibited in New York's Judson Memorial Church, Oldenburg's assemblage of scavenged cardboard, newspaper and graffiti conjured street vagrancy, anticipating Michael Harrington's book *The Other America* (1962), which similarly excavated beneath the nation's surface affluence and found one-fifth of Americans living in poverty.[8] Meanwhile, popular music by African American artists spread the word to white youth that a vibrant, volatile black consciousness – a 'soul' that could be heard in the soulless suburbs – was emanating from black urban neighbourhoods. Martha and the Vandellas'

Motown hit 'Dancing in the Street' (1964), for example, acquired multi-layered meanings in the wake of the Harlem riot of July 1964.[9]

All of this recommended the city to the growing ranks of the politicized among America's white, middle-class youth. The radical sociologist C. Wright Mills had urged the New Left to abandon the Old Left's 'labor metaphysic' and look beyond the organized working class for the agent of social transformation.[10] With factories relocating to the suburbs, many young activists believed organized labor had joined the comfortably co-opted. For the college radicals of Students for a Democratic Society (SDS), the largest New Left organization, the city held exciting possibilities for reaching new social constituencies. While some in SDS prioritized on-campus organizing and accused opponents of 'ghetto-jumping', increasing numbers responded to a nagging anxiety that the campus was an insular, privileged site by moving into 'the community'. In 1963, SDS resolved to launch 'An Interracial Movement of the Poor'. Looking to the millions of Americans left out of affluence, it found them, above all, in the nation's cities. By 1965, SDS's Economic Research and Action Project (ERAP) and its affiliates had established thirteen project bases in Baltimore, Chicago, Philadelphia, Boston, Newark, Trenton, Hoboken, New Haven, Cleveland, Louisville, Oakland, Chester (Pennsylvania) and Cairo (Illinois).[11]

Living and working in neighbourhoods of poor whites, African Americans and Latinos, teams of ERAP volunteers set out to forge a mass interracial movement and demand full employment or a guaranteed minimum income. They were soon forced to adjust to demands from neighbourhood activists, especially the women who became the backbone of many of the projects, to mobilize around the immediate manifestations of the urban crisis: deficient housing and welfare services, urban renewal and police brutality. For many student activists, the choice to go 'to the community' and the goal of creating an interracial movement spoke to a deep, personal need to transcend the gulf separating them from the 'Other America'. As Doug Rossinow has argued, the 'search for authenticity' and 'search for community' that animated the American New Left reflected the Christian existentialist notion that individuals, and indeed the 'whole world', were 'broken and in need of healing'. For white, middle-class students raised in a society torn by divisions between races, between cities and suburbs, between the affluent and the poor, going 'to the community' – especially to marginalized inner-city communities – seemed a chance to heal their own and their society's wounds.[12]

By early 1968, however, ERAP was collapsing. Disillusionment among volunteers and residents had set in quickly in some projects as tangible gains proved difficult to achieve and obstacles to interracial unity more stubborn than anticipated. Low-income whites – often southern migrants – frequently resisted appeals for interracial cooperation, while the massive black uprisings in Newark and Detroit in 1967 and the rise of Black Power further limited the scope for interracial mobilization. Within SDS, internal debates ebbed back towards campus-based activism during 1967 with the brief popularity of Carl Davidson and Gregory Calvert's 'new working-class theory'. At a moment when urban community activism seemed fraught with difficulty, the theory helped rationalize a return to campus by identifying students as 'trainee' members of a stratum of alienated, disempowered white-collar workers who would themselves become the agents of societal transformation.[13]

Yet the allure of the city remained. In the autumn of 1967, *New Left Notes* carried pleas for students to 'come off the campus' and 'become people again', and by June 1968, a new SDS leadership including Bernadine Dohrn and Mike Klonsky had renounced the new working-class theory, as had Carl Davidson. Amid the factional warfare that destroyed SDS in 1968–9 even as its membership exceeded 100,000, one of the loudest positions, eventually endorsed by the national council in April 1969, was that the black liberation movement, and specifically the Black Panther Party, constituted 'the vanguard in our common struggles against capitalism and imperialism'. As black urban insurrection captured the revolutionary imagination and the Panthers articulated their role as the US arm of Third World revolution, SDS leaders' 'affirmations of fealty to "black leadership"' substituted for the earlier, now unfeasible commitment to interracial organizing in the cities. For Weatherman, the SDS offshoot that would maintain this rhetorical fealty most doggedly after 1969, urban guerrilla actions, including bombings, assumed priority, and the romance of urban violence reached a new intensity. When the dwindling group moved underground, the city furnished both hiding spaces and a theatre of operation.[14]

If the viability of going 'to the community' had diminished by 1968, going 'to the streets' had assumed ever greater importance as the Vietnam War became a crucial focus of New Left activism. Campus teach-ins had been among the first protests against escalation of US military action in 1965, but by 1967 the antiwar movement increasingly looked to massive street mobilizations to signal, in a visually arresting way, the scale of public opposition: 400,000 marched in New York and 75,000 in San Francisco on 15 April that year. With activists turning their attention to the Democratic National Convention (DNC) that would open at Chicago's International Amphitheater on 26 August 1968, the dramatic possibilities of street protest again fired imaginations. Particularly attuned to the performative dimensions of urban demonstrations were the Yippies, a group founded by Jerry Rubin and Abbie Hoffman in New York late in 1967 with the aim of bringing the playful, irreverent spirit of the youth counterculture to the DNC protests.[15]

The Yippies were admirers of the Diggers, an avant-garde street theatre collective in San Francisco that called for 'the families, communes, black organizations and gangs of every city in America to coordinate and develop Free Cities', urban enclaves that would become nuclei of an alternative society. In similar fashion, the Yippies explained their 'theatre-in-the-streets' or 'guerrilla theatre' as part of a 'cross-fertilization of the hippie and New Left philosophy', a meeting of 'pot and politics'. Announcing plans for Convention week, they urged likeminded people to 'Rise up and abandon the creeping meatball!' by joining their 'Festival of Life' in Chicago:

> We are there! There are 500,000 of us dancing in the streets, throbbing with amplifiers and harmony . . . We will create our own reality, we are Free America. And we will not accept the false theatre of the Death Convention. We will be in Chicago. Begin preparations now! Chicago is yours! Do it!

Like visual artists such as Oldenburg, the Yippies understood the unique potential of the urban environment to dissolve boundaries between life and art. Only the densely populated city could provide a ready-made audience for roving, spontaneous political theatre. As Rubin explained: 'The street is the stage. You are the star of the show.' The exhortation to fill the city's streets and the insistence that 'Chicago is yours!' invoked the image of the city *as its people*, a refusal of 'the City' of Mayor Daley and his police force. For the publicity-savvy Yippies, the presence of the world's media at the DNC would afford an opportunity to expose both the coercive might and the vulnerability of American power. Protesters, Rubin predicted, would 'roar like wild bands through the streets, forcing the president to bring troops home from Viet Nam to keep order in the city while he is nominated under the protection of tear gas and bayonets'.[16]

Sceptical of what they saw as the Yippies' juvenile absurdism but equally convinced of the power of occupying the streets were Tom Hayden, Rennie Davis and David Dellinger, the key protest organizers of the National Mobilization Committee to End the War in Vietnam ('the Mobe'). From the New Left's perspective, both the DNC and Daley's municipal patronage machine were prime examples of America's sham democracy: for them real democracy was in the streets. The Mobe's plans for Convention week, outlined early in 1968, envisaged 'clogging the streets of Chicago with people demanding peace, justice and self-determination'. Meanwhile, Daley's plans involved denying permits to the protesters and bolstering his 12,000 police with 5000 National Guards and 6000 US Army troops to create a force equipped with machine guns, bayonets and flame-throwers. The showdown began in earnest on Sunday 25 August, when police clubbed demonstrators who had refused to vacate Lincoln Park. Spilling into the surrounding neighbourhood, protesters chanted 'the streets belong to the people'.[17]

Three days later, the bloody denouement arrived when police began attacking some of the 10,000 or more demonstrators gathered in Grant Park. Jerry Rubin's speech shortly beforehand had signalled how, for some white radicals, urban protest evoked the possibility of reunification with the black freedom movement. 'That's how we are going to join the blacks', Rubin insisted, 'by joining them on the streets'. By the time Tom Hayden's turn at the microphone came, police were lashing out at the crowd after a teen-ager started lowering the stars and stripes from a flagpole. A furious Hayden declared:

> This city and the military machine it has aimed at us won't permit us to protest . . . Therefore we must move out of this park in groups throughout the city and turn this excited, overheated military machine against itself. Let us make sure that if blood is going to flow let it flow all over this city. If gas is going to be used, let that gas come down all over Chicago and not just all over us in the park. That if the police are going to run wild, let them run wild all over this city and not over us. If we are going to be disrupted and violated, let this whole stinking city be disrupted and violated . . . I'll see you in the streets.

In this extraordinarily pressurized moment, what power Hayden believed the protesters had lay in the creation of an urban spectacle. By flooding the streets throughout the city with themselves, their blood and the violence of the 'machine' as it pursued them, they would not only subvert 'the City' that had denied their right to the streets, but make all Chicago a giant stage on which the brutality of American government would reveal itself. When, hours later, demonstrators on Michigan Avenue pointed at the gathered media's cameras, which were trained on policemen beating already felled protesters, and shouted 'the whole world is watching', they believed they had enticed the American state into the role of villain in an impromptu street theatre performance before a global audience.[18]

Chicago further fractured the New Left, however. For Rennie Davis, the protesters had shown what real democratic action looked like under oppressive conditions: 'Don't vote', he implored the day after Hubert Humphrey's nomination for President of the United States, 'join us in the streets of America'. But for Todd Gitlin and others who clung to SDS's early, nonviolent ethos, the 'fetishism of the streets' that had culminated in over 1000 injuries in Chicago had unleashed 'adolescent machismo fantasies' that could only alienate the American public and divert the movement from its original aims.[19]

Even as the organized New Left was splintering in 1968, other movements rooted in American cities began to surge forward. Feminist activists, often repelled and radicalized by male chauvinism within civil rights and antiwar groups, formed organizations that clustered disproportionately in major cities. What became known as 'radical feminism' – which identified gender, rather than class, as the foundational axis of human oppression – sprang to prominence in 1968 through the work of activists in New York. Its first programmatic statement, *Notes from the First Year: Women's Liberation*, was published in June 1968 by New York Radical Women, whose members, particularly Kathie Sarachild, pioneered 'consciousness-raising'. The centre of the nation's publishing industry, New York exerted a particular pull for activists who were eager to define and promote their causes through magazines and books.[20]

As with other major cities, New York's size offered dissenting minorities the chance to band together in significant numbers and its ethnic diversity had engendered a cosmopolitan milieu comparatively accommodating of alternative lifestyles and mores. For these reasons, gay men and lesbians had long congregated in large cities and had succeeded in establishing partially above-ground communities and institutions, though always under threat of arrest and harassment. As the Stonewall riot in Greenwich Village would demonstrate in June 1969, contestation of urban space was critical to the gay liberation movement that gathered force at the decade's end. While circumstances and dynamics differed, gay men and lesbians, as well as racial minorities, hippies and others, fought police and other City authorities for the right to occupy and control their urban spaces. Nothing better illustrates how the public spaces of the city had become the key terrain for establishing visibility and signifying self-assertion than the gay liberation slogan 'Out of the closets, into the streets', or these lines from Fran Winant's poem 'Christopher Street Liberation Day, June 28, 1970':

we are together
we are marching
past the crumbling old world
that leans toward us
in anguish from the pavement

our banners are sails
pulling us through the streets
where we have always been
as ghosts
now we are shouting our own words.[21]

The City as a Focus of Protest

While the city was providing a stage for, and shaping the form of, demonstrations ranging from antiwar mobilizations to gay liberation marches, the nature of life in the city also lay at the heart of many American protests of the late 1960s. Indeed, a great deal of the violence and militancy that erupted in 1968 can be understood as responding to the inequalities and deprivation that characterized the urban crisis. Racialized minorities became, to a significant degree, inheritors of many of America's major cities just when the industrial city that had offered employment and the possibility of homeownership to generations of European immigrants or their offspring yielded to the postindustrial city of disinvestment and managed decline. Not only the Black Power movement but also the Latino, Asian American and even Native American radicalisms that were catalysed in the late 1960s and early 1970s were deeply rooted in urban grievances and in the segregation that created affluent, all-white suburbs and depressed inner cities.

The postwar US had experienced internal migration on a vast scale. The nation's industrial base shifted away from the cities of the Northeast and Midwest as new factories, often stimulated by government defence spending and highway construction, opened in outlying suburbs or in the fast-growing Sunbelt cities of the South and West, with their low-tax, anti-union 'business climate'. The net migration of white Americans to suburbs totalled 3.6 million during the 1950s, while these expanding sites of opportunity fortified themselves against non-whites through restrictive covenants and discriminatory mortgage lending. During the same decade, the black exodus from the rural South and an upsurge in Puerto Rican migration spurred a net movement of 4.5 million non-white people into the twelve largest US cities. Crowded into segregated neighbourhoods, most migrants faced a sharp disjuncture between

their hopes of high-wage jobs and the realities of the deindustrial-
izing American city: job discrimination and high unemployment;
exploitative rents for dilapidated housing; displacement through
'urban renewal' and incipient gentrification; failing schools and
social services; police harassment and brutality. Out of this matrix
came the urban uprisings and, in large measure, the Black Power
movement, both of which proliferated dramatically in 1968.[22]

Beginning shortly after Lyndon Johnson signed the Civil Rights
Act in July 1964, a wave of rioting engulfed hundreds of black
urban communities over successive summers, most dramatically in
Harlem (1964), the Watts neighbourhood of Los Angeles (1965)
and Newark and Detroit (1967). The civil rights and voting rights
legislation of 1964–5 did little to alter racialized poverty, segregation and police violence in the swelling black neighbourhoods of
northern cities, and participants in these spontaneous uprisings –
mostly prompted by incidents of police brutality – chose ripping
up the fabric of the city, rather than marching with banners, as their
urban medium of communication. They succeeded in reorienting
America's public conversation about race away from the Jim Crow
South and towards the 'ghettos' of major northern cities, and in
redirecting Martin Luther King's campaigning to Chicago, even as
they triggered a massive, sometimes lethal response from armed
police and soldiers. By the time of King's assassination on 4 April
1968, the script for these events had been rehearsed over a period of
four years: window smashing, looting, arson and missiles directed
against police, mostly within the confines of the black 'ghettos'
that residents attacked as concrete expressions of their marginaliza-
tion and oppression. The night of King's death witnessed the most
widespread racial violence in US history, with riots erupting in
125 cities. A week of insurrection saw the deployment of 130,000
troops and National Guards, 46 deaths (41 of African Americans),
20,000 arrests and 2600 fires that caused more than $100 million
of property damage.[23]

A few weeks earlier, on 29 February, the National Advisory
Commission on Civil Disorders had attributed the 1967 Newark
and Detroit uprisings to the 'destructive environment' of the 'racial
ghetto', in which 'white society is deeply implicated'. Yet its call
for massive investment in black urban communities, backed if

necessary by new taxes, was never likely to gain President Johnson's approval; his War on Poverty programmes, underfunded from the outset in 1964, were being further eroded by the escalation in military spending during the Vietnam War. Few African Americans had high expectations of the War on Poverty by now. Instead, increasing numbers found hope in the Black Power organizations springing up in many cities, which were formulating responses to the urban crisis that went beyond the anguished destruction of the riots.[24]

The largest and most influential of these organizations had started with a membership of two. In October 1966, Huey Newton and Bobby Seale founded the Black Panther Party for Self-Defense and drew up its 'Ten Point Program', which, in demanding community empowerment, full employment, decent housing and an end to police brutality, squarely addressed the conditions plaguing their West Oakland neighbourhood. Newton and Seale were working-class migrants from the South. Both had studied at nearby Merritt College but had become frustrated with the campus-bound mentality of its black Soul Students Advisory Council. They determined to take their activism 'to the streets', and to organize those whom Marx had disparaged as the 'lumpen proletariat' but whom they celebrated as the 'brothers on the block'. The streets were, indeed, the vital arena for their early recruitment and activism. By mounting conspicuous, armed patrols to deter police harassment, the Panthers, as Joe Street has argued, created a 'performative' and 'participatory' street politics. Through displays of defiance that challenged the power of the police – whom Newton defined as a colonial 'occupying army' – over black urban space, their actions transformed community members from passive onlookers to willing participants and recruits. For the Panthers, no less than the Yippies or the Mobe, street theatre afforded an essential, highly visual means of performing and promoting an identity grounded in resistance to the authority of the City.[25]

A multitude of new groups were shaping and contesting the politics of Black Power, including Ron Karenga's US Organization in Los Angeles and the Republic of New Africa in Detroit. But the movement's remarkable growth during 1968 was driven primarily by the expansion of the Black Panther Party, which in April still comprised a single chapter in Oakland, but which ended the year with chapters in twenty cities, from Seattle to New York via Denver, Omaha, Chicago and Philadelphia. King's assassination and the vehement suppression of the April uprisings led to a surge in support for the Panthers, who insisted that armed self-defence was indispensable to the Black Power struggle for self-determination and community control of black urban space. Yet, if the movement's growth was propelled by the same militant spirit that had ignited the riots, its leaders and activists rarely advocated rioting. In March 1968, Amiri Baraka warned in Baltimore that rioting 'only leaves black people dead in the streets', while Newton advocated surgical, armed 'guerrilla warfare' rather than 'spontaneous rebellions' that gave 'racist cops' the 'chance to murder unarmed black people'.[26]

Following Newton's arrest on a murder charge in October 1967, the Panthers, like other Black Power groups, focused increasingly on the immediate needs of black urban communities and on securing control of institutions that affected their lives. As violent, sometimes deadly repression by police and intelligence agencies increased, the Panthers harnessed their thousands of new members, many of them women, to 'serve the community'. In the autumn of 1968, the decision was taken to launch a free breakfast programme that was soon feeding tens of thousands of schoolchildren across multiple cities, and was later joined by free health clinics, legal aid, rent assistance, pest control, plumbing, food distribution and other programmes, all addressing the conditions of the urban crisis by substituting for inadequate, discriminatory government services. Meanwhile, in Ocean Hill–Brownsville, Brooklyn, black activists waged a fierce campaign for community control of public schools. In Newark, Baraka developed a Black Power response to systemic spatial inequalities by calling in 1968 for a city payroll tax on commuters whose earnings from city jobs fed tax revenues in wealthy, all-white suburbs. His Committee for Unified Newark played a major role in registering and mobilizing black and Puerto Rican voters, culminating in the election of Kenneth Gibson in 1970 as one of a new generation of African American mayors. And in Memphis, the strike by black sanitation workers that had drawn King's support troubled neat distinctions between civil rights and Black Power in rejecting the 'plantation mentality' and the institutionalized inequality that rural migrants encountered in the city.[27]

The discontents of urbanization and conditions of urban crisis were equally vital to the growth of Latino, Asian American and Native American radical groups in the late 1960s, which frequently acknowledged the inspiration they drew from Black Power. The Brown Berets, a Mexican American nationalist organization, emerged at the end of 1967 in response to police brutality in Los Angeles. With a paramilitary style indebted to the Panthers' street patrols, they established ninety chapters from coast to coast within a single year and launched services including free medical clinics. The revolutionary Young Lords Organization, founded in Chicago in September 1968, emerged from a Puerto Rican street gang, much as the Panthers' Southern California chapter had its beginnings among the LA Slausons. Police brutality, which had prompted rioting among Chicago's Puerto Rican youths in June 1966, was again a primary concern for the Young Lords, as was the job and housing discrimination that beset their deprived, dilapidated Lincoln Park neighbourhood, where migrants from Puerto Rico had arrived since the late 1940s seeking work.[28]

Native Americans, half of whom lived in urban areas by the late 1960s, felt the disappointments of urbanization as keenly as anyone. Pressured to migrate to cities by postwar federal 'relocation' policies and enticed by assurances about high-wage manufacturing jobs, Native Americans found, in cities such as Los Angeles, Denver, Phoenix and Dallas, the same circumscribed opportunities and bleak conditions as other minorities. 1968 marked a watershed for Native American radicalism with the establishment of the American Indian Movement (AIM) in July. Initiated by urban Chippewa activists in Minneapolis, by 1973 AIM had seventy-one chapters in the US and eight in Canada.[29]

A common cause and focus of protest for all these movements was the displacement wrought by urban renewal. In the early 1960s, a preservationist movement with the architectural journalist Jane Jacobs as its figurehead had captured attention by opposing the 'bulldozer renewal' that replaced traditional streets and row houses in supposedly 'blighted' neighbourhoods with superblocks and modernist towers. By 1968, however, the dominant forces opposing renewal were Black Power and other ethnic radicalisms, which rejected 'slum clearance' schemes as naked attempts to remove impoverished minority communities from their potentially lucrative central-city locations. As the following two chapters elaborate, students and Harlem residents joined together in the spring of 1968 to block Columbia University's attempts to build a gymnasium in Morningside Park and the City's plans to redevelop an adjacent section of Harlem. Blurring divisions between campus and urban protest, they highlighted universities' powers as urban landlords and developers as well as the determination of urban communities of colour to resist gentrification and displacement.[30]

Indeed, few objectives propelled the rise of ethnic radicalisms in the late 1960s as much as the defence of urban neighbourhoods. According to one member of the Young Lords, serial displacement of Puerto Rican families in Chicago by urban renewal – 'It happened once. It happened twice. It happened three times. Each time the family had to move' – was the main reason 'why the kids have become more political'. In San Francisco, a campaign that began in October 1968 to prevent eviction of elderly Filipino tenants from the International Hotel placed the defence of Chinatown and the remnants of Manilatown against gentrification at the forefront of California's growing Asian American movement. Contestation of urban space lay at the heart of many of the radical mobilizations of 1968 and, for black students at Columbia and Asian students at Berkeley and San Francisco State, offered a means to reconnect with 'the community' and 'serve the people'.[31]

Conclusion: Urban Legacies

'As we look at America', Richard Nixon intoned in his speech accepting the Republican presidential nomination, 'we see cities enveloped in smoke and flame'. The image of the city on fire was central to Nixon's electoral appeal in 1968, and his promise to restore 'law and order' to America's streets became a fulcrum of the enduring political realignment that saw white working-class voters decamp from the Democratic to the Republican party in large numbers. A rising neoconservative urbanism, hostile to liberal social programmes, found a willing audience in the new administration and was crisply summarized in Daniel Moynihan's suggestion that 'the issue of race could benefit from a period of "benign neglect"'.

Favoured policy intellectuals such as Edward Banfield urged vigorous law enforcement as the only guarantor of urban order, laying groundwork for the 'zero tolerance' policing adopted by mayors including Rudy Giuliani during the 1990s.[32]

The conditions of urban crisis only deepened during the 1970s, when New York verged on bankruptcy and rising violent crime encouraged further waves of suburbanization. For some radicals and counterculturalists, the allure of the city diminished in the wake of the violence and racial polarization of 1967–8. As the proliferation of rural communes in the late 1960s and early 1970s suggests, a good deal of the energy that had turned urban neighbourhoods such as the East Village into hippie and New Left enclaves was now transplanted to back-to-the-land experiments like Montague Farm in western Massachusetts and Total Loss Farm in southeastern Vermont. Significant numbers of dissenting white youth no longer believed they could reach 'the community', and the punishments meted out in Chicago during the DNC turned some away from street protest and towards small, prefigurative communities removed from the centres of a corrupt society. Black Power and other radical ethnic movements were targeted with severe repression by police and intelligence agencies, exemplified by the assassination of Chicago Panther leader Fred Hampton in December 1969, which weakened key organizations at the same time that SDS's implosion removed the main unifying force of the white New Left.[33]

Yet urban protest was far from spent. Movements that were just acquiring momentum, including gay liberation, took to the streets to inscribe their demands and identities much as activists had done in 1968. Earth Day demonstrations, African Liberation Day rallies and anti-apartheid protests would all use human congregation in urban space to create spectacles of power and unity during the 1970s and 1980s, just as antiwar protests would in cities across the US and much of the world in 2003 and the Occupy movement would from 2011 onwards. Although leading Black Power and ethnic radical organizations succumbed to state repression and ideological schism during the 1970s, the neighbourhood activists who had formed their ranks, and those of ERAP, often continued to protest the conditions of urban crisis through the National Welfare

Rights Organization and tenants' rights groups. And while the spate of black urban uprisings abated after the late 1960s, rioting has re-emerged periodically in response to persistent police harassment and brutality, most notably in Los Angeles in 1992 and Ferguson, Missouri, in 2014–15. Violent, discriminatory policing remains, as in the late 1960s, the most explosive issue in American race relations.[34]

Meanwhile, two legacies of 1960s urban dissent increasingly stand in opposition to one another. The embrace of the city by white radical and countercultural youth during that decade, as the realm of authenticity and variety, pointed the way for developers and City agencies to promote the urban renaissance of the late twentieth and early twenty-first centuries, including a renewed vogue for city living among American professionals. From San Francisco's Mission District on the West Coast to Harlem on the East, impoverished communities of colour are waging rearguard campaigns to stem the tide of gentrification displacing them from their neighbourhoods. As in the 1960s, the contested spaces of the city reveal some of the sharpest fault-lines of the United States' inequalities and divisions, and generate some of the nation's fiercest protests.[35]

Notes

1. Daniel P. Moynihan, 'Has This Country Gone Mad?', *Saturday Evening Post* (4 May 1968); David Farber, *Chicago '68* (Chicago: University of Chicago Press, 1988), 94.

2. See Victor Gruen, *The Heart of Our Cities: The Urban Crisis: Diagnosis and Cure* (New York: Simon & Schuster, 1964), and Robert A. Beauregard, *Voices of Decline: The Postwar Fate of U.S. Cities* (New York: Routledge, 2003).

3. Morton White and Lucia White, *The Intellectual versus the City: From Thomas Jefferson to Frank Lloyd Wright* (Cambridge, MA: Harvard University Press, 1962); John Winthrop, 'A Modell of Christian Charity' (1630), in David A. Hollinger and Charles Capper (eds), *The American Intellectual Tradition: A Sourcebook: Volume I: 1630–1865*, 2nd edn (New York: Oxford University Press, 1993), 15; *The New-Ark*, dir. LeRoi Jones (Harlem Audio-Visual, 1968).

4. Charles Baudelaire quoted in Marshall Berman, *All That is Solid Melts into Air: The Experience of Modernity* (London: Verso, [1982] 2010), 316. On the history of modern street demonstrations, see Martin Reiss (ed.), *The Street as Stage: Protest Marches and Public Rallies since the Nineteenth Century* (Oxford: Oxford University Press, 2007).

5. Frank Kusch, *Battleground Chicago: The Police and the 1968 Democratic National Convention* (Chicago: University of Chicago Press, 2008), 155; 'Poll Shows 71.4% find Police Action Justified in Chicago', *New York Times* (31 August 1968); Robert B. Semple, Jr., '400,000 Welcome Nixon During a Tour of Chicago', *New York Times* (5 September 1968); Daniel Walker, *Rights in Conflict: Convention Week in Chicago, August 25–29, 1968: A Report Submitted by Daniel Walker, Director of the Chicago Study Team, to the National Commission on the Causes and Prevention of Violence* (New York: E. P. Dutton, 1968), 5.

6. Ellen Sander, *Trips: Rock Life in the Sixties* (New York: Charles Scribner's Sons, 1973), 9–11.

7. See George Lipsitz, 'Who'll Stop the Rain? Youth Culture, Rock 'n' Roll, and Social Crises', in David Farber (ed.), *The Sixties: From Memory to History* (Chapel Hill: University of North Carolina Press, 2012), 213–14; Doug Rossinow, *The Politics of Authenticity: Liberalism, Christianity, and the New Left in America* (New York: Columbia University, 1998), 281; David McBride, 'Death City Radicals: The Counterculture in Los Angeles', in John McMillian and Paul Buhle (eds), *The New Left Revisited* (Philadelphia: Temple University Press, 2003), 110–36.

8. Berman, *All That is Solid Melts into Air*, 320; Richard H. Axsom and David Platzker, *Printed Stuff: Prints, Posters, and Ephemera by Claes Oldenburg: A Catalogue Raisonné, 1958–1996* (New York: Hudson Hills Press, 1997), 12; Michael Harrington, *The Other America: Poverty in the United States* (New York: Macmillan, 1962), 182.

9. See Richard Iton, *In Search of the Black Fantastic: Politics and Popular Culture in the Post-Civil Rights Era* (New York: Oxford University Press, 2008), 23–4.

10. C. Wright Mills, 'Letter to the New Left', *New Left Review* 5 (September–October 1960), 18–23.

11. Tom Hayden and Carl Wittman, *An Interracial Movement of the Poor?* (New York: Students for a Democratic Society, 1963), available at: michiganintheworld.history.lsa.umich.edu/antivietnamwar/items/show/37 ; Jennifer Frost, *'An Interracial Movement of the Poor': Community Organizing and the New Left in the 1960s* (New York: New York University Press, 2001), 8, 36–37, 45, 190 n.3.

12. Ibid. 4, 69, 144; Rossinow, *Politics of Authenticity*, 7–8. My attention to the urban as a perceived realm of the 'real' complements Rossinow's attention to the perceived authenticity of 'prairie power', as invoked by the SDS chapter at the University of Texas, Austin.

13. Frost, *Interracial Movement of the Poor*, 145–53; Gregory Calvert, 'In White America: Radical Consciousness and Social Change' (1967), in Massimo Teodori (ed.), *The New Left: A Documentary History* (London: Jonathan Cape, 1970), 417.

14. Alice Echols, *'Daring to Be Bad': Radical Feminism in America, 1967–1975* (Minneapolis: University of Minnesota Press, 1989), 39; Peter B. Levy, *The New Left and Labor in the 1960s* (Urbana: University of Illinois Press, 1994), 121; Joshua Bloom and Waldo Martin, *Black Against Empire: The History and Politics of the Black Panther Party* (Berkeley: University of California Press, 2013), 3; David Barber, 'Leading the Vanguard: White New Leftists School the Panthers on Black Revolution', in Jama Lazerow and Yohuru Williams (eds), *In Search of*

the *Black Panther Party: New Perspectives on a Revolutionary Movement* (Durham, NC: Duke University Press, 2006), 223–34; Jeremy Varon, *Bringing the War Home: The Weather Underground, the Red Army Faction, and Revolutionary Violence in the Sixties and Seventies* (Berkeley: University of California Press, 2004).

15. Simon Hall, *Peace and Freedom: The Civil Rights and Antiwar Movements in the 1960s* (Philadelphia: University of Pennsylvania Press, 2006), 22–3; Farber, *Chicago '68*, 69.

16. Bradford D. Martin, *The Theater Is in the Street: Politics and Performance in Sixties America* (Amherst: University of Massachusetts Press, 2004), 86–124; [The Diggers,] 'The Post-Competitive, Comparative Game of a Free City', *The Realist* 81 (August 1968), 15, reprinted in Teodori, *New Left*, 376; Abbie Hoffman, 'The Yippies are Going to Chicago', *The Realist* 82 (September 1968), 23–4, 1: www.ep.tc/realist/82/01.html; Farber, *Chicago '68*, 17, 20–1.

17. Walker, *Rights in Conflict*, 27; Farber, *Chicago '68*, 181–2; Bloom and Martin, *Black Against Empire*, 207.

18. Farber, *Chicago '68*, 195–7, 200.

19. Farber, *Chicago '68*, 204, 206–7. Bloom and Martin, *Black Against Empire*, 209.

20. Echols, *Daring to Be Bad*, 3, 103, 72–4, 299 n.4, 83–84, 20; Shulamith Firestone, *The Dialectic of Sex: The Case for Feminist Revolution* (New York: William Morrow, 1970); Kate Millett, *Sexual Politics* (Garden City, NY: Doubleday, 1970).

21. George Chauncey, *Gay New York: Gender, Urban Culture, and the Making of the Gay Male World, 1890–1940* (New York: Basic Books, 1994); Jeffrey Weeks, *The Languages of Sexuality* (New York: Routledge, 2011), 26; Fran Winant, 'Christopher Street Liberation Day, June 28, 1970', in Karla Jay and Allen Young (eds), *Out of the Closets: Voices of Gay Liberation* (New York: New York University Press, [1972] 1992), 5.

22. Thomas J. Sugrue, *The Origins of the Urban Crisis: Race and Inequality in Postwar Detroit* (Princeton, NJ: Princeton University Press, 1996); Amy Scott, 'Cities and Suburbs', in David Farber and Beth Bailey (eds), *The Columbia Guide to America in the 1960s* (New York: Columbia University Press, 2001), 264; Elizabeth Tandy Shermer, *Sunbelt Capitalism: Phoenix and the Transformation of American Capitalism* (Philadelphia: University of Pennsylvania Press, 2013).

23. Stephen Tuck, *We Ain't What We Ought to Be: The Black Freedom Struggle from Emancipation to Obama* (Cambridge, MA: Harvard University Press, 2010), 338; Robert Weisbrot, *Freedom Bound: A History of America's Civil Rights Movement* (New York: Norton, 1990), 270.

24. *Report of the National Advisory Commission on Civil Disorders* (New York: Bantam Books, 1968), 2; Anthony S. Campagna, *The Economic Consequences of the Vietnam War* (New York: Praeger, 1991), 61–2.

25. Donna Jean Murch, *Living for the City: Migration, Education, and the Rise of the Black Panther Party in Oakland, California* (Chapel Hill: University of North Carolina, 2010), 127–42; Joe Street, 'The Black Panther Party and Street Protest in the 1960s', unpublished paper delivered at Historians of the Twentieth Century United States annual meeting, Reading, UK (7 September 2014); Huey

P. Newton, 'Functional Definition of Politics' (1967), in Huey P. Newton, *The Genius of Huey P. Newton* (San Francisco: Ministry of Information, Black Panther Party, 1970), 29.

26. Bloom and Martin, *Black Against Empire*, 159. Untitled FBI report, 21 March 1968, Box 9, 2nd FBI file, Amiri Baraka Papers, Moorland-Spingarn Research Center, Howard University, Washington, DC. Huey P. Newton, 'In Defense of Self-Defense' (1967), in Huey P. Newton's *Essays from the Minister of Defense, Huey Newton* (n.p.: Black Panther Party, 1968), 10, 5.

27. Bloom and Martin, *Black Against Empire*, 181, 184; Jerald E. Podair, *The Strike that Changed New York: Blacks, Whites, and the Ocean Hill–Brownsville Crisis* (New Haven: Yale University Press, 2002); Daniel Matlin, *On the Corner: African American Intellectuals and the Urban Crisis* (Cambridge, MA: Harvard University Press, 2013), 175; Laurie B. Green, *Battling the Plantation Mentality: Memphis and the Black Freedom Struggle* (Chapel Hill: University of North Carolina Press, 2007), 275–87.

28. 'Interview with Cha-Cha Jimenez' (1969), in Darrel Enck-Wanzer (ed.), *The Young Lords: A Reader* (New York: New York University Press, 2010), 27–8; Laura Pulido, *Black, Brown, Yellow, and Left: Radicalism in Los Angeles* (Berkeley: University of California Press, 2006), 116; Lilia Fernández, *Brown in the Windy City: Mexicans and Puerto Ricans in Postwar Chicago* (Chicago: University of Chicago Press, 2012), 163, 173–205; Bloom and Martin, *Black Against Empire*, 144.

29. Paul Chaat Smith and Robert Allen Warrior, *Like a Hurricane: The Indian Movement from Alcatraz to Wounded Knee* (New York: New Press, 1996), 51, 7–9, 22, 117, 127; Dennis Banks with Richard Erdoes, *Ojibwa Warrior: Dennis Banks and the Rise of the American Indian Movement* (Norman: University of Oklahoma Press, 2004), 64.

30. Christopher Klemek, *The Transatlantic Collapse of Urban Renewal: Postwar Urbanism from New York to Berlin* (Chicago: University of Chicago Press, 2011), 109–28; Stefan M. Bradley, *Columbia vs. Harlem: Black Student Power in the Late 1960s* (Urbana: University of Illinois Press, 2010).

31. Fernández, *Brown in the Windy City*, 173; Estella Habal, *San Francisco's International Hotel: Mobilizing the Filipino American Community in the Anti-Eviction Movement* (Philadelphia: Temple University Press, 2007), xiii, 2–3.

32. Robert Mason, *Richard Nixon and the Quest for a New Majority* (Chapel Hill: University of North Carolina Press, 2004), 29; Peter Kihss, '"Benign Neglect" on Race Is Proposed by Moynihan', *New York Times* (1 March 1970), 1; Edward C. Banfield, *The Unheavenly City: The Nature and Function of Our Urban Crisis* (Boston: Little, Brown, 1968); Themis Chronopoulos, *Spatial Regulation in New York City: From Urban Renewal to Zero Tolerance* (London: Routledge, 2011), 147–80.

33. Steven Conn, 'Back to the Garden: Communes, the Environment, and Antiurban Pastoralism at the End of the Sixties', *Journal of Urban History* 36 (November 2010), 831–48; Bloom and Martin, *Black Against Empire*, 237–39.

34. David Bird, 'Earth Day Plans Focus on City', *New York Times* (20 April 1970); Francis Njubi Nesbitt, *Race for Sanctions: African Americans against*

Apartheid, 1946–1994 (Bloomington: Indiana University Press, 2004), 78–80; Tuck, *We Ain't What We Ought to Be*, 352–70; Donna Murch, 'Ferguson's Inheritance', *Jacobin* (8 May 2015): www.jacobinmag.com/2015/08/ ferguson-police-black-lives-matter/

35. On connections between the counterculture and the urban renaissance, see Lipsitz, 'Who'll Stop the Rain?', 231.

SIX

Centring The Yard:
Student Protest on Campus in 1968

Stefan M. Bradley

On 12 April 1968, the President of Columbia University, Grayson Kirk, stated emphatically: 'Our young people, in disturbing numbers, appear to reject all forms of authority . . . and they have taken refuge in a turbulent and inchoate nihilism whose sole objectives are destructive.'[1] The president of the Ivy League institution was both accurate and inaccurate in his assessment of the baby-boomer youth. He was accurate insofar as, at that moment, young people – especially students – were rejecting forms of authority they had no say in appointing. They presumed that blind faith in authority and the established system had brought them to this point of turbulence. Kirk, again, was accurate in that some young people were nihilistic in their approach to life, but this analysis of youth had been true for generations. And, he was correct in that some youth sought to destroy the established systems. However, what Kirk got wrong was that many young Americans, especially students in higher education, did not want to destroy their institutions literally; they wanted to dismantle the models of stale complacency regarding race, class and gender that had been maintained for centuries. In 1968, those young learners wanted their institutions to be *relevant* to the current problems of the United States and not to contribute to the oppression of people at home or abroad.

The broad span of universities and colleges, then, became a symbol of American society. In 1968, famed academician and a colleague of Grayson Kirk at Columbia, Jacques Barzun, wrote that the American university 'has ceased to be a sheltered spot for study only; has come into the market place and answered the cries for help uttered by government, industry, and the general public; . . . has served the country by carrying on research for national goals'. He also added that the university has 'recognized social needs by undertaking to teach the quite young, the middle-aged, the disabled, the deprived, the misdirected and the maladjusted'.[2] In short, he revealed, universities had finally been exposed to the complexities of American social life, and had opened their doors to the economically poor and working class, black citizens and women – those with whom higher education institutions had been unfamiliar.

While many eighteen to twenty-four-year-old men took their place in the armed forces, their peers at university challenged their institutions to distance themselves from the war effort altogether. Students-turned-activists focused on removing Reserved Officer Training Corp (ROTC) programmes – which the Department of Defense frequently funded – from their campuses, as was the case at historically black Southern University in Louisiana.[3] Additionally, these students (sometimes physically) challenged military, FBI and CIA recruiters when they arrived on campus, as was the case at the University of Wisconsin in May 1965. Others used their curiosity and research skills to reveal the contracts that their universities kept with private corporations like the Dow Chemical Company.[4] Students on campuses took inspiration from young people like Muhammad Ali who refused induction into the US Army in April 1967 or those youth who organized a march on Washington DC in October to oppose US military involvement in Vietnam. They thought idealistically about their educational institutions and did not believe that there was room for strategies of destruction, which is what they believed the Institute for Defense Analyses (IDA) cultivated. As the research wing of the Department of Defense, IDA was a consortium to which many leading higher education institutions belonged.

At the same time that some students on American campuses voiced their disdain for the Vietnam conflict, others pushed against what they viewed as institutional racism. During the period, activist Julius Lester wrote his 1969 book titled *Look Out Whitey!: Black Power's Gon' Get Yo' Mama!* The author may have well warned universities and colleges to look out because Black Power had come to campus, and many students – both black and white – welcomed the movement.[5] The calls for Black Power during the late 1960s meant self-determination regarding a number of key issues affecting black communities: closing ranks along racial lines to build unity and then coalescing with groups outside their race; reclaiming and celebrating the history and culture of black people; and defending blackness and black people.

The institutional racism that students battled on campus took the form of low recruitment of black students, faculty and administrators; hostile cultural environments on campus; and institutions using their power to take advantage of neighbours who lived near these campuses. Until recently, scholars of the 1960s have characterized the student movement as a primarily white affair that featured leaders like Mario Savio at Berkeley and Mark Rudd at Columbia.[6] The reality was that black students were very active during the period. If the Vietnam War was one of the main catalysts of student activism, so too was the black freedom movement. To complete the story of the campus movement, the role of black student activists needs to be infused into the historical narrative. Undoubtedly, those youth agitators drew upon 'Black Student Power' – their status as students combined with their race – to bring the struggle for freedom onto campus.[7]

The antiwar movement, the battle against institutional racism and the campaigns for co-education and women's rights on campuses represented different aspects of the New Left movement, and more particularly pointed to the need for student empowerment.[8] On the campuses of what today are known as Predominantly White Institutions (PWIs), where in 1968 more black students attended than ever before, and Historically Black Colleges and Universities (HBCUs), where most black students still attended, young people manoeuvred to have their voices heard in the governance of their educational institutions.

In order to 'centre the yard' in a reappraisal of 1968, the discussion here focuses on the campus as the representative space and students as the key players that acted within and beyond its microcosm. To reframe 1968 is to place black university students near the centre of activism. Also, reframing the year requires that female student activists garner more attention for their efforts than is often credited. As such, this essay addresses aspects of the student movement that have been overlooked or lightly treated but are nonetheless essential to the retelling of 1968.

Outside Agitation: The Influence of Black Power on Students

The Black Campus Movement has garnered scholarly attention, especially since the turn of the millennium.[9] In 1968, black students took the offensive regarding their presence at PWIs by moving beyond tactics of survival and assimilation to create an environment that either welcomed them or became uncomfortable for all university affiliates. They took cues not only from domestic black freedom struggles but also those abroad. Students followed the activism and scholarship of figures such as Pan-Africanists Walter Rodney in Guyana and Frantz Fanon in Martinique, who challenged the oppressed and working classes to overthrow the racial and economic ruling class. In addition to Fanon's *Wretched of the Earth* (1961), they read the searing criticisms of institutional racism and economic deprivation in *The Autobiography of Malcolm X* (1965), Stokely Carmichael and Charles Hamilton's *Black Power: The Politics of Liberation* (1967), Harold Cruse's *The Crisis of the Negro Intellectual* (1967) and Martin Luther King, Jr.'s *Where Do We Go from Here?* (1967). By January 1968, Nathan Wright, Jr.'s *Black Power and Urban Unrest* was available. That year, socially conscious and intellectually curious students read books like *The Black Power Revolt: A Collection of Essays*, edited by Floyd Barbour. In an attempt to extend their international political understanding, some students were reading Karl Marx's *Das Kapital* and Mao Tse-Tung's *Quotations from Chairman Mao Zedong* (Little Red Book), a favourite of the Black Panthers. Through their reading, students, attempted to grasp the meaning of revolution and sought to apply revolutionary principles to their own struggles.[10]

On college campuses, despite their rhetoric, students were largely reformist in their campaigns of 1968. Recent scholarship has described black campus activism as revolutionary, but even many students understood that they wanted to improve rather than extirpate the institutions they attended. Bill Sales, a history major at Columbia, attempted to link the world revolutions into what was happening at his university during the spring and fall of 1968 when Columbia student activism seemed to epitomize the broader currents at play across American campuses. On the initial day (23 April) of the building takeovers that dominated activities at Columbia that spring, white student Hilton Obenzinger remembered Sales telling a crowd of students that when 'you strike a blow at the gym [that Columbia officials attempted to build in the mostly black patronized Morningside Park], you strike a blow for the Vietnamese People. You strike a blow at Low Library [where the administration was housed] and you strike a blow for the freedom fighters in Angola, Mozambique, and South Africa'.[11] Black students saw themselves as being part of the long continuum of the black freedom movement that featured various approaches to struggle: revolution, rebellion and resistance. Sales, who, in addition to checking the university's ambition to build a gymnasium in nearby Morningside Park, also advocated the need to bring Black Studies to Columbia, months later explained: 'we knew this was not the revolution, per se, but that it was part of an ongoing struggle to improve the lives of black students and black people in general'.[12]

Figure 6.1 Columbia University Students' Afro-American Society leader Bill Sales addresses occupiers of Hamilton Hall with Students for a Democratic Society (SDS) leader Mark Rudd to his immediate right. Images of Stokely Carmichael (left) and Malcolm X (right) adorn the back wall. 23 April 1968. Courtesy of Gerald S. Adler.

Figure 6.2 Predominantly white students on Low Library Ledge during its week-long occupation, 28 April 1968 (CAPA551). Courtesy of University Archives, Rare Book & Manuscript Library, Columbia University, New York City.

With social turbulence on the rise, some young people did actually believe a revolution was at hand. At Columbia, white student and Students for a Democratic Society (SDS) leader Mark Rudd had actually visited Cuba in March and believed that perhaps the struggles on campus were part of a revolution. He said: 'Cuba seemed to me a society inspired by a new morality . . . I wandered around Havana in a euphoric haze . . . Cuba's socialism was the moral and political wave of the future. I was stoned on socialism.'[13] He could not wait to return to New York and challenge the social status quo via the work of SDS. 'I bought into the fantasy of revolution', Rudd admitted two decades after the 1968 rebellion at Columbia.[14] Rudd's fellow student Obenzinger thought that apocalypse must have been imminent when he saw members of the militant Harlem Mau Maus not being molested by – but rather escorted by – the police across campus. When a white professor, who had taught Obenzinger about Karl Marx, pleaded with the student activist to stop his occupation of Columbia's Low Library, the student only felt sadness for the professor because the professor 'couldn't *live* the revolution; couldn't put his life, his career, on the line'.[15] At that moment, students engaged in protest were putting their futures at risk.

As well as taking some of its impetus from freedom struggles abroad, student activism in the United States inspired protest around the nation and world. As one essayist and poet who witnessed the uprising at Columbia put it, 1968 was 'The Year of the Rebel'.[16] The zeitgeist of the historical moment provoked student agitators from across the globe to follow each other. Students in Germany, France, Czechoslovakia, Mexico and the Caribbean pressed their educational institutions to reform. Activists abroad chanted 'Two, Three, Many Columbias!', referring to the student rebellion in New York that April.

Administrators throughout the nation struggled to appease demonstrating students, who were prone to agitate at any moment. University officials, sometimes anxiously, worked with students to bring controversial figures onto campus for lectures. At times, this proved successful and, at others, the invited figures stirred trouble.[17] Former leader of the Student Non-Violent Coordinating Committee (SNCC) Stokely Carmichael, as much as any other singular figure, influenced students' conceptions of activism. Scholar Peniel Joseph described Carmichael as 'the most important black radical activist of his generation'.[18] By 1968, Carmichael had published *Black Power* and the Black Panther Party had appointed him as prime minister in the hopes of creating a coalition of SNCC and the Panthers.

Carmichael was a student favourite on the university lecture circuit, and that caused a certain amount of anxiety for school officials. For instance, in October 1968, on Howard University's campus in Washington DC (where Carmichael spent his undergraduate days), he met with John Carlos, the Olympic sprinter, who, after receiving his bronze medal at the Mexico City Olympics earlier that month, raised his fist as a sign of Black Power and in protest against the United States' oppression of poor black people.[19] The two icons shared their thoughts on the movement with the hundreds of onlookers. During 1968, Carmichael travelled to dozens of campuses, where he warned students to be prepared to face institutional anti-black racism and liberal white people who 'want to hold hands without punishing the guilty and violence' of racists.[20] Some of the white liberals to which Carmichael referred were administrators. Many students took the young leader's message to heart.

Malcolm X, like Carmichael, was an important figure in the student movement, despite (and in some ways because of) his assassination four years earlier. When black students took over Hamilton Hall at Columbia, they renamed the building Malcolm X Hall. The building had been officially named after Alexander Hamilton, who was an alumnus of King's College, which was the precursor of Columbia College and Columbia University. Similarly, after protesting at Duke, students helped to create Malcolm X Liberation University as an alternative to the elite institutions that focused nearly exclusively on western civilization. One scholar explained that, even after his death, Malcolm X's message provided the 'theoretical framework for the Black Student Movement and the development of independent Black educational institutions'.[21] Undoubtedly, Malcolm X greatly influenced young people.

Perhaps an overemphasized element of Malcolm X's message was violence. The nuanced role of violence made the student movement unique. Where nonviolence remained a way of life for many activists during the early 1960s, self-defence and tactical violence became a more attractive option for agitators in the late 1960s. One New York University student asked: 'if nonviolence doesn't work, what is there left for blacks to do', adding that 'black people will come to violence only with sincere [white] racist help'.[22] Malcolm X could not have stated it better. The prospect of lethal violence on campus captured the minds of activists and administrators alike.

Students in 1968 were mostly safe from the kind of violence that their peers confronted in Vietnam and on the streets of urban America. Even when police encroached on campus, law enforcement rarely employed lethal violence (police officers killed three black student activists in Orangeburg, South Carolina, in February at an off-campus protest). Sometimes the mostly white police officers wanted to teach the protesters a lesson. One, who was called in to remove students from an occupied building, stated: 'these kids need to be spanked'.[23] At the University of California, Santa Barbara in February, protesters hurled rocks at police cars during an action and trapped policemen in a bank near campus to dramatize their critique of capitalism. The officers exited the building unscathed, and miraculously no students died from their action against the police officers.[24]

Though they were roughly the same age as college agitators, Black Panther Party members like Bobby Hutton, who confronted police on the street, were much less fortunate than college activists. In April 1968, Hutton was shot twelve times after he and other members allegedly ambushed police in Oakland.[25] Hutton's shoot-out was just one of the violent confrontations that involved black youth and law enforcement in off-campus settings. That year, Huey Newton faced trial for the alleged murder of a policeman, and three other Panthers had been involved in a shootout in Los Angeles. The stakes in Black Panther and law enforcement confrontations seemed higher than those between students and authorities on campuses. There, faculty members tried to interpose themselves between law enforcement and their students.[26] Similarly, in spite of the trouble students ran into by protesting, school officials made attempts to keep them from becoming eligible for the draft. Faculty members sometimes assigned higher grades so that students ranked better in their class. A City University of New York professor remembered that she and other members in the history department 'gave all A's to our students as a protest'.[27] Those efforts were fortuitous for some university students, but for those not so privileged the call to the war beckoned much louder.

There was relative safety on campuses, but that did not mean that violence was nonexistent. Columbia University called in a thousand uniformed and plain-clothes police officers to remove students who were occupying five buildings after a week-long demonstration. The episode of 30 April soon turned violent. Students in one building, along with national SDS leader Tom Hayden, resisted arrest physically. As the following chapter in this volume discusses, the police removed barricades, pounced on demonstrators, and dragged them down the steps of the building by their hair. Violence radicalized moderate students and observers, who could not fathom such a scene on an American campus.[28]

The presence of police and violence led some students to demand the removal of presidents and other administrators. That autumn, Columbia's president, Grayson Kirk, resigned, as did two presidents of San Francisco State College, John Summerskill and

Robert Smith, and chancellor William Sewell of the University of Wisconsin. Other leaders followed suit because they became symbols of establishment America. Administrators' jobs became part of the collateral damage in the larger war against the establishment.

Yard Work: Campus Protest Germinates

In spite of previous major protests at places like the University of California Berkeley in 1964, campus activists caught their institutions by surprise in 1968. Students believed they had to disrupt the normal operation of their institutions, as Berkley Free Speech Movement leader Mario Savio suggested years earlier.[29] Still adhering to the principles of *in loco parentis* and enforcing parietals, university officials could not fathom students bringing the actions used in the outside movement onto campus. Surprise worked in the students' favour. That combined with the leadership styles at some of the educational institutions gave students a chance to advance their goals. Students pushed against liberal administrators including James Perkins of Cornell University, John Dickey of Dartmouth College and John Summerskill of San Francisco State with the same vigour that those pushed against more conservative administrators, legislators and communities. Then, sometimes at co-educational institutions but often at women's colleges, activists pushed progressive agendas that charted women's freedom and also inspired men at other institutions.

Campus demonstrations also differed depending on the location and type of institution. Protesters at private schools faced different circumstances than those at public schools.[30] Additionally, private institutions necessarily relied upon tuition dollars; whereas, public institutions answered to state legislatures that provided a sizable amount of funds to university and college coffers. Whether the school was historically black or predominantly white also made a difference in the contours of students' campaigns.

The region in which the students found themselves influenced their activism as well, particularly in the Black Campus Movement. In the Northeast, where some of the oldest institutions of higher education in the nation resided, students enjoyed a level racial and ethnic diversity beyond the iron gates and ivy-laden walls, but they battled against the liberalism and ineffectiveness of President Lyndon Johnson's Great Society policies and legislation that proved unsuccessful in economically poor communities adjacent to their institutions. Yale black students supported the Black Coalition, a confederacy of New Haven's black community organizations that contested the university's expansion into poor and working class black neighbourhoods.[31] Students, viewing themselves as representatives of the black community, stood on behalf of the Black Coalition when it charged the university with paternalism and land grabbing. After King's assassination, at Rutgers University, New Jersey, students captured the American flag at Douglass Residential College and raised it upside down to indicate the emergency of violent racism. At the University of Pennsylvania, members of the Students Afro-American Society acted on behalf of the neighbouring community in West Philadelphia when they blocked the entrances and exits of a bank that did not hire black workers and also when they delivered signatures for open housing in the state house of representatives.[32]

In the Midwest, institutions like Northwestern University, the University of Missouri, the University of Michigan and the University of Wisconsin witnessed student upheaval. At Northwestern near Chicago, on 3 and 4 May, a group called For Members Only and the Afro-American Student Union, which included now famed Black Studies luminary James Turner, occupied the university's business offices, pressuring the institution to respond to demands for resources the students made at the end of the previous month.[33] At the University of Missouri, black students formed one of the first Legion of Black Collegians student government bodies to be acknowledged by a university. Ann Arbor, birthplace of 1962's Port Huron Statement, witnessed black students and white supporting activists staging a sit-in at the administration building to protest the paucity of black students and faculty members on campus.[34] At the University of Wisconsin, students intensified their activism when conservatives and radicals clashed ideologically and physically. When the local SDS chapter coalesced with the city's draft resistance group, conservative forces vandalized a building housing the antiwar protesters. Subsequently, the antiwar contingent intensified its efforts by firebombing the university's administration building

(South Hall).[35] The student battle at the University of Wisconsin and elsewhere was about who could control the university.

In the South, at the University of Alabama, students appealed to the university president to have speakers like Tom Hayden (author of the Port Huron Statement), Eldridge Cleaver (before his hasty exit from the United States), communist scholar Herbert Aptheker and Jerry Rubin of the Yippies come to campus, but the president denied their request.[36] At historically black LeMoyne–Owen College in Memphis, students, still reeling from the assassination of King and the uprising that ensued, seized campus buildings calling for lowered tuition and Black Studies.[37] At Duke University, which desegregated in 1964, black students led a campaign to ban segregated facilities on campus and supported the black cafeteria workers' efforts to unionize, which was no small task in the South.[38] At the Atlanta University Center (which housed Morehouse College, Spelman College, Clark Atlanta University, Morris Brown College and Interdenominational Theological Center), scholar-activists Vincent Harding, Gerald McWhorter and others planted the seeds for the Institute of the Black World that sprouted in the following years.[39] Similarly, Howard Fuller in North Carolina helped to organize black university students at universities like Duke and North Carolina A&T in Greensboro to build institutions for the nearby black communities.[40]

Out West, where working-class black people migrated to participate in the airplane industry, the transition to higher education was troublesome.[41] Scholar Donna Murch described the evolution toward consciousness that students at Merritt Community College experienced during the Black Power Movement. This activist spirit inspired Bobby Seale and Huey Newton to create the Black Panther Party in 1966 and influenced black students along the West Coast. At San Jose State University, student-athletes led protests against the mistreatment of black players who had trouble finding housing.[42]

In urban areas, students could seek outside help from community members in their campaigns for black freedom and push against the war. In light of the long hot summers of the mid-1960s, campuses had to take notice because officials could observe the destruction around them. As a reminder, H. Rap Brown, the leader of the SNCC at the time of the Columbia protests, noted: 'If the university doesn't deal with our brothers in there, they're going to have to deal with the brothers out on the streets.'[43] Rap Brown indicated that community members and organizations stood in support of the campus activists.

Students in rural areas could not rely much on the assistance of the outside community, and so they had to protect their own interests. That was the case at Dartmouth College in Hanover, New Hampshire, and Cornell University in Ithaca, New York, where there was no significant black community in proximity to campus to influence the institutions to accommodate black students. In these instances, the students had to negotiate their own movement.[44]

The spirit of resistance encouraged activists at Howard University to take over campus buildings. Building takeovers was a preferred tactic of activists during the year. Other methods included walk-outs and sit-ins or teach-ins like those at Brown University and Pembroke College. Violent rebellion in the way of destruction and physical scuffles crept onto both PWI and HBCU campuses. The mostly white chapters of SDS and the Southern Student Organizing Committee sought to expose their fellow students to the atrocity of war with the teach-ins and sit-ins they held. In April, SDS led a one-day class national strike to draw attention to the war and inequality; nearly a million students participated.

The intensity of the moment and the use of violence was enough to splinter SDS by the close of 1968. Young radicals battled over the ideology of participatory democracy and Maoism, as well as the philosophy of sociologist C. Wright Mills. The result of the ideological scrimmages was a loosening of the bond of activists and the formation of isolated actions. At national conventions the Revolutionary Youth Movement of SDS challenged the Worker-Student Alliance Party, which was associated with the Progressive Labor faction. Controversy erupted over whether to mobilize on campuses or in the streets among the working classes. Campus rebels agreed that pressing and disrupting the politicians at the Democratic National Convention in Chicago that September was essential. By then, however, some SDS members had formed another organization called the Weathermen. Subsequently, SDS's base fractured and eventually could not survive.[45]

Who Runs The Yard? Black Campus Activism and Institutional Change

At the same time that students protested institutional links to the war, black students moved 'toward a black university' – a protest phrase and conference title that students at Howard used in 1968.[46] One scholar noted: 'Black colleges faced a separate set of *intra*-institutional debates regarding the responsibilities of a *black* college in society.'[47] Although HBCUs like Howard had existed since American Reconstruction, there was little curricular emphasis on the black experience. In an age when the Black Consciousness and Black Arts Movement thrived, it chafed young admirers of Audrey 'Queen Mother' Moore and Malcolm X to not be able to learn about their heritage in a scholarly way.

Students at HBCUs and PWIs believed they had an obligation to contextualize the black experience. At HBCUs especially, students decided that their institutions would be relevant to the needs of the black community. As Howard officials attempted to seal the university's reputation as the 'Black Harvard' students charged that it lost touch with the black masses, and that the institution was not even the 'Black Howard'. To actualize a black university, students at Howard took over campus buildings in the spring and held a conference in the fall.

The push toward a black university extended to PWIs. 'As black students we pledge to use our talents in black communities for the benefit of the black man', a student declared.[48] That statement represented the stance of many black students in the late 1960s. In the decades and years before 1968, black students had been on the defence in their attempts to survive culturally and mentally at elite institutions of higher education. By 1965 black students only made up 4.8 per cent of all students enrolled in universities in the United States, and, according to two scholars, 'only 1 per cent the enrollments of selective New England colleges in 1965'.[49] Essentially, there was no black presence. Barry Beckham, a 1966 graduate of Brown University, remembered there being eight black students of 659 in his class. He and the few other black students had not yet come to the point where they demanded a change in the curriculum.

The demand for increased black admissions was also common. In spite of the increased effort to admit more black students, life could still be difficult for new students. A black student who was a sophomore in 1968 remembered Princeton as a 'lonely place', where he felt at times 'unwelcome' and 'under attack'.[50] He was not alone in his sentiment, however, and that is the reason for the development of Black Student Unions and similar organizations such as the Association of Black Collegians at Princeton. Carl Fields, one of the first black administrators in Princeton's more than 200-year history, helped the Association to organize a national conference, inviting black students from mostly elite PWIs. As they discussed the 'Negro Undergraduate', the goals were to increase black admissions and to hire black administrators and professors.[51]

In moving toward a black university, black students welcomed the support of white peers. In 1968, black women activists at Pembroke College in Providence, Rhode Island, initiated a demonstration for increased black admissions. They demanded that the college admit at least the percentage of black people in the United States (11 per cent) at the time. Leading the charge, Sheryl Grooms, attempted to help her college with recruitment strategies: 'They've [Pembroke] got to have a black admissions officer to go into the ghettos and compete for the students.'[52] She wanted the institution to go beyond its traditional pools for students (which usually meant private white preparatory academies in the Northeast) and traditional methods of employing white admissions recruiters. Adding pressure, Grooms and her fellow black student activists from Pembroke, as well as black men at Brown, decided to 'boycott' their institution until the schools could focus on the needs of black people. Hundreds of white students and some faculty stood in solidarity with the black protesters.[53]

Despite the fact that they played significant roles in the struggle for freedom, black women (and women in general) have rarely been featured in the narratives of campus activism. Leaders such as Grooms, Kathryn Ogletree of Northwestern University's For Members Only black student organization, and Gwenn Patton of the National Student Association and later the National Association of Black Students have been overlooked in the literature.[54] They took their cues from leading women like Elaine Brown, Kathleen

Cleaver and Angela Davis of the Black Panther Party, who struggled against racism, patriarchy and capitalism at once.[55] Those leaders (on and off campus) headed up their campaigns and received the support of sympathetic black and white activists, who added resonance to their causes.

As the experience of black students went from presence to protest, Black Studies became a primary issue. In addition to what they would learn, students believed that Black Studies would give them a sense of belonging at their institutions. Barry Beckham from Brown University noted that, by 1968, black students were ready for 'a piece of the action'.[56] Historian Heyward 'Woody' Farrar documented his experience as a black student at the University of Maryland in 1968. He said students who were 'deprived of chance to fight the system in the streets of Baltimore, Washington, Philadelphia and elsewhere . . . looked forward to fighting it on the campuses of their colleges'.[57] That fight included the infusion of black history and culture in the curriculum.

The Black Studies campaign linked students from disparate institutions and ideologies. As students at San Francisco State College, a public state institution that served mostly working-class learners, engaged in a strike for a Black Studies department, students at Yale, an elite and exclusive Ivy League institution, also struggled to bring the discipline to their campus. At San Francisco State, students aligned themselves with Black Panthers like George Murray and observed the actions of militant groups in the Bay Area. Black students at Yale organized a 'Black Studies in the University' conference that featured various thought leaders on the role of the curriculum in advancing the larger freedom movement. Diverse movement activists like cultural nationalist Maulana Karenga, social critic Harold Cruse, Spelman faculty member Gerald McWhorter, director of Black Studies at San Francisco State College Nathan Ware, Harvard administrator Martin Kilson and others opined on the need for inclusion at PWIs.[58] At Yale, scholars and activists alike made it clear that Black Studies was as much a manifestation of activism as it was of intellectual decolonization. The efforts of those at San Francisco, Yale and elsewhere worked because within five years of the first programme being established, 5611 courses were being taught at nearly half the universities and colleges in the nation.[59]

There was a conservative backlash against the campus movements. Politically, Nixon took advantage of the 'silent majority' by pointing out the lawlessness and threat that student protesters posed to the nation. Similarly, he focused his southern strategy to appeal to the fears that many white Americans had of a black uprising. At the local level, politicians tried to curb the activism of activists as well. In response to demonstrations at Penn, Temple University, Cheyney College and Pennsylvania State University, Pennsylvania state legislators (Democratic and Republican alike) proposed a Bill to cut funding to universities that did not punish student protesters by 'throwing them out of school or in jail'.[60] On campuses, there were also counter-protesters for most of the major demonstrations. One consistently conservative contingent was the Young Americans for Freedom, which launched its own campaigns on campus. Although its methods differed from groups like SDS and the BSU, the Young Americans for Freedom led campaigns to bring awareness to the struggle for control that was occurring in higher education.[61] Members questioned if black students and members of leftist organizations should have the power to determine the educational experience of all other students.

After the campus uprisings of 1968, university and college officials learned how to respond quickly to demonstrations or suffer consequences. The responses of those officials sometimes had deadly implications, as was the case at Jackson State University and Kent State University in May 1970. Calling law enforcement early in a demonstration was a tactic to subdue student protest, but one that often turned students against administrators. Another tactic was to begin negotiations as quickly as possible while being as amenable as necessary to encourage students to end their occupations or demonstrations. In an attempt to be proactive about student concerns, some universities established liaison positions for students on institutional executive committees and boards of trustees. In an ad hoc way, that relationship rose from bodies like the tripartite committee at Columbia and the quadripartite committee at Penn. More permanently, entities like the university senate at Columbia solidified the voices of students in decision making. Another legacy of 1968 and the campus rebellions was the creation of community outreach divisions that led communication efforts of urban universities and colleges. The intention was to prevent the types of controversies that occurred that year over institutional expansion at places such as Columbia, Penn and Chicago.[62]

Conclusion: The Campus Resurrection of 1968

One of the most enduring legacies of 1968 can be found in the curricula of American universities and colleges. These institutions, after that year, featured Black Studies courses, programmes, departments and centres. The rise of Black Studies directly influenced the arrival of Women's Studies and Ethnic Studies. As the number of black students and professionals rose on PWIs, HBCUs unfortunately lost access to some black talent. Universities and colleges also admitted women and became co-educational, which helped to equalize access but also led to the closure of some women's colleges. A major legacy of 1968 was the sustained courage to confront ties between higher education, the military and war. Student activists in the antiwar movement, as much as anyone or anything else, could claim responsibility for the nation's withdrawal from the conflict.

As of 2016, almost eighty universities and colleges face the demands of protesting students.[63] In many cases, the student activists resubmit the demands of student demonstrators from 1968. The demands of the newer generation of agitators cover many themes of the past. There are calls for increased black and Latino enrolment; the addition of black and Latino faculty; the renaming of buildings that feature now controversial historical figures. Students today, learning from the activism of 1968, demand that administrators be terminated for not addressing their needs or for acting insensitively with regard to race or gender. Again, many university officials were not prepared for the uprisings that occurred on their campuses, and as a result, student-activists have benefited from the element of surprise. Just as the issues of society invaded campuses in 1968, issues such as the abuse of police power, institutional racism and gender bias all made their way onto campus. This time, instead of Black Power, students join in the Black Lives Matter movement to protest the police-involved deaths of young people such as Michael Brown, Jr., Tamir Rice, Sandra Bland, Jacquan McDonald, Alton Sterling,

Philando Castille and others. The current student protesters enjoy the advantages of technology like Twitter, YouTube, Snapchat, Vine and Facebook, which has allowed them to share their struggles on their own terms without the filter of mainstream media. That has worked to create unity among students from different institutions, as demonstrators can support each other virtually. The technology is new, but the same spirit of resistance existed in 1968. As was the case then and now, 'the whole world is watching'.[64]

Notes

1. Grayson Kirk, quoted in Jules Witcover, *The Year the Dream Died: Revisiting 1968 America* (New York: Grand Central, 1997), 188.

2. Jacques Barzun, *The American University: How it Runs, Where It Is Going* (New York: Harper & Row, 1968), 6.

3. Marcus Cox, '"Keep Our Warriors out of the Draft": The Vietnam Anti-War Movement at Southern University, 1968–1973', *Educational Foundation* 20 (Winter/Spring, 2006), 123–44.

4. Milton Mankoff and Richard Flacks, 'The Changing Social Base of the American Student Movement', *The Annals of the American Academy of Political and Social Science* 395 (May 1971), 54–67.

5. Julius Lester, *Look Out, Whitey!: Black Power's Gon' Get Yo Mama* (New York: Grove, 1969).

6. Robert Cohen, *Freedom's Orator: Mario Savio and the Radical Legacy of the 1960s* (Oxford: Oxford University Press, 2009); Mark Rudd, *Underground: My Life with SDS and the Weathermen* (New York: William Morrow Press, 2010).

7. Stefan Bradley, *Harlem vs. Columbia University: Black Student Power in the Late 1960s* (Champaign: University of Illinois Press, 2009), 4.

8. See Kelly Morrow, 'Sexual Liberation at the University North Carolina', in Robert Cohen and David Snyder (eds), *Rebellion in Black and White: Southern Student Activism in the 1960s* (Baltimore, MD: Johns Hopkins University Press, 2013), 195–217. See Faith Holsaert et al., *Hands on the Freedom Plow: Personal Accounts of By Women in SNCC* (Urbana: University of Illinois Press, 2012); Anne M. Valk, *Radical Sisters: Second-Wave Feminism and Black Liberation in Washington, D.C.* (Urbana: University of Illinois Press, 2008); Bettye Collier-Thomas and V. P. Franklin, *Sisters in the Struggle: African-American Women in the Civil Rights-Black Power Movement* (New York: New York University Press, 2001).

9. The literature surrounding black student activism on white campuses has grown greatly in the last decades. See Wayne Glasker, *Black Students in the Ivory Tower: African American Student Activism at the University of Pennsylvania, 1967–1990* (Amherst: University of Massachusetts Press, 2002); Joy Ann Williamson, *Black Power on Campus: The University of Illinois, 1965– 1975* (Champaign: University

of Illinois Press, 2003); Carl Fields, *Black in Two Worlds* (Princeton, NJ: Red Hummingbird Press, 2006); Fabio Rojas, *From Black Power to Black Studies: How a Radical Social Movement Became an Academic Discipline* (Charlottesville: University of Virginia Press, 2007); Stefan Bradley, 'Black Power and the Big Green: Dartmouth College and the Black Freedom Movement, 1945–75', *Journal of Civil and Human Rights* 1 (Fall/Winter 2015), 25–55; Stefan Bradley, 'The Southern-Most Ivy: Princeton University from Jim Crow Admissions to Anti-Apartheid Protests, 1794–1969', *American Studies* (Fall/Winter 2010), 109–30; Martha Biondi, *The Black Revolution on Campus* (Berkeley: University of California Press, 2012); Ibram H. Rogers, *The Black Campus Movement: Black Students and the Racial Reconstitution of Higher Education, 1965–1972* (New York: Palgrave Macmillan, 2012).

10. Frantz Fanon, *Wretched of the Earth* (New York: Grove Press, 1963); Malcolm X (as told to Alex Haley), *The Autobiography of Malcolm X* (New York: Grove Press, 1965); Stokely Carmichael and Charles Hamilton, *Black Power: The Politics of Liberation* (New York: Vintage Books, 1967); Harold Cruse: *Crisis of the Negro Intellectual* (New York: Morrow Press, 1967); Nathan Wright, *Black Power and Urban Unrest* (New York: Hawthorn Press, 1968); Floyd Barbour, *The Black Power Revolt: A Collection of Essays* (New York: Collier Books, 1968).

11. Bill Sales, quoted in Hilton Obenzinger, *Busy Dying* (Tucson, AZ: Chax Publishing, 2008).

12. William Sales, 'Response to a Negro Negative', *Columbia Daily Spectator* (14 March 1969).

13. Mark Rudd, *Underground: My Life with SDS and the Weathermen* (New York: Morrow, 2009), 40–1.

14. Keith Moore, 'Only Make-Believe Says Student Rebel', *New York Daily News* (22 April 1988).

15. Obenzinger, *Busy Dying*, 82, 85.

16. Stephen Spender *Year of the Young Rebels* (New York: Vintage, 1969).

17. See Jeffrey A. Turner, *Sitting In and Speaking Out: Student Movements in the American South, 1960–1970* (Athens: University of Georgia Press, 2010), 177.

18. Peniel E. Joseph, *Stokely: A Life* (New York: Basic Civitas, 2014), 231. For another thorough treatment of Carmichael see Michael Thelwell, *Ready for Revolution: The Life and Struggles of Stokely Carmichael (Kwame Ture)* (New York: Simon & Schuster, 2003).

19. See Harry Edwards, *The Revolt of the Black Athlete* (New York: Free Press, 1969), and Amy Bass, *Not the Triumph but the Struggle: The 1968 Olympics and the Making of the Black Athlete* (Minneapolis: University of Minnesota Press, 2004).

20. Joseph, *Stokely: A Life*, 275.

21. Richard Benson II, *Fighting for Our Place in the Sun: Malcolm X and the Radicalization of the Black Student Movement, 1960–1973* (New York: Peter Lang, 2014), 2. See also Manning Marable, *Malcolm X: A Life of Reinvention* (New York: Viking Press, 2011).

22. Quoted in William Exum, *Paradoxes of Protest: Black Student Activism in a White University* (Philadelphia: Temple University Press, 1985), 47.

23. Bradley, *Harlem vs. Columbia University*, 94.
24. Alexander Bloom and Wini Breines (eds), *Takin' It to the Streets: A Sixties Reader*, 3rd edn (Oxford: Oxford University Press, 2011), 340.
25. Bobby Seale, *Seize the Time: The Story of the Black Panther Party and Huey Newton* (Chicago: Black Classic Press, 1991), 228–36.
26. Such was the case at Columbia University during the 1968 student rebellion: *Crisis at Columbia: Report of the Fact-Finding Commission on Columbia Disturbances* (New York: Random House, 1968), 107.
27. 'The Vietnam War on Campus, Revisited': 150.as.cornell.edu/vietnam.cfm (accessed 4 June 2016).
28. Bradley, *Harlem vs. Columbia University*, 96–111.
29. See Robert Cohen, *Freedom's Orator: Mario Savio and the Radical Legacy of the 1960s* (Oxford: Oxford University Press, 2009).
30. Joy Ann Williamson, *Radicalizing the Ebony Tower: Black Colleges and the Black Freedom Struggle in Mississippi* (New York: Teachers College Press, 2008), 3–4; Williamson, *Black Power on Campus*.
31. 'Yale to Provide Funds to Ghetto in New Haven', *The Harvard Crimson* (13 April 1968): www.thecrimson.com/article/1968/4/13/yale-to-provide-funds-to-ghetto/
32. Richard McCormick, *The Black Student Protest Movement at Rutgers* (New Brunswick, NJ: Rutgers University Press, 1990), 24–5; Glasker, *Black Students in the Ivory Tower*, 40. For information regarding student protest at the University of Pennsylvania, see John Puckett and Mark Lloyd, *Becoming Penn: The Pragmatic American University, 1950–2000* (Philadelphia: University of Pennsylvania Press, 2015).
33. 'Sit-in, Negotiation Continues; No Accord Reached on Demands', *Daily Northwestern* (4 May 1968), 1, 3. Rogers, *The Black Campus Movement*, 119; Biondi, *The Black Revolution on Campus*, 82–93.
34. Kellie Woodhouse, 'A Look Back at Political Activism Empowered by the Port Huron Statement', *The Ann Arbor News* (3 November 2012): www.annarbor.com/news/post-199/
35. 'Protests and Social Action at UW-Madison during the 20th Century' collection, 1968–1969 file, UW Archives and Records Management, University of Wisconsin-Madison Libraries: www.library.wisc.edu/archives/exhibits/campus-history-projects/protests-social-action-at-uw-madison-during-the-20th-century/1960-1969/
36. Gary Sprayberry, 'Student Radicalism and the Antiwar Movement at the University of Alabama', in Robert Cohen and David Snyder (eds), *Rebellion in Black and White*, 152–3.
37. Quoted in Shirletta Kinchen, *Black Power in the Bluff City: African American Youth and Student Activism in Memphis, 1965–1975* (Knoxville: University of Tennessee Press, 2015), 127.
38. Russell Rickford, *We Are an African People: Independent Education, Black Power, and the Radical Imagination* (Oxford: Oxford University Press, 2015), 170–2; Turner, *Sitting in and Speaking Out*, 194.
39. See Derrick White, *The Challenge of Blackness: The Institute of the Black World*

and Political Activism in the 1970s (Gainesville: University Press of Florida, 2011).

40. Regarding Malcolm X Liberation University, see Richard Benson II, *Fighting for Our Place in the Sun*; Jelani Favors, 'North Carolina A&T Black Power Activists and the Student Organization for Black Unity', in Robert Cohen and David Snyder (eds), *Rebellion in Black and White*, 255–76.

41. See Donna Murch, *Living for the City: Migration, Education, and the Rise of the Black Panther Party in Oakland* (Chapel Hill: University of North Carolina Press, 2011).

42. Edwards, *The Revolt of the Black Athlete*, 42–4.

43. Arthur Kokot, 'Black Leaders Support Strikers', *Columbia Daily Spectator* (27 April 1968).

44. Daniel Bell and Irving Kristol (eds), *Confrontation: The Student Rebellion and the Universities* (New York: Basic Books, 1968), 139–41; Donald Alexander Downs, *Cornell '69: Liberalism and the Crisis of the American University* (Ithaca, NY: Cornell University Press, 1999), 68–72.

45. On SDS see Kirpatrick Sales, *SDS* (New York: Random House, 1973); James Miller, *Democracy is in the Streets: From Port Huron to the Siege of Chicago* (New York: Simon & Schuster, 1987); Dan Berger, *Outlaws: The Weather Underground and the Politics of Solidarity* (Chico, CA: AK Press, 2006). Some of the former members of SDS and the Weathermen have penned important biographies as well. They include David Gilbert, Bill Ayers, Mark Rudd, Tom Hayden, Todd Gitlin and others (see Chapter 4 of this volume for discussion).

46. See Jocelyn Imani Cole, '"We're a Winner": Howard University and Student Activism in the Era of Black Power', unpublished PhD thesis, Howard University, Washington DC, 2015, 42–63.

47. Joy Ann Williamson, *Radicalizing the Ebony Tower: Black Colleges and the Black Freedom Struggle in Mississippi* (New York: Teachers College Press, 2008), 147.

48. Exum, *Paradoxes of Protest*, 49.

49. William Bowen and Derek Bok, *The Shape of the River: Long-Term Consequences of Considering Race in College and University Admissions* (Princeton, NJ: Princeton University Press, 1998), 4–7.

50. See Melvin McCray's 2009 documentary, *Looking Forward: Reflections of Black Princeton Alumni*. The film was premiered at a 'Coming Back and Moving Forward' alumni conference at Princeton University, October 2009, and is available at: alumni.princeton.edu/learntravel/lectures/videodetail/index.xml?videoid=124

51. Bradley, 'The Southern-Most Ivy', 120.

52. Robert Reinhold, 'Negroes at Brown U. Begin Boycott of Classes', *New York Times* (6 December 1968).

53. Ibid.

54. Bill Harsh, *The Daily Northwestern* (22 April 1968). For more information on Gwenn Patton see Richard Benson II, 'Interview with Gwen Patton', *Journal of Civil and Human Rights* 1 (Fall/Winter 2015), 182–9.

55. See Elaine Brown, *A Taste of Power: A Black Woman's Story* (New York: First Anchor Books, 1994), and Kathleen Cleaver and George Kastiaficas (eds),

Liberation, Imagination, and the Black Panther Party: A New Look at the Panthers and Their Legacy (New York: Routledge Press, 2001), 123–7; Angela Davis, *Angela Davis: An Autobiography* (New York: Random House, 1974). See also Kim Springer, *Living for the Revolution: Black Feminist Organizations, 1968–1980* (Durham, NC: Duke University Press, 2005).

56. Barry Beckham, 'Listen to the Black Graduate, You Might Lear Something', *Esquire* (September 1969), 197.

57. Peter Wallenstein (ed.), *Higher Education and the Civil Rights Movement: White Supremacy, Black Southerners, and College Campuses* (Gainesville: University of Florida Press, 2008), 141.

58. Armstead Robinson et al., *Black Studies in the University* (New Haven: Yale University Press, 1969).

59. 'The Plight of Black Studies', *Ebony* (December 1973), 128.

60. Paul Levy, 'Mullen Warns Colleges to Control Disorders', *Evening Bulletin* (Philadelphia) (20 February 1969).

61. Regarding the Young Americans for Freedom see Christopher Huff, 'Conservative Student Activism at the University of Georgia', in Robert Cohen and David Snyder (eds), *Rebellion in Black and White*, 174.

62. See Bradley, *Harlem vs. Columbia University*, 178–85; Judith Rodin, *The University and Urban Revival: Out of the Ivory Tower and into the Streets* (Philadelphia: University of Pennsylvania Press, 2007); Davarian Baldwin, 'The "800-Pound Gargoyle": The Long History of Higher Education and Urban Development on Chicago's South Side', *American Quarterly* 67 (March 2015), 81–103; John Fish, *Black Power/White Control: The Struggle of the Woodlawn Organization in Chicago* (Princeton: Princeton University Press, 1973).

63. Stefan M. Bradley, 'Black Activism on Campus', *New York Times* (1 February 2016).

64. This is a reference to the chant that young people shouted in the late 1960s as well as a reference to Todd Gitlin, *"The Whole World is Watching": Mass Media in the Making and Unmaking of the New Left* (Los Angeles: University of California Press, 1980).

SEVEN

The Ceremony is about to Begin: Performance and 1968

Martin Halliwell

A bare-chested young man with an open sheepskin jacket is bound to a heavy wooden stake on a sunny beach. His long hair and unshaven face accent his anguish, mixed with a hint of defiance as he awaits execution by firing squad. Just as the military command and drum roll seal his fate, he opens his eyes and turns his head to the right for a brief moment of recognition before blacking out. We hear the rifle shot and see his body crumple. His neck goes instantly limp and blood pours from his mouth in thick streams.

Anyone unable to recognize the face of Jim Morrison, the wild front man of Los Angeles rock band The Doors, would have little difficulty once the soundtrack begins again. An eerie organ note suspends the moment and heralds Morrison's unmistakable, mournful voice: 'Make a grave for the unknown soldier / Nestled in your hollow shoulder'. The camera cuts to a shot of blood dripping over funeral flowers and then zooms out to reveal the three other band members arced around the death scene, playing an Indian tanpura and drums with the ocean behind them. This ritualistic scene of mourning ends abruptly as the music bursts back into life. The cadence is cacophonous and Morrison's voice aggressive, accelerating into a fast-paced montage that combines colour footage of the Vietnam War with monochrome images of jubilation from VJ Day over twenty years earlier – this includes some jarring images, one showing a young Asian boy waving an American flag as ticker tape falls around him. The tempo eventually slows, we hear a clock chiming, and the film ends with the three musicians walking away along the shore line, with a dog in place of the deceased Morrison.

This short film was released as a promo for The Doors' March 1968 single 'The Unknown Soldier' and links the rising body count in Southeast Asia to the Californian counterculture. The film's location, perhaps symbolically, is the Los Angeles playground of Santa Monica Beach, by Pacific Ocean Pier that had been dismantled the previous year.[1] *Time* magazine proclaimed 'The Unknown Soldier' an 'antiwar philippic', but in its ambiguous symbolism it is not easy to classify as a straightforward protest song.[2] It is certainly not the kind of rallying antiwar song epitomized by Country Joe and the Fish's 'I-Feel-Like-I'm-Fixin'-to-Die Rag' which, on its commercial release in November 1967 and through live performances in 1968, became a potent hippie anthem.[3] Instead, 'The Unknown Soldier' hinges on juxtaposition. The first verse looks sombrely to a postwar moment, conveyed by the empty image in the line 'nestled in your hollow shoulder', but the song also recalls the communal Human Be-In of January 1967 in Golden Gate Park. The Doors had been there for what was billed as a tribal gathering. However, maybe because they never felt comfortable with the San Francisco psychedelic scene (despite Jim Morrison having lived there as a child and the band seeing-in 1968 as the headline act of the 6 Days of Sound festival in the Upper Fillmore neighbourhood), the pastoral image of the film is an unsettling one. We see three shots of a young couple lying in the grass: in the first two they are entwined; in the third they lie slightly apart with twisted postures, as if petrified or lifeless.[4] The juxtaposition works similarly in the song's compressed and queasy image of middle-class family life – 'television children fed' – that gives way to the oxymoronic line 'unborn living, living dead', shattering this apparent moment of domestic comfort.

This juxtaposition of the quotidian and metaphysical captures Morrison's and keyboardist Ray Manzarek's cinematic aspirations as University of California, Los Angeles (UCLA) film students (they graduated in 1965), here played out through a mix of live and filmed images that cluster around the central sacrificial ritual. The Vietnam conflict is not only the song's most obvious context, then, but it is restaged at a moment when graphic images of the Tet Offensive meant that it was increasingly difficult for either

Figure 7.1 6 Days of Sound poster advertising performances by the Doors at the Winterland Ballroom, San Francisco, 26–8 December 1967, designed by Bonnie MacLean. Image courtesy of the Victoria and Albert Museum, London.

politicians or the public to ignore the brutality and moral confusion of the war. Just as underground filmmaker Emile de Antonio deployed montage and irony to explore the historical roots and systems of power that undergirded the war in his 1968 documentary *In the Year of the Pig*, so The Doors used similar techniques to dramatize an explosive moment in which these forces settle on an image of a band destroying itself.

'The Unknown Soldier' is not just an example of the mixed-mode aesthetic that fascinated West Coast artists at the time, but it is a song in which opposing instinctual forces – that had been articulated by Herbert Marcuse in *Eros and Civilization* (1955) and Norman O. Brown in *Life Against Death* (1959) – take on corporeal form. The Doors' Hollywood Bowl concert of 5 July, for example, saw Morrison (son of a naval admiral who commanded a fleet during the Gulf of Tonkin incident of August 1964) intone the firing-squad commands as he reaches for a final drag of his cigarette, before collapsing theatrically when lead guitarist Robbie Krieger shoots him with his electric guitar and drummer John Densmore drops his reverb unit. The mixed meanings of warfare are captured both in the carnivalesque performance and the impressionistic lyrics of 'The Unknown Soldier'. This is emphasized in the off-harmonies of the coda when it is not clear if 'it's all over' means that war is at an end or if the re-enactment has led to the destruction of civilization.

The song was in tune with the spirit of '68, even though its origins can be traced back to 1966 when Morrison was experiencing nightmares about bombs and napalm; it was recorded in late 1967, before appearing as a single in March 1968 and as the final track of side one of the *Waiting for the Sun* album in July. In essence, the song is a microcosm of a divided America, caught between military engagement and antiwar protest. But the firing-squad sequence crosses aesthetic and moral lines as the band enacts its self-destruction, with Morrison playing both the commander and the victim. This makes 'The Unknown Soldier' more disturbing than Phil Ochs's equally powerful folk song 'The War is Over' (which he wrote for a Los Angeles rally in July 1967 and released as a single the following summer) that insists ceasefire is a moral imperative.[5]

The Doors were rarely as politicized as Ochs, even though countercultural politics are to be glimpsed in their 1968 song 'Five to One' and Morrison appeared to have a political strategy when he claimed the previous November that 'I'm interested in anything about revolt, disorder, chaos'.[6] Nonetheless, Morrison's lyrics and Manzarek's hypnotic organ together create an 'angry sign' (to borrow Ochs's phrase) that evoked instincts and energies which were more visible than ever in 1968, exposing the rifts that historian Howard Brick has traced through the 1960s. What makes The Doors a compelling case is that they brought to the surface what Brick calls 'social tortion' in a poetic, theatrical and musical idiom that steered between the esoteric and the offensive, between introspective individualism and participatory action.[7]

This did not mean that the band were universally acclaimed as visionaries during their six years in the public eye: Joan Didion commented ironically that in their mythical emphasis on Eros and Thanatos The Doors were 'missionaries of apocalyptic sex' and 'the Norman Mailers of the Top Forty'.[8] But The Doors were nevertheless one of the most powerful performers of 1968 and, as this chapter explores, can be usefully contrasted with three other groups who fused aesthetic and political performance across a range of cultural expressions: the Youth International Party (or Yippies), which began life on Manhattan's Lower East Side in the winter of 1967–8; the Living Theatre, which had its roots in the mid-1940s but found new direction in the tumult of the late 1960s; and a group of transatlantic filmmakers engaging with the aesthetics of protest (including Emile de Antonio, Jonas Mekas, Bruce Conner, Lindsay Anderson and Jean-Luc Godard) – a group represented here via British filmmaker Peter Whitehead's feature-length experimental New York film *The Fall*, one of the most potent cinematic readings of the unrest and possibilities of 1968.

Performance and The Resistance Experience

Christopher Crenshaw has argued that The Doors were never about univocal political opposition. Instead, the band represented 'another side of the resistance experience' to the folk community, 'a side fascinated with self-expression, darkness and release, sex and death'.[9] This does not mean that Ochs's 'The War is Over' is straightforward protest either, certainly compared with the folk revivalist Pete Seeger and the Student Nonviolent Coordinating Committee (SNCC) quartet the Freedom Singers. In fact, when he introduced a performance of the song at Lund University, Sweden, on 6 June 1968 – the day that Senator Robert F. Kennedy died from an assassin's bullet – Ochs asserted that the 'numbing' caused by recent events meant that 'straight moral protest' was harder to maintain than a few years earlier.[10] The Doors adopted a more provocative tack, though, moving beyond the 'numb surprise' of their early song 'Soul Kitchen' towards an existentially charged realm that harked back to Morrison's reading of Friedrich Nietzsche and Albert Camus as a Florida high-school student. A mixture of sensuality, absurdity and ritual were vehicles for urging the band's audience to confront unsettling cultural and ideological forces. Thus, the coda of 'The Unknown Soldier' can be read as a 'climax of ecstatic release' that only temporarily relieves the struggle between irreconcilable forces clashing in Vietnam – a conflict that the former Students for a Democratic Society (SDS) leader Todd Gitlin has called a 'phantasmagorial war (with real corpses)'.[11]

The Doors sometimes critiqued social values in straightforward terms: at an Arizona State Fair concert in November 1968 Morrison derided the announcement of Richard Nixon's victory in the presidential campaign and in the long title track of their July 1969 album *The Soft Parade* the band reject a bourgeois life of sweating and saving.[12] At others, they eschewed public action for a hedonistic world, such as during their 'Rock is Dead' jam session that February at which Morrison encouraged dropping out rather than tuning-in: 'I want to see my people non-political', and a few moments before, 'I don't want to hear no talk about no riots, no demonstrations, no calcitrations [sic] . . . we're here to have a good time, let's roll'.[13] So, while Ochs played 'The War is Over' through 1968 – including a rendition on 27 August at an 'Unbirthday Party for LBJ' held at the Chicago Coliseum to protest the Democratic National Convention – The Doors' concerts explored an alternative public realm of mixed messaging.[14] Chiming with Ochs's view that 'the use of the theatrical' is a way of 'changing reality in your head', play-acting for Morrison was an aesthetic means for dealing with

Figure 7.2 Phil Ochs performing at the Chicago Coliseum, 27 August 1968. Courtesy of Michael Ochs at the Woody Guthrie Center, Tulsa, Oklahoma.

the whirling confusion of forces that was splintering the participatory politics of the New Left, leaving more confrontational guerrilla tactics in its wake, as Ochs found when the Democratic Convention became engulfed in street riots.[15]

For The Doors, this embodiment functioned on visceral and psychological levels, especially as Manzarek worried that Morrison was drinking too much in early 1968, did not always know 'whom he was fighting', and was developing a split-persona that placed the poet and the rebel at odds with each other. On a first take the contrast between Ochs and Morrison seems stark. Between 1967 and 1969 Morrison pushed his audience to the brink of revolt (he failed to stir up a mass riot though, despite police provocation), whereas Ochs mourned the rioting he saw around him in Chicago. However, although the two held different views about social engagement, there is an uncanny resemblance in the way their lives unfolded. The pair died within five years of each other after theatrically faking their deaths in 1968: Morrison's death by firing squad in 'The Unknown Soldier' was only slightly more dramatic than Ochs's inscription on his *Rehearsals for Retirement* album, 'Born: El Paso, Texas, 1940; Died: Chicago, Illinois, 1968'.

Dispirited by events in Chicago and the flagging fortunes of the New Left, this mock epitaph prefigured Ochs's faked death in his final months at the hands of a recently emerged second self, the violent doppelganger John Butler Train – an act that foreshadowed his actual suicide of April 1976.

This comparison of Morrison and Ochs raises an important question for reframing 1968: how potent was public performance as a vehicle of social transformation, both as a means of insurgency and as a new aesthetic? One could argue either way, but participation was undeniably central, even if there were differing views about how organized participatory politics needed to be, or to what extent the lines between performer/audience and leader/group should be blurred.[16] The Diggers and the Living Theatre were two radical collectives that showed it was possible to erase these lines whilst remaining a cohesive group, but the assorted performers and activists that engaged in street theatre tactics in the second half of the decade were often in danger of fragmenting into factions with divergent philosophies. As Daniel Matlin's chapter discusses, this was particularly true of the Yippies' revolutionary action theatre of 1968–9 that yoked together differing performance styles: guerrilla, pantomime, absurdism and surrealism.[17]

The 'revelatory and sensory explosion' that Paris was to witness in May 1968 had a similar intellectual lineage, linking to what Mark Kurlansky describes as mode of 'shocking modernism' that thrived on aesthetic provocation even if its politics were not always clear.[18] However, whereas class conflict underpinned many of the events in Paris, in the United States the spectacle threatened to swallow the political content, as it did in Chicago when the Yippies (aided by Phil Ochs) nominated Pigasus the Pig for president.[19] The absurdist pig imagery was in contrast to the imperialistic caricatures that students from the newly formed Vincennes University brought to life in the subways and streets of Paris in 1969. There they enacted a modernized medieval morality play in which the characters of the Third World Peasant and the Guerrillero murder the Army Officer and the Ugly White Man, described in their manifesto as 'Nixon, the Ruler, the Wall Street King' (stimulated by Nixon's meeting with Charles de Gaulle that February).[20] The choice of a pig as the Yippies' ironic icon resonated with the colloquial insult for an aggressive police force, which the Paris group burlesqued through the figure of the 'capitalist cop' who literally beat down protestors in the French capital in early May 1968. But, whereas Vincennes students had tight solidarity with the proletarian struggle, for the Yippies politics and art often strained against each other.[21]

The Yippie pig harked back to Antonin Artaud's short avant-garde essay 'All Writing is Pigshit . . .' in which the French surrealist rejects all ideological 'vantage points' in an effort to tap into sub-terranean 'states which have no name'.[22] This anarchic spirit was embodied in Abbie Hoffman's pronouncement that 'the concept of pig as our leader was truer than reality'. Hoffman had used guerrilla theatre as a marketing stunt for Jerry Rubin's failed bid for mayor of Berkeley in 1966, and the pair enshrined their countercultural politics in the sentiments of the Yippie Election Day: 'You name it. You do it. Everyone participates – every man is a creator.'[23] The Manifesto asserted that the Yippies would forge a 'new reality' via confrontational tactics, such as encouraging activists to release 'hundreds of greased pigs in pig uniform' and create mayhem in the streets, a stunt that seemed to be halfway between gimmickry and anarchy. There were not so many pigs in Chicago. Nonetheless, events turned chaotic when the Yippies arrived on 28 August with two pigs; and when a third pig was seen running through Lincoln Park the following day, it suggested that the power of the spectacle was in danger of turning into chaos or farce.[24]

This explosive mixture was captured by *Chicago Review* editor Eugene Wildman that summer in his claim that words should 'explode off the page, leap into consciousness and actuality' and that expression should be 'integral to life, embedded in experi-ence and not merely descriptive of it'.[25] This statement had roots in the avant-garde practices of the Dadaists and Futurists, but in this late 1960s context it gave rise to a messy and chaotic aes-thetic that was driven by desire and instinct rather than conscious craft. It also linked to countercultural literature of the time: the moral chaos of Allen Ginsberg's July 1968 poem 'Violence', with its woozy mixture of bodies, machines and capitalist exploitation, and William Burroughs's attempts in the Nova Trilogy (1961–7) to expose what he called the 'reality studio' that creates a monopoly on what goes under the name of reality. Wildman, similarly, saw a city like Chicago as being 'a form of make-believe' and he thought it important that street theatre boldly challenged the veneer of reality:

> the theater that is emerging today is turning similes into metaphors, is destroying those lines of demarcation behind which we all, habitually, hide our true natures. And insofar as art inevitably becomes moral, it is destroying the masks behind which we hide ourselves from our true selves.[26]

This attempt to awaken the audience from a state of passivity links electoral guerrilla theatre to the disruption techniques that Burroughs propounded in the second book of the Nova Trilogy, *The Ticket that Exploded* (1962), in which he incites the reader 'to infiltrate, sabotage and cut communications – Once machine lines are cut the enemy is helpless'.[27] Burroughs realized that simply opposing forces of power can lead to the same power play in reverse. For him, disrupting communication channels was the only viable strategy, suggesting that lawlessness and confrontation were more effective than nonviolent protest, however strategic its aims. But there is a significant risk. In the confusion of faces and bodies meaningful critique may merge with symptom, and revolution might become reaction.

We can see this in Jim Morrison's live spectacles, exemplified by his epic 1968 song 'Celebration of the Lizard', originally planned for the *Waiting for the Sun* album, but not performed in its fifteen-minute entirety until July 1969 at San Francisco's Aquarius Theatre. The Morrison persona in 'Celebration of the Lizard' flees the 'chaos & disorder' of the dystopian American city to face a different set of unruly forces south of the border.[28] Urban bestial imagery in the first verse (roaming lions, rabid dogs, a caged beast) is broken by the insistent bard-like call 'Is everybody in? Is everybody in? Is everybody in? The ceremony is about to begin.' This line echoes Morrison's claim to *Time* magazine that Los Angeles 'is looking for a ritual to join its fragments' and prompted him to command the audience to 'Wake up!' from their foggy state of forgetting.[29] The ritualistic ceremony is complicated by the spilling over of creaturely energies that centres on the ambiguous image of a lizard. This lizard imagery is at once vital and primitive (contrasted with the 'dead president's corpse' in a limousine), sinister (echoing the reptilian mugwumps of Burroughs' *Naked Lunch*), sexually ambiguous (the lizard's gender is constantly morphing) and regal (given that Morrison adopted the moniker of 'the Lizard King').[30] Such a metamorphosis can be read as a Nietzschean overcoming via self-transformation or as a recreation of the mythical ouroboros that eats its own tail as a means of renewing itself.[31] Either way, the act paves the way for a vision of a noble Kingdom that might replace the fallen Republic. However, whilst Morrison's reptilian imagery has the capacity to shock listeners and defamiliarize habitual ways of seeing, it is hard to build a participatory politics from it.

Channelling Radical Energies: The Living Theatre

If Morrison's revisioning cannot easily reconcile personal and participatory elements, it points to both the possibilities and dangers of performance in the late 1960s: it might renew language and refresh perceptions, but its artistry was in danger of spilling over, as it did with the Yippies in Chicago. Another strong influence on Morrison was the Living Theatre, spearheaded by Julian Beck and Judith Malina, who had shifted from their avant-garde modernist performances of the 1950s that challenged the hegemony of Broadway towards a more revolutionary practice that attacked agents of power. There is a direct line between the Living Theatre's attempt to dissolve the fourth wall and The Doors' live spectacles. Morrison saw the Living Theatre at the Nourse Auditorium, San Francisco, in March 1968, he assisted the group financially, and his notorious drunken performance in Coconut Grove, Miami, the following March (when local police claimed he exposed himself on stage) could be interpreted as a botched attempt to realize the provocation of the Living Theatre.[32]

Whereas Morrison found it difficult to control these energies in live performances, Beck and Malina kept in check political and aesthetic impulses, as embodied by their radical street theatre experiment *Paradise Now*. The couple had left the United States for Europe as tax exiles four years earlier and had written the play's outline early in 1968 in Rome and Sicily, before honing its contemporary relevance by joining in the events of Paris that May, including the symbolic occupation of the Paris Odéon Théâtre de France on the 15th.[33] The four-and-a-half-hour play, which opened its American run at Yale Repertory Theatre on 16 September, might seem a confusing spectacle to watch, but it strives to balance order and release. Influenced by Martin Buber's mystical philosophy of beholding, its structure is based on the eight rungs of a Hasidic ladder (each one combining a rite, a vision and an action) which Beck and Malina linked to a release of sexual and spiritual energy that they believed could tear through the veil of repression and lead to a social and spiritual rebirth.[34] The emphasis on freeing the audience from a script (embodied in lines such as 'Do whatever you want with the capitalist culture of New York . . .') links the anarchism of guerrilla theatre to a strategy of nonviolent direct action that could be taken into the streets and recreate the utopianism of the occupation of the Odéon that May.[35]

Sections of *Paradise Now* are calm and meditative, such as elements of The Rites of Prayer and Study, but the performance is

Figure 7.3 The Rite of Study from *Paradise Now*, 'Paradise Now 68–69', Living Theatre Records, Beinecke Rare Book and Manuscripts Library, Yale University, New Haven, Connecticut.

remembered for the revolutionary zeal of the later sections. This fusion of the personal and political not only echoed Bertolt Brecht's and William Burroughs' attempts to expose those who control 'reality', but it tapped into the revolutionary potential of the orgasm, as elaborated by Wilhelm Reich in his mystico-psychological work *The Discovery of the Orgone* in the mid-1940s, as well as exposing passive bourgeois conformity that Reich had identified in *Listen, Little Man!* (1945) and that twenty years later Herbert Marcuse reprised in *One Dimensional Man* (1964). Beck and Marcuse both appeared at the Dialectics of Liberation Conference held in July 1967 in Belsize Park in Northwest London, but the pacifist Beck was more optimistic than Marcuse about the potential of revolutionary consciousness, believing that participatory performance could create a new gestalt that would revolutionize social relations.[36] Artaud was again a key reference point for Beck, particularly his idea of the 'uncivilized man' who, through his incivility, can slip the knot of the social contract and utter a scream that could 'smash the great prison society'.[37] In *Paradise Now* it was a ceremonial erotic rebirth as well. This was symbolized by the mass of naked bodies of the Rite of Universal Intercourse, amongst which it was virtually impossible to distinguish between performer and spectator.

The revolutionary energy of the Yale premiere of *Paradise Now* surged into the streets of New Haven, leading to the arrest on the charge of public indecency of ten performers and audience members. Yet, for some commentators the play was 'too arty' and for others 'an unbearably self-indulgent catharsis' that failed to integrate aesthetics and politics.[38] And, however radical *Paradise Now* seemed, theatre guru Richard Schechner claimed it was not radical enough as a performance form. So while Beck and Malina provoked audiences to take the play to the streets, Schechner sought to reorganize space entirely; his 'environmental theater' conceived of performance areas as 'islands or continents in the midst of the audience' where action flows in multiple directions.[39] This made participation the bedrock of performance and ensured that there were 'no settled sides' that could reify into fixed positions. Such radical reorganization was appealing for leftists and anarchists, but the danger was, as Jim Morrison found in his audience experiments, that without anchors it is hard to channel energies or to prevent being swept along by the flow.

A focus on the human face was one way of controlling energies. This theme was taken up by African American dramatist Ed Bullins (the Black Panthers' Minister of Culture) in his efforts to explain street theatre in terms of its purpose (communication), method (drawing a crowd) and duration (short). Writing for *The Drama Review*, Bullins claimed that when one thinks of contemporary America it is always about faces: 'faces moving, faces facing upwards, faces in crowds, faces in dynamic mobs – expanses of faces in the streets'.[40] Schechner took this idea further by seeing in facial manipulation a method for channelling bodily energies and broadening the expressive range. Not only can the individual grow in self-awareness by practising facial exercises, Schechner argued, but the command of facial movement can lead to 'extraordinary improvisations and confrontations' at the bodily level.[41] However, although this emphasis on face and body could release the performer from the bonds ·of etiquette, Schechner maintained that performance spaces were ultimately choreographed by a director inside a theatre, rather than being 'director-less' in the streets, as the Living Theatre and the Yippies encouraged.

Reality Under Siege: Peter Whitehead's *The Fall*

One of the most important visual–theatrical texts of 1968 that put the role of the director under the spotlight was British filmmaker Peter Whitehead's *The Fall*, which premiered at the Edinburgh Film Festival the following summer. Whitehead's two-hour film has taken on cult status in its fusion of aesthetics and politics by means of montage, overexposure, psychedelic disorientation, blackouts, and *cinéma-vérité* techniques. It also, notably, portrays the filmmaker as a participant in the drama. Whitehead is seen early on in the film in a television interview and as a cameraman, and he reappears at important moments: we see him filming and interacting with his Italian girlfriend, Alberta Tiburzi, assembling and editing film stock, and switching through TV channels as the dramatic events of spring 1968 unfold. At times, the film feels mournful in charting 'the fall' from the high ideals of the mid-1960s (signalled by an excerpt from Eric Burdon and the Animals' brooding spring 1967 single 'When I Was Young'), but Whitehead retains the possibility that authentic action might emerge from dismay, even as he seeks to critique forms of ineffective protest.

Shot in New York City over nine months, from October 1967 to June 1968, *The Fall* extends Whitehead's countercultural interests that led him to film the famous Beat poetry readings at the Albert Hall of 11 June 1965 (released as *Wholly Communion*) and the 1967 London underground music scene (as *Tonite Let's All Make Love in London*), as well as his *Benefit of the Doubt* documentary that captures the improvised agitprop theatre of Peter Brook's production of Denis Cannan's 1966 play *US. Benefit of the Doubt*, in particular, was important for conveying the antiwar spirit that was to influence other theatrical responses, such as Donald Sutherland and Jane Fonda's Free the Army (or FTA) Tour of 1971 that mixed vaudeville, cabaret and stand-up comedy in an effort to raise awareness of the peace movement among US troops. Brook's ensemble production of *US*, as performed by the Royal Shakespeare Company at the Aldwych Theatre in October 1966, turns Cannan's play into what Brook called a 'theatre of provocation', blending word, drama, music and visuals to indict a political system that had betrayed Americans, Europeans and Asians alike.[42]

The Fall can be interpreted as a culmination of these three films, not to create a well-wrought production, nor to maintain the high moral tone of *US*, but to develop a mixed-mode aesthetic in an attempt to channel political and imaginative impulses. Whitehead started out with the aim of making a film 'about protest and violence' in 'a city, a people, a culture, a society that was falling apart', but in the process he realized that *The Fall* should not just observe this moment in time but also capture 'what ought to be done'.[43] It is an intensely personal film in the respect that Whitehead's face reappears, sometimes realistically as a filmmaker in action, and at others as a spectral apparition on a monitor screen. But it is also a panoramic exploration of the ways in which reality was under siege in 1968, prompting Whitehead to look 'behind the scenes' rather than simply offering a visual presentation of the cultural 'scene in New York'.[44] His critique of contemporary culture did not mean that he thought that avant-garde expressions necessarily held the

answer though. The film includes a number of experimental performances such as a Robert Rauschenberg radical ballet, the *commedia
dell'arte* performances of the San Francisco Mime Troupe, the antiwar spectacle of the Bread and Puppet Theater, and an example of
Raphael Ortiz's deconstruction art that involves beating a chicken
to death against a smashed-up piano. The insertion of these performance pieces gives them documentary validity within the events
of 1967–8, but also conveys Whitehead's view that they are all
'impotent to effect radical change'.[45]

The early part of the film is dominated by a series of perspectival
shots of New York City reminiscent of the modernist city sym-
phony films of the early century, but set against The Nice's electric
(and ironic) version of 'America' from *West Side Story*, released in
June 1968 with the title 'America (2nd Amendment)'. The montage
seems to be enraptured by the most cosmopolitan of American
cities, but at the same time it critiques what Whitehead saw as the
'fragmentation and aggression' of Manhattan.[46] *The Fall* is about
media spectacle as much as it probes the mediated reality of 1968.
It is a music film in many ways (including Jim Morrison shouting
'We want the world and we want it / Now'), but it is also a personal
poem and a public performance. This is signalled by clips of Arthur
Miller reading the unpublished poem 'What Blood-Red Law' at
the Poets for Peace event at New York Town Hall on 12 November
1967, Allen Ginsberg performing an extract from 'These States: Into
L.A.', and Robert Lowell reciting his two-part 'The March' that captures the poet's participation in the march on the Pentagon on
27 October.[47] The film explores the intersections between public
and private spaces, signalled both by these three public readings
and by the image of a book cover seen in Whitehead's car, phi-
losopher William Barrett's *Irrational Man: A Study in Existential
Philosophy*, a 1958 study which helped to popularize existentialism
in America. The presence of Barrett's book intertextually links the
title of Whitehead's film *The Fall* to Albert Camus' novel *La chute*
and to Martin Heidegger's formulation of *Dasein* or 'thrownness
into being'.[48]

The first section of *The Fall* introduces the filmmaker searching
for information that could help him to make sense of a world in
which existential and sensual energies jar with news footage of civil

Figure 7.4 Alberta Tiburzi's photograph of Peter Whitehead filming a scene for *The Fall* in Newark, New Jersey, April 1968. Courtesy of Peter Whitehead Archive, De Montfort University, Leicester.

unrest. Television news plays an important bridging role between the aesthetics and politics of the film – in his diaristic notebook of the time Whitehead describes the news as 'so much larger than life, so much more hideous and dramatic and foreboding than anything I could write and make up and dream up and film'.[49] The second part retains a focus on the news, but it is more episodic in charting the antiwar demonstrations at the Pentagon the previous October through to public and media reaction to the assassination of Martin Luther King, Jr. on 4 April, including President Johnson's sombre statement four days later in which he offered a riposte to Malcolm X's retaliatory 'The Ballot or the Bullet' speech of 1964.[50] If the first section revives the countercultural possibilities of 1967, then the national fall of the second section – especially the race riots that followed King's death – leads to its most tangible subject in the third part: the Columbia University student sit-in.

The three sections of the film appear to be structured dialectically. The first part is titled 'Word', the second part 'Image' and the third part 'Word & Image' that together address *The Fall*'s subtitle 'A Film as a Series of Historical Moments seeking Synthesis'. Given that the third section moves beyond media images and the revolutionary potential of violence to engage directly with the events at Columbia in spring 1968 might suggest an instinctive or unmediated form of cinema, but the roughness of the first two sections lingers. This includes a forty-five-minute sequence when the police raided Hamilton Hall on 30 April after the week-long student occupation, a violent scene that is conveyed by a series of blurred and disconnected frames (Whitehead had to throw some film stock out of the window to escape confiscation).[51] Influenced by Jean-Luc Godard's 1967 protest film *La Chinoise* (which criticizes de Gaulle's and Johnson's foreign policies), the third section can be read as the most theatrical too in documenting the unfolding drama of the sit-in and police raid. Not that there is a well-choreographed performance that synthesizes the three causes behind the student protests: Columbia University's affiliation with the Institute for Defense Analyses; the suspension of six students for conducting antiwar demonstrations indoors; and the building of a private gymnasium on public land in the black neighbourhood of Morningside Park.

The ensuing demonstrations at Columbia lack the gimmickry of the Yippies, the poetic charge of The Doors and the deep ritual of the Living Theatre. Instead, the events prompted a coalition of activists to grasp a moment when it was possible to protest capitalism, racism and foreign policy simultaneously. There are three different moods on display during the sit-in: the nonviolent tenor of the civil rights movement (signalled by a brief snatch of 'We Shall Overcome' and a modified version of the spiritual 'He's Got the Whole World in His Hands'); the militant direct action of the Black Panthers (the former and current SNCC leaders Stokely Carmichael and H. Rap Brown are shown speaking outside Hamilton Hall); and the agitation of a key organizer Mark Rudd (who transitioned from leader of Columbia's SDS chapter to co-founder of the Weather Underground in 1969).

What makes *The Fall* especially interesting is that Whitehead tries to occupy a middle ground between sympathy with the student cause and the director of a probing film that had the potential to revolutionize perception. Whitehead appears frequently in earlier sections in both real and mediated form, but until the coda we see him only twice in the third part: the first time he is filming through a window and the second he appears as a choric figure straddling the roof of the Mathematics Building, speaking very ominously about the three causes that led to the sit-in. But he is also spatially (and culturally, given his very British accent) removed from the scenes that unfold inside and on the streets below as passers-by stop to listen to the students' singing and pass up food parcels. Not only does this choric scene lend a deliberately staged moment to the complex forces that brought together diverse protestors, it also hints that these forces are likely to unravel. So, although the drama culminates in the police raid on Hamilton Hall and footage of battered student bodies on the ground outside, this further example of intolerance and violence (that led to 700 arrests) does not mask the feeling that this loose coalition of activists was likely to splinter.

Rather than a synthesis of collective action, then, the film's third part hovers between a respect for the activist spirit and an inquiry into whether the main organizing bodies – SDS and SAS (Columbia's Student Afro-American Society) – were robust enough for a sustainable vanguard against authorities with power and weapons.[52] The film does not end with the arrests or with a second occupation in mid-May led by Mark Rudd to protest the disciplinary action against six student leaders. Instead, in the coda we move forward to news of Robert Kennedy's assassination on 5 June and – set against a haunting reading of Russian poet Andrei Voznesensky's antiwar poem 'I Am Goya' – return to the ghostly face of Whitehead on a Steenbeck monitor. The face fuzzes and the screen turns black, recalling previous moments of darkness and silence and reminding the viewer of two things: that reality in the late 1960s is mediated and that a neat synthesis might well be just a fantasy.[53]

Conclusion: Radical Performance after 1968

Looking back on 1968 performance one is struck by its remarkable vibrancy. The mixed-mode aesthetic and the blurring of high and low cultural forms were elements of its appeal, but also meant it was often difficult to pull back from the fray and retain the critical distance that Whitehead enacted in his rooftop commentary in *The Fall*. The consumption of Jim Morrison by forces that swirled around and inside him, and that led to his mysterious death in Paris in July 1971, is one bookmark to the decade, but so too is Whitehead's abandonment of radical cinema after *The Fall*. He experienced a mental collapse soon after returning to Britain on the day of Kennedy's assassination; he managed to edit and assemble the film from sixty hours of footage, but then gave up filmmaking in 1973 for writing and falconry.[54]

The emergence of feminist collectives such as It's All Right to Be Woman Theatre (1970–6) and the transnational activities of the Living Theatre were two legacies of the burgeoning performance culture of the late 1960s. But, despite the Living Theatre's working-class cycle of plays *The Legacy of Cain* (staged in outdoor and industrial spaces in the mid-1970s) and their 1979 London production of *Prometheus* (in which actors and audience recreated the communist storming of the Winter Palace before marching by the Holloway–Pentonville prisons), the group appeared out of step with a fractious decade. Similarly, although the Yippies seemed part of a passing moment, they persisted into the 1970s, clashing with police at a New Nation Conference in Madison, Wisconsin, in April 1971 and, following their Pig for President stunt, nominating the mysterious 'Nobody' as Democratic presidential candidate in 1976. Nevertheless, the Yippies seemed progressively irrelevant (and more like a stunt-based sideshow), even though Hoffman and Rubin staged a series of 'Yippie versus Yuppie' debates on university campuses in 1984–5, and local chapters continued beyond their deaths in 1989 and 1994 respectively.

Arguably, the Living Theatre has had the most lasting afterlife. Under the leadership of Judith Malina (following Beck's death in the mid-1980s), not only did they continue to create uncommercial low-budget productions Off-Off Broadway, but plugged into a new wave of anti-globalization activism that inspired protests at the Seattle World Trade Organization convention in November 1999. There is a direct link between the re-flowering of the Living Theatre and the Occupy movement, including the troop's Occupy Your World performance on 8 October 2011 in Washington Square Park. Reviving the utopian spirit of *Paradise Now*, but with an eye on environmental issues and a bankrupt capitalist system, the performance paid homage to Occupy's grassroots organization and conjured the ceremonial theatre of the late 1960s. 'The Money Song' the following week in Washington Square, for example, includes a choric figure who ritually condemns capitalism while performers stagger around as if blinded, before four of them spin in a mesmerizing circle chanting about unholy associations between time and money.[55] The spectacle both enacts and denounces, but, as Doug Rossinow argues in the opening chapter of this volume, it is perhaps surprising that such performances had developed little in aesthetic terms since the late 1960s. However, the fact that *The Fall* was screened in January 2012 at an Occupy Cinema festival in New York City is a clear sign that Occupy activists see 1968 as one of the key reference points.[56]

To what extent, then, did 1968 witness 'the Death of a Culture', to quote Julian Beck's theatrical claim of 1970?[57] Escalation in Vietnam, political chaos in the aftermath of President Johnson's decision not to seek re-election and the assassinations of two beacons of hope were clear reasons why Peter Whitehead chose the myth of the fall to filter the year's events. All the cultural practitioners discussed here attempted, in different ways, to confront these events head on whilst trying to expose the mediated nature of reality. Whitehead's film is instructive in this respect, but perhaps because he experienced exhilaration, confusion and desperation in equal measure (as he described it), his search for historical synthesis was necessarily a frustrated one.[58] By the time *The Fall* premiered in summer 1969, the coalition that staged the Columbia University protests had splintered into radical factions and the participatory democratic politics of the New Left seemed moribund. However, even though Beck's claim that 'The death is not outside us. It is inside each one of us' played out in the fate of Jim Morrison and Phil Ochs – in their feigned deaths of 1968 and in their actual deaths a few years later – the spectacular fusion of politics and art has a complex prelude and a resonant epilogue that goes well beyond the acts of 1968.

Notes

1. The February 1968 promo film of 'The Unknown Soldier', directed by Mark Abramson and Edward Dephoure, is available on The Doors, *R-Evolution* DVD (Eagle Rock, 2013).
2. 'Swimming to the Moon', *Time* (24 November 1967). See Greil Marcus, *The Doors: A Lifetime of Listening to Five Mean Years* (New York: Faber & Faber, 2012), 92.
3. See James E. Perone, *Songs of the Vietnam Conflict* (Westport, CT: Greenwood, 2001), 40–1, and Doug Bradley and Craig Werner, *We Gotta Get Out of This Place: The Soundtrack of the Vietnam War* (Amherst: University of Massachusetts Press, 2015), 96–102. See also Sarah Hill, '"This is My Country": American Popular Music and Political Engagement in "1968"', in Beate Kutschke and Barley Norton (eds), *Music and Protest in 1968* (Cambridge: Cambridge University Press, 2013), 46–63.
4. Ray Manzarek, *Light My Fire: My Life with the Doors* (New York: Arrow, 1999), 231–4.
5. Phil Ochs wrote 'Have You Heard? The War is Over!' for the *Los Angeles Free Press* in June 1967; it was reprinted in the *Village Voice* in November 1967.
6. Howard Brick, *Age of Contradiction: American Thought and Culture in the 1960s* (Ithaca, NY: Cornell University Press, 1998), 22.
7. Ibid. xiii.
8. Joan Didion, *The White Album* (New York: Farrar, Straus and Giroux, 1979), 21.
9. Christopher Crenshaw, 'Five to One: Rethinking the Doors and the Sixties Counterculture', *Music and Politics* 8(1) (Winter 2014), 3.

10. Ochs, 'The War is Over', Lund University, Lund, Sweden, 6 June 1968.
11. Todd Gitlin's foreword to John Schultz, *No One Was Killed: The Democratic National Convention, August 1968* (Chicago: University of Chicago Press, [1969] 2009), vii.
12. Manzarek, *Light My Fire*, 289. For the tirade against Nixon see Stephen Davis, *Jim Morrison: Life, Death, Legend* (New York: Penguin, 2004), 292.
13. 'The Rock is Dead' session of 25 February 1969 was unreleased until a sixteen-minute edit appeared on *The Doors: Box Set* in 1997.
14. See Marc Eliot, *Death of a Rebel: A Biography of Phil Ochs* (New York: Citadel, 1994), and Michael Schumacher, *There But for Fortune: The Life of Phil Ochs* (New York: Hyperion, 1996).
15. The quotation is from Ochs's introduction to 'The War is Over', Lund, 6 June 1968.
16. Bradford D. Martin, *The Theater is in the Street: Politics and Public Performance in Sixties America* (Amherst: University of Massachusetts Press, 2004), 6, 160.
17. Susanne Shawyer, 'Radical Street Theatre and the Yippie Legacy: A Performance History of the Youth International Party, 1967–1968', unpublished PhD thesis, University of Texas, Austin, 2008.
18. Mark Kurlansky, *1968: The Year that Rocked the World* (New York: Random House, 2005), xix.
19. Jean-Jacques Lebel, 'Note on Political Street Theatre, Paris: 1968, 1969', *The Drama Review* 13(4) (Summer 1969), 112.
20. Ibid. 116.
21. On police powers in Paris see Kristen Ross, *May '68 and its Afterlives* (Chicago: University of Chicago Press, 2002), 27–31.
22. Antonin Artaud, *Artaud Anthology*, ed. Jack Hirschman (San Francisco: City Lights, 1965), 38–9. For Artaud's influence on the Yippies see Naomi Feigelson, *The Underground Revolution: Hippies, Yippies, and Others* (New York: Funk & Wagnalls, 1970), 178–81.
23. Stew Albert et al., 'Yippie Election Day Manifesto', in Massimo Teodori (ed.), *The New Left: A Documentary History* (Indianapolis, IN: Bobbs-Merrill, 1969), 364–5. See Jerry Rubin, *Do It: Scenarios of the Revolution* (New York: Simon & Schuster, 1970), 47–50.
24. See Schultz, *No One Was Killed*, 53.
25. Eugene Wildman, 'Reality Theater in Chicago', *Chicago Review* 42(3/4) (1996), 91 (originally in the summer 1968 issue of *Chicago Review*). See also Theodore Shank, 'The Theatre of the Cultural Revolution', trans. Wyley L. Powell, *Yale French Studies* 46 (1971), 167–85, and Theodore Shank, *Beyond the Boundaries: American Alternative Theatre* (Ann Arbor: University of Michigan Press, [1988] 2002).
26. Wildman, 'Reality Theater in Chicago', 92.
27. William Burroughs, *The Ticket That Exploded* (New York: Grove Press, [1962] 1991), 111.
28. Jim Morrison, 'Celebration of the Lizard', *The American Night: The Writings of Jim Morrison, Volume 2* (New York: Vintage, 1990), 39.
29. 'Swimming to the Moon', *Time* (24 November 1967).

30. Morrison, *The American Night*, 43, 45.

31. See Laurence Coupe, *Beat Sound, Beat Vision: The Beat Spirit and Popular Song* (Manchester: Manchester University Press, 2007), 173–4.

32. See John Tytell, *The Living Theatre: Art, Exile, and Outrage* (New York: Grove Press, 1997), 256–7, 400–1.

33. Gerd-Rainer Horn, *The Spirit of '68: Rebellion in Western Europe and North America, 1956–1976* (New York: Oxford University Press, 1997), 20, and Julian Jackson et al. (ed.), *May 68: Rethinking France's Last Revolution* (London: Palgrave, 2011), 301–13.

34. Tytell, *The Living Theatre*, 225–42; Martin, *The Theater is in the Street*, 70–4.

35. Judith Malina and Julian Beck, *Paradise Now: Collective Creation of the Living Theatre* (New York: Random House, 1971), 23.

36. See David Cooper (ed.), *The Dialectics of Liberation* (London: Verso, [1968] 2015). For links between gestalt therapy and the Living Theatre see Daniel Belgrad, *The Culture of Spontaneity: Improvisation and the Arts in Postwar America* (Chicago: University of Chicago Press, 1998), 149–50.

37. Julian Beck, *Signals Through the Flames* (Mystic Fire Video, 1983); quoted in David Callaghan, 'Ritual Performance and Spirituality in the Work of the Living Theatre, Past and Present', in Edward Bert Wallace (ed.), *Theatre Symposium, Vol. 21: Ritual, Religion, and Theatre* (Tuscaloosa: University of Alabama Press, 2013), 37.

38. Lebel, 'Note on Political Street Theatre', 116. Renfreu Neff, *The Living Theatre: USA* (Indianapolis, IN: Bobbs-Merrill, 1970), ix.

39. Richard Schechner, *Environmental Theater* (Montclair, NJ: Applause, [1973] 1994), 38.

40. Ed Bullins, 'A Short Statement on Street Theatre', *The Drama Review* 12(4) (Summer 1968), 93.

41. Schechner, *Environmental Theater*, 146.

42. *Wholly Communion* and *Benefit of the Doubt* are available on the BFI release *Peter Whitehead and the Sixties*. Brooks released his own film adaptation of the play in 1968 with the title *Tell Me Lies*.

43. 'Peter Whitehead Talks about his New Film – *The Fall*', *Cinema* (December 1968), 18–21.

44. '*The Fall*: Treatment for Full Length Documentary/Feature Film' (1968), ii, Peter Whitehead Archive, Cinema and Television History Research Centre, De Montfort University, Leicester.

45. Ibid. See also Peter Whitehead, 'I Destroy Therefore I Am . . .', *Films and Filming* 15(4) (January 1969), 14–19.

46. Whitehead described Manhattan as 'extraordinary' but also 'aggressive and demanding': Peter Whitehead, 'The Fall Dossier: Extracts' (10 October 1967), *Framework* 52(1) (Spring 2011), 487.

47. Ginsberg's poem is part of the sequence 'Thru the Vortex West Coast to East 1965–66', *The Fall of America: Poems of These States 1965–1971* (San Francisco: City Lights, 1972), 9–13. Lowell's 'The March 1' and 'The March 2' were published in *The New York Review of Books* on 23 November 1967.

48. See Tina Rivers, 'From Alienation to Hallucination: Peter Whitehead's *The*

Fall and the Politics of Perception in the 1960s', *Framework* 52(1) (Spring 2011), 439. Whitehead was reading Camus's 1951 treatise *L'Homme révolté* at the time, and on 31 December 1967 railed against the idea of the 'pedantic' Luchino Visconti's film adaptation of Camus's *L'Etranger*: 'The Fall: Dossier A', *The Fall* File, 101–2, Peter Whitehead Archive.

49. 'The Fall: Dossier A', 106.

50. A montage sequence includes the headline of Gloria Steinem and Lloyd Weaver's report on the race riots: 'The City on the Eve of Destruction', *New York* magazine (22 April 1968).

51. See Philip Drummond, 'Peter Whitehead and *The Fall*', *Isis* (21 May 1969). As the twenty-year anniversary of the occupation approached, Whitehead wrote to the Dean of Columbia University on 25 September 1987 to explain that he had five hours of unused footage of the events: *The Fall* File, Peter Whitehead Archive. Some of this footage will be included as extras on the high-definition 2018 DVD release of *The Fall* (the film was not available commercially until 2016 due to contested music rights).

52. See Stefan Bradley, *Harlem vs. Columbia University: Black Student Power in the Late 1960s* (Champaign: University of Illinois Press, 2009).

53. Rivers, 'From Alienation to Hallucination', 448–50.

54. Whitehead made one further film, his post-1960s 'comedown' film *Fire in the Water* (1977), a project he initially called 'Requiem for the Sixties'. For an early treatment see Whitehead, '*Requiem for the Sixties*, Film Proposal, 1974', *Framework* 52(2) (Fall 2011), 667–73.

55. The Living Theatre was again forced to close their performance space on Clinton Street, Lower East Side, in 2013 for financial reasons (Malina died two years later).

56. *The Fall* was screened on 8 January 2012 as part of an Occupy Cinema festival in collaboration with Anthology Film Archives.

57. Julian Beck, *The Life of the Theatre: The Relation of the Artist to the Struggle of the People* (San Francisco: City Lights, 1972), 109. Beck wrote this short fragment in Rio de Janeiro in September 1970.

58. Whitehead, '*The Fall* Dossier: Extracts' (1 May 1968), 491.

EIGHT

1968: A Pivotal Moment in Cinema

Sharon Monteith

That 1968 was pivotal in US culture is axiomatic. Retrospective analysis of a year that has been described as 'the most turbulent twelve months of the postwar period' has elicited bold claims from cultural commentators, who locate it as 'the moment when all of a nation's impulses towards violence, idealism, diversity, and disorder peaked to produce the greatest possible hope – and the worst imaginable despair'.[1] The idea that 1968 was the culmination rather than a continuation of 'the sixties' textures memoirs and histories: Maurice Isserman and Michael Kazin and journalist Charles Kaiser assert that '1968 was the pivot of the American decade' and 'the pivotal year of the sixties'.[2] The defining events took shape on the screen in a critical year for film production. The Production Code that had remained in place since 1930 was finally overturned, modernizing as well as liberalizing the industry and affording more freedom to filmmakers, with the opportunity to both diversify and specialize. In this respect, it was a moment of rapid and decisive change and the industry found in the counterculture a new subject and a new audience.

In 1968 the film industry cultivated a particular youth market by targeting 'the counterculture' which had emerged out of the convergence of political and cultural rebellions, including the radicalization of civil rights and antiwar activists: students protested for free speech and against defence-related research and Reserve Officer Training Corps (ROTCs) on campuses; black nationalists championed Black Power; anti-imperialists challenged the government's continuation of its war in Vietnam and its foreign policy; and anti-capitalists and environmentalists 'turned on, tuned in and dropped out'. Hippies, 'long hairs' and 'flower children' discovered a philosophical vantage point in communal living, mysticism, sexual liberation, LSD (outlawed in 1966), and the drug culture generally. In *The Return of the Vanishing American* (1968), Leslie Fiedler asserted that the fifties beatnik had transformed into a hippie: 'one more wild man seeking the last West of Haight-Ashbury in high-heeled boots and blue jeans'.[3] Yippies protested in the form of 'happenings' that pushed rebellion into disruption. It was popularly understood that more than half of the population was below the age of twenty-five in 1968, as conveyed through sound bites about 'The Generation Gap'. Sociological studies such as Theodore Roszak's *The Making of the Counter Culture* (1969), journalistic works including Nicholas von Hoffman's *We Are the People Our Parents Warned Us Against* (1967) and Joan Didion's 'Slouching Towards Bethlehem' (1968), and fictions by Richard Brautigan, Kurt Vonnegut and Thomas Pynchon, among others, exemplified that the counterculture had found not only cultural visibility but also an audience.

The Beat generation identified on the cover of Jack Kerouac's *On The Road* (written in 1951 and published in 1957) as 'today's wild youth' undertaking a 'frenetic search for Experience and Sensation' was one precursor of the counterculture. Another was rebellious sixteen-year-old Holden Caulfield in J. D. Salinger's best-selling cult teenage novel *The Catcher in the Rye* (1951). Caulfield's lone rebellion against 'phoniness' would not be adapted for the screen, however, because Salinger would not sell the rights. In the movie *Making It* (1971), students mock a teacher for trying to teach them the novel: in their view it is sentimental and passé rather than risqué. Much had changed in the intervening years. Cultural discourse no longer identified 'youth' by age or separated 'teenage' experience from 'youth culture'. The changing contours can be traced in cinema. Marlon Brando in *The Wild One* (1954) and James Dean in *Rebel Without a Cause* (1955) had epitomized the rebel on screen: when Brando's Johnny is asked what he is rebelling against, he replies 'Whaddya got?' Charles Webb opened his 1963 novel *The Graduate* with a scene that echoed fifties-style rebellion when Benjamin Braddock unable to articulate the 'problem that has no name' locates it in the family home and in the elite business world to which his father belongs: 'You're grotesque . . . I'm grotesque. This house is grotesque. It's just this feeling I have all of a sudden. And I don't know why!'[4] The novel's tagline was 'This is Benjamin. He's a little worried about his future.' By the end of the decade, such understatement risked being underwhelming. With Mike Nichols directing thirty-year-old Dustin Hoffman's performance in his first screen role, though, the film would be a breakthrough in the representation of youth culture in a pivotal moment for the industry.

The Transition: Youth Culture on Screen

The executive producer of *The Graduate* (1967), legendary showman and promoter Joe E. Levine, financed the film after the option was turned down by multiple studios, but remained unclear how to market it, suggesting titillating exploitation-style publicity. Dustin Hoffman recalled that:

> I got a phone call that he wanted me to pose with Ann Bancroft. She would be sitting on a bed, and I would be facing her, standing up – naked – and she would have her hands around me, holding my buttocks! The only reason it didn't happen was that Nichols found out about it and put an end to it.[5]

Levine did make Hoffman and Nichols tour university campuses to drum up audiences but graduate students demanded to know why the film did not feature opposition to the war in Vietnam. Levine was a master publicist for art cinema and 'teenpics' but had yet to understand that a subculture had evolved into a politicized youth culture. *The Graduate* would be the highest grossing film of 1968 precisely because it bore no relation to a teenpic. Nor did Benjamin, an honours student and a member of his university's debating team, resemble a teenpic protagonist or, indeed, any character that Brando or Dean had played.

By 1968 the impulse to rebel was represented not solely, or even, as juvenile delinquency or a disdain for phoniness. Instead, restless agitation was expressly political with identified sources of rage, resistance and rebellion. In 1960 in 'The Revolt of Youth' Kenneth Rexroth had already discerned that

> A head of steam was building up, the waters were rising behind the dam; the dam itself, the block to action, was the patent exhaustion of old forms. What was accumulating was not any kind of programmatic 'radicalization', it was a moral demand.[6]

Benjamin challenges the affluent society in which a female graduate, Elaine (Katharine Ross), can be married off to a wealthy peer she does not love and whose career she will be expected to support instead of forging her own. The film's final scene addresses Betty Friedan's thesis of a 'feminine mystique' when, just married and still in her bridal gown, Elaine runs away with Benjamin to board a bus to somewhere, anywhere, else.

The Graduate was a transitional film marking the moment when 'youth culture' was perceived as a collectivist construction rather than Oedipal rebellion. It was the first film to include previously released songs and Simon and Garfunkel's soundtrack ensured an audience in a way Levine had not predicted. Students at Columbia University were sneaking out from sit-in demonstrations in April to catch the film at theatres and the counterculture would evolve a more complex political sensibility, as likely to lie in distinguishing the New Left from the Old, or the forging of radical politics against a hardened democratic pragmatism, as cross-generational rebellion. Progressive figures over thirty – as different as Martin Luther King, Jr., Benjamin Spock, Robert F. Kennedy, Michael Harrington and Eugene McCarthy – could be co-opted into 'the counterculture' in one moment or derided for failing to signify the vanguard in the next. When Louis Menand returned to the term 'counterculture' in 'Life in the Stone Age' (1991), it was to discern in it a media-made commercialism, but he allows that it was also 'imaginative and infectious, and it touched a nerve'.[7]

Television drama would not capture the political tensions inherent in the youth rebellion until the 1970–1 season but films in production in 1968 and released in 1968–9 were already dramatizing countercultural preoccupations and demands.[8] Among them were *Midnight Cowboy, Planet of the Apes, The Born Losers, Finian's Rainbow, Wild in the Streets, Greetings, Night of the Living Dead, Easy Rider, Medium Cool, Barbarella, 2001: A Space Odyssey, Uptight* and *Alice's Restaurant*. Of these, *Wild in the Streets* and *Easy Rider* moved the exploitation movie from drive-in to mainstream appeal and *Night of the Living Dead* inaugurated a gorefest that would prove a model for filmmakers for decades. *Greetings* and *Easy Rider* would prove that films focused on avoiding the military draft and embracing hippie culture would sell to audiences – even when made on B-movie budgets.

In film history, the 1968 cinema moment is revealing of industry shifts that made political dissent and the counterculture commercial. It would presage a 'New Hollywood' in the 1970s. Many of the New Hollywood's most successful directors served apprenticeships with prolific entrepreneur Roger Corman who, by 1968, was allied with American International Pictures (AIP), a B-movie operation. AIP were 'intuitive demographers', as Thomas Doherty has demonstrated, and their primary audience was eighteen- to twenty-four-year-olds.[9] Corman and AIP influenced filmmakers who directed inaugural fiction films in 1968, including Peter Bogdanovich (*Targets*), Brian De Palma (*Greetings*), William Friedkin (*Good Times*), Alan J. Pakula (*The Sterile Cuckoo*) and Haskell Wexler (*Medium Cool*) to name a few. In *Easy Riders and Raging Bulls* (1999), Peter Biskind would extend this moment in film culture when he described 1967–80 as the last time that Hollywood promoted risky work that eschewed traditional heroes and dared to end unhappily – and 'the last time there was an audience to sustain it'. However, with the focus on a single year, it is possible to trace how the film 'community' diversified, specialized and presaged what Timothy Corrigan called a 'cinema without walls', redefining the role of the director outside of the industrial apparatus of the classical Hollywood system.[10]

A Shift in Content and Censorship

The Production Code, self-regulatory guidelines that enforced compliance with what was deemed acceptable to show on screen, weakened in the 1950s. In 1966, in the wake of fractious debate about violence in *Bonnie and Clyde* (1967), Jack Valenti, President of the Motion Picture Association of America (MPAA), met producers, writers and studio heads to advocate 'increased restraint and heightened responsibility in portraying violence'; but, in reinforcing responsibility, he sought to liberalize the Code's application.[11] Valenti was a politician, a White House aide in the Johnson administration until 1966, and aware of the stranglehold the Code had on an industry that needed to diversify. On 1 November, he jettisoned the Code and introduced a 'rating system' that would change the industry from 'the *only* communications art medium that turns away business at the box office . . . and denies itself additional business in order to serve a public pledge'.[12] The prudish Code protecting audiences from moral ambiguity was dismantled. Adult material, whether in the form of sex, drugs or violence, no longer needed to be hidden in symbolism or innuendo: it could be X-rated. In practice, a film could fix its rating post-production, as when a scene in which a man's throat is cut in *The Wild Bunch* excised a spurt of blood to ensure an R-rating (children under sixteen could watch if accompanied by a responsible adult) rather than an X-rating, which disallowed any person under sixteen, regardless of parental monitoring.

Valenti promoted the system through what it heralded for a new kind of filmmaker: 'young . . . sensitive . . . dedicated . . . reaching out for new dimensions of expression', and a 'new style in filmmaking matched by a new audience'.[13] Directed by Brian De Palma, *Greetings* was the first film to be awarded an X-rating. It was also the first to address explicitly civil disobedience around conscription to fight in Vietnam and the Warren Report's findings on the assassination of President Kennedy. It is a fast and furious statement on the times, with the opening fifteen minutes a tour de force in which three young men (including Robert De Niro in his first major role) test whether it is more effective to avoid the draft by performing right-wing bigotry, rampant homosexuality or insanity. It made a $1 million return on its $39,000 budget.

Ownership of the change in the industry's image was associated with 'new' and 'authentic' countercultural directors and actors – De Palma, Dennis Hopper, Jack Nicholson and Peter Fonda – even though established filmmakers would 'authenticate' the counterculture in Hollywood, including Stanley Kramer and Arthur Penn. Even veteran director William Wyler threw himself and Columbia behind *The Liberation of L. B. Jones* (1970). This cynical story of the small-town 1960s South included an adulterous affair between a white supremacist police officer and the black wife of a pillar of the community: the revenge plot leads to the death of both men with no justice served. The film was, screenwriter Stirling Silliphant worried, 'enough to scare a senator or a studio chief', but Wyler eschewed a Hollywood ending – even Jesse Hill Ford's 1965 source novel ends with more hope.[14] In December, another veteran of the studio system, Otto Preminger, released *Skidoo*, an anarchic romp in which a clutch of established Hollywood stars (Jackie Gleason, Carol Channing, Groucho Marx, Mickey Rooney, Caesar Romero and George Raft) satirised the counterculture to absurd effect.

In 1968, renegades and mavericks on the edges of the film industry, including Haskell Wexler and George Romero, consolidated a place at its heart. Bob Rafelson and Bert Schneider edged their way into television and film; they put The Monkees on screen in an Emmy-award winning NBC series and Rafelson directed *Five Easy Pieces* in 1970. Rafelson and Schneider collaborated with Steve Blauner on BBS Productions, creating a lucrative relationship with Columbia Pictures. Corporate mergers of studios with distribution and media conglomerates had been in process since the Paramount decision of 1948 but now the last of the studio moguls were selling up or retiring, as Jack Warner did in 1967 and Darryl Zanuck in 1970.[15] In 1969, *Midnight Cowboy*, John Schlesinger's first American film, would become the only X-rated film to ever win an Oscar. With unprepossessing protagonists, a would-be gigolo (Jon Voight) and a consumptive con man (Dustin Hoffman) living in a New York City squat, it was a revisionist critique of Hollywood product from within the industry.

Nevertheless, throughout the 1960s, family musicals like *My Fair Lady* (1964) and *The Sound of Music* (1965) secured the best box office receipts, and sometimes critical acclaim, epitomized by *Oliver!* winning the Best Film Oscar in 1968. *West Side Story* (1962) was an indicator that young protagonists, contending with violence and exploring sex while in conflict with tradition and authority, could win audiences regardless of the genre in which the story was told.[16] However, by the end of the decade there were enough costly failures in the mix – *Doctor Dolittle* (1967) lost $10.8 million despite nine Oscar nominations and *Camelot* (1967) bombed to the tune of $15 million – to prompt a rethink. Cross-generational audiences had bottomed out with television the bastion of family entertainment and radio the medium of choice for young Americans. *Finian's Rainbow*, which lost to *Oliver!* at the Golden Globes and the Oscars, was an attempt to combine 'countercultural' cinema with its 'parent', the classical Hollywood musical.

In *Finian's Rainbow*, Francis Ford Coppola blended the 1947 stage musical (one of John F. Kennedy's favourite films, dismissed by Pauline Kael as 'decaying material that reeks of old Broadway'[17]) with a socially-conscious, even 'hip', critique of white supremacy. It would be the final musical in which sixty-nine-year-old Fred Astaire would dance and sing – as Finian McLonergan fleeing Ireland with daughter Sharon (Petula Clark) to escape a leprechaun he robbed of a pot of gold. It signalled the end of the studio-era musical and, in 2012, when Clark revealed she and Astaire smoked cannabis on the movie, Astaire could even be co-opted retrospectively as a happy convert to what was deemed coolly countercultural.[18] The McLonergans join the countercultural community of 'Rainbow Valley', an island of integration in segregated 'Missistucky', a sharecropping and tobacco-growing cooperative, and Sharon defies bigotry when she magically turns a racist southern senator into a black itinerant – in which form he learns the meaning of democracy. Coppola's fantasy was a poignant coda to a utopian dream of interracial coalition.

That the counterculture was making it to the screen in the new dispensation highlights that Hollywood had been slower to see financial merit in the civil rights movement. *Guess Who's Coming to Dinner* (1967) could not have been further removed from the pernicious reality that brought *Loving vs. Virginia* before the Supreme Court in the same year. Instead, it used the safer cliché of the 'Generation Gap' to avoid confronting racist laws that ensured that Mildred and Richard Loving could be imprisoned for marrying across 'the color line'. While television news and journalism were essential media channels for civil rights organizations, 'civil rights' as a theme was only explored in Hollywood's shadow cinema – or

Figure 8.1 Fred Astaire at the West Coast premiere of *Finian's Rainbow*, Los Angeles, 16 October 1968. Photograph by Harold P. Matosian. Courtesy of AP/ Press Association Images.

'paracinema' in Jeffrey Sconce's definition of genres that coalesce as marginal 'trash' – which exploited racial terrorism.[19] Civil rights did provide suggestive texture in genres as different as horror (*Night of the Living Dead*) and musical (*Finian's Rainbow*), but it is striking that there were more acid trips than civil rights demonstrations in fiction films.

George Romero's *Night of the Living Dead* reinvigorated the horror film. Men and women mutate into flesh-eating predators in a Cold War fantasy that shifts the battle between humans and aliens typical of 1950s 'teenpics' into a national civil war against a backdrop of contemporary anxieties. Romero's film helped to turn 'midnight movie' screenings into a commercial phenomenon that thrived in the 1970s and established generic expectations for the zombie film. The closest it has to a hero is a young African American, Ben (Duane Jones), who, with a motley group of survivors, holds out in a farmhouse against a mob of living dead. Despite his skill and ingenuity, white men resent Ben's leadership and conflict overwhelms the survivors' ability to fend off incursions. The Cooper family is destroyed when daughter Karen (Kyra Schon) turns into a zombie, hacks her parents to death and feasts on them. Karen literally pinions and consumes the grotesque that *The Graduate*'s Benjamin Braddock believes lies at the heart of the complacent white nuclear family; *Variety* would call it 'an unrelieved orgy of sadism'.[20] Roger Ebert warned that *Night of the Living Dead* had slipped into cinemas as a Saturday matinee the month before the rating system was introduced and that children were terrified.[21]

Romero's first movie would be field-defining. It came in below his budget of $114,000 but grossed $12 million with international distribution bringing in $18 million. *Night of the Living Dead* was a cult success and a scathing comment on race relations, the police, the military, and a clever satire on the nation's defence system and 'space race'. Survivors learn from the radio that experts believe the ghouls are the result of NASA purposely exploding a space satellite that emits such dangerous levels of radiation that corpses are reanimated as murderous cannibals. When a journalist despairs that 'somewhere on this planet there has to be something better than man', he echoes George Taylor (Charlton Heston), the stranded astronaut in *Planet of the Apes*, word for word.

Romero would refuse to change the ending though he lost Hollywood distributors as a result. Ben, the only character to respond intelligently to a deadly situation, survives until a national guardsman sees 'a black man', assumes he is a ghoul and shoots Ben dead. The guardsman is told: 'Hit him in the head, right between the eyes. Good shot. Okay, he's dead. Let's go get him.

That's another one for the fire.' Watched now, in the 2010s, the final frames are an ironic commentary on the situation the Black Lives Matter movement is campaigning against fifty years later.

'I'm Hip about Time': From *Greetings* to *Easy Rider*

Thomas Doherty called *Easy Rider* 'an over-the-hill teenpic featuring actors adolescent in attitude only' but 'teenpics' focused on juvenile delinquency and moral panics while films of countercultural rebellion drew on an ideology that challenged the idea of society itself. *Easy Rider*, a disquisition on the utopian and apocalyptic sensibilities of the counterculture, demonstrated that youth was a concept and a mood and little to do with adolescence.[22] Made for just $330,000, it earned $20 million in the summer of 1969 and was touching $50 million the following summer. When Wyatt aka 'Captain America' (Peter Fonda) says lazily 'I'm hip about time', the phrase resonates for the moment in which the counterculture became hip in cinema. A collaboration between Fonda, Dennis Hopper, Terry Southern, who contributed to the screenplay, and Bob Rafelson producing, it elicited a bravura performance from Jack Nicholson that kick-started his career and it exploited the youth audience the industry had secured by 1968.

Easy Rider's timing was perfect. In 1970, Paul Warshow declared 'the film's "news" about America is at least five years old. But as an expression of a certain shared feeling about this country, *Easy Rider* is a fragile but lovely lyric poem.' Warshow takes as read that there is 'a new filmgoing generation' and that countercultural ideas 'fit very snugly into the fashionable thinking of an under-thirty generation' and those 'who sympathize with that generation, and share much of its thinking'.[23] He could do so because in 1968 film culture acknowledged the conceptual shift from adolescence to a more broadly conceived counterculture. Moved by the film's sincerity, and its 'truth', which he believed was 'told in a way that is controlled, unexaggerated, and unhysterical', Warshow captured how *Easy Rider* distils preoccupations that were laid down courageously in *Greetings* but remained frenetic in a frantically paced barrage of contemporary issues. Warshow concluded that *Easy Rider* was 'probably the first above-ground movie which treats the culture

Figure 8.2 Peter Fonda as Wyatt ('Captain America') in *Easy Rider*. Courtesy of Topham Picturepoint/Press Association Images.

mainly from the viewpoint of the youth of that culture'.[24] It was characteristic of the counterculture and inseparable from it.

Production of the film was fraught with tensions that were the result of the values that gave rise to its success. Fonda even tried to halt it:

> Tapes exist on which Dennis weeps, screams, curses, pleaded for almost seven hours without stopping. The cameraman finally threw a TV set at Dennis, and Dennis decked him with a karate kick. Next morning 17 members of the company quit.[25]

Off screen, the filmmakers grappled with drugs, each other and project organization; on screen they captured the zeitgeist. They also included lyrical representation of constituencies that located themselves outside the mainstream and which continue to be neglected in the historiography of the counterculture: Wyatt and Billy's road trip includes stopovers at communes, hippie encampments and farm cooperatives, some of which are struggling to survive. By 1971, it was calculated that more than 3 million people were living in communes around the country. Dropping out and 'taking a stand' in this way was not easy, as *Easy Rider* depicts, but it caught this movement tenderly and thoughtfully.[26] The camera caresses the protagonists and their motorcycles as it glides over them but it is made achingly clear from the first that there is danger inherent in the kind of freedom promised by the counterculture. Captain America hides ill-gotten drug money in his gas tank that could blow at any moment – just like the nation.

From Tet to The Streets

The Vietnam War would be hard to sell on screen. The first half of the decade saw largely peaceful protests against the war the United States was waging in Vietnam but in the aftermath of the Tet Offensive of January 1968, the public's faith in victory turned to a majority belief that if the war could be brought to an end, the best that could be hoped for would be stalemate. Between November 1967 and February 1968, the number of Americans who believed the US was making progress dropped from 52 to 32 per cent; and by the beginning of April, for first time, polls showed that the majority of Americans no longer supported the war.[27] In the moment that public support was plummeting, Universal released *The Green Berets* by arch-Republican and President of the Motion Picture Alliance for the Preservation of Ideals, John Wayne. What television journalist Jeff Greenfield would summarize as a generational faultline was also challenged by this intergenerational project produced by Wayne's thirty-two-year-old son Michael.[28]

The Tet Offensive – during which the National Liberation Front (NLF) attacked scores of cities in South Vietnam and the US Embassy in Saigon – changed the way the war could be reported in the US. It was a television newscaster, CBS's Walter Cronkite, who, having returned from Vietnam, forecast on 27 February that America's war could end only in a stalemate and described its escalation as approaching 'the brink of cosmic disaster'. The release in June of pro-military and pro-war *The Green Berets* would prove an ironic rejoinder to Cronkite's prediction and President Johnson's televised speech on 31 March in which he announced a partial halt to bombing, a willingness to negotiate with the North, and his decision not to run for election that year. While *The Green Berets* was shot in 1967, it was edited after the Tet Offensive, but John Wayne, lead actor as well as executive producer, had promised Johnson, as early as 1965, that his film would 'help our cause throughout the world' and 'inspire a patriotic attitude on the part of fellow Americans'.[29] The most overt symbol of this aim is a journalist (David Janssen) who arrives 'in country' opposed to the war and is converted to a hawk. The film was so jingoistic in the aftermath of Tet that New York Congressman Benjamin S. Rosenthal accused Wayne and the military of conspiring to make it.[30] It made $16 million on release but was picketed around the country, which was unsurprising since in the first five months of 1968, demonstrations against the war increased significantly and by December, forty-one cases of arson on university campuses were recorded as student protest against the draft.[31]

Scenes that provoked criticism include an ARVN officer describing his goal 'to kill all the stinking Cong and go home' and a US pilot discharging bombs observing matter-of-factly that 'it only takes a minute', with the truth of his statement illustrated by 'enemy Viet Cong' burning and writhing in torment. The implication was clear: barbaric Asians die screaming while Americans die with dignity and stoic courage for a righteous cause. The film closes on Wayne's character, Colonel Kirby, comforting a Vietnamese boy orphaned by the war by telling him that he is 'what this war is all about'. If the filmmakers attached no irony to the propaganda, many audiences did. Articles in *Photoplay*, compiled to promote interviews with Wayne, included the story that he defied death while signing autographs in Chu Lai when sniper fire hit the ground around him: 'On the firing line, the legend came alive. Whatever he may have felt inside, Wayne lived up to his image.'[32] Nevertheless, Richard Schickel's description of *The Green Berets* as 'dead on arrival' because 'in the age of the global village, we know too much', summarizes what most film critics felt and it was too late for most viewers to be swayed by bravado.[33] It was the last time that such a hawkish image of America's war in Vietnam would be seen in cinema.[34]

When *The Green Berets* is viewed alongside other films released in 1968 it seems anachronistic. Marxist Emile de Antonio's *In the Year of the Pig* (1968) included footage of General S. Patton IV

Figure 8.3 John Wayne during the filming of *The Green Berets*, 11 November 1967. Courtesy of AP/Press Association Images.

describing his troops as 'a bloody good bunch of killers' in glaring counterpoint to antiwar demonstrations and veteran testimony. David Loeb Weiss's 16mm documentary *No Vietnamese Ever Called Me a Nigger* recorded African American protestors in Harlem on 15 April 1967 whose platform was the Spring Mobilization to End the War, a week after Martin Luther King, Jr. delivered his speech 'A Time to Break Silence' at New York's Riverside Church in which he accused 'the greatest purveyor of violence in the world today – my own government' of prolonging the war.[35] Weiss fused interviews with angry and impassioned men and women with testimony from black veterans interviewed after the Tet Offensive. The veterans frame the film and when Dalton James describes his development from solider-recruit to militant opponent, he locates the shift in a longer history of the black freedom struggle:

> Four little girls died in a Sunday school. The man who laid the charge was a National Guardsman.[36] Yet the white people in this United States have the nerve to get shaken up when I say I will use my skills to fight for a revolt for four hundred years of racism . . . I will be out in the damn streets and won't be wearing a fatigue uniform.

James begins quietly but becomes increasingly direct. His denunciation of the military is simultaneously a rejection of nonviolent direct action symbolized by King and a turn toward armed resistance catalysed by the war:

> Lyndon Baines Johnson is busy bombing the hell out of Vietnam – don't nobody talk about nonviolence. White people beat up black people every day – don't nobody talk about nonviolence. As soon as black people start to move, the double standard comes into being.

If these documentaries 'brought the war home', three very different fiction films took issues to the streets. In May, in Barry Shear's *Wild in the Streets* rock star Max Frost (Christopher Jones) is elected president on the platform that 'we're fifty-two percent'. He makes thirty the age of mandatory retirement to 'Paradise Camps' in which LSD 'treatment' is administered to render older people non-disruptive. Max's election is the result of political game-playing over the voting age which slides in competing campaigns down to fourteen. The hippie and would-be-revolutionary president dismantles what previous generations put in place, disbanding the military and dissolving security forces and intelligence agencies. In the final frame, a child tells Max he is already too old to lead the nation at twenty-four and that 'We're going to put everybody over ten out of business'. The consequences of rule according to generational divide are made frighteningly clear. Produced in around three weeks, *Wild in the Streets* was a timely satire. Exploitation movies could secure large audiences in 1968 once youth was represented as a process of politicization and in 'Trash, Art, and the Movies' (1969) Pauline Kael would extol *Wild in the Streets* for breaking down taste distinctions between mass and 'high' entertainment.[37] Corman's *Gas-s-s-s, or It Became Necessary to Destroy the World in Order to Save It* (1970), in which a poisonous gas kills everyone over twenty-five, reinforced what *Wild in the Streets* achieved. With AIP's biggest budget to date at $700,000, it too moved the exploitation movie into the mainstream, its subtitle an ironic reworking of the US Army's reported statement on bombing Ben Tre in Vietnam: 'it became necessary to destroy the town in order to save it'.[38]

If the exploitation movie matured in 1968, *Medium Cool*, Haskell Wexler's semi-documentary indictment of August's Democratic National Convention in Chicago, was unprecedented. A television cameraman (Robert Forster) embraces a distant and purely professional attitude to his subject but is made increasingly aware of the politics of his representational practice until he crosses the line of supposed objectivity into sympathy with the protestors he is depicting. In the final frame, when a camera pans to Wexler himself, he turns his camera on the audience. In a disquieting and complicitous shot he poses the film's central question: how can a filmmaker or a viewer remain unaffected by what they have witnessed? During the week of the convention 660 people were arrested, 1000 were injured and Dean Johnson, a seventeen-year-old Native American, was shot dead by police who said he pulled a gun. December saw the release of the Walker Report, the *National Commission on the Causes and Prevention of Violence*, that declared the episode a 'police riot', and film critic Vincent Canby praised Wexler's film as 'a picture of America in the process of exploding into fragmented bits of hostility, suspicion, fear and violence'.[39]

Wexler's carefully planned but largely improvised film, supported by Paramount, was one of the clearest rebuttals to the assumption that the sixties cultural revolution would not find a place on the screen. Wexler filmed news being made and NBC and CBS cameras rolling while NBC's Dan Rather was punched to the convention floor. Television networks would be castigated by Democrats for having covered violent confrontations on the streets outside the International Amphitheatre more than the political contest taking place within, and went so far as to imply that television media had cost Hubert Humphrey the election.[40] Wexler inadvertently captured a military intelligence film unit reporting events to Washington and *Medium Cool*'s narrative was played out for real when Mayor Richard J. Daley ordered police to release tear gas on demonstrators. Wexler kept his cameras rolling then too, even though he and another camera operator would suffer the effects. The line the cameraman shouts, 'Look out, Haskell, it's real', was added in post-production and signals the moment when *cinéma-vérité* flips into melodrama, but only in order to dramatize what had been a real experience. In this way, *Medium Cool* was groundbreaking.

In April and August, the murders of Martin Luther King and Robert Kennedy were tragic evidence that political assassination was becoming as prevalent as it was pernicious and would also define the decade. The Kerner Commission reported the nation was moving toward 'two societies, one black, one white – separate and unequal', a bellwether for the integrationist civil rights movement which had achieved so much since the 1950s.[41] *Uptight* was the first big budget film to depict militant black nationalism and the radicalization of the civil rights movement in the aftermath of King's death when 130 cities saw disturbances and riots. *Uptight* begins the day of King's funeral, 9 April 1968, in Cleveland (whose African American mayor, Carl Stokes, allowed Jules Dassin to film across the city). In taking to the streets, the industry began to have the courage to explore African American anger and armed resistance.

That Paramount funded *Uptight* was more interesting to contemporary reviewer Stanley Kauffman than the film itself. He asserted that 'there isn't a militant statement in *Uptight* that will be news to readers of *Look* and *Life* or to viewers of CBS and NBC and NET'.[42] However, the film is suggestive of the ways in which FBI operations like COINTELPRO (COunter INTELligence PROgram), not yet fully exposed in 1968, divided radical groups. It was also indicative of a trend that forged films of black militancy out of former studio system hits. Carol Reed's *Odd Man Out* (1947) was transformed by Robert Alan Arthur into *The Lost Man* in 1969, with Sidney Poitier a committed black nationalist planning to burgle a white factory to raise funds for families of jailed black militants. African American actors would become visible big screen heroes in Blaxploitation films and this trend too was evident in 1968. *The Split*, originally envisaged as a vehicle for Lee Marvin, starred instead former full-back for the Cleveland Browns, Jim Brown, signalling a further trend in which black sporting heroes were turned into action stars. In this moment, Hollywood finally realized that Sidney Poitier's star image was sufficiently robust to be broken open to include less safely middle-class roles, and began to diversify the image of black actors in a way that Poitier himself relished: 'I was there at the box office putting down my $3 to see Jim Brown and Fred Williamson . . . beating up on white guys for a change . . . Not only did I like watching the revenge syndrome at work, I also liked watching my fellow actors at work. Suddenly after too many years . . . came a profusion of movies with black stars, male and female.'[43] It was a very late beginning but by 1969, as Mel Watkins attested, 'Black' would be marketable.[44]

Conclusion: That Was Then

The passage of the 26th Amendment that lowered the voting age from twenty-one to eighteen in 1971 demonstrated unequivocally that the youth-led social movements of the 1960s had impacted popular as well as political culture in precise ways, not least in the film industry. American cinema in 1968 was as variegated and contradictory as the national picture was conflicted. *Barbarella*, for example, verged on soft porn, especially in the scene in which Jane Fonda's forty-first-century 'astronautical aviatrix' beats a machine designed to kill her with an overdose of erotic pleasure. The film's director, and Fonda's husband in 1968, Roger Vadim, would describe it as 'a kind of sexual Alice in Wonderland of the future' and it would be a countercultural hit. But, at the same time, it gained mainstream appeal and Fonda featured as Barbarella on the cover of *Life* and was photographed nude inside its covers. *Life* described Barbarella as 'a new kind of movie' for the daughter of Henry Fonda living 'a new kind of life'.[45]

The film made of the actress a sex goddess in the same year that the Miss American pageant was targeted by 'Women's Liberation

Figure 8.4 Jane Fonda on the set of *Barbarella*, 1 September 1967. Courtesy of AP/ Press Association Images.

Movement' protesters as a degrading sexualized spectacle. The 'Freedom Trash Can' into which protestors threw girdles, bras and false eyelashes (see Chapter 11) contained the tools of the actress's trade in *Barbarella*. While *Barbarella* was a comedy spoof of a French comic strip and Fonda a fine comedy actress, 1968 would be a turning point: *Barbarella* was the last in the series of similar movies she had made with Vadim since 1964's *La Ronde*. By 1969 and *They Shoot Horses, Don't They?* Fonda was acclaimed as a serious actress with an Academy Award nomination and – more significantly for her 'new life' – her politicization, underway in 1968, would make her more (in)famous than her films by 1970. The political Fonda would even become the subject of a countercultural, if somewhat spiteful, movie: *Letter to Jane*, directed by Jean-Luc Godard in 1973.

By the end of the decade, too, the avant-garde docu-drama and improvisational qualities of *Medium Cool* had presaged documentary-style dramas that included *Zabriskie Point* (1970) and *Punishment Park* (1971) wherein generic markers were dissolved. Their self-conscious meta-commentary on the counterculture would enforce their distance from the industry in which *Medium Cool* had found a place in 1968. Dennis Hopper's *The Last Movie* (1971), shot in a remote village in the Andes, would prove a step too far. The premise of the film echoes something of Wexler's project insofar as the crew shooting a Western about Billy the Kid is made as visible as the actors on screen. Once the shoot is over, a stuntman (Hopper) remains behind to discover villagers are re-enacting the film's narrative, without any film in home-made bamboo cameras; it is an increasingly violent ritual in which the remaining American will play Billy the Kid to his death. Funded $850,000 by Universal based on the success of *Easy Rider*, Hopper told *Life* that 'if I foul up now, they'll say *Easy Rider* was a fluke'.[46] This intriguing essay-style film won the Grand Jury Prize at the Venice Film Festival, but Universal hesitated to release it. *The Last Movie* was too far from the industry's acclimatization to countercultural values in 1968 – and was a film about US cinema destroying its own myths and legends.

1969 saw the beginning of a 'recession' in Hollywood and *Variety* judged industry losses from 1969 to 1971 as $600 million.[47] Overproduction of films for a family audience was impacted by the loss of that audience to television. The industry would not stabilize in financial terms until the 1970s. Films produced in 1968, though, created new and successful markets on low budgets and through new directorial approaches there emerged aesthetics that reflected European and art cinema more than the Hollywood studio system, as Andrew Sarris explored in *Confessions of a Cultist* (1970). Writers and directors introduced outlaw countercultural heroes that influenced New Hollywood, and an economic turn that derived from a new filmmaking constituency and audience with a sense of urgency for social change. As Rexroth had predicted in 1960, the waters had risen, and while by 1970 the riptide of youth-led cultural revolution was deemed to be going out, its co-option by the industry and even its paroxysms and demise, set the style for stories patterned on cult hits of '68. Burt Reynolds, the top grossing male film star in the 1970s, gained fame as an outlaw hero and in *White Lightning* (1973), when his countercultural activist brother is murdered by a southern sheriff, it was a nod to *Easy Rider*. The *Smokey and the Bandit* cycle echoed *Easy Rider* too by pairing Bandit (Reynolds) and Snowman (Jerry Reed).

Television was catching up fast. The rise of the television movie, first airing on NBC in 1964, ensured that controversial themes could begin to find an audience in the home, with, for example, NBC's World Premier movies designed to explore new subject matter and television critic Elayne Rapping judging that, 'more than any other fictional form', as the genre consolidated, TV movies 'call on us to think and act as citizens in a public social sphere'.[48] ABC's *Carter's Army* (1967) tackled racism in the military during the Second World War and NBC's *My Sweet Charlie*, filmed over four weeks in 1968, was nominated for ten Emmy awards, winning five.

In 1968, though, the film industry had been bolder. While some activist groups were disappointed in political cinema – Appalshop was formed in 1969 to continue waging the War on Poverty and the New Orleans Video Access Center, founded by VISTA (Volunteers in Service to America), was inaugurated in 1972 – the end of a political era was captured forcibly in cinema, especially in *Medium Cool* and *Easy Rider*. *Wild in the Streets* self-consciously exploited media-made panics over the counterculture and satirized the media in which they were promulgated and *Uptight* spoke to anger and insurgency, dramatizing the moment of Dr King's assassination as declension. By 1972, the potential malfunctioning of the new film rating system would be the subject of vigorous debate and media critics would decide that representation of the counterculture had institutionalized an otherwise subversive phenomenon as 'a popular subject for cheap horny flicks'.[49] In 1968, though, the counterculture and a new film-rating system coincided in a pivotal year for the industry, offsetting the decline of its studio system and traditional audiences. The events of 1968 and a dynamic political milieu provided creative opportunities for a film industry endeavouring to change with the times.

Notes

1. Charles Kaiser, *1968 in America* (New York: Weidenfeld and Nicolson, 1988), xv.
2. Maurice Isserman and Michael Kazin, *America Divided: The Civil War of the 1960s*, 3rd edn (Oxford: Oxford University Press, 2008), 232; Kaiser, *1968 in America*, xv.
3. Leslie Fiedler, *The Return of the Vanishing American* (London: Paladin, 1972), 23.
4. Charles Webb, *The Graduate* (London: Penguin, 1968), 12.
5. Dustin Hoffman in Sam Kashner, 'Here's to You Mr. Nichols: The Making of The Graduate', *Vanity Fair* 571 (March 2008), 430.
6. Kenneth Rexroth, 'The Students Take Over', *The Nation* (2 July 1960).
7. Louis Menand, 'Life in the Stone Age', *New Republic* (7 January 1991), 42.
8. Aniko Bodroghkozy enumerates the 'season of social relevance' in *Groove Tube: Sixties Television and the Youth Rebellion* (Durham, NC: Duke University Press, 2001), 199–235.
9. Thomas Doherty, *Teenagers and Teenpics* (Boston: Unwin Hyman, 1988), 194.
10. Peter Biskind, *Easy Riders and Raging Bulls: Coppola, Scorsese and Other Directors* (New York: Simon and Schuster, 1999), 17; Timothy Corrigan, *A Cinema Without Walls: Movies and Culture After Vietnam* (New Brunswick, NJ: Rutgers University Press, 1992).
11. Jack Valenti, 'Statement before the National Commission on the Causes and Prevention of Violence' (19 December 1968), in Stephen Prince (ed.), *Screening Violence* (New Brunswick, NJ: Rutgers University Press, 2000), 65.
12. Valenti, 'Why Jack Valenti Still Sleeps Soundly . . . Because All's Well with Exxon, LBJ, Hollywood, That's Why', *Texas Monthly* (July 1974), 72.
13. Valenti, 'Statement', 65.
14. Stirling Silliphant in Axel Madsen, *William Wyler: The Authorized Biography* (New York: Thomas Y. Crowell, 1973), 398.
15. One of the best studies of this era is Richard Maltby's *Harmless Entertainment: Hollywood and the Ideology of Consensus* (Metcheun, NJ: Scarecrow, 1983) and on television see Les Brown's *Television: The Business Behind the Box* (New York: Harcourt, Brace, Jovanovich, 1971).
16. Variety reported an $11million receipt for *West Side Story* on release: *Variety* (9 January 1963), 13.
17. Sharon Monteith, *American Culture in the 1960s* (Edinburgh: Edinburgh

University Press, 2008), 154; Pauline Kael 'Trash, Art, and the Movies', *Going Steady: Film Writings 1968-1969* (New York: Marion Boyars, 1994), 96.

18. Petula Clark in *The Telegraph* (29 August 2012).

19. Jeffrey Sconce, 'Trashing the Academy: Taste, Excess and an Emerging Politics of Cinematic Style', *Screen* 36(4) (Winter 1995), 373; Sharon Monteith, 'Exploitation Movies and the Freedom Struggle of the 1960s', in Deborah Barker and Kathryn McKee (eds), *American Cinema and the Southern Imaginary* (Athens: University of Georgia Press, 2011), 194–216.

20. *Variety* (31 December 1968).

21. Roger Ebert, *Chicago Sun Times* (5 January 1969); Ebert, 'Just Another Horror Movie – Or Is It?', *Reader's Digest* (June 1969), 128.

22. Doherty, *Teenagers and Teenpics*, 192.

23. Paul Warshow, 'Easy Rider', *Sight and Sound* (Winter 1969–70), 36.

24. Ibid. 37–8.

25. Brad Darrach, 'Easy Rider Runs Wild in the Andes', *Life* (19 June 1970), 56.

26. Associated Press, *The World in 1971: History As We Lived It* (New York: Associated Press, 1972), 123.

27. Edward Jay Epstein, *Between Fact and Fiction: The Problem of Journalism* (New York: Vintage, 1975), 224; Michael X. Delli Carpini, 'US Media Coverage of the Vietnam Conflict in 1968', in Michael Klein (ed.), *The Vietnam Era: Media and Popular Culture in the US and Vietnam* (London: Pluto, 1990), 38.

28. Jeff Greenfield, *No Peace, No Place: Excavations along the Generational Fault* (New York: Doubleday, 1973).

29. John Wayne in Edward Jay Epstein, *The Big Picture: Money and Power in Hollywood* (New York: Random House, 2005), 328.

30. 'John Wayne as the Last Hero', *Time* (8 August 1969), 56.

31. Delli Carpini, 'US Media Coverage', 38.

32. 'John Wayne Talks About His Toughest Battle', *Photoplay* (March 1969) (UK edition), 42. The battle is the one he fought to beat cancer in 1964.

33. Richard Schickel, 'Duke Talks Through His Green Beret', *Life* (19 July 1968), 8.

34. Marshall Thompson, who played the friendly veterinarian in CBS's *Daktari* (1966–9) directed and starred in the pro-war *A Yank in Vietnam* (1964) and starred in *To the Shores of Hell* (1966).

35. Martin Luther King, Jr., 'A Time to Break Silence', in Reese Williams (ed.), *Unwinding the Vietnam War* (Seattle, WA: Real Comet Press, 1987), 429.

36. The case was closed in 1968 with none of the four men identified convicted. James may be referring to Frank Cherry, finally convicted in 2002, who had been in the Marine Corps.

37. Kael, 'Trash, Art, and the Movies', 98.

38. Philip Jones Griffiths, *Vietnam Inc.* (London: Phaidon, [1971] 2005), 84.

39. Vincent Canby, 'Real Events of '68 Seen in Medium Cool', *New York Times* (28 August 1969). See Lewis Chester, Godfrey Hodgson and Bruce Page, *An American Melodrama: The Presidential Campaign of 1968* (London: André Deutsch, 1969), and David Farber, *Chicago '68* (Chicago: University of Chicago Press, 1988).

40. Brown, *Television*, 30.

41. Otto Kerner et al., *Report of the National Advisory Commission on Civil Disorders* (New York: Dutton, 1968).
42. Stanley Kauffman, *Figures of Light: Film Criticism and Comment* (New York: Harper and Rowe, 1971), 123, 124.
43. Sidney Poitier, 'Walking the Hollywood Color Line', *American Film* 5(6) (April 1980), 26.
44. Mel Watkins, 'Black is Marketable', *New York Times* (16 February 1969).
45. *Life* (29 March 1968), 66.
46. Quoted in Darrach, 'Easy Rider Runs Wild in the Andes', 57.
47. *Variety* (2 July 1974).
48. Elayne Rapping, *The Movie of the Week: Private Stories, Public Events* (Minneapolis: University of Minnesota Press, 1992), xii.
49. Stephen Farber, *The Movie Rating Game* (Washington DC: Public Affairs Press, 1972); Tommy Tinker, 'Image Media as a Cultural Medium', *Los Angeles Free Press* (4 April 1969).

Part Three

Identities and Protest

NINE

1968: End of The Civil Rights Movement?

Stephen Tuck

On Sunday 7 April 1968 the United States held a national day of mourning for the Reverend Dr Martin Luther King, Jr. In New York City that afternoon some 5000 people marched from Harlem to Central Park to join an open-air memorial service to commemorate the civil rights leader who had been murdered in Memphis three days earlier. The march was sombre and subdued. In a show of solidarity, Charles Kenyatta, leader of Harlem's Mau Mau group, walked arm in arm with New York's Governor Nelson Rockefeller. One man at the front of the march held a large picture of Malcolm X. The woman next to him carried a smaller picture of Martin Luther King.

As the platform party made its way to the stage, James Forman, a prominent student leader, stood up on his seat in the front row and called on Rockefeller to tell the president to 'Free Rap Brown', the high profile Black Power leader who was on hunger strike to protest his imprisonment on the charge of threatening the life of an FBI officer.[1] Forman was joined by colleagues who each had a picture of Brown pinned to their chests. As the African American newspaper, the *New York Amsterdam News* put it, Forman brought the tribute to King 'to a halt even before it began'.[2] Forman stopped his protests when Kenyatta invited him to join the speakers on the stage. Rockefeller, speaking first, compared Martin Luther King to Jesus Christ, a man who gave his life 'so we may live in brotherhood ourselves'. The following day, the governor would ask the state legislature to agree legislation to fund urban regeneration projects, including a $10 million office in Harlem to be named the 'Dr. Martin Luther King State of Office Building'.[3]

While the main tribute was in Harlem and Central Park, there were parades across the city in memory of King. In Brooklyn, Reverend Elijah Pope told one such parade that their first march up the streets of their neighbourhood would not be their last, but rather it marked a 'new era for East New York'. Standing on an upturned garbage can, the pastor told the crowd of 200 'we're going to march on the Police Department, we're going to march on the Sanitation Department' and demand more services.[4]

The events in New York pointed to some of the headline themes of 1968 in regard to the black freedom struggle. The death of the civil rights movement's most famous leader, and the prominence of those committed to Black Power during the commemoration, seemed to signify the passing of a particular phase of protest.[5] So too did violent confrontations in over 100 cities across the country following news of King's death. 'The philosophy of nonviolence died with Dr. King, the last prince of nonviolence', declared one prominent African American activist, Floyd McKissick, with tears in his eyes, the day after the assassination.[6] Another headline ran: 'When white America killed Dr. King it declared war on us. We have to retaliate.'[7]

Meanwhile, Rockefeller's call for commemorative legislation at the state level was followed on Thursday 11 April by the passage of a Civil Rights Act at the federal level, popularly known as the Fair Housing Act. 'Dr. King would have smiled approvingly at this development', argued a syndicated editorial in the black press, noting how unlikely the passage of a wide-ranging bill had been before King's death, 'for, he spared neither intellectual nor physical energy in the struggle for abolition of residential segregation'.[8] But with hindsight, the Act would also mark the final major congressional response to the civil rights movement, following the Civil Rights Act of 1964 and Voting Rights Acts of 1965.

Furthermore, the Poor People's Campaign that would follow soon after the day of mourning in Washington DC during May and June 1968 (as discussed in Chapter 12) would mark the last major campaign run by King's organization, the Southern Christian Leadership Conference (SCLC). Championed by King during early

1968, the Campaign attracted at least 3000 people to construct and live in a tented city on the National Mall, who were joined by some 50,000 people for a Solidarity Day Rally for Jobs, Peace and Freedom on 19 June. The protests drew attention to the problem of poverty, which had become a central focus of King's concern in his final years, and won plaudits in the black press. But the mainstream media focused as much on leadership divisions and the bad weather. By the time the police cleared out the tented city on 24 June, wrote Keith Mantler, a historian of the campaign, 'Martin Luther King Jr.'s last dream lay pulverized amid the rain-driven, ankle-deep mud of Resurrection City and the fractious and polarized politics of the late 1960s'.[9]

The momentous events of 1968, then, mark the end of the classic years of the civil rights era that had started with Martin Luther King's rise to prominence at the Montgomery bus boycott in 1955. Looking back on the year 1968, an editorial in the influential African American newspaper the *Chicago Defender* concluded: 'this has been a year in which events of irresistible force have focused attention more on the Black Power movement than on civil rights per se'. Or as historian David Chappell begins his 2014 study of protest after the assassination of King:

> In retrospect his death often appears to be the tragic, sudden end of the triumphal story of progress in civil rights, a story that Americans associate with King's career. After the major victories of the civil rights movement in the 1960s, most Americans remember a dreary story from that point forward.[10]

Looking ahead, then, there were many reasons why the years after 1968 might seem to be a dreary story of protest compared with the so-called King years. The hard won legislative successes of the 1960s movement encouraged some activists to work within the system, to move from 'protest to politics'.[11] Others became disillusioned, especially as no single figure replaced Martin Luther King.[12] In his survey of a century of black protest, the historian Adam Fairclough concluded that 'in the years since 1968, black leadership has become increasingly fragmented and uncertain' as many of the major civil rights organizations, like the SCLC, fell into decline.[13] Instead Black Power protest dominated the headlines as the political climate turned against support for civil rights. In this vein, in his 2009 study of the impact of King's death, historian Clay Risen noted that candidates from both political parties responded to the ensuing urban disorder by prioritizing 'law and order'.[14] Republican Richard Nixon was elected president in November 1968 after running what one black newspaper editorial called a 'white campaign'.[15]

Thus the first histories of the civil rights movement tended to move from a period of progress to a period of decline, from a period when activists forced change to a period when change was forced upon them. But the New York commemoration also points to a more complicated story, one that lacks such clear distinctions between the years before and after the assassination in Memphis on 4 April. It was, after all, a tribute where adjacent marchers carried pictures of Malcolm X and Martin Luther King, and, following widespread urban disorder, a Black Power leader walked arm in arm with a Republican governor who then demanded anti-poverty legislation.

Indeed, the reason the *Chicago Defender* reflected on 1968 as a year that saw the passing of the civil rights era and the triumph of Black Power was because of the effectiveness of Black Power as a movement rather than any negative connotations. It was not just the assassination of 'the great apostle of rights through interracial unity and peace', the editorial noted, but rather, the 'substantive gains' that were made by Black Power mayoral candidates at the ballot box and by Black Power student activists on campuses during 1968 that gave the movement 'the impetus it needed to establish itself . . . as a workable principle'. In his ground-breaking 2011 history of Black Power, historian Peniel Joseph agreed. 'Black Power loomed over the year 1968', noted Joseph, but he argued that although 'future histories would look back at 1968 as, effectively, the end of the democratic surges inspired by civil rights struggles . . . actual events suggest the exact opposite'.[16]

Indeed, recent studies at the national and especially the local level have revealed numerous examples of protest continuing in diverse ways in diverse places after King's death.[17] For Will Campbell – a clergyman who had worked with King – the protest that he joined in a small Southern town in 1974 'sparkled as it had in Birmingham, Selma, Albany, Montgomery' and other sites where King had campaigned.[18] Most local protests after 1968 combined tactics that were associated with both the civil rights movement and Black Power protest.[19] In Northern Mississippi during 1974–9, for example, tens of thousands of people joined the United League to challenge white supremacy. 'In a period generally considered a low point of Black insurgency', noted the historian of Mississippi protest, Akinyele Umoja, in 2013, 'the United League organized successful boycotts utilizing self-defense and bold rhetoric embracing armed resistance'.[20]

On this evidence, the overall story of the diverse forms of African American protest that developed after 1968 is not so much one of fragmentation as one of proliferation. Some contemporary African American commentators welcomed the diversity of protest on offer. As Carl Holman, president of the National Urban Coalition observed approvingly a decade after the death of King, 'what's happened in the last ten years is that black leadership has diversified.

Figure 9.1 Peaceful protest felt anachronistic during the civil discord that followed Martin Luther King, Jr.'s assassination. Here King prays against the Vietnam War with other religious leaders at the Arlington National Cemetery, Virginia, 6 February 1968. Courtesy of Harvey Georges AP/Press Association Images.

There's no single figure who bestrides the landscape as Martin King did. We've got people working different vineyards.'[21]

In many ways, African American activism continued to make advances after the supposed end of the civil rights movement precisely because it built upon the many examples and achievements of 1960s protest. Or, as one protester in Northern Mississippi put it in 1968: 'we are taking up where the movement of the 1960s left off'.[22] Throughout the twentieth century (not to say before), African Americans sought to build a better world and resist those who interfered. But the 1960s changed the terrain of this long struggle for equality. The civil rights movement and Black Power protests provided a variety of models for, and won victories that would empower, subsequent activism.

This chapter will illustrate the proliferation and power of African American activism in the decade after 1968 by surveying two characteristics of the struggles for equality and justice. In the first place, the chapter will explore the way that the legislative victories around voting and the workplace gave activists new opportunities to make their demands. Indeed, in some workplaces and smaller communities, the gains of the 1960s actually provided the springboard for unprecedented confrontational protest. The chapter will then consider the protests of previously sidelined groups. The celebrated figures of the 1960s were often civil rights clergymen, middle-class students or young male militants. But after the classic years of the civil rights movement, groups such as welfare activists, feminists and the imprisoned were able to make demands for their distinctive causes with unprecedented force.

The Strengthening of Grassroots Activism

On 1 January 1968 Richard Hatcher was sworn in as the first African American mayor of Gary, Indiana – one of the first elected black mayors of a major city in the United States.[23] Just over four years later, in March 1972, 8000 African Americans delegates headed to Gary for the first convention of the National Black Political Assembly. The delegates represented a wide range of politically engaged African Americans from moderate supporters of integration to militant black nationalists. Militancy won the day. Moderates joined the chant 'It's Nation Time!' The convention concluded with a 'challenge to consolidate and organize our own Black role as the vanguard in the struggle for a new society'.[24] Delegates seemed optimistic that they could meet the challenge – a view that led historian Manning Marable to conclude that 'Gary represented, in retrospect, the zenith . . . of the entire black movement during the Second Reconstruction'.[25] But for Marable and many other commentators, it was all downhill after Gary. Within weeks, most black elected politicians distanced themselves from the convention's call for an independent black political party. However, the end of the convention movement did not mean the end of political action or even the end of political gains. African American protest had led to the Voting Rights Act. In turn the Act empowered activists to use politics to unprecedented effect in the struggle for equality.

At the national level, the Congressional Black Caucus (CBC) was established in 1971 with a dozen members, and almost doubled in size during the decade. This still left African American voters vastly underrepresented in Congress. But the CBC was able to lobby the Democratic Congress in ways that many previous generations of civil rights leaders could have barely dreamed of. The first chairman of the CBC, Rep. Charles Diggs, earned the nickname 'Mr. Africa' for his championing of the anti-apartheid movement on the Foreign Relations Committee.[26] In 1977, CBC chairman Parren Mitchell added the minority set-aside requirement as an amendment to the Public Works Employment Act. The historian of federal civil rights policy Hugh Davis Graham concluded that the PWEA was 'one of the most significant turning points in modern civil rights history'.[27]

At the local level, African American candidates made spectacular progress. Within a decade of Hatcher's 1968 victory in Gary, over 200 cities had black mayors. To be sure, this did not mean race ceased to be an issue in local elections. Rare indeed was the African American candidate who won more than 15 per cent of the white vote. Rare too was the African American mayor who had formerly been prominently involved in any kind of civil rights activity. Worst of all, most mayors drank from the cup of municipal victory at precisely the moment it became something of a poisoned chalice. Suburbanization and deindustrialization cut the tax base. A reduction in federal grants compounded the problem. In city after city, downtown became a ghost town. Hatcher's campaign slogan had been 'Gary: A City on the Move'. Some cynics replied 'Yes, everyone's moving out'.[28]

But the fact remains that African American mayors usually worked for a more equitable or even compensatory distribution of resources. Cedric Herring concluded in his study of the impact of black political empowerment: 'those Blacks who live in cities with Black mayors tend to fare better than those who live in cities with non-Black mayors'.[29] The proportion of African Americans in the municipal workforce during the 1970s tended to rise furthest in those cities with a black mayor. The cities of Atlanta, Chicago, Cleveland, Detroit, Gary, Newark and Washington DC had African American police chiefs within five years of their first black mayor. Some mayors took a lead in minority set-aside programmes. For example, when Maynard Jackson was elected mayor of Atlanta in 1973, less than 1 per cent of city business went to African American companies. By the end of his second term, it was one third.[30] Such local set-aside programmes provided the model for the federal PWEA amendment.

There was progress in the rural Southern black belt, too. In 1979, the primary election in majority-black Marshall County, northern Mississippi, home of the United League, was the first in the history of the county to have African Americans officiating. Such progress had to be campaigned for. In the case of Marshall County, United League members defended themselves with guns and the head of the League was arrested on polling day for disorderly conduct – which local people presumed was an attempt to intimidate voters (seven black candidates won their primary election in the county).[31] As with municipal elections, successful black candidates in the rural South inherited costly social problems. Georgia's State NAACP president Robert Flanagan accepted that during the 1970s, a common complaint was 'you told me to vote and, hell, I'm still hungry and I look up there and see the sky through my house'.[32] Black elected officials were unable to overturn the recession of the 1970s, but they did seek to ensure that the recession was not disproportionately harsh on African Americans.

Protest about fair employment led to the Civil Rights Act and a programme that was introduced under Lyndon Johnson in 1967 and adopted by Richard Nixon in 1969 that came to be known as the Philadelphia Plan.[33] In turn, the Civil Rights Act and Philadelphia Plan gave workers new power in their long pursuit of workplace equality. For example, Title VII of the Act prohibited employment discrimination, while the Philadelphia Plan provided for affirmative action in federal hiring. At the same time, however, the limits of 1960s employment legislation also left workers with little option but to continue to protest for economic rights. The legislation did not establish adequate enforcement mechanisms, and the language of the legislation was somewhat ambiguous. For example, the Civil Rights Act and Philadelphia Plan did not define what employment discrimination or affirmative action actually were.[34]

As in the 1960s, African American workers focused on the textile industry in the South and the construction industry in the North and West. During the 1970s seemingly each mill and each building site had its own story of confrontation and litigation. Take the case of A. C. Sherill, the lead plaintiff in a 1973 class action suit against the J. P. Stevens textile company in North Carolina. Sherill's persistent requests for promotion had led to harassment, threats, assault and then redundancy. Before Title VII, Sherill would have been powerless to act. But the new law enabled Sherill to take on the company, and win.[35] Sherill was just one of thousands of plaintiffs, many of whom joined together through local civil rights organizations to form class action suits.[36] Meanwhile, in Washington DC in early 1970 a coalition of thirty-one organizations threatened to block the construction of the new Metro subway system unless African Americans received three quarters of the jobs.[37] (In many other towns, African American demonstrators did block construction sites.) Such demands built on the Philadelphia Plan's precedent for minority employment proportional to local populations.

As in the 1960s, activists on the frontline received support from civil rights lawyers. Clifford Alexander, a former chair of the federal Equal Employment Opportunity Commission (EEOC), represented the Washington coalition.[38] In the South, the National Association for the Advancement of Colored People (NAACP) supported the struggle for the integration of the textile industry. Reflecting on the major legal battles of the civil rights era, lead NAACP lawyer Jack Greenberg argued that the struggle for textile integration was 'almost on a par with the [NAACP] campaign that won *Brown* [*vs. the Board of Education*]' (the seminal 1954 Supreme Court decision that outlawed segregated schooling).[39]

By the 1970s workers received significant support from the state, too. As the number of cases and evidence of resistance mounted, both the courts and the bureaucracy came out in favour of industry-wide solutions, looking at results not intent.[40] Whereas Title VII had called for 'prospective and not retrospective change', the Court held that it was an 'affirmative duty . . . to undo past discrimination'. In 1971 a federal judge ruled the seniority system 'illegal' because it perpetuated prior racial discrimination.[41] In the same year, in a case brought by thirteen black janitors, the Supreme Court ruled against race neutral tests that led to under-representation of racial minorities.[42] Meanwhile, after Congress approved the Philadelphia Plan, the Labor Department applied the plan to all federal contractors. In 1977 Congress passed the PWEA that set aside 10 per cent of federal contracts for Minority Business Enterprises.[43]

Following a series of successful class action suits, some companies acted to pre-empt a legal challenge. Many signed Consent Decrees that promised affirmative hiring practices. For example, in 1974 the major steel companies faced 408 cases pending with the EEOC. With the prospect of paying out enormous compensatory sums hanging like Damocles' sword over the industry, the companies and the union signed a Consent Decree with the federal government. The Decree established goals and timetables for the admission of minorities and women to skilled jobs, and provided over $30 million as compensatory back pay. The NAACP suspected that negotiators had sought to do the minimum necessary to offset litigation. Still, the minimum necessary was a major advance. One worker noted approvingly: 'the Consent Decree has been the most significant and just thing to happen to the American working people in 40 years.'[44]

The struggle for workplace equality had mostly positive results. Black managers and professionals made significant gains in firms covered by the EEOC.[45] Minority hiring in steel rose quickly after the Consent Decree.[46] The integration of textiles was nothing short of historic. From being white-only in 1960, some 20 per cent of workers were African Americans in 1980 (and half were women).[47]

The construction industry proved to be more resistant. The proportion of carpenters who were African American almost doubled between 1965 and 1980. But the proportion of African Americans in others crafts only increased from 6.5 to 7.8 per cent.[48] Many construction jobs required lengthy training, and the absence of large companies and the quick turnover of jobs undermined the litigation process.

Overall, black workers moved into skilled and semi-skilled industrial work at a faster rate than at any time in American history. Unfortunately, African American workers made their greatest gains in industries that were beginning to decline. Worse still, increased residential segregation meant that black workers were unable to claim jobs in the new industries in the suburbs. The disastrous effect of deindustrialization and recession of black employment is well documented.[49] Nevertheless, the protest of African American workers in the industries that they could influence ameliorated some of the worst effects of the recession.

The Prominence of Previously Marginalized African American Groups

On 3 February 1968 Martin Luther King met leaders of the National Welfare Rights Organization (NWRO) to seek their involvement in his forthcoming Poor People's Campaign. The campaign was a major new development from King, reflecting his increasing focus on jobs and economic justice. But the welfare leaders were frustrated that, despite previous efforts at dialogue on their part, King's campaign had not addressed their concerns. The spokeswoman for the group was Joanne Tillmon. With a grandchild on her lap, Tillmon asked King some specific questions about welfare. King was nonplussed. 'You know, Dr. King, if you don't know about these questions, you should say you don't know, and then we could go on with the meeting.' King's colleague Andrew Young thought that the welfare mothers 'jumped on Martin like no one ever had before'. King confessed, 'we are here to learn'.[50]

Tillmon was in a good position to teach. She explained, 'I'm a black woman. I'm a poor woman. I'm a fat woman. I'm a middle-aged woman. And I'm on welfare. In this country if you are any one of those things . . . you count less as a human being. If you're all those things, you don't count at all.'[51] Having grown up picking cotton, Tillmon moved to Los Angeles where she worked in a series of poorly paid jobs. With the onset of various chronic illnesses, and six children to care for, she needed welfare support. In Watts, Tillmon began to organize welfare mothers to work together. During her speech at the Poor People's Campaign march, Tillmon celebrated 'mother power'.[52] By 1973, the NWRO claimed a total membership of more than 125,000, on a par with the membership of the best known civil rights organization of the day, the NAACP (Tillmon became NWRO president in 1973).[53]

As Tillmon's encounter with King showed, the welfare activists represented a group that had been sidelined by the major organizations during the 1960s. Andrew Young later admitted, 'I guess in the back of our minds we thought asking for welfare was tactically unsound'.[54] Hence welfare mothers took up their own cause. The NWRO's goals were 'dignity, justice, full citizenship and an adequate income to all welfare recipients'.[55] Ultimately they didn't achieve these goals. After all, Ronald Reagan famously deployed the image of a black Cadillac-driving welfare queen to powerful effect in his 1976 campaign to be the Republican presidential nominee. But the roll back of welfare rights did not occur until the 1980s. Before then, welfare activists were able to have an influence on welfare provision. 'We have won some major battles', Tillmon asserted in 1973, 'and we plan to keep on fighting'.[56]

When she spoke of major battles, no doubt Tillmon had in mind Nixon's Family Assistance Plan (FAP) of 1970. Some civil rights organizations initially supported the plan. Although it was far from ideal, it was better than they had expected. The NWRO, by contrast, denounced the plan. The proposed welfare allowance worked out to be less than the sum total of the various allowances already available. NWRO activists also denounced workfare requirements that had no guarantee of adequate childcare. A cartoon character in the NWRO magazine called the FAP 'F*** America's Poor'.[57] Thus the NWRO determined to 'ZAP FAP'.

The testimony of welfare mothers in Congress made little positive impact on conservative senators such as Russell Long, who scoffed: 'If they can find time to testify and march . . . they can find time to do some useful work', like 'picking up litter'.[58] But the NWRO did persuade many civil rights groups to oppose FAP, and these groups in turn influenced liberal senators wary of alienating African American voters or provoking a riot. Some civil rights groups resented the NWRO tactic of making 'everyone who supported [FAP] feel immoral'.[59] Nonetheless, liberal opposition to Nixon's plan, coupled with conservative opposition, left FAP well and truly zapped.

The NWRO's ability to oppose FAP was not matched by an ability to push through a federal welfare equivalent of the Civil Rights. For the most part, though, welfare targeted local change. At the end of August 1970 NWRO members sat-in the Washington office of HEW Secretary Robert Finch.[60] In Las Vegas in 1971, welfare mothers stormed Caesar's Palace to protest the cutback of state welfare payments. And by the mid-1970s such protests translated into significant local and state gains, leading Nevada to reverse its welfare cutbacks.[61] The NWRO's publicity prompted tens of thousands of eligible mothers to apply for welfare, and local chapters helped many candidates with the application process. One commentator credited the NWRO with increasing the amount of welfare claimed four fold.[62]

By the mid-1970s the NWRO had fallen apart. Many commentators jumped to the conclusion that welfare activism ground to a halt.[63] In fact, the welfare struggle continued locally, with some success, throughout the decade. The NWRO also spawned other anti-poverty movements. The Nevada anti-poverty effort, Operation Life, brought hundreds of thousands of dollars into the community each year during the 1970s.[64] The Arkansas Community Organizations for Reform Now (ACORN) would develop into one of the key champions of low wage workers and workfare employees into the twenty-first century.[65] As Tillmon summed up in 1980, 'I hear people saying that the welfare rights movement is dead. It is not dead. It has changed since those early days of agitating and protesting in the streets. The movement is different but still alive in many parts of the country.'[66]

As with welfare activists, African American feminists also came to the fore in the 1970s (indeed there was some overlap between the two). Like the welfare activists, many African American women had sought to spotlight women's issues during the 1960s. But as with welfare activists, they had often been sidelined within the major organizations. In the 1970s, however, black women found that they had new opportunities to take the lead. A plethora of organizations sprang up. Deborah Gray White observed in her survey of black women's groups in the twentieth century that 'if ever the nation could see the variety of black womanhood, now was the time'.[67]

As many national (usually male-led) organizations declined after 1968, community issues, and thus (often women-led) community groups, came to the fore. In the wake of the civil rights and Black Power movements, they were able to adopt more aggressive tactics. In Harlem, Mothers Against Drugs (MAD) formed to call the police to account for their lack of action against drug dealers. One MAD leader told reporters that 'the best news I've heard in a long time is that more white kids are getting hooked on heroin'.[68] This way, she reasoned, the drugs issue would get attention. This was a far cry from the politics of respectability that was the hallmark of organizations such as the National Association of Women's Clubs earlier in the century.[69]

In addition to leading community groups, some African American women articulated a distinct black feminist position. They defended themselves against the charge of holding back black men. Los Angeles community activist Margaret Wright explained, 'we're helping them get their liberation. It's the white man who's oppressing, not us. All we ever did was scrub floors so they could get their little selves together.'[70] Many also distanced themselves from the emerging white feminist movement. One welfare activist wrote to the National Organization of Women in 1973, saying: 'You speak of freedom and we are starving, begging, selling ourselves, scrounging for our very survival . . . How dare you call yourselves Sisters?'[71]

Several specifically feminist groups developed during the 1970s. In 1973 the National Black Feminist Organization held its first conference in New York City with some 400 women. For the most part the organization's chapters engaged in discussion groups and education sessions. On occasion local organizers ran confrontational campaigns. For example, the Atlanta chapter protested against the popular television show *That's My Mama*, where Eloise 'Mama' Curtis was a large, domineering mother. By portraying African American women as 'castrating matriarchs', said Atlanta chapter chairwoman Sandra Flowers, the show 're-popularized the concept of the devious . . . black woman . . . by design'.[72]

As with the NWRO, the National Black Feminist Organization fell as quickly as it rose. But as with welfare activism, the collapse of a national organization did not mean the end of mobilization. A wide variety of local groups continued. Prominent black feminists also sharpened their critique of American society. Witness the outpouring of black women's literature by the end of the decade, such as some of the enduring classics in the field: Michelle Wallace, *Black Macho and the Myth of the Superwoman* (1978); bell hooks, *Ain't I A Woman* (1981); Angela Davis, *Women, Race and Class* (1981); and Barbara Smith, *All the Women Are White, All the Men are Black, But Some of us are Brave* (1981).

In response to the urban rebellions of the late 1960s, the federal government – through the work of COINTELPRO (Counterintelligence Program) – used prison to repress African American militants. COINTELPRO's tactics were as disreputable as they were devastating. Take the case of the Charlotte Three. In 1972 federal agents sought the arrest of Jim Grant, T. J. Reddy and Charles Parker. The three men had agitated, with success, for the establishment of a Black Studies program at UNC-Charlotte. In 1971, a local stable – known for its refusal to allow black riders – burned down. Fifteen horses died.[73] Agents suspected the three activists. Their only difficulty was they had no evidence whatsoever. So they arranged for two African American prisoners, convicted of murder and armed robbery, to meet in a cell to concoct a story for court. The convicted criminals were soon released (and given an all-expenses paid trip to the beach for three months). The innocent activists were imprisoned for a total of fifty-five years.[74]

As the name the Charlotte Three suggests, many came to see themselves, and be seen by some others, as political prisoners and used their plight to draw attention to excessive and questionable jurisprudence more generally. For example, the Wilmington Ten (sentenced to 282 years in prison for burning a grocery store in February 1971) were the subject of a *Sixty Minutes* documentary.

Their case was taken up by Amnesty International. The convictions were overturned in 1980. Most famously of all, Angela Davis's story gained sympathy around the world. Davis was a brilliant scholar, a former student activist who began working with black prisoners including George Jackson, an outspoken militant accused of murdering a guard. When Jackson's younger brother Jonathan used Angela Davis's gun in a courtroom shootout in 1970, Davis found herself on the FBI's most wanted list. She fled, but was captured in New York. Davis's picture was emblazoned on posters and T-shirts. The Rolling Stones responded by releasing 'Sweet Black Angel' in April 1972 and John Lennon and Yoko Ono included 'Angela' on their *Some Time in New York City* album in June. In response to public pressure, Davis was acquitted that same month.

The imprisonment of militants had a wider impact on the African American community. For example, in 1975, a panel of black lawyers, church leaders and politicians gathered in Chicago to reconsider the evidence of three such cases, in order to make a judgement about 'seven years of alleged crimes by the US and various state governments against the Black Movement'.[75] This belief that there was a state-led conspiracy to destroy the movement led some mainstream civil rights leaders to support militants that they may have previously kept a distance from. For example, members of Chicago's Coalition on Civil Rights opposed the imprisonment (for alleged murder) of local gang leaders Bobby Gore of the Conservative Vice Lords and Leonard Sengali of the Black P. Stone Nation. C. T. Vivian, a former colleague of King, was incensed when he discovered that police had offered Sengali a reduced sentence if he would accuse Vivian of being a communist.[76]

Meanwhile black prisoners sought to mobilize protest within prisons. As with welfare and black feminism, this too had a long tradition. But as with welfare activists and black feminists, the post-King years saw an unprecedented level of collective activism. Black Power rhetoric helped individual prisoners to see their incarceration as part of a systematic assault on African Americans. George Jackson was a case in point. Sent to Soledad prison in 1969 for armed robbery, Jackson joined the Black Panthers and quickly set about persuading his cellmates that prisons were a means of white repression. When Jackson and two inmates were accused of

killing a prison guard, they became well-known as political prisoners, referred to as the Soledad Brothers. They were acquitted in
August 1971, but Jackson was shot dead soon afterwards (the guard
claimed that Jackson had a gun hidden in his hair).[77]

Throughout the system, prisoners mobilized. Davis led cellmates
to demand a bail programme for impoverished prisoners. Reverend
Benjamin Chavis, one of the Wilmington Ten and future head of
the NAACP, had a 129 day 'vegetable broth only' fast to draw media
attention to the 'ever increasing necessity to struggle against racism
in its many forms' (he also used the day-release programme to earn
a degree).[78] In Attica, New York, on 9 September 1971, more than a
thousand prisoners took over the prison and demanded better conditions including the end of censorship of letters, better education,
a drug treatment programme, religious freedom and adequate food
and sleeping arrangements.

Prison protest did not lead to significant reform. In Attica, the
governor sent in the National Guard. Twenty nine prisoners and
ten guards died – soldiers used blood to smear epithets on the walls
such as 'Black blood will flow'. Only prisoners were prosecuted.[79]
The Wilmington Ten were not released until 1980. Nevertheless,
such a public challenge to prison authority was a new departure.
Considering the rapidly rising numbers of young black men in
prison, this activism had wider significance. African American
prison reform and prisoner support groups grew in number during
the rest of the century.[80]

Conclusion: Black Activism after 1968

The persistence of protest after 1968 is a reminder that African
American activism was a response to increased opportunity as well
as to increased oppression. As scholars have demonstrated, the
long freedom struggle, in the North and South, was as much about
seeking jobs, decent housing and voting power and opposing white
violence, police brutality and imperialism as it was about legal segregation. In other words, activists did not need to be educated about
the problem of racism in order to identify racism, they needed sufficient power to oppose it. Because of the legislative gains of 1960s,
and because of the example of 1960s protest, and even because

of the impact of King's death and urban disorder in 1968, many grassroots activists were able to confront persistent racial inequality with new power.

The history of activism in the decade after 1968 also suggests that historians should be wary of lumping these post-King years with the so-called Reagan revolution that followed as a post-civil rights era of reversal. Throughout the 1970s, many activists were still seeking to extend the rights of African Americans rather than simply defend previous gains. Surveys from the mid-1970s showed that African Americans in the lower-middle class and above had never been more optimistic, and poorer African Americans were no more pessimistic than previously.[81]

Furthermore, for much of the 1970s, the cultural revolution that was born in the 1960s reached new heights, from distinctive African American music to changes in school and university curricula. The end of the 1970s also saw the first stirrings of the movement for environmental justice, and the rise of the anti-apartheid movement. To be sure, we now know that urban crisis was set to stay. We know too that the turn of public opinion and political rhetoric against African American goals would develop into a hostile policy environment during the Reagan era and beyond. But the actual rollback of some African American advances – such as cutbacks in state provision for welfare to Supreme Court rulings against affirmative action – did not begin until the 1980s. Thus the hope of many African Americans that continued protest would lead to tangible gains in the decade after the civil rights movement was not blind faith. In the first years after the death of Martin Luther King, nothing was certain, and many things still seemed possible.

Notes

1. 'H. Rap Brown Vows Fast During Long Jail Term', *Chicago Defender* (24 February 1968).
2. '"Militant" Uproar Menaced King Rally in Central Park', *New York Amsterdam News* (20 April 1968); 'Mourning Is Led by President: Marches and Services are Held', *New York Times* (8 April 1968).
3. 'Pope, Other World Figures Join in Tributes to Dr. King', *Washington Post* (8 April 1968); 'Rockefeller Asks Funds to Erect Harlem Offices', *New York Times* (8 April 1968).

4. 'Violence Eases in Pittsburgh; Dr. King Mourned in the Nation', *New York Times* (8 April 1968).
5. For discussion of King's engagement with economic issues, see Thomas Jackson, *From Civil Rights to Human Rights: Martin Luther King, Jr., and the Struggle for Economic Justice* (Philadelphia: University of Pennsylvania Press, 2009).
6. 'Non-Violence Dies with King', *New York Amsterdam News* (20 April 1968).
7. 'When White America Killed Dr. King it Declared War on Us. We Have to Retaliate', *Chicago Daily Defender* (8 April 1968). See also 'Demonstration in New York', *Times of India* (7 April 1968).
8. 'Freedom of Residence', *Chicago Defender* (15 April 1968); *Pittsburgh Courier* (27 April 1968).
9. Gordon Keith Mantler, 'Black, Brown and Poor: Martin Luther King Jr., The Poor People's Campaign and its Legacies', unpublished PhD thesis, Duke University, 2008, 5; Elizabeth Hayes Turner, 'Gone to Washington: Mobilizing the 1968 Poor People's Campaign', in Constante González Groba (ed.), *Unsteadily Marching On: The U.S. South in Motion* (Valencia: Universitat de València, 2013), 123–34; 'Poor People's March a Giant Step', *The Chicago Defender* (22 June 1968).
10. David L. Chappell, *Waking From the Dream, The Struggle for Civil Rights in the Shadow of Martin Luther King* (New York: Random House), xi.
11. Bayard Rustin, 'From Protest to Politics', *Commentary* 39(2) (February 1965), 25–31.
12. See, for example, Jackie Robinson, *I Never Had It Made* (New York: Putnam, 1972), 98.
13. Adam Fairclough, *Better Day Coming: Blacks and Equality, 1890–2000* (New York: Viking), 330.
14. Clay Risen, *A Nation on Fire: America in the Wake of the King Assassination* (Hoboken, NJ: Wiley, 2009).
15. See 'Nixon's Anti-Riot Recipe', *Chicago Defender* (12 March 1968), and Jackie Robinson, 'Nixon Candidacy Imperils America', *Chicago Defender* (7 September 1968).
16. Peniel E. Joseph, *Waiting 'Til the Midnight Hour: A Narrative History of Black Power in America* (New York: Henry Holt, 2006), 205.
17. For helpful survey overviews see Simon Hall, 'Framing the American 1960s: A Historiographical Review', *European Journal of American Culture* 31(1) (April 2012), 5–23; Barbara Keys et al., 'The Post-Traumatic Decade: New Histories of the 1970s', *Australasian Journal of American Studies* 33(1) (July 2014), 1–17; Jacquelyn Dowd Hall, 'The Long Civil Rights Movement and the Political Uses of the Past', *Journal of American History* 91(4) (March 2005), 1233–63.
18. Will D. Campbell, *Forty Acres and a Goat: A Memoir* (Atlanta, GA: Peachtree, 1986), 249.
19. See, for example, 'The Path of Reason', *New York Amsterdam News* (4 January 1969).
20. Akinyele Omowale Umoja, *We Will Shoot Back: Armed Resistance in the*

Mississippi Freedom Movement (New York: New York University Press, 2013), 10.

21. 'Black Voices Speak Up', *Time* 112 (18 December 1978), 31.

22. Betty Norwood Chaney, 'Tupelo, Hometown in Turmoil', *Southern Changes* 1(3) (1978), 18.

23. Material in the later sections of this essay is drawn (with permission) from Stephen Tuck, 'We are Taking Up Where the Movement of the 1960s Left Off', *Journal of Contemporary History* 43(4) (October 2008), 637–54.

24. 'The Gary Conference Report', *Black World/Negro Digest* (October 1972), 30.

25. Manning Marable, *Race, Reform and Rebellion: The Second Reconstruction in Black America, 1945–1982* (Jackson: University Press of Mississippi, 1984), 132.

26. Francis Njubi Nesbitt, *Race for Sanctions: African Americans against Apartheid, 1946– 1994* (Bloomington: Indiana University Press, 2004), 73.

27. Hugh Davis Graham, 'The Civil Rights Act and the American Regulatory State', in Bernard Grofman (ed.), *Legacies of the 1964 Civil Rights Act* (Charlottesville: University Press of Virginia, 2000), 53–4.

28. James Lane, 'Black Political Power and Its Limits: Gary Mayor Richard G. Hatcher's Administration, 1968–87', in David R. Colburn and Jeffrey S. Adler (eds), *African-American Mayors: Race, Politics, and the American City* (Urbana: University of Illinois Press, 2001), 63.

29. Cedric Herring (ed.), *African Americans and the Public Agenda: The Paradoxes of Public Policy* (Thousand Oaks, CA: Sage 1997), 49.

30. Colburn and Adler, *African-American Mayors*, 14.

31. 'Pushing the Klan Aside in Mississippi': wpconvo.com/pushing-the-klan-aside-in-mississippi-my-memory-of-alfred-skip-robinson-by-akinyele-umoja/; 'Seven Blacks Win Primary Votes in Mississippi Election', *Jet* (4 October 1979), 5. See also Umoja, *We Will Shoot Back*.

32. Stephen Tuck, *Beyond Atlanta: The Struggle for Racial Equality in Georgia, 1940– 1980* (Athens: University of Georgia Press, 2001), 237.

33. See Thomas J. Sugrue, 'Affirmative Action from Below: Civil Rights, the Building Trades, and the Politics of Racial Equality in the Urban North, 1945– 1969', *Journal of American History* 91(1) (June 2004), 145–73.

34. Paul Burstein, 'The Impact of EEO Law', in *Legacies of the 1964 Civil Rights Act*, 129–55.

35. Nancy MacLean, *Freedom is Not Enough: The Opening of the American Work Place* (Cambridge, MA: Harvard University Press, 2006), 86. See also Timothy J. Minchin, *Hiring the Black Worker: The Racial Integration of the Southern Textile Industry, 1960–1980* (Chapel Hill: University of North Carolina Press, 1999).

36. Tuck, *Beyond Atlanta*, 239.

37. 'Washington Coalition', *Chicago Defender* (2 February 1970).

38. Ibid.

39. MacLean, *Freedom is Not Enough*, 87.

40. Nicholas Pedriana and Robin Stryker, 'The Strength of a Weak Agency: Enforcement of Title VII of the 1964 Civil Rights Act and the Expansion of State Capacity, 1965–1971', *American Journal of Sociology* 110(3) (November 2004), 709–60.

41. *United States v. Bethlehem Steel Corp.*, 446 F.2d 652, 659 (2d Cir. 1971).
42. *Griggs v. Duke Power Co.*, 401 U.S. 424, 431 (1971).
43. Graham, 'The Civil Rights Act and the American Regulatory State', 52–4.
44. Bruce Nelson, *Divided We Stand: American Workers and the Struggle for Black Equality* (Princeton: Princeton University Press, 2001), 281.
45. James Smith and Finis Welch, 'Black Economic Progress after Myrdal', *Journal of Economic Literature* 27(2) (June 1989), 554.
46. Casey Ichniowski, 'Have Angels Done More? The Steel Industry Consent Decree', *Industrial and Labor Relations Review* 36(2) (January 1983), 182–98.
47. Gavin Wright, 'The Civil Rights Revolution as Economic History', *Journal of Economic History* 59(2) (June 1999), 277.
48. MacLean, *Freedom is Not Enough*, 103.
49. See Thomas J. Sugrue, *Origins of the Urban Crisis: Race and Inequality in Postwar Detroit* (Princeton: Princeton University Press, 2014).
50. Deborah Gray White, *Too Heavy A Load: Black Women in Defense of Themselves, 1894–1994* (New York: Norton, 1999), 215; Michael Honey, *Going Down Jericho Road: The Memphis Strike, Martin Luther King's Last Campaign* (New York: Norton, 2007), 183. Mantler, 'Black, Brown, and Poor', 119; Annelise Orleck, *Storming Caesars Palace: How Black Mothers Fought Their Own War on Poverty* (Boston: Beacon, 2005), 114.
51. White, *Too Heavy a Load*, 234.
52. 'Poor People Vow', *Jet* (4 July 1968).
53. 'Mrs Tillmon heads NWRO', *Chicago Defender* (23 January 1973).
54. White, *Too Heavy a Load*, 233.
55. Carolyn DuBose, 'Champion of Welfare Rights', *Ebony*, 25(6) (April 1970), 29.
56. 'Mrs Tillmon heads NWRO'.
57. James T. Patterson, *America's Struggle against Poverty in the Twentieth Century* (Cambridge, MA: Harvard University Press, 2000), 189.
58. Anne M. Valk, '"Mother Power": The Movement for Welfare Rights in Washington D.C., 1966–1972', *Journal of Women's History* 11(4) (Winter 2000), 40.
59. Marisa Chappell, 'Rethinking Women's Politics in the 1970s', *Journal of Women's History* 13(4) (Winter 2002), 163.
60. 'So This Is Washington', *Chicago Defender* (29 August 1970).
61. Orleck, *Storming Caesar's Palace*.
62. 'Black Focus', *Chicago Defender* (8 September 1973).
63. See Frances Fox Piven and Richard A. Cloward, *Poor People's Movements: Why They Succeed, How They Fail* (New York: Vintage, 1979).
64. Orleck, *Storming Caesar's Palace*, 261.
65. Steven Kest, 'ACORN and Community–Labor Partnerships', *Working USA* 6(4) (March 2003), 84; 'Wages of Workfare', *New York Times* (7 July 1997).
66. Cited in Todd C. Shaw, 'We Refused To Lay Down our Spears', in Ollie Johnson and Karin Stanford (eds), *Black Political Organizations in the Post-Civil Rights Era* (New Brunswick, NJ: Rutgers University Press, 2002), 183.
67. White, *Too Heavy a Load*, 216.
68. 'Blacks Declare War on Dope', *Ebony* 25(8) (June 1970).

69. See Evelyn Brooks Higginbotham, *Righteous Discontent: The Women's Movement in the Black Baptist Church, 1880–1920* (Cambridge, MA: Harvard University Press, 1993).

70. Robin Kelley and Earl Lewis, *To Make Our World Anew* (New York: Oxford University Press, 2000), 273.

71. Chappell, 'Rethinking Women's Politics', 155.

72. White, *Too Heavy a Load*, 245.

73. J. Christopher Schutz, 'The Burning of America: Race, Radicalism, and the "Charlotte Three" Trial in 1970s North Carolina', *North Carolina Historical Review* 76(1) (January 1999), 44.

74. Ibid. 53.

75. 'Black Panel Hears Claims of Crimes', *Chicago Defender* (11 February 1975).

76. 'It's Still a Plot', *Chicago Defender* (31 December 1969).

77. Kelley and Lewis, *To Make Our World Anew*, 271.

78. 'Wilmington 10 Leader', *Jet* (30 September 1976); Signe Waller, *Love and Revolution: A Political Memoir* (Lanham, MD: Rowman and Littlefield, 2002), 132.

79. See Heather Ann Thompson, *Blood in the Water: The Attica Prison Uprising of 1971 and its Legacy* (New York: Penguin, 2016).

80. Ginny Looney, 'Segregation Order at Reidsville Prison', *Southern Changes* 1(6) (1979), 19–21.

81. Bart Landry, *The New Black Middle Class* (Berkeley: University of California Press, 1987), 133; John Langston Gwaltney, *Drylongso: A Self-Portrait of Black America* (New York: Vintage, 1980).

TEN

Gay Liberation and The Spirit of '68

Simon Hall

1968 is, it seems, destined to be forever cast in popular imagination as a magical year of rebellion and revolution; an extraordinary twelve months in which students and activists took to the streets of West Berlin, Chicago, Mexico City, Paris, Prague, among other cities, occupied buildings, denounced imperialism, called for freedom and equality and dared to dream that a new and better world was possible.[1] When it comes to the United States, the contribution of New Leftists, antiwar activists, draft resisters, Black Power revolutionaries and feminists to the year's radical hue has been widely recognized. But, in both the historiography and historical memory of the gay liberation movement, 1968 remains something of a 'forgotten year', eclipsed by the drama of the Stonewall riots of June 1969 – the movement's 'Bastille Day'. Stonewall's aftermath certainly witnessed an unprecedented explosion of gay and lesbian organizing.[2] By the end of July, activists in New York had formed the Gay Liberation Front or GLF (their counterparts in other cities soon followed suit), gay newspapers, bookstores, telephone helplines and speakers' bureaus sprang up across the country, and there was an extraordinary flowering of gay culture and activism. Fifty gay rights organizations had existed in 1969; within just a few years, there were more than 800. Meanwhile, tens of thousands of gays and lesbians had become actively involved in the struggle for gay liberation.[3] Little wonder that the pioneering gay historian John D'Emilio has argued that, 'for many gay men and lesbians, the "sixties" happened in the 1970s'.[4]

In fact, at times during 1968 it appeared as if gay rights activists were marching to a markedly different beat than their counterparts in the New Left, antiwar and civil rights movements. On 4 July 1968, for instance, dozens of gay men and lesbians gathered outside Independence Hall in Philadelphia – just as they had for the previous three years – to call for equal rights.[5] Some at this 'annual reminder' quietly handed out fliers, which asked: 'Are we guaranteeing to all of our citizens the rights, the liberties, the freedom, which took birth and first form in the Declaration of Independence?'[6] A strict dress code stipulated jackets and ties for the men, and skirts for the women, and the protesters were required to behave in a dignified and orderly fashion.[7] This was a very different type of demonstration to the raucous street theatre and civil disobedience that characterized contemporaneous protests against the Vietnam War. Then, between 11 and 18 August, scores of delegates representing more than thirty organizations gathered in Chicago, for the annual convention of the North American Conference of Homophile Organizations (NACHO) – whose predilection for parliamentary procedure contrasted sharply with the chaos that engulfed the Windy City during the Democratic National Convention at the end of the month.[8] Amid the formal debates, and detailed discussions about the organization's future structure, the conference endorsed a 'Homosexual Bill of Rights'. The document reflected the liberal, integrationist approach that had been the hallmark of the so-called 'homophile movement' since the 1950s:

1. Private consensual sex between persons over the age of consent shall not be an offense.
2. Solicitation for any sexual acts shall not be an offense except upon the filing of a complaint by the aggrieved party, not a police officer or agent.
3. A person's sexual orientation or practice shall not be a factor in the granting or renewing of federal security clearances or visas, or in the granting of citizenship.
4. Service in and discharge from the Armed Forces and eligibility for veteran's benefits shall be without reference to homosexuality.
5. A person's sexual orientation or practice shall not affect his eligibility for employment with federal, state, or local governments, or private employers.[9]

Notably, the 1968 convention also adopted 'Gay is Good' as the movement's official slogan. Coined by the veteran gay rights campaigner Frank Kameny, and inspired by the 'Black is Beautiful' ethos of Black Power, 'Gay is Good' signalled the movement's increasing assertiveness, and prefigured the coming era of 'Gay Pride'.[10] Not everyone, though, was impressed. Writing to Kameny in October, Randy Wicker – a prominent gay rights activist who also ran a business that produced political buttons – complained that the slogan was 'wishy washy', 'absolutely colorless', and that it 'soft sells rather than puts the idea over with a punch'. Noting that he already produced an 'It's Great to be Straight' button, Wicker (who was unaware of his friend's involvement in coining the slogan) lamented a missed opportunity: 'why', he wondered, 'didn't they at least decide "Gay is Great"'.[11]

But for those who were looking, there were signs that the movement was beginning to embrace a more radical approach; early hints that, in its style, approach and ideology, the gay liberation movement would come to embody the revolutionary spirit of 1968.[12] Inspired by the Human Be-In that had taken place in San Francisco's Golden Gate Park in January 1967, gay activists in Los Angeles staged a series of 'Gay-Ins' during 1968. The first, which took place on Sunday 17 March (St Patrick's Day), and featured 'a throng' of several hundred homosexuals, was described by the *Advocate*'s P. Nutz as 'one of the maddest scenes of the year':

> boys in tight pants were careening on skateboards down the hairpin curves of the park like Olympic skiers. Such a group of delightfully outrageous queens I wouldn't have believed – some in rags, some in tags, and some in velvet gowns! There were lavish pants, fluffy sweaters, fur hats, beads, earrings, and flowers everywhere.

Although plans to drop several tons of sequins from a hired airplane failed to materialize, the 'flamboyant festivities' were led by 'The Duchess' – described by Nutz as a 'truly mad, mad woman' with 'finger curls, broad-brimmed bonnet, Audrey Hepburn sunglasses, and semi-psychedelic pantaloons' – who welcomed new arrivals, poured out the punch, and handed out slices of cake. Gay-Ins were joyous, fun occasions, but there was a serious political point, too. As Nutz noted, 'it was encouraging to see all these people asserting their right to gather in public for a family outing, to come out of their dark shadows of fear and paranoia, and to establish themselves as free American citizens engaged in "the pursuit of happiness"'; the second Gay-In saw participants denounce the LAPD's fondness for entrapment.[13]

A more direct, confrontational style also began to creep into gay protest. In August, when the vice squad raided *The Patch*, a popular gay bar in the Los Angeles suburb of Wilmington, its owner – the comedian Lee Glaze – leapt to the stage, declaring: 'It's not against the law to be homosexual, and it's not a crime to be in a gay bar!' Rallying the 500 or so patrons to fight for their rights, he pledged to post bail for the two men who had been arrested. A group of some two dozen activists then marched to a flower shop that was owned by one of the bar's customers, bought up all of the gladioli, mums, carnations, roses and daisies (but not the pansies) and, at 3 a.m., delivered the bouquets to the nearby police station. Two hours later, the first of the prisoners walked free, whereupon, as the *Advocate* reported, he was 'immediately covered with the bouquets, and pandemonium reigned. The same thing happened when victim number two was released a half hour later.' For the historians Lillian Faderman and Stuart Timmons, this camp demonstration of flower power signalled that gay Angelinos were no longer willing to 'accept harassment as part of the built-in cost of being gay'.[14]

The gay press, meanwhile, began to run articles that called for a more militant approach, and that advocated solidarity with African American, New Left, and antiwar activists.[15] In September 1968, for instance, the *Ladder* (published by the Daughters of Bilitis, the nation's leading lesbian organization) declared:

> The Negro has stopped running scared. He has opted for his own identity. Black is beautiful. He has nothing to lose? Everybody has something to lose. Even the poor of Appalachia, even the Mexican grape harvester. But they have a world to win. So have homosexuals. A right to walk in the sunlight of full freedom, unmasked, upright, unashamed. We are a viable minority. With an identity. With a cause . . . You can't pick up a magazine, conservative or liberal, at this moment of history and not read 'this is a time of change'.
> Are homosexuals going to let it pass them by?[16]

There were signs of change, too, on the cultural front. Writing in *New York* magazine on 23 December, the film critic Judith Crist cited the explicit love scene between Coral Browne and Susannah York in Robert Aldrich's *The Killing of Sister George* to argue that 1968 had been 'the year of the third sex . . . with girls and girls together paving the way (and seasoning the public palate) for the boys-and-boys togetherness that several of the new year's films will be concerned with'.[17] A few weeks later, in a column that adorned the front page of the *New York Times'* Arts and Leisure section, Donn Teal (writing under the pseudonym 'Ronald Forsythe') declared that 1968 had been a 'banner year' for the popular portrayal of homosexuals in culture:

Some of its films – notably 'The Killing of Sister George' and 'Queen' – dealt compassionately with the homosexual as a human being . . . 1968 even made some advances toward giving the homosexual a happy ending – 'Staircase' on Broadway last spring (and soon to be seen on film) made the greatest steps in that direction.

Nevertheless, Teal bemoaned how, in general, 'writers and producers still feared to let the public see two homosexuals happily in love', and he appealed for the arts to become more inclusive:

the American homosexual . . . does not believe his life must end in tragedy and would like to see a change in the image reflected in the entertainment he pays to see and the books he buys to read. Like any minority group, he, too, would like his 'Place in the Sun.' He has been striving for it in *life* by seeking the revocation of laws that harass him unjustly; he would like also to achieve it in the creative worlds of the novel, plays, films, music, art, and television.[18]

In calling for culture that would inspire and empower homosexuals, Teal made passing mention of the growing political activism of gay Americans. But as well as pressing for greater equality, gay people were also involved in many of the year's iconic protests. In the spring, the Student Homophile League (the nation's first officially recognized gay student group) joined the Columbia University student strike – which had erupted over the institution's links with the military and its plans to expand into the predominantly African American neighbourhood of Morningside Park. Citing the 'irresponsible and capricious use of power by the current Administration in attempts to suppress and discredit this organization', SHL called for 'student control of student organizations' and a 'student bill of rights', and demanded the resignation of the University's vice-president and provost, David B. Truman.[19]

On Saturday 7 September, as Anne Valk discusses in the following chapter, New York Radical Women staged its celebrated protest at the Miss America Pageant in Atlantic City. More than 100 feminists picketed the contest, denounced the exploitation of women, and paraded a sheep (which they later crowned 'Miss America') on the city's historic boardwalk in order to 'parody the way the contestants (all women) are appraised and judged like animals at a county fair'.[20] Cynthia Funk, who founded Radicalesbians, the pioneering feminist lesbian group, in 1970, not only played a leading role in organizing the protest, but was also assigned responsibility for returning the sheep safely to the New Jersey farm from where it had been rented![21]

Meanwhile Kiyoshi Kuromiya – an architecture student, veteran of the New Left and civil rights movements, and participant in the first 'annual reminder' – won notoriety in the spring of 1968 after organizing an antiwar demonstration in which he threatened to napalm a dog. At the end of August, he was among the thousands who protested outside the Democratic National Convention in Chicago, and was arrested for distributing a 'Fuck the Draft' poster.[22] Leo Laurence, a thirty-six-year-old reporter with San Francisco's KGO radio station, was also in Chicago, and was profoundly radicalized by what he witnessed there. Within months, he was writing for the underground *Berkeley Barb*, and was soon appointed editor of *Vector*, which was published by the Society for Individual Rights – a leading homophile organization. The cover of the April 1969 edition featured a provocative picture of Laurence's twenty-year-old lover, Gale Whittington, 'wearing nothing but low-slung cutoffs as he smiled and motioned the reader toward a bed', under the headline, 'An Invitation'. But it was what was written inside that ultimately cost Laurence his post.[23] In his piece 'Gay Revolution', Laurence denounced the homophile movement's 'timid' and egotistical middle class leaders, who were 'too afraid to become militant'. He called on all gays to 'open up', 'say you're gay at work, at home, church, wherever you go', and to 'come out from behind a double-life of straight at work and home, but gay at night'. Laurence offered his support to those who believed that '1969 is our year, it's a time to move, to be militant, to demand our rights', and lauded the new, courageous 'breed of young gay kids', who were threatening to 'really create a gay revolution'.[24]

Gay Liberation and The Spirit of '68

In the event, the 'gay revolution' that was launched (symbolically, at any rate) by the Stonewall riots swept away much of the homophile old guard amidst a new clamour for 'gay liberation'. The most famous organization to emerge in the immediate aftermath of Stonewall was New York's GLF. Founded by veterans of the New Left and antiwar movements, the organization (whose name was inspired by the National Liberation Fronts of Algeria and Vietnam) pledged solidarity with the struggles of other oppressed peoples and embraced the revolutionary rhetoric that was then all the rage.[25] The GLF memorably proclaimed that it was:

> a revolutionary homosexual group of men and women formed with the realization that complete sexual liberation for all people cannot come about unless existing social institutions are abolished. We reject society's attempt to impose sexual roles and definitions of our nature . . . We are going to be who we are. At the same time, we are creating new social forms and relations, that is, relations based upon brotherhood, cooperation, human love, and uninhibited sexuality. Babylon has forced us to commit ourselves to one thing . . . revolution.[26]

Scores of groups, with a similarly radical outlook, soon emerged in cities across the United States.[27] In Philadelphia, for instance, the GLF declared that homosexuals had 'burst their chains and abandoned their closets'. 'Battle-scarred and angry', they were now intent on overthrowing the 'sexist, racist, hateful society' and challenging 'the incredible hypocrisy of your serial monogamy, your oppressive sexual role-playing, your nuclear family, your Protestant ethic, apple pie and Mother'.[28] In Louisville, gay activists proudly declared that they were 'Freaking Fag Revolutionaries' while the Los Angeles based GLF proclaimed 'Gay Power to Gay People. Right on with the Revolution. All Power to All People'.[29]

Like the '68ers, many gay liberationists envisioned a radical new world, and they saw themselves as part of a wider movement that would transform American society. Street Transvestite Action Revolutionaries (STAR), which was founded in 1970 by two young 'street queens', Sylvia Rivera and Marsha Johnson, following a GLF occupation at New York University, demanded a 'revolutionary people's government, where transvestites, street people, women, homosexuals, puerto ricans, indians, and all oppressed people are free, and not fucked over by this government who treat us like the scum of the earth and kills us off like flies, one by one . . .'.[30] Similarly, Boston's GLF called for 'the self-government and self-determination of all peoples irrespective of national, sexual, party, race, age or other artificially imposed categories'. It also argued that, 'our liberation cannot be complete as long as any person is the property or the slave of another in any way. All coercion and dominance must end, equality must be established and we must search together for new forms of cooperation.'[31] In Houston, meanwhile, activists demanded the creation of 'people's courts' and the abolition of the nuclear family, and denounced organized religion for practising 'genocide' against homosexuals.[32]

In contrast to the single-issue politics of their homophile predecessors, gay liberationists sought to build radical coalitions that would advance their broader revolutionary agenda, and participated enthusiastically in protests organized by the Young Lords (a Puerto Rican nationalist organization), the United Farm Workers, the Black Panthers, the National Welfare Rights Organization, and other groups.[33] In September 1970, for instance, scores of gay men and lesbians joined with Yippies, Weathermen, New Leftists, feminists, antiwar activists, and black militants at the Revolutionary People's Constitutional Convention (RPCC). Its avowed purpose was to write a new American Constitution and remake the nation. Convened in Philadelphia by the Black Panther leader, Huey P. Newton, it marked the high point of gay liberationists' attempts to forge a revolutionary united front.[34]

Newton had called for an alliance between the Black Panthers and the 'revolutionary brothers and sisters' of the gay and women's liberation movements in an open letter, published in the *Black Panther* newspaper that August. Urging his followers to set aside their 'insecurities' about homosexuality and feminism, and insisting that offensive terms, such as 'faggot', 'should be deleted from our vocabulary', the Panthers' 'Supreme Commander' argued for the full inclusion of the gay and women's liberation movements in demonstrations and rallies, and enjoined his fellow Panthers to 'try to unite with them in a revolutionary fashion'.[35] During the RPCC there were some indications that the construction of what Newton had termed a 'working coalition' might be possible. On Saturday 5 September, for instance, the 'Male Homosexual Workshop' convened in a local church where, according to one report, a number of men 'dressed in drag . . . and rapped to some Panthers who came over'.[36] After several hours of discussions a manifesto was approved, which declared 'the revolution will not be complete until all men are free to express their love for one another sexually', and demanded that the 'struggle against sexism be acknowledged as an essential part of the revolutionary struggle'. It also saluted the Black Panther Party as 'the vanguard of the people's revolution in Amerikkka'. Specific demands included 'the right to be gay, any time, any place', the abolition of the nuclear family, gay representation at all levels of government, and 'that all people share equally the labor and products of society, regardless of sexual orientation'.[37] When Philadelphia's Kiyoshi Kuromiya read the statement to the assembled delegates in Temple University's gymnasium on the evening of Sunday 6 September, gay activists chanted 'Gay Power to the Gay People, Black Power to the Black People, Red Power to the Red People, Woman Power to the Women People, Children Power to the Children People' and 'Ho-Ho Homosexual, the Ruling Class is Ineffectual!' Although there were a few sniggers, Kuromiya's remarks drew enthusiastic applause; 'Dijon', an African American gay liberationist, recalled that, 'it was such a beautiful thing to hear Kiyoshi . . . and to be acknowledged by people that we considered to be our peers and even our idols'.[38]

It was, though, not all plain sailing. Among the lesbian delegates, for instance, there were widespread concerns about Panther chauvinism and militarism, and deep reservations over the party's highly masculinized brand of nationalism.[39] The demands of the 'lesbian workshop' focused on sexual autonomy, the destruction of the nuclear family, the communal care of children, and 'control of all production and industry' – including commerce, education, transport, and health facilities – 'that would ensure one hundred percent [control] over our own destinies'.[40] But they notably failed to follow their gay male counterparts in acknowledging the Panthers' leadership of the revolution. A number of lesbian feminists – citing 'threats of violence' and an 'atmosphere of sexism' – eventually walked out in disgust. As they explained, 'if women continue to struggle for their liberation within contexts defined by sexist male mentalities, they will never be free . . . we had attempted to negotiate on enemy territory and found it oppressive and unworkable.' A few months later, beset by logistical problems, state repression, and ideological splits among the Panther leadership, the RPCC project itself fizzled out.[41]

It was not just in its embrace of militant rhetoric and revolutionary politics, though, that the gay liberation movement embodied the spirit of '68. In promoting the virtues of 'coming out' – not only as a private act that would help to overcome feelings of self-loathing and low self-esteem, but as a public act that promoted gay visibility and solidarity, and challenged societal prejudice – many gay liberation activists championed the notion that the 'personal' was 'political'. The movement also sought to undermine traditional gender norms and celebrated sexual liberation, which, as the historian Marc Stein has pointed out, 'in some contexts . . . meant defending and celebrating anonymous sex, casual sex, group sex, intergenerational sex, public sex, sex work, pornography, promiscuity, sadomasochism, and sex for minors'.[42] Gay liberation activists, moreover, displayed an enthusiasm for local organizing and the building of alternative institutions (including newspapers and community centres) that owed much to the participatory democratic ethos of the 1960s New Left; some even talked about carving out 'free territory' within 'Amerika' in which gay people would be able to 'govern ourselves, set up our own institutions, defend ourselves, and use our own energies to improve our lives'.[43] Given that many of its leading lights were veterans of the antiwar and student movements, it is not surprising that gay liberation organizations also took a prominent part in protests against the war in Vietnam. Activists in Berkeley, for instance, staged a play, *No Vietnamese Ever Called Me a Queer!*, and the November 1969 Moratorium demonstrations in San Francisco saw some 15,000 gay and lesbian protesters join the chants of 'Ho Ho Ho Chi Minh, Dare to Struggle, dare to Win'.[44]

The gay liberation movement was also defined by its confrontational, colourful and theatrical protests. The Los Angeles GLF, for instance, warned cruising gay men about police surveillance by placing stickers, featuring crossbones superimposed over the head of a pig, in restrooms and on telegraph poles; picketed a restaurant until it removed a 'Fagots (sic) Stay Out' sign; 'liberated' a gay bar that vigorously enforced a 'no touching' rule; and infiltrated an international medical conference on behavioural modification. Rushing the stage at the downtown Biltmore hotel during a talk on gay aversion therapy, GLF activists shouted, 'We're sick all right – sick of having ourselves defined by sexist straight psychiatrists.'[45] In New Orleans, more than seventy GLF activists picketed City Hall to protest police entrapment and harassment. Armed with placards that declared 'Lesbians Are Loveable' and 'We're Not Freaks, We're Human', they explained how:

> Over the years, we have watched as our brothers and sisters were carried off to jail, beaten, and tortured. We have watched as judges, politicians, and police extorted millions of dollars from fearful, innocent Gay people. We have watched as agents of the Vice Squad broke all the laws they were supposedly out to enforce. We have watched silently. Now, we have had enough.[46]

In New York, activists staged a skit that saw a drag queen hand a five dollar bill to a bar owner, who passed it to an official from the State Liquor Authority, who in turn passed it on to the mafia, who gave it to a police officer. The performance ended with the officer assaulting the drag queen with his nightstick. 'Zaps' (direct action protests, usually directed at short notice against politicians and other public figures, and often involving an element of spectacle or theatre designed to generate media coverage) and 'Kiss-ins', meanwhile, became hallmarks of the gay liberation movement's tactical repertoire.[47]

From Revolution to Reform

In the event, though, the radical era of gay liberation proved to be relatively short-lived. As early as the summer of 1971 New York's GLF was in a state of near collapse. According to the sociologist and gay rights activist Laud Humphreys, by the end of the year, 'gay liberation as a branch of the New Left alliance' was 'in disarray'. In part, this reflected the wider decline of the radical movement. As John D'Emilio has put it, 'the soil that fertilized the GLF, the radicalism of the 1960s, was drying up rapidly. The belief that a revolution was imminent and that gays and lesbians should get on board was fast losing whatever momentary plausibility it had.' Indeed, as American politics shifted to the right, and as the nation endured a deepening economic crisis, radicals' room for manoeuvre quickly became heavily circumscribed.[48]

The move away from the politics of revolution was also borne of activists' personal experience. Jim Owles, of New York's GLF, recalled that when gay activists attended other demonstrations and protests,

> they went as a kind of auxiliary unit. To me, they were begging for the same kind of acceptance they had accused some of the older homosexuals of wanting . . . *And they were still getting spit at.* The word *faggot* was still being used at them. And they were relegated to 'back' roles, and were told, 'Don't come out in front! We don't want our groups to be known as homosexual things'.

The New Left, Owles declared, was 'viciously anti-homosexual'.[49]

At the end of 1969, Owles, together with three other disillusioned GLFers, founded the Gay Activists Alliance (GAA). Abandoning the chaotic, 'structureless structure' of the GLF, it adopted a conventional organizational approach, with formal rules and a paid membership. It also rejected multi-issue politics to focus 'solely and completely' on gay rights. While it pledged to confront and disarm 'all mechanisms which unjustly inhibit us: economic, social, and political', the GAA proved much more amenable than its radical predecessors to working within the existing system in order to achieve meaningful reforms. The GAA, which was one of the most important gay rights organizations of the early 1970s, provided a model for activists across the nation. As an *Advocate* editorial of September 1971 noted approvingly:

> between the hard conservatives and the intolerant radicals, young Gays are finding the middle ground productive. From coast to coast, they are building new organizations . . . The formula: just enough structure and planning to have a sound foundation but not so much that action is impossible.

The newspaper also explained that the majority of these new groups were 'limiting their activity to gay-oriented issues, rather than tackling all the world's ills at once'.[50]

Rather than seeking to create a 'people's government', or to over-throw what the GLF (NY) had denounced as 'the dirty, vile, fucked up capitalist conspiracy', the focus of much gay rights activism during the early 1970s was on political and legal reforms (especially the repeal of anti-sodomy statutes, securing legal protections against employment discrimination, and ending police harassment), securing more favourable media coverage, winning the support of professional organizations (especially those involved in science, medicine and the law), and celebrating gay identity, culture and 'pride'.[51] This narrower approach also, it should be said, more accurately reflected the political outlook of most gay men and women (many of whom were no more enthusiastic about overthrowing the American Republic than their straight friends and neighbours). As Marc Stein has put it,

> gay liberation had attracted thousands to its demonstrations and dances, but the vast majority of lesbians and gays were not radicals. Gay liberation had convinced many to come out, but most who did so came to think of themselves as members of a sexual minority group rather than radical critics of sexual categories.[52]

In the view of some, however, this more liberal, pragmatic approach came at a high cost – the exclusion of gay people of colour, those who openly defied standards of middle-class 'respectability', and other marginalized members of what would become known, by the 1990s, as the LGBT community. Bob Kohler, an African American activist and GLF supporter, claimed that:

> the dirty little secret of the gay movement is how and why the GAA was formed . . . They wanted white power. And so they let the freaks, the artists, the poets, the drag queens, the street people, the street queens, the blacks, the colored people keep the GLF. We're going to form this thing that is going to change laws. That is a good idea. Change laws. But it was mainly reformist. The vision was broken. The vision went.[53]

Nothing better encapsulates the gay liberation movement's retreat from the radical 'spirit of '68' than the fact that, in 1975, Leonard P. Matlovich – a highly decorated Air Force sergeant who had served three tours of duty in Vietnam – became a 'poster boy' for the gay rights cause. On 6 March, Matlovich wrote to his commanding officer at Langley Air Force Base to explain that, 'my sexual preferences are homosexual, as opposed to heterosexual'. He also made it clear that he would contest any move to forcibly discharge him from the armed forces. Matlovich's public challenge to the military's blanket ban on gay service personnel soon became a cause célèbre – he was interviewed by the *New York Times* and the major television networks and, in September, became the first openly gay man to appear on the front cover of *Time* magazine. Many leading gay rights strategists saw Matlovich as the ideal candidate for a test case. After all, here was a bone fide military hero (recipient of the Bronze Star and Purple Heart) who challenged widespread stereotypes of gay men as effeminate and deviant. Indeed, with the sole exception of his sexual orientation, Matlovich embodied traditional conservative values – he foreswore cigarettes and alcohol, expressed his desire to settle down in a stable and loving monogamous relationship, and extolled the virtues of the American Dream.[54] As one Associated Press report put it, 'he could be your next-door neighbor . . . He wants what you want: a decent job, a comfortable home, love.'[55] He also had an unimpeachable record of service to his nation. The National Gay Task Force (which had been founded in 1973 to lobby and advocate for gay rights), drew attention to Matlovich's distinguished military record as part of its own efforts to change the military's policy, describing him as a 'courageous man, winner of the Purple Heart and many other medals, [who] gives hope and pride to countless lesbians and gay men through his fight to integrate the armed forces and society'.[56]

Matlovich's emergence as a gay rights hero was, at one level, astonishing. Not only were many of the founders of the gay liberation movement veterans of the struggle to end the war in Vietnam, but opposition to that war – together with what the historian Justin David Suran has described as a 'radical antimilitarism' – had been integral to the creation of gay identity during the late 1960s.[57] Just three years before Matlovich appeared on the cover of *Time* magazine, for instance, Boston GLF leader Charles Shively had addressed the Platform Committee at the Democratic National Convention in Miami, dressed in a leopard-skin robe, to call for 'the *total* withdrawal of all United States and United States-supported air, land or naval forces from Vietnam' and 'an end to all aggressive armed forces'.[58] Others had argued (or simply assumed) that gay liberation was, by definition, antiwar.[59] Yet now here was Matlovich – who had fought and killed in Vietnam, who held robust views about the conflict itself ('if Vietnam was worth being there, we should have fought to win it'), and who expressed his 'love' for the military – being celebrated as the public face of the gay rights movement.[60]

While some activists viewed Matlovich as an inspiration, and saluted his courage in challenging the military's homophobia, others were appalled by the movement's support for the Air Force sergeant. Matlovich found himself denounced as a 'napalmer' and a 'baby-bomber' and heckled at rallies; some refused to support his legal challenge. Indeed, for those who held true to the radical roots of gay liberation, the whole episode represented a betrayal of the movement's founding ideals.[61] As one activist put it, 'the struggle that some gay persons seem to be undertaking to get into or remain in . . . an organization of murderers' – was 'unworthy of Gay Liberation and treasonous to our common humanity'.[62]

Conclusion: Beyond a Gay '68

Gay radicalism did not, of course, disappear. For one thing, the heyday of lesbian feminism (as embodied by groups like The Furies and Radicalesbians) actually coincided with the decline of New York's GLF and other revolutionary organizations. Moreover, the Combahee River Collective, which was committed to 'struggling against racial, sexual, heterosexual, and class oppression', and which saw its 'particular task [as] the development of integrated analysis and practice based upon the fact that the major systems of oppression are interlocking', was at its most influential during the second half of the so-called 'Me decade'.[63]

The radical strain persisted elsewhere in the movement, too. On 18 June 1977, less than two weeks after Anita Bryant's victory in overturning a gay civil rights ordinance in Dade County, Florida, Charles Shively delivered the keynote speech at Boston's gay pride parade. At a time when many gay leaders were advocating the politics of respectability to counter the growing power of the religious right, Shively issued an impassioned call to arms:

WE CANNOT COMPROMISE; WE CANNOT SINK INTO RESPECTABLITY.
Some among us may think you don't have to worry.
   those who are Christian can blame our troubles on the atheists and Jews
   those who are rich can blame our problems on the poor
   those who are white can blame the Black and Third World peoples who are in struggle
   those who are conservative can blame the radicals
   those who are well-dressed can blame the sloppy dressers
   those who are educated can blame the uneducated
   those who are alcoholics can blame the sober
   those in their closets can blame the out-front for our troubles
   those who have sex in private can blame those in public places
   those who are monogamous can blame the promiscuous
   those who are celibate can blame the sexual
   those who are bisexual can say they only did it for a lark.
We cannot remain alone and terrorized and divided. Because we face a test: a test to see who among us is the weakest, who among us will go first, who among us will be destroyed first.
   Some say let the weirdos go, and we will be safe. Perhaps let the radicals go, others say . . . Some say send the pornographers to jail.
But when the time comes, we are not going to be asked what degrees we

have, how rich we are, who we know or what we have accomplished. They will only ask, 'Are you queer?' And when they come for the queers, they are going to come for all of us. So. WE MUST COME TOGETHER OR WE WILL SURELY BE DESTROYED.[64]

During the 1980s and 1990s, meanwhile, the militant rhetoric and confrontational style of groups like ACT UP–New York and Queer Nation signalled powerful continuities with the gay liberation tradition. Queer Nation, which deployed high visibility, in-your-face protests, to protest anti-gay violence and to challenge homophobia, declared that 'Rights are not given they are taken, by force if necessary'. They also argued that:

being queer is not about a right to privacy . . . It means everyday fighting oppression; homophobia, racism, misogyny, the bigotry of religious hypocrites and our own self-hatred . . . Being queer means leading a different sort of life. It's not about the mainstream, profit-margins, patriotism, patriarchy or being assimilated. It's not about executive directors, privilege and elitism. It's about being on the margins, defining ourselves; it's about gender-f--- and secrets, what's beneath the belt and deep inside the heart; it's about the night.[65]

Nevertheless, the past twenty years have seen the growing ascendancy of the so-called 'neo-liberal' approach to gay rights – embodied by organizations like the Human Rights Campaign (HRC) and the prominent writer and blogger Andrew Sullivan. According to its critics, this approach amounts to little more than the politics of assimilation and the veneration of the mainstream.[66] In making the case for gay marriage, for instance, some activists and organizations have emphasized the importance of monogamy, commitment, stability, and responsibility – thereby echoing the arguments of conservatives, and denigrating (if only implicitly) the unmarried and those in non-conventional relationships.[67] This is, of course, a world away from gay liberationist attacks on the nuclear family 'as a microcosm of the fascist state' and vision of a society in which child rearing would be 'the common responsibility of the whole community', with parental legal rights 'dissolved' and 'each child . . . free to choose its own destiny'.[68] Meanwhile, in its attempts to secure the right of gay and lesbian Americans to serve openly in the military, the National Gay and Lesbian Task Force cast aside any doubts about US foreign policy to testify before Congress in February 2010 that, in the context of the War on Terror, 'our nation can ill-afford to squander the contributions of brave and loyal Americans who volunteer to serve in the U.S. Armed Forces'.[69] The contrast with the movement's earlier denunciations of 'Amerikan imperialism', its fierce opposition to the war in Vietnam, and its demand for the 'disbanding of all armed forces' could hardly have been more striking.[70]

The repeal of Don't Ask, Don't Tell (2010), and the Supreme Court's decision, in *Obergefell vs. Hodges* (2015), that state-level bans on same-sex marriage were unconstitutional represent landmark victories in the struggle for gay rights, and offer much cause for celebration. But for those who had once marched to chants of 'Two, four, six, eight, smash the church, smash the state!' the retreat from the 'spirit of '68' is a cause for regret.[71] Speaking in 2012, Martin Duberman lamented the fact that 'the gay movement no longer represents a genuinely transformative politics'. Criticizing the likes of HRC for prioritizing the needs of the gay white middle and upper middle classes at the expense of the poor, the black and the Latino, the veteran activist, playwright and historian voiced 'deep concern' that the contemporary gay rights movement was 'essentially devoted to winning inclusion into an unequal, greed-haunted, oppressive society'. Warning that the 'assimilationist-minded' gay rights movement was now 'in danger of becoming part of the problem', Duberman called for 'the gay movement, and the country as a whole, to refocus its agenda'. 'What is needed', he declared, 'is nothing less than a massive antiracist, pro-feminist, economic justice movement'.[72] A return, if you will, to the spirit of 1968.

Notes

1. Claire Brewster, 'Mexico 1968: A Crisis of National Identity', in Ingo Cornils and Sarah Waters (eds), *Cultural History and Literary Imagination: Memories of 1968* (Bern: Peter Lang, 2010), 149; Martin Klimke and Joachim Scharloth, '1968 in Europe: An Introduction', in Klimke and Scharloth, *1968 in Europe: A History of Protest and Activism, 1956–1977* (New York: Palgrave Macmillan,

2008), 1–2; Gerd-Rainer Horn, *The Spirit of '68: Rebellion in Western Europe and North America, 1956–1976* (Oxford: Oxford University Press, 2007), 1; Mark Kurlansky, *1968: The Year That Rocked the World* (New York: Ballantine, 2004), xvii–xix. Deborah Cohen and Lessie Jo Frazier, 'Love-In, Love-Out: Gender, Sex, and Sexuality in '68', in Cohen and Frazier(eds), *Gender and Sexuality in 1968: Transformative Politics in the Cultural Imagination* (New York: Palgrave Macmillan, 2009), 1.

2. Charles Shively, '*Fag Rag*: The Most Loathsome Publication in the English Language', in Ken Wachsberger (ed.), *Insider Histories of the Vietnam Era Underground Press, Part 2* (East Lansing: Michigan State University Press, 2012), 97. Elizabeth Armstrong and Susan M. Crage, 'Movements and Memory: The Making of the Stonewall Myth', *American Sociological Review* 71(5) (October 2006), 724–51.

3. Simon Hall, *American Patriotism, American Protest: Social Movements Since the Sixties* (Philadelphia: University of Pennsylvania Press, 2011), 34–6; John D'Emilio, 'After Stonewall', in *Making Trouble: Essays on Gay History, Politics, and the University* (New York: Routledge, 1992), 241–4; John D'Emilio, *Sexual Politics, Sexual Communities* (Chicago: University of Chicago Press, 1998), 232–9.

4. John D'Emilio, 'Placing Gay in the Sixties', *The World Turned: Essays on Gay History, Politics, and Culture* (Durham, NC: Duke University Press, 2002), 210.

5. D'Emilio, *Sexual Politics, Sexual Communities*, 223.

6. Marc Stein, *City of Sisterly & Brotherly Loves: Lesbian and Gay Philadelphia, 1945–1972* (Chicago: University of Chicago Press, 2000), 273.

7. Martha Shelley, 'Our Passion Shook the World', in Tommi Avicolli Mecca (ed.), *Smash the Church, Smash the State! The Early Years of Gay Liberation* (San Francisco: City Lights, 2009), 93.

8. 'News in Brief', *Mattachine Midwest Newsletter*, July/August 1968 (National Conference Issue), 5 in Mattachine Society, Inc. of New York Records, 1951–1976, New York Public Library, Humanities and Social Sciences Library, Manuscripts and Archives Division, microfilm edition (hereafter MSNY Records), Series II. Topical Files, Box 5, Folder 4 'North American Homophile Conference 1967–1968', reel 13; St. Sukie de la Croix, *Chicago Whispers: A History of LGBT Chicago before Stonewall* (Madison: University of Wisconsin Press, 2012), 271–2.

9. 'A Homosexual Bill of Rights', prepared and distributed by the Society for Individual Rights, in MSNY Records, Series II. Topical Files, Box 5, Folder 4 'North American Homophile Conference 1967–1968', reel 13.

10. Franklin Kameny's foreword to James T. Sears, *Rebels, Rubyfruit, and Rhinestones: Queering Space in the Stonewall South* (New Brunswick, NJ: Rutgers University Press, 2001), x.

11. Kameny to Randy Wicker and Peter Ogren, 23 August 1968, and Wicker's reply of October 2, in *Gay is Good: The Life and Letters of Gay Rights Pioneer Franklin Kameny*, ed. Michael G. Long (Syracuse, NY: Syracuse University Press, 2014), 165–6.

12. Susan Stryker, 'Militant Foreshadowings', in Mecca (ed.), *Smash the Church,*

Smash the State!, 3–9. On '1968' as a 'symbol for a far larger moment in time' or an 'idea' see Sarah Waters, 'Introduction: 1968 in Memory and Place', in Ingo Cornils and Sarah Waters (eds), *Memories of 1968: International Perspectives* (Oxford: Peter Lang, 2010), 2.

13. P. Nutz, 'Ultra High Camp at First Gay-In', in Mark Thompson (ed.), *Long Road to Freedom: The Advocate History of the Gay and Lesbian Movement* (New York: St Martin's Press, 1994), 10; Lillian Faderman and Stuart Timmons, *Gay L.A.: A History of Outlaws, Power Politics, and Lipstick Lesbians* (New York: Basic Books, 2006), 157.

14. Faderman and Timmons, *Gay L.A.*, 157–8; Bill Rand, 'Patch Raids Police Station', in Thompson, *Long Road to Freedom*, 6.

15. D'Emilio, *Sexual Politics, Sexual Communities*, 227; Rodger Streitmatter, *Unspeakable: The Rise of the Gay and Lesbian Press in America* (Boston: Faber and Faber, 1995), 82–115.

16. James Colton, 'The Homosexual Identity', *The Ladder* (September 1968), 8.

17. Judith Crist, 'The Word for the Holiday is S-x', *New York* (23 December 1968), 56.

18. Ronald Forsythe (Donn Teal), 'Why Can't "We" Live Happily Ever After, Too?', *New York Times* (23 February 1969).

19. SHL/CU #113, 'Student Homophile League Joins Strike', in MSNY Records, Series III. Gay Organizations, Box 8, Folder 3 'Student Homophile League (Columbia University) 1968–1969, reel 18; David Eisenbach, *Gay Power: An American Revolution* (New York: Da Capo, 2006), 51–79.

20. Alice Echols, *Daring to Be Bad: Radical Feminism in America, 1967–1975* (Minneapolis: University of Minnesota Press, 1989), 92–3.

21. Ibid. 214–17. Ellen Shumsky, 'The Radicalesbian Story: An Evolution of Consciousness' and 'The Woman Identified Woman Manifesto', in Mecca (ed.), *Smash the Church, Smash the State!*, 190–202; 'Funk, Cynthia Ellen (1941–), in Barbara J. Love (ed.), *Feminists Who Changed America, 1963–1975* (Champaign: University of Illinois Press, 2007), 164.

22. Liz Highleyman, 'Kiyoshi Kuromiya: Integrating the Issues', in Mecca (ed.), *Smash the Church, Smash the State!*, 17–19; Roger Vaughan, 'The Defiant Voices of SDS', *Life* (18 October 1968), 90, 92.

23. D'Emilio, *Sexual Politics, Sexual Communities*, 230; Strietmatter, *Unspeakable*, 99–100.

24. Leo E. Laurence, 'Gay Revolution', *Vector* (April 1969), 11, 25.

25. Hall, *American Patriotism, American Protest*, 35.

26. Stephan L. Cohen, *The Gay Liberation Youth Movement in New York: 'An Army of Lovers Cannot Fail'* (New York: Routledge, 2008), 26–7.

27. Marc Stein, *Rethinking the Gay and Lesbian Movement* (New York: Routledge, 2012), 82.

28. Stein, *City of Sisterly & Brotherly Loves*, 322.

29. Sears, *Rebels, Rubyfruit, and Rhinestones*, 61; Faderman and Timmons, *Gay L.A.*, 172.

30. Cohen, *The Gay Liberation Youth Movement in New York*, 2, 37.

31. Charles Shively, '*Fag Rag*', 103.

32. Sears, *Rebels, Rubyfruit, and Rhinestones*, 64.

33. Stein, *Rethinking*, 88.
34. Stein, *City of Sisterly & Brotherly Loves*, 330-1; Hall, *American Patriotism, American Protest*, 18-19.
35. Huey P. Newton, 'A Letter from Huey to the Revolutionary Brothers and Sisters About the Women's Liberation and Gay Liberation Movements' (21 August 1970), in Mark Blasius and Shane Phelan (eds), *We Are Everywhere: A Historical Sourcebook of Gay and Lesbian Politics* (New York: Routledge, 1997), 404-6.
36. Stein, *City of Sisterly & Brotherly Loves*, 333-4.
37. 'Statement of the Male Homosexual Workshop' (1970), Revolutionary People's Constitutional Convention, in Blasius and Phelan (eds), *We Are Everywhere*, 402-3.
38. Stein, *City of Sisterly & Brotherly Loves*, 334.
39. Ibid. 335-7.
40. 'Demands of the Lesbian Workshop' (1970), RPCC, in Blasius and Phelan (eds), *We Are Everywhere*, 403-4.
41. Stein, *City of Sisterly & Brotherly Loves*, 336, 338, 339-40.
42. Stein, *Rethinking*, 84.
43. Carl Wittman, 'A Gay Manifesto' (1970), in Karla Jay and Allen Young (eds), *Out of the Closets: Voices of Gay Liberation* (New York: New York University Press, 1992), 339.
44. Stein, *Rethinking*, 85; D'Emilio, *Making Trouble*, 242; Randy Shilts, *Conduct Unbecoming: Lesbians and Gays in the U.S. Military, Vietnam to the Persian Gulf* (New York: St Martin's, 1993), 96.
45. Faderman and Timmons, *Gay L.A.*, 172, 174-77.
46. Sears, *Rebels, Rubyfruit, and Rhinestones*, 71.
47. Stein, *Rethinking*, 86, 89, 98.
48. Elizabeth A. Armstrong, *Forging Gay Identities: Organizing Sexuality in San Francisco, 1950-1994* (Chicago: University of Chicago Press, 2002), 90-1; Stein, *Rethinking*, 79, 90.
49. Armstrong, *Forging Gay Identities*, 93-4.
50. Ibid. 97.
51. Stein, *Rethinking*, 100-14. GLF quotation from D'Emilio, 'After Stonewall', 242.
52. Stein, *Rethinking*, 90.
53. Armstrong, *Forging Gay Identities*, 95.
54. Simon Hall, 'Leonard Matlovich: From Military Hero to Gay Rights Poster Boy', in Simon Wendt (ed.), *Warring over Valor: How Race and Gender Shaped American Military Heroism in the Twentieth and Twenty-First Centuries* (New Brunswick, NJ: Rutgers University Press, forthcoming).
55. Michael Bedwell, 'And a Discharge for Loving One – 34 Years and Counting: Leonard Matlovich', *Gay Military Signal: The Voice of the Military Rainbow Community*, 2009, available at: www.gaymilitarysignal.com/0907Bedwell.html
56. 'Join The People of NGTF', advertisement printed in *The Advocate* (19 October 1977), 25. Stein, *Rethinking*, 114.
57. Justin David Suran, 'Coming Out Against the War: Antimilitarism and the Politicization of Homosexuality in the Era of Vietnam', *American Quarterly* 53(3) (September 2001), 456-9, 463-4.

58. 'Boston GLF's 10-Point Demands Presented to the Democratic Convention in Miami Beach, July 1972', in Shively, 'Fag Rag', 103.

59. Allen Young, 'Out of the Closets, Into the Streets' (1971), in Jay and Young (eds), Out of the Closets, 20.

60. Hall, 'Leonard Matlovich'.

61. Ibid.

62. Neil Miller, 'Anti-military Backlash Surfaces', Gay Community News (27 December 1975), 3. John Kyper, 'Largest Conference Ever', Gay Community News (13 December 1975), 1.

63. Yamissette Westerband, 'Lesbian Feminism': sitemaker.umich.edu/lesbian. history/lesbian_feminism

64. Shively, 'Fag Rag . . .', 110. On the hostile conservative political climate see, Martin Duberman, 'Feminism and the Gay Academic Union (GAU)', in The Martin Duberman Reader (New York: The New Press, 2013), 269, and Stein, Rethinking, 115–17, 138–42.

65. Queer Nation Manifesto, 1990, available at: www.actupny.org/documents/ QueersReadThis.pdf

66. Lisa Duggan, The Twilight of Equality? Neoliberalism, Cultural Politics, and the Attack on Democracy (Boston: Beacon Press, 2003), 50. Martin Duberman, 'Coda: Acceptance at What Price? The Gay Movement Reconsidered' (acceptance speech for Kessler Award from Center for Lesbian and Gay Studies, 5 December 2012), in Duberman Reader, 365–66.

67. Lisa Duggan, 'Holy Matrimony!' (2004), in Lisa Duggan and Nan D. Hunter, Sex Wars: Sexual Dissent and Political Culture (New York: Routledge, 2006), 227–8. Duberman, 'Coda', 368; Andrew Sullivan, 'Here Comes the Groom: A (Conservative) Case for Gay Marriage', The New Republic, 28 August 1989.

68. 'Demands of the Lesbian Workshop' (1970); 'Boston GLF's 10-Point Demands'.

69. Testimony of the National Gay and Lesbian Task Force Action Fund For the Hearing: 'Don't Ask, Don't Tell' Policy, Committee on Armed Services United States Senate, Room SD-G50, Dirksen Senate Office Building Tuesday, 2 February 2010 available at: www.thetaskforce.org/static_html/downloads/ release_materials/tf_dadt_020210.pdf

70. 'Boston GLF's 10-Point Demands . . .'; Chicago Gay Liberation, 'Working Paper for the Revolutionary People's Constitutional Convention' (1970), in Jay and Young (eds), Out of the Closets, 346.

71. Mecca, 'Introduction', in Mecca (ed.), Smash the Church, Smash the State!, xi.

72. Duberman, 'Coda', 368, 369, 371.

ELEVEN

Women's Movements in 1968 and beyond

Anne M. Valk

On 7 September 1968 members of New York Radical Women gathered activists in Atlantic City, New Jersey, to protest the annual Miss America pageant. Several hundred women gathered on the boardwalk to 'protest the image of Miss America, an image that oppresses women in every area in which it purports to represent us'.[1] Although the organizers refused to communicate with male reporters, they garnered extensive publicity through brilliant use of guerrilla theatre. They paraded sheep down the boardwalk before crowning one the new Miss America, hoping to show how the contest displayed and judged women like farm animals at a county fair. Women set up a 'Freedom Trash Can' into which they threw girdles, bras and other restrictive clothing; make-up and other so-called beauty products; and popular publications that targeted women readers through selling cosmetic or domestic products or exploited them for men's sexual pleasure. From inside the pageant hall, television cameras rolled as protestors draped a large women's liberation banner over a balcony.[2] Journalists claimed the Miss America protesters had burned their bras; even though the reports mischaracterized what occurred, the 'bra-burner' label stuck. One otherwise sympathetic commentator, for example, described women's liberation movement participants as women who 'give up make-up; a lot of them fret over whether to give up depilation in favor of furry legs. A few of them are a bouncy-looking lot, having given up diets and foundation garments. And virtually all of those in the movement light their own cigarettes and open their own doors.'[3]

Figure 11.1 'Freedom Trash Can', Miss America protest, Atlantic City, New Jersey, September 1968. Alix Kates Shulman Papers, David M. Rubenstein Rare Book and Manuscript Library, Duke University. Photograph copyright Alix Kates Shulman.

The Miss America demonstration now is considered an iconic event of the post-World War II feminist movement. At the time, the protest received wide coverage by journalists, mostly dismissive in tone. It also became the subject of extensive analysis in the nascent feminist press, where it was lauded for 'launch[ing] Women's Liberation in the public consciousness'.[4] In the years since, feminist activists and women's historians solidified the action's importance in subsequent publications. Robin Morgan's 1970 groundbreaking anthology *Sisterhood is Powerful* reprinted the demands issued by the New York Radical Women in a section of 'Historical Documents'.[5]

Nearly ten years later, in one of the movement's first book-length histories, Sara M. Evans called the protest the 'explosive debut' of the 'new feminist movement'.[6] Over time other scholars have continued to recognize the importance of the protest in garnering attention for women's liberation and demonstrating activists' media savvy. Estelle Freedman, in her sweeping history of feminism, described the protest as the 'first publicity coup' of US radical feminists and cited it as an example of activists' realization that issues related to 'women's bodily confinement' could generate attention in the press and help expand their movement. Historian Ruth Rosen noted that the demonstration showed how mass media became a double-edged sword for feminists: on the one hand, the pageant 'seemed to sum up everything these women rejected – woman as spectacle, woman as object, woman as consumer, woman as artificial image' – but, on the other hand, the media's focus on bras was a 'sexy trope' that typified how corporations used female sexuality to sell products.[7]

'Feminist Movements, Plural': Liberals, Radicals and More

By shaping the depiction of feminism in the United States, the Miss America protest brought attention to many of the demands and tactics of one branch of the movement. Women's liberation was the emerging ideology of a generation of women who had become politically active in New Left, antiwar and civil rights movements earlier in the decade. New York Radical Women (NYRW), organizers of the Atlantic City protest, along with other self-defined women's liberation groups, focused on eradicating sexism through upending marriage, heterosexuality, family, childrearing and childbearing, and other relations that perpetuated unequal power between women and men. Insisting that the 'personal is political', they scrupulously examined their own experiences as fodder for an analysis of women's oppression, a process known as consciousness raising. Mostly white and young, these 'bouncy' activists established hundreds of new groups – generally small and decentralized in structure – that became places where feminists could read, write and plan actions designed to spread their ideas and topple patriarchy.

In their analysis of women's oppression, women's liberationists (often called radical feminists) stood ideologically apart from so-called liberal feminists, such as those in the National Organization for Women (NOW). Founded in fall 1966, NOW billed itself as a civil rights organization for women and prioritized women's equality in law and the economy. Fuelled by a powerful vision statement laid out by Betty Friedan and Pauli Murray, in its first two years NOW coordinated pickets at corporations that discriminated in their hiring and employment practices. NOW's members, women and men, campaigned particularly to end newspapers' use of sex-segregated job listings by lobbying the newly formed Equal Employment Opportunity Commission to outlaw this practice. In contrast to NOW, other feminists struggled internally over questions of whether to build a separate women's movement. Was it more politically expedient to organize within the left, tackling capitalism as the cause of women's oppression, as many so-called politicos advocated? Or should women's liberation be subsumed in the fight against race-based oppression, poverty or other social inequities? If women organized separately around their own liberation, how would that impact the other movements and causes they supported? To what extent did women constitute a specific class or caste that faced sex-based discrimination that transected their other differences? And, if so, could 'sisterhood' become a source of solidarity and community among women? Becoming the 'most vital and imaginative force within the women's liberation movement', one scholar has claimed, radical feminism 'succeeded in pushing liberal feminists to the left and politicos toward feminism'.[8]

In 1968, such debates over the meaning of women's liberation and strategies to gain women's rights proliferated with dizzying speed and enormous consequences. The multiple streams that made up the women's movement become apparent when reconsidering the demands expressed by NYRW in Atlantic City and by examining other events in 1968. Of course, any attempt to recount the events of a historical period, especially in a short essay, will inevitably be selective. As with other topics in this volume, delimiting the women's movement to a single year risks over-accentuating the importance of these episodes or elevating the significance of a short phase that had been long in unfolding and broad in its goals. That is not my point. Instead, by examining three specific moments, I aim to suggest how the events of 1968 reveal many of the currents then shaping women's demands for rights and equality under the law, as well as the social and cultural changes that feminists hoped to precipitate. These influences include both intersections and links across organizations as well as fissures that separated those organizing to expand women's economic, social and political opportunities. Emerging, converging and diverging in the late 1960s, these strands all made up the women's movement of that era.

Making the Miss America protest central to the birth of women's liberation overemphasizes the centrality of radical feminism to the larger movement. It also perpetuates a view that feminists prioritized life-style choices – the right to go braless, for instance – over more transformative structural and cultural changes to expand women's opportunities and shift gender relations. In addition, this narrative of second-wave feminism eclipses other synchronous events that contributed to the political streams shaping the movement for women's rights in the 1960s and 1970s. Over the past decade, careful scholarship has transformed the prevailing historical narrative of so-called second-wave feminist activism in the United States. Looking at individual communities and singular groups, historians have complicated the chronology, composition, theories and methods that drove feminist activists. Although the media concentrated on a small number of white 'movement stars', including Betty Friedan, the first president of NOW, and Gloria Steinem who started *Ms.* Magazine, feminism's vibrant growth took place due to the energies of thousands of women working at the local level and often dodging media attention. At this level, the movement varied greatly in Dayton, Memphis, Gainesville, Minneapolis and Washington DC, for example, as activists came together to address local issues, bringing with them distinctive ideas about the most effective ways to make change.[9] The struggle for abortion rights, for instance, spread throughout the country, but before the Supreme Court's decision in *Roe v. Wade* (1973), access to abortion varied widely depending on state legislation and the practices of individual hospitals. Without a national organization dedicated to fighting for abortion rights and facing a patchwork of state rights, feminists primarily worked in city or state-wide groups to reform and over-turn restrictive laws.[10]

Through short-term alliances and inter-organizational coalitions, activists often blurred the boundaries that separated diverse strands of feminist thought in order to tackle specific issues including ending sexual violence and abortion rights.[11] Other scholars have offered histories of black feminism that challenge its depiction as an offshoot of, and response to, white feminism. African American women such as Florynce Kennedy, Pauli Murray, Shirley Chisholm and Aileen Hernandez joined NOW in its early years. Other women of colour joined predominantly white women's groups and took part in feminist campaigns in the 1960s.[12] In addition, as Kimberly Springer, Benita Roth and others have shown, a distinctive black and Third World feminism emerged simultaneously with radical feminism. Despite their willingness to tackle gender oppression, many feminist women of colour rejected articulations of feminism that subsumed differences of race and economic status to a search for universal sisterhood. Instead, they built a movement that oper-ated largely independently of white feminists, often working within the context of mixed-sex organizations. Feminists of colour played an important role in advancing theoretical understandings of the ways that race and class both compounded and distinguished the kinds of oppression women of colour experienced.[13]

Historians' recognition of the presence of African American, Chicana and Asian activists, as well as those coming from labour, religious and welfare organizations, has shed light on a new cast of participants into the 1960s women's movement and showed how feminist ideas were both developed and reinterpreted by other concurrent movements.[14] Together, this scholarship has provided complex evidence of a feminist movement extended over time and with divergent streams. Historian Nancy Hewitt surmised that:

> in the 1960s and 1970s, campaigns for welfare rights and economic-jus-tice issues occurred alongside and in collaboration with the more famil-iar feminist movements; working-class women and women of colour played central roles in defining and challenging sexual harassment and other forms of workplace discrimination; and battles over pornography, prostitution, and lesbian rights erupted locally and nationally.[15]

As a result of these many influences, feminism developed as a multi-pronged movement, encompassing diverse understandings, and often conflictual understanding, about the causes of and solutions to women's oppression. As Roth concluded, travelling 'separate roads' in the 1960s and 1970s, activists produced 'feminist movements, plural'.[16]

From Woman Power to Women's Liberation

These multiple threads were very much in evidence in 1968. As other chapters in this volume detail, it was a time when world and national events demanded activists' passionate and urgent responses. Like their political brothers, women made up the foot soldiers of the black freedom, American Indian, and free speech movements, the community workers fighting a war on poverty, the crowds protesting against the war in Vietnam and the US military build-up, and the pioneers of the sexual revolution. Participation in these campaigns gave women chances to hone both their skills as political organizers and their understanding of political theory. They also sharpened their anger at inequality and injustice, including the sexism they sometimes experienced in the New Left, antiwar, and student movements and in society more generally.[17] Those women who aspired to tackle sexism in public life or to otherwise improve women's opportunities and civic participation could turn to numerous organizations that had worked for decades to represent women's interests. The National Women's Party, for example, had helped to secure woman suffrage in 1920 and it continued to push Congress to pass an Equal Rights Amendment that would eliminate sex-specific references in laws.[18] Gender equality was advanced, too, by passage in 1964 of the Civil Rights Act, in which Title VII banned discrimination in employment whether on racial or gender grounds. The National Council of Negro Women, the Women's International League for Peace and Freedom, the League of Women Voters and myriad religious, labor and community groups had mobilized women to work on behalf of the betterment of their communities and established the validity of women's civic participation, even if their efforts also revealed how race and class differences made it impossible to articulate any shared set of 'women's interests'. When NOW and NYRW formed at the end of the 1960s, they benefitted from and aimed to build on – and go beyond – such previous accomplishments.[19]

For groups dedicated to uniting women around any cohesive feminist agenda, the year began inauspiciously. In mid-January, Women Strike for Peace (WSP) convened women in Washington DC, to show their opposition to the war in Vietnam. Since its founding in 1960, WSP had campaigned for cessation of the US arms build-up in response to the Cold War. The march at the start of 1968 was deliberately designed to broaden this campaign by pulling in women civil rights activists, church women and young militants. Exemplifying this reach, a number of prominent women agreed to sponsor the protest, including black feminist lawyer Flo Kennedy and civil rights activists Ella Baker, Rosa Parks, Coretta Scott King and Fannie Lou Hamer, along with celebrities and wives of male celebrities, elected politicians, and labour and religious leaders. Reflecting this broader constituency, the WSP connected the human and economic costs of the war to issues of domestic poverty; surprisingly, however, it failed to recognize how lack of opportunity particularly pressed men of colour into military service. About 5000 women – named the Jeanette Rankin Brigade in honour of the pacifist congresswoman (the first to serve in a high elected government office) – showed up to exercise their 'Woman Power'. Dressed in black for mourning, they demanded that the new Congress act quickly to 'end the war in Vietnam, use its power to heal a sick society at home, make reparation for the ravaged land we leave behind in Vietnam, and refuse the insatiable demands of the military-industrial complex'.[20] Despite WSP's effort to build an inclusive Brigade, tensions among participants unsettled the day's action. Initial disagreement focused on organizers' choice of tactics. Politicos, militant women coming from the New Left, draft resistance and antiwar movements, considered Congress ineffectual and engagement with elected officials unlikely to change the nation's military course. On the day of the Brigade, however, the most disruptive disagreements related to a broader question: should women be organizing to stop the war or to end their own oppression?[21]

For feminists, the Jeannette Rankin Brigade proved a critical moment when the attempt to unite women around a common agenda – in this case, the role of women in the antiwar movement – resulted in a noticeable fracturing. Differing in theory, methods and experiences, WSP women parted ways with radical activists about the role of women in the antiwar movement and in society more broadly. In particular, radicals objected to WSP's maternalist approach to politics. 'Until women go beyond justifying themselves in terms of their wombs and breasts and housekeeping abilities', a statement released by women's liberationists from Chicago and New York argued, 'they will never be able to exert any political power'.[22] Disagreeing with WSP's emphasis on women's traditional roles, radical young women from NYRW and other groups broke off to hold their own counter-demonstration. Employing dramatic tactics, the counter-demonstrators staged a theatrical funeral procession meant to signify the burial of traditional womanhood. The struggle to end the war in Vietnam also needed to incorporate a struggle to change gender roles and to catalyse women to muster a fuller range of personal and political power.[23]

Marilyn Salzman Webb, who attended the Brigade, considered it a failure from which women could learn valuable lessons. 'It attempted national action based on a coalition without a base', Webb concluded. She went on to stress that,

in order for a coalition of women to ever work in the future we as radical women have to organize ourselves so we have a clearly defined sense of who we are and what we represent . . . We need power; we need a base; and most of all, we need to develop an analysis of ourselves in a society that is oppressive to everybody.[24]

After the Rankin Brigade members of NYRW, Webb, and other radicals attempted to build this base by mobilizing a separate women's liberation movement. At the national convention of Students for a Democratic Society in June, they demanded that SDS incorporate a demand for women's liberation into its priorities. The hostile response they received provided more evidence that women needed to organize independently to combat sexism, including sexism coming from within leftist organizations. Connected by personal relationships built through participation in antiwar, New Left and black freedom campaigns, the women's liberationists saw themselves as the radical branch of a larger feminist movement. In this way they parted from WSP, which remained largely outside of this movement. But the event planted seeds of feminist consciousness within WSP. By 1970, WSP joined in events organized by feminist organizations including NOW and explicitly identified as part of both the women's movement and the antiwar movement.[25]

The Brigade established a pattern that recurred throughout 1968 when moments of convergence among women activists resulted in a sense of greater divergence. Acutely aware of race, class and ideological distinctions among women, activists nonetheless sought commonalities that could be the basis of a unified movement. Many movement participants and other observers found in these divisions signs of weakness: intellectual confusion that left the women's movement open to criticism from the general public and from male comrades in movements for black freedom and the New Left. Disagreements about whether women's oppression could be the basis of its own movement produced anxious analyses about the sources of conflict and ways to resolve it. Marlene Dixon, a scholar and participant in Chicago's women's liberation movement in the late 1960s, observed that in 1968 movement events were characterized by struggles 'between totally rebellious "independent" women and the radical women who work primarily within women's caucuses' of the New Left. She referred to these divisions as '"consciousness raising" vs. "radical" or "bourgeois" vs. "revolutionary" camps'. Dixon concluded that this conflict would lead liberalism to transcend within the new women's movement. 'Unless the radical women get themselves together, in the interests of their own oppression and the oppression of all their sisters', Dixon predicted, 'a mass movement dominated by an ideology of "let us in" (and not "set us free") will develop in the next few years'.[26] Journalist Martha Lears, writing about the rise of second-wave feminism for the *New York Times*, similarly noted divisions in 1968 but without Dixon's radical bias. She explained to the paper's readers that the pragmatic 'evolutionaries' of NOW focused on 'concrete issues, tied primarily to employment'. In contrast, radicals who had split off from SDS and other leftist groups were the movement's 'theoreticians – atypical but they are interesting because they are the movement's intellectual hip, the female version of

Black Power'. Equating radical feminists with participants in organizations such as the Black Panther Party, Lears captured the fervour and militant style that both groups shared. But her categorization may have oversimplified the pragmatic and political distinctions swirling within feminism; and Lears's assessment definitely overlooked the presence of women who simultaneously allied with Black Power and radical feminist movements. To Lears, such divisions perhaps explained why feminism had the distinct burden to be 'the only civil-rights movement in history which has been put down, consistently, by the cruelest weapon of them all – ridicule'.[27]

Although such differences caused confusion, they also reflected the vitality of the movement. Feminism was fertile if not unified, thanks to hearty debates, an influx of new participants, the growth of new organizations and a blossoming women's media. Political disagreements, even with others who identified as feminist, spurred activists to refine their goals and approaches. Moreover, despite being fervent such differences seldom created an impassable barrier between organizations or concurrent movements. Instead, ideas about theory and tactics spread from group to group, and sometimes activists with common or compatible goals but opposing approaches to social change showed up to support and learn from each other's campaigns. Rather than diluting feminism, this dynamic broadened and expanded it.[28]

Five months after the Brigade, on 12 May, women assembled in Washington DC for the start of the Poor People's Campaign. The initiative had been called by Martin Luther King, Jr. and it proceeded despite his assassination the month before. King's organization, the Southern Christian Leadership Conference (SCLC), spearheaded the campaign, signalling a shift from race-based discrimination as a focus of civil rights to economic issues, especially widespread American poverty. As Reverend Ralph Abernathy, who succeeded Dr King as president of the SCLC, explained of the campaign: 'What does it profit a man if he has the right to eat at a lunch counter, if he can't pay the bill?'[29] Thousands of participants from across the country came to an encampment on the Mall where their temporary presence could force the nation and its elected officials to see the many problems resulting from poverty, including a lack of food, healthcare and housing, substandard schools and high unemployment. The campaign intended to emphasize, too, that poverty existed in urban and rural areas and was shared by people of all races.

The Poor People's Campaign did not, however, call particular attention to poverty as a women's issue. But leaders of the new National Welfare Rights Organization (NWRO) played a central role in voicing the concerns of poor women and ensuring that the larger march incorporated their perspectives. Meeting with Dr King and other SCLC representatives prior to the campaign's start, activists in NWRO insisted that welfare issues must be included in the campaign for poor people's rights. It is significant that NWRO did not then define itself as a women's or feminist organization. Founded in DC in 1967, NWRO members – mostly black women who received welfare benefits including food stamps and other assistance with the cost of raising their children – framed the struggle for welfare reform as intimately linked to their roles as mothers and the heads of families. NWRO deemed the welfare system 'anti-mother' because it provided insufficient assistance and forced recipients to prove their eligibility for benefits by putting up with requirements that destabilized their families, limited their rights as parents, and demeaned them as women. NWRO did not seek to reject 'traditional womanhood', as radicals at the Jeanette Rankin Brigade had; neither did they completely embrace WSP's depiction of women solely as mothers and wives. Instead, NWRO members recognized that racism and poverty, as well as sexism, restricted their opportunities. By acting collectively, they sought to ensure that poverty and dependence on welfare did not rob women of their right to decide whether to be mothers and how to balance work and family life.[30]

As impoverished men, women and children streamed in from across the country, the Poor People's Campaign kicked off with a Mother's Day march organized by the NWRO. While honouring mothers, the event also focused on the particular role that women could, and should, shoulder in the movement against poverty. That day some 4000 to 5000 women paraded through the capital, led by Coretta Scott King, recently widowed after the murder of her husband. In her address to the crowd, King called on 'black women, white women, brown women and red women – all the women of this nation' to join a 'campaign of conscience' to ameliorate poverty and expand opportunities for low-income Americans. That campaign should include serious efforts to reform the welfare system, King declared, urging women to pressure Congress to repeal newly enacted welfare requirements that made it more difficult for families to qualify for assistance while lowering benefits. Marchers organized by NWRO carried signs calling for 'Bread and Justice, Now', 'Income, Dignity, Justice, Democracy', and, following King's theme, asserting 'Woman Power'. Leaders of other women's organizations also joined the march. Betty Friedan, a founder of NOW and author of the groundbreaking *The Feminine Mystique* in 1963, carried a sign urging 'Free Women from Poverty Now'. Marchers also represented Women Strike for Peace and two organizations established decades earlier, the Women's International League for Peace and Freedom and the National Council for Negro Women. The self-defined women's liberation groups did not have a visible role in the march, although individual activists affiliated with such groups no doubt participated.[31]

Despite NWRO's prominence in the Mother's Day march and subsequent actions, including marches outside of the Capitol, the overall Poor People's Campaign paid little attention to women's specific demands or the cause of welfare reform.[32] The campaign nonetheless helped integrate welfare issues into the larger women's rights agenda. A Women's Bill of Rights composed by NOW during the summer of 1968, for example, demanded revision of welfare laws and jobs programmes to make them more favourable for poor women. Women should be able to seek job training and welfare allowances 'without prejudice to a parent's right to remain at home to care for her children; there should be revision of welfare legislation and poverty programs which deny women dignity, privacy, and self-respect', the document avowed, echoing NWRO's own arguments.[33]

NWRO's involvement in the 'Woman Power' movement within the Poor People's Campaign showed the welfare organization's growing influence; their participation also gave welfare activists the opportunity to coalesce with a wide array of civil rights and women's groups. For NWRO, such opportunities became part of its gradual shift to a more explicitly feminist stance. As historian Premilla Nadasen has shown, by 1970 black welfare activists in NWRO put forth an insightful critique of the welfare system and the ways in which it controlled and regulated the sexuality and lives of women. Even welfare activists who were more reluctant to identify as feminists nevertheless articulated economic demands that increasingly asserted a critique of gender roles, patriarchy, and proscribed sexuality.[34]

Miss America Reconsidered

Within this context of mounting conversations – and disagreements – about the meaning of women's liberation and the role of women within movements for economic and racial opportunity and against the war, the NYRW planned its action against the Miss America pageant. Putting this now iconic event within a broader framework makes clear that the Atlantic City protest was exceptional in several ways. Most of the women in attendance were white and young, although it included some older women and some African American women, including activist-lawyer Flo Kennedy, one of the notable endorsers of the Rankin Brigade, who helped plan the protest. Men, however, were excluded from joining in the protest and organizers vowed to only give interviews to women journalists. In addition, the Miss America protest did not bring together women for a public march through city streets or target public policy. Instead NYRW organizers used guerrilla theatre and other dramatic and humorous 'zap actions' to attack the pageant promoters and to seize people's attention.[35]

Most strikingly, the Miss America protest rejected the notion of 'woman power' based in women's domestic and familial roles and instead directly opposed these roles and the culture that perpetuated them. The ten-point list of demands that NYRW released focused especially on ways that consumerist beauty culture objectified women and elevated Miss America as an ideal to which all women should subscribe. Most women of colour could not attain this stature – none had ever been selected as a Miss America finalist and women who were not young or who were too 'tall, short, over or under ... weight' didn't match the standards by which contestants were judged. The ideal also forced women into competition with each other, striving to win men's approval. Protestors linked the exploitation and objectification of women to racism and militarism, too, arguing that Miss America represented a 'mascot for murder', trotted out by the US military to entertain troops and therefore support the nation's wars.[36]

The Miss America protest generated both enthusiasm and criticism from movement activists. One of the NYRW organizers recalled that the event catalysed a lot of positive action: 'We were deluged with letters, more than our small group could possibly answer . . . Taking the Women's Liberation Movement in to the public consciousness gave some women the nudge they needed to form their own groups. They no longer felt so alone and isolated.'[37] But on reflection, organizers also faulted some of the tactics employed to protest the 1968 pageant. In particular, they believed the protest blamed women for their quest of the feminine ideal rather than focusing on the systems that forced women to desire it. Zap actions might be effective in getting attention and conveying messages to men, but they would not topple patriarchy, they concluded. Other activists believed the event risked trivializing the cause. To NOW president Betty Friedan, the protest focused attention on cultural and social issues and detracted from more serious demands for economic and educational opportunities or legal equality for women.[38]

Like the Mother's Day March, the protest also revealed the complicated relationship that African American women had to feminism. Flo Kennedy worked hard to recruit other black women and supporters. Yet the media generally overlooked their presence.[39] In addition, some activists objected that the protest ignored the significance of a Miss Black America pageant that took place only four blocks away. A first of its kind, that pageant embraced some aspects of feminine beauty culture but also defied the stereotypes that Miss America endorsed. Unmoved by the feminist critique of the pageant, winner Saundra Williams nonetheless shared some of NYRW's criticisms when she explained, 'Miss America does not represent us because there has never been a black girl in the pageant'. In contrast, her crown conveyed the message that African American women are also 'beautiful, even though they do have large noses and thick lips'.[40] By failing to acknowledge that Miss Black America constituted an achievement in the movement for racial equality, the pageant protest inadvertently suggested that feminism and black liberation were at odds.

The following September, 200 women returned to Atlantic City for a repeat action against the Miss America pageant. This time pageant officials and law enforcement were prepared to contain the protest. Police seized activists' posters and issued an injunction preventing congregating outside the convention hall and other disruptive activities including public burning of materials and the use of loud or offensive language. Without the novelty and dramatic flair of the first protest, the 1969 event failed to gain much visibility. The women's movement also had changed in the intervening year. Public demonstrations and heightened media contributed to a growth in feminism, with an estimated 10,000 to 50,000 active women's groups in cities and universities across the land.[41] This number included the Black Women's Liberation Caucus, a subgroup within the Student Non-violent Coordinating Committee that formed in 1968 (renamed the Third World Women's Alliance), focused on fighting the combined forces of racism, sexism and imperialism.[42] Membership in NOW numbered about 1200, about one-third coming from the New York City chapter.[43] Similarly, membership in NWRO swelled, climaxing in 1968 with 30,000 members and dwarfing its feminist counterparts.[44]

Yet even as the women's movement grew in visibility and size, activists continued to raise the kinds of questions asked in 1968 regarding the commonality of women's experiences and the best strategies for achieving change. By the early 1970s, activists' analyses had grown more complicated and subsumed a greater range of priorities and approaches. If women were constrained to particular roles – 'secretary, sexpot, sow, spender, civic actor and sickie' in the words of radical Marilyn Webb – then women's liberation would require social, political, cultural, legal and economic changes.[45] The women's movement included self-described radical feminists, socialist feminists, Third World feminists, lesbian feminists, cultural feminists, and womanists, sometimes united and sometimes divided by their differences.[46] The Women's Equity Action League split from NOW in 1968 with an agenda to focus specifically on advancing women's equality in education, employment and economics. It was joined by other feminist groups that sought reform, not revolution, including the National Women's Political Caucus (established in 1971) which promoted women's entry into electoral politics and 9to5 (established in 1973) which organized for fair pay and equitable treatment in the workplace. A National Black Feminist Organization (1973) convened women to address topics such as media representations that belittled or degraded African American women. Other activists tackled previously taboo issues including reproductive rights, sexual intimacy and the division of labor within families. Rape crisis centres, battered women's shelters, women's health facilities, and Take Back the Night marches created an infrastructure of enduring services to improve women's lives and to advocate for new public policy.

Conclusion: (Mis)Remembering 1960s Feminism

Looking closely at some episodes from 1968 and reflecting on their impact provides an opportunity to reconsider historical narratives of feminism and to recognize the diverse organizations, ideas, events and experiences that contributed to the larger women's movement. These moments belie the centrality of the Miss America pageant protest to feminism's origins. In popular consciousness, however, the stereotype of feminists as young, white 'bra burners' persists, even as subsequent feminist activism has moved far beyond the goals and actions of 1968. Indeed, the notion of 'bra burning' hangs on despite a general amnesia about the event that birthed the stereotype.[47] This persistence offers a reminder of the difficulty of changing historical narratives. Feminism's post-1960s narrative has been shaped both by insiders – activists themselves – and by outsiders including journalists and scholars. Women's liberation activists, including members of the NYRW, ensured that the protest would be documented and preserved through their published reflections and the incorporation of demands in early second-wave anthologies. It says much about the power of guerrilla theatre that the trope of feminist bra burners lasts even when the range of demands voiced at the Miss America protest and the other events of the year have been forgotten. At the same time, the inability of NYRW to control the media message in Atlantic City and the jeering or querulous tone of the news coverage speaks to the extent of public resistance to women's liberations' demands.

But it is more difficult to explain the wider failure to remember the diverse streams of women's organizing for sex, race and economic equality that merged to create the feminist agenda of the 1960s and 1970s. Throughout the twentieth and twenty-first centuries, the writing of feminist history has been a political project. Activist-scholars, including Sara Evans, Rosalyn Baxandall, Jo Freeman and Marlene Dixon, all participants in 1968 campaigns, have uncovered evidence of the efforts of women's activists from the past and preserved historical documents from their own generation's women's movement.[48] Through such chronicles feminists have sought to define their activism in relation to that of other movements and earlier generations. In doing so, they sought to better understand the movement and to share its principles with potential participants. Moreover, as historian Nancy Hewitt has observed, by looking to demonstrate how their movement improved on those of the past, feminists have emphasized the failures and shortcomings of prior efforts to achieve equality and end sexism. In other words, when activists looked back to the 1960s from the 1980s and beyond, they stressed the failure of their foremothers to understand the intersections of gender, race and class and to launch organizations and campaigns that attacked women's oppression across a broad front.[49] In contrast, other authors have argued that by the early 1970s, the women's movement had become divided in ways that were personally painful to activists and destructive to the movement. Historian Alice Echols, for example, contends that 'by 1970, the rhetoric of universal sisterhood (that characterized radical feminism from 1968 to 1970) had given way to wrenching discussions of women's differences . . . [and] excoriations of the movement as racist, classist, and heterosexist became routine if not obligatory at feminist gatherings'. In this telling, the growing attention that activists paid to differences is associated with a collapse of the radical wing of the movement and an overall decline as liberal feminism became the movement's dominant strain.[50]

All of these assessments remind us that the consequences of telling movement history are both scholarly and political. Pulling the Jeanette Rankin Brigade and NWRO's Mother's Day March into the story of feminism in the 1960s, as this chapter has outlined, offers one step toward transforming the narrative. Of course, the events of 1968 provide only a partial picture of a movement that extended over decades and incorporated a diverse array of people, ideas, causes, tactics and theories. Yet 1968 reminds us of both the importance of looking at intersections and links, as well as understanding the boundaries that activists drew to distinguish and define their movements.

Notes

1. 'No More Miss America!', Redstockings: www.redstockings.org/index/php/miss-america-protest-1968/

2. 'WLM vs Miss America', *Voice of the Women's Liberation Movement* (October 1968), 1, 5: www.cwluherstory.org/cwlu-newsletter-october-1968.html; Alice Echols, *Daring to be Bad: Radical Feminism in America, 1967–1975* (Minneapolis: University of Minnesota Press, 1989), 92–6; Carol Hanish, 'Two Letters from the Women's Liberation Movement', in Rachel Blau DuPlessis and Ann Snitow (eds), *The Feminist Memoir Project: Voices from Women's Liberation* (New York: Random House, 1998), 197–202.

3. Helen Dudar, 'Women's Lib: the War on "Sexism"', *Newsweek* (23 March 1970), 34. See also Mary Wiegers, 'Beneath Those Charred Bras Revolution Smolders', *Washington Post* (8 March 1970).

4. 'No More Miss America!'.

5. Robin Morgan (ed.), *Sisterhood is Powerful: An Anthology of Writings from the Women's Liberation Movement* (New York: Vintage, 1970), 521–4.

6. Sara M. Evans, *Personal Politics: the Roots of Women's Liberation in the Civil Rights Movement and the New Left* (New York: Vintage, 1979), 213–14.

7. Estelle B. Freedman, *No Turning Back: The History of Feminism and the Future of Women* (New York: Ballantine Books, 2002), 214–15, and Ruth Rosen, *The World Split Open: How the Modern Women's Movement Changed America* (New York: Viking, 2000), 159–60. For a similar take, see also Flora Davis, *Moving the Mountain: The Women's Movement in America Since 1960* (New York: Simon & Schuster, 1991), 106–8.

8. Echols, *Daring to be Bad*, 3–4. Many contemporary articles tried to sort out the disparate branches of the movement, often using different names. For example, see Martha Lears, 'The Second Feminist Wave', *New York Times* (10 March 1968), 50–1.

9. Judith Ezekiel, *Feminism in the Heartland* (Columbus: Ohio State University Press, 2002); Stephanie Gilmore, *Groundswell: Grassroots Feminist Activism in America* (New York: Routledge, 2012); Melissa Estes Blair, *Revolutionizing Expectations: Women's Organizations, Feminism, and American Politics 1965–1980* (Athens: University of Georgia Press, 2015); Finn Enke, *Finding the Movement: Sexuality, Contested Space, and Feminist Activism* (Durham, NC: Duke University Press, 2007); Anne M. Valk, *Radical Sisters: Second-Wave Feminism and Black Liberation in Washington, DC* (Urbana: University of Illinois Press, 2008).

10. On local activism around abortion see Valk, *Radical Sisters*; David Cline, *Creating Choice: a Community Responds to the Need for Abortion and Birth Control* (New York: Palgrave, 2006); Jennifer Nelson, *Women of Color and the Reproductive Rights Movement* (New York: New York University Press, 2003); Gilmore, *Groundswell*.

11. Stephanie Gilmore (ed.), *Feminist Coalitions: Historical Perspectives on Second-Wave Feminism in the United States* (Urbana: University of Illinois Press, 2008).

12. Pauli Murray, a lawyer, had worked on NAACP civil rights cases and was pivotal in shaping NOW's approaches to the fight against sex discrimination. Lawyer Flo Kennedy became a prominent supporter of feminist and black radical activists. Shirley Chisholm, who ran for president in 1972, was an outspoken advocate of reproductive and women's rights; in 1968 she became the first African American woman elected to the House of Representatives. Aileen Hernandez was the first woman appointed to the Equal Employment Opportunities Commission, established in 1965 to enforce the 1964 Civil Rights Act; she served as NOW's executive vice president for three years, before succeeding Betty Friedan as the organization's president in 1970.

13. For examples of this analysis see Toni Cade (ed.), *The Black Woman: An Anthology* (New York: New American Library, 1970); Cherrie Moraga and Gloria Anzaldua (eds), *This Bridge Called My Back: Writings by Radical Women of Color* (New York: Persephone Press, 1981); Michele Wallace, *Black Macho and the Myth of the Superwoman* (New York: Dial, 1979); Audre Lorde, *Sister Outsider: Essays and Speeches* (New York: Crossing Press, 1984); and Barbara Smith (ed.), *Home Girls: A Black Female Anthology* (New York: Kitchen Table Women of Color Press, 1983).

14. Kimberly Springer, *Living for the Revolution: Black Feminist Organizations, 1968–1980* (Durham, NC: Duke University Press, 2005); Benita Roth, *Separate Roads to Feminism: Black, Chicana, and White Feminist Movements in America's Second Wave* (Cambridge. Cambridge University Press, 2004); Premilla Nadasen, *Welfare Warriors: the Welfare Rights Movement in the United States* (New York: Routledge, 2004); Dorothy Sue Cobble, *The Other Women's Movement: Workplace Justice and Social Rights in Modern America* (Princeton, NJ: Princeton University Press, 2005); and Becky Thompson, 'Multiracial Feminism: Recasting the Chronology of Second Wave Feminism', *Feminist Studies* 28(2) (Summer 2002), 337–60.

15. Nancy Hewitt (ed.), *No Permanent Waves: Recasting Histories of U.S. Feminism* (New Brunswick, NJ: Rutgers University Press, 2010), 6.

16. Roth, *Separate Roads to Feminism*, 3.

17. On women's experiences in these other movements see, for example, Faith S. Holsaert et al., *Hands on the Freedom Plow: Personal Accounts by Women in SNCC* (Urbana: University of Illinois Press, 2010), and DuPlessis and Ann Snitow (eds), *The Feminist Memoir Project*.

18. The NWP helped introduce the ERA into Congress in 1923 and thereafter. In 1972, with the backing of NOW and other feminist groups, both houses of Congress finally passed the ERA. Hotly contested throughout the 1970s, it failed to win ratification by a necessary two-thirds of states and the amendment

guaranteeing that states could not deny equal rights on the basis of sex was never added to the US Constitution.

19. Nancy F. Cott, *The Grounding of Modern Feminism* (New Haven, CT: Yale University Press, 1987); Deborah Gray White, *Too Heavy a Load: Black Women in Defense of Themselves, 1894–1994* (New York: Norton, 1999); Nancy MacLean, *Freedom is Not Enough: the Opening of the American Workplace* (Cambridge, MA: Harvard University Press, 2006); Cobble, *The Other Women's Movement*.

20. Quoted in Amy Swerdlow, *Women Strike for Peace: Traditional Motherhood and Radical Politics in the 1960s* (Chicago: University of Chicago Press, 1993), 137.

21. On the Brigade, see Echols, *Daring to be Bad*, 54–9, and Andrea Estepa, 'Taking the White Gloves Off: Women Strike for Peace and "the Movement", 1967–73', in Stephanie Gilmore (ed.), *Feminist Coalitions: Historical Perspectives on Second-Wave Feminism in the United States* (Urbana: University of Illinois Press, 2008), 84–112.

22. Quoted in Swerdlow, *Women Strike for Peace*, 140.

23. Radical Woman's Group, 'Burial of Weeping Womanhood', leaflet, Baxandall/Gordon papers, Tamiment Institute Library, New York University Bobst Library; reprinted in Rosalyn Baxandall and Linda Gordon (eds), *Dear Sisters: Dispatches from the Women's Liberation Movement* (New York: Basic Books, 2000), 25.

24. Marilyn Salzman Webb, 'Call for a Spring Conference', *Voice of the Women's Liberation Movement*, 1 (March 1968), 4–5. See also Marilyn Salzman Webb, 'Women: We Have a Common Enemy', *New Left Notes* (10 June 1968), 15, and 'Women's Liberation', *Washington Free Press* (29 February 1968), 4.

25. Estepa, 'Taking the White Gloves Off', 102. For other connections between WSP and feminist organizations, see Dana Densmore, 'A Year of Living Dangerously', in DuPlessis and Snitow (eds), *The Feminist Memoir Project*, 71–3.

26. Marlene Dixon, 'On Women's Liberation', *Radical America* 4(2) (February 1970), 27–8, 33.

27. The mainstream media paid ample attention to feminist divisions. For example, see Martha Lears, 'The Second Feminist Wave', *New York Times* Magazine (10 March 1968), 24–5, 50–3; Elizabeth Shelton, 'Women's Group Split Over Meaning of Feminism', *Washington Post* (24 October 1968), and Karlyn Barker, 'Divisions Slow Women's Lib Drive', *Washington Post* (14 November 1971).

28. Gilmore, *Groundswell*; Valk, *Radical Sisters*.

29. Willard Clopton, 'Campaign Goal: "Escape from Prison of Poverty"', *Washington Post* (23 May 1968).

30. Welfare activists objected to 'no-knock' policies that allowed welfare officials to conduct surprise investigations of recipients' homes in order to determine that no men or husbands lived there; and coerced sterilization of poor women. On the NWRO, see Guida West, *The National Welfare Rights Movement: the Social Protest of Poor Women* (New York: Praeger, 1981); Nick Kotz and Mary Lynn Kotz, *A Passion for Equality: George A. Wiley and the Movement* (New York:

Norton, 1977); Nadasen, *Welfare Warriors*; White, *Too Heavy a Load*; Annelise Orleck, *Storming Caesar's Palace: How Black Mothers Fought Their Own War on Poverty* (Boston: Beacon, 2005).

31. Ben A. Franklin, '5,000 Open Poor People's Campaign in Washington', *New York Times* (13 May 1968), and Elsie Carper, '3000 March in Opening of Drive by Poor', *Washington Post* (13 May 1968). Coretta Scott King made similar calls to women to take part in a campaign against poverty during a Solidarity Day event in Washington DC in late June. Judith Martin, 'Coretta King Stresses Soul in Solidarity', *Washington Post* (20 June 1968), and Phyl Garland, 'Coretta King: In Her Husband's Footsteps', *Ebony* (October 1968), 154–6.

32. 'March', *Washington Post* (24 May 1968).

33. Carol Kleiman, 'N.O.W. Wants Action on Women's Bill of Rights', *Chicago Tribune* (18 August 1968); 'Women Plan a "Militant 1969" to Fight for Job Equality', *Chicago Daily Defender* (14 December 1968).

34. Premilla Nadasen, 'Expanding the Boundaries of the Women's Movement: Black Feminism and the Struggle for Welfare Rights', *Feminist Studies* 28(2) (Summer 2002), 272.

35. Charlotte Curtis, 'Miss America Pageant is Picketed by 100 Women', *New York Times* (8 September 1968), 81; Pauline Tai, 'Miss America Pageant Chosen as the Latest Target of Protesters', *Wall Street Journal* (6 September 1968), 4; 'Women with Gripes Lured to Picket "Miss America"', *New Pittsburgh Courier* (21 September 1968), 3; 'The Miss America Protest: 1968' and Redstockings Archives, op. cit.

36. New York Radical Women, 'No More Miss America', in *Sisterhood is Powerful*, 521–4.

37. Hanish, 'Two Letters from the Women's Liberation Movement', 200.

38. Marilyn Salzman Webb and Pat Rourke, 'Women Hit Pageant Promoters', *The Guardian* (20 September 1969). On the impact on NYWR, see Echols, *Daring to be Bad*, 92–101.

39. Sherie M. Randolph, *Florynce 'Flo' Kennedy: The Life of a Black Feminist Radical* (Chapel Hill: University of North Carolina Press, 2015), 156–60.

40. Judy Klemesrud, 'There's Now Miss Black America', *New York Times* (9 September 1968), 54; Carol Hanisch, 'A Critique of the Miss America Protest', reprinted in Barbara A. Crow (ed.), *Radical Feminism: A Documentary Reader* (New York: New York University Press, 2000), 378–81.

41. The October 1968 issue of *Voice of the Women's Liberation Movement*, for instance, mentioned groups in Seattle, Chicago, New York City, Los Angeles, San Francisco, New Haven, Cambridge, and at UCLA and the University of Chicago. See also Mary Wiegers, 'Beneath Those Charred Bras' and 'Women's Lib: the War on "Sexism"', *Newsweek* (23 March 1970), 33–9.

42. Springer, *Living for the Revolution*, 47–50.

43. Elizabeth Shelton, 'Women's Group Split over Meaning of Feminism', *Washington Post* (24 October 1968).

44. Nadasen, 'Expanding the Boundaries of the Women's Movement', 276.

45. Marilyn Salzman Webb, 'Woman as Secretary, Sexpot, Spender, Sow, Civic Actor, Sickie', *Motive*, 29(6–7) (March/April 1969), 48–59.

46. Sara M. Evans, 'Women's Liberation: Seeing the Revolution Clearly', *Feminist Studies* 41(1) (Spring 2015), 139–40.

47. For an attempt to debunk the bra-burning myth by a journalist who covered the Miss America protest, see Lindsay Van Gelder, 'The Truth About Bra-Burners', *Ms.* (September 1992), 80–1.

48. Evans, *Personal Politics*; Baxandall and Gordon (ed.), *Dear Sisters*; Jo Freeman, 'The Tyranny of Structurelessness', *The Second Wave* 2(1) ([1970] 1972): www.jofreeman.com/joreen/tyranny.htm; and Dixon, 'On Women's Liberation'.

49. Nancy Hewitt has written about the difficulty of changing narratives about feminist history. Nancy A. Hewitt, 'Feminist Frequencies: Regenerating the Wave Metaphor', *Feminist Studies*, 38(3) (Fall 2012), 658–80.

50. Echols, *Daring to be Bad*, 203.

TWELVE

Organizing for Economic Justice in The Late 1960s

Penny Lewis

In the weeks before his assassination, Martin Luther King, Jr. was in the process of organizing a Poor People's Campaign set to bring thousands of the nation's destitute to Washington DC later that spring. Given the recent urban rebellions and the rise of radicalized race politics, the tactic and philosophy of nonviolent direct action that had been a hallmark of the civil rights movement seemed increasingly obsolete. 'No one is listening to it', Dr King imagined his critics believing.[1] Reacting to the cracks in the movement, King's organization, the Southern Christian Leadership Conference (SCLC), supported the campaign as an effort to create a 'middle ground between riots on the one hand and timid supplications for justice on the other'.[2]

As conceived by King, the Poor People's Campaign would involve a multi-racial coalition dedicated to mass civil disobedience – highway blockades, school boycotts, disruption to government offices – actions 'as dramatic, as dislocative, as disruptive, as attention-getting as the riots without destroying property'.[3] Its core demand was that the federal government pass an Economic Bill of Rights, encompassing a right to a job, basic income, decent housing and an end to enforced segregation, adequate education and healthcare, and a right for those affected by these programmes to participate in decision-making processes.[4] In early 1968, addressing a crowd in Mississippi, King reminded his listeners:

It didn't cost the nation one penny to integrate lunch counters. It didn't cost the nation one penny to guarantee the right to vote. But now we are dealing with issues that cannot be solved without the nation spending billions of dollars and undergoing a radical redistribution of economic power.[5]

By the late 1960s, in word and in deed, a growing number of social justice activists working in varying arenas echoed King's call for a 'radical redistribution of economic power'. In February 1968, unionized African American sanitation workers walked off their jobs, whilst images of strikers filing narrowly along Memphis, Tennessee, sidewalks, carrying signs asserting 'I Am A Man', graphically illustrated the connection between racial and economic dignity. Public sector unions, like Memphis sanitation's American Federation of State, County and Municipal Employees (AFSCME), had been organizing over the course of the 1960s, including those representing teachers, nurses and other state workers. By the end of the decade both public and private sector workers were engaging in militant actions, demanding everything from union recognition to an end to internal racial barriers, from better pay to work rule changes, from occupational safety to union democracy. New organizations among the poor also took root, such as the Young Patriots Party in Chicago's Uptown, allied with the Black Panther Party and the Puerto Rican Young Lords, who explained in 1968: 'We see that our allies are those who have nothing and our enemies are those who have too much.'[6] That same year, members of National Welfare Rights Organization occupied the offices of the New York City social services commissioner for three days, as one welfare recipient explained to the commissioner that she wanted her 'children to be decently clad, decently fed, and decently housed – just like your children'.[7] In addition, the Vietnam antiwar movement after 1968 was joined by increasing numbers of working-class and poor war opponents, as well as organizations whose membership base and demands focused on the class implications of the war.[8]

Such class-oriented analyses, demands and action did not appear out of nowhere. The successes and limitations of other ongoing struggles inexorably brought liberals as well as radicals, newcomers as well as experienced activists to confront the problems of economic power and resources. By 1968, poverty, unemployment and welfare – as well as access to jobs, education, housing and healthcare – were coming to be seen as inseparable from the problems of racism, the war and opportunities for women. In the midst of the peace protest, youth revolts and the new rights revolution, economic justice and opportunity were also demands on the table.

This chapter examines how the social movements of the 1960s reckoned with the problems of poverty, class oppression, economic inequality and insecurity. As Chapters 3 and 9 discuss, many accounts mark 1968 as the beginning of the end of the antiwar movement and the civil rights movement; the moment when a more hopeful New Left movement gave way to more splintered and violent social action. But 1968 is also an early year of a period when economic claims came closer to front stage. Relatedly, from 1966 to 1973, greater numbers of working-class and poor people were participating in the movements for social change, marking a few brief years when issues of economic power and social class joined other issues at the forefront of the upsurges. It was this economic turn that in part infused a new rhetoric of revolution through the movement, helped make the late 1960s the most radical of the decade, and agitated government agencies towards new reforms as well as greater levels of repression.

For a period, then, the social movements of the 1960s, taken together, foregrounded the interpenetration of capitalism, multi-faceted oppressions and war. Looked at fifty years later, it is clear that today's social movements are once again grappling with the unfinished business unearthed by their 1968 forerunners. Economically oriented movements like Occupy and fights for a living wage, the fervent insistence that Black Lives Matter in the face of ongoing police repression and the violence of poverty, the immigrant Dreamers seeking college educations whose 'illegal' and second-class status threatens their chances of decent lives, directly echo the critiques, aspirations and challenges of the previous era.[9] A reclamation of this history is therefore all the more relevant, even urgent. In what follows, I pay particular attention to both the breakthroughs and difficulties faced by these predecessors, joining scholars and activists alike who are turning to the economically oriented efforts of the end of the 'long sixties' for lessons and inspiration today.

From *The Affluent Society* to *The Other America*

Politics in the 1960s are often understood as having a 'post-scarcity' flavour. Depression-era legislation establishing minimal retirement pensions and unemployment insurance, ensuring a minimum wage and other employment standards, and assuring the right to private sector union representation, together combined with progressive taxation to create the regulatory groundwork for less unequal, more secure and stable economic conditions for large numbers of Americans. As the industrialized nation least affected by the devastation of the two world wars, the US was also the leading contributor to, and beneficiary of, the postwar economic boom. For the better part of three decades, the productive capacity of the global economy was expanding and the consumption of American-made goods was on the rise. Together, social policy, strong unions and an improving economy resolved many of the worst effects of class inequality. From World War II through the early 1970s, average income roughly doubled for rich and poor alike. This widely shared prosperity was unprecedented, and social scientists wrestled with the implications of such generalized well-being. John Kenneth Galbraith's *The Affluent Society* (1958) was perhaps the most influential study discussing these changes. While it, in fact, problematized the country's preoccupation with wealth and private gain, *The Affluent Society* was taken up in popular culture as a more celebratory description of the kind of society the United States was becoming.

Cutting against such optimistic projections was another, less visible, set of realities for millions of Americans. Legislation passed during the 1930s had created a two-tier rights and benefits system, with labor rights granted for production, service and transport workers in the private sector, and income assistance flowing to the male and employed through unemployment insurance and social security. Meanwhile, public sector, domestic and agricultural workers – usually women and people of colour – were denied union rights and largely excluded from social security and unemployment insurance. Indigent non-working unmarried women received fairly stingy, means-tested and morality-policed outlays. During the boom, African Americans saw their income rise at similar rates to whites, but their overall income was around half that of whites, which meant continued poverty and degraded living standards for millions of families despite improvements. Economic restructuring and local job losses spurred a mass migration of Puerto Ricans that brought nearly half a million migrants to the US in the 1950s, with hundreds of thousands emigrating in the next two decades as well, many of them facing poverty and low wages. Between 1942 and 1964, the Bracero Program brought millions of contract farmwork-ers from Mexico to work in US agribusiness. These 'guestworkers' were paid substandard wages, which served to depress the wages of agricultural workers as a whole while barely maintaining the Braceros in desperate poverty. Women workers also received a little over half the pay of white men, with rates falling to less than half for women of colour. Lacking the same entitlements as families led by white men, all of these groups experienced little by way of public assistance or loans; discriminatory housing policy, in particular, denied families of colour access to housing loans, perpetuating pat-terns of unequal wealth. Geographically, large pockets of poverty existed, in cities among recent migrants and in rural areas that were starved for jobs and decent wages.[10]

In 1962, Michael Harrington described this set of realities *The Other America*, a book in which he lyrically described the over 40 million Americans, one in four, who lived on incomes below $3000 a year.[11] His goal in the slim volume was to make this pov-erty visible, and through this revelation perhaps lend the poor a public voice:

> It is one of the cruelest ironies of social life in advanced countries that the dispossessed at the bottom of society are unable to speak for them-selves. The people of the other America do not, by far and large, belong to unions, to fraternal organizations, or to political parties. They are without lobbies of their own; they put forward no legislative program. As a group, they are atomized.[12]

An official from the John F. Kennedy administration credits Harrington's book with creating a focus for the disparate social policy initiatives that the federal government was developing in 1962 and 1963.[13] Why was the administration in a position to recognize that poverty was something that warranted attention? Certainly economic growth provided the means for liberal leaders to envision the nation's capacity to 'wage an unconditional war on poverty', as President Lyndon Johnson described it in 1964 as he took up the poverty campaign imagined by Kennedy. Given ongoing Cold War competition, many liberals were quick to point out that the US could little afford *not* to demonstrate that guns and butter were simultaneously achievable in a dynamic welfare capitalist society.[14] Liberals forecast an ever-expanding pie, with ongoing economic growth that could pay for income supports and expanded social services that would together provide more universal opportunity.

But other external factors were also pushing the federal government to act. The black struggle in the South, and a closely coordinated effort of labor and civil rights movement organizations had forced the issues of poverty and joblessness to centre stage. It was the longstanding efforts of movement activists across the country, and his own attention to them, that had set the stage even for Harrington's initial interest. Speaking of *The Other America*, Harrington recalled decades later, 'that book belonged to the movement, which contributed so much more to me than I to it'.[15]

Economic Organizing in the Early 1960s

Fighting economic exclusion had long been a cornerstone of the African American movement, as well as the efforts of other racially excluded groups.[16] Historians describe the 'dual agenda' of the civil rights movement, while economic inclusion has been described as one of twin pillars of citizenship, with voting rights as the other.[17] Through World War II, civil rights efforts recurrently focused on universal, federal programmes to ensure equal job rights and social welfare programmes. Cold War anti-communism that took hold in the late 1940s, however, 'devastated organizing for economic inclusion'.[18] Like nearly all progressives in the US between the 1940s and the early 1960s, civil rights leaders and organizations distanced themselves from anyone or anything that might taint their work as communist.

The near exclusive focus on political rights and representation (and exclusion of economic demands) in the early movement in the South reflected this Cold War anti-communist climate, and at the same time, its often middle-class base. Blacks in the South faced combined racial and economic oppressions, and their efforts to overthrow the former were frequently met with white resistance via the latter. Facing attacks from groups like the White Citizens' councils and others including the denial of employment, credit, mortgages and access to other goods and services, civil rights movement participants in urban areas tended to hold slightly more secure economic roles than the jobs and positions more typical in the black community as a whole. By dint of the density of the black community in places like Birmingham, Montgomery and Selma where they often served as clergy, professionals or business owners, the leaders of the urban movement were frequently less economically dependent on the white power structure than city workers or rural residents. Voting and an end to Jim Crow segregation were middle-ground demands that liberals and more radical activists could agree to. The political demands, if won, would have profound economic effects, as their supporters well understood. But they were not usually put forward in the context of redistribution or economic justice.

Yet the class composition of the movement changed depending on location. Early leaders, like Septima Clark, connected the problem of basic education and voting rights in the 'citizenship schools' she helped create in South Carolina for illiterate rural blacks. These schools were supported by the Highlander Folk School, a labor school in Tennessee whose orientations towards class and the self-activity of the oppressed were echoed in the work of the pre-eminent new left organization, the Student Non-Violent Coordinating Committee (SNCC), formed in 1960. SNCC's first work was voter registration, but they organized widely among the rural poor. Organizing voter registration in the Delta and elsewhere, SNCC had to contend with the fact that people could lose it all: they might need food, shelter and clothing as a result of movement action. The deep connections forged between the SNCC organizers and the communities they worked in sensitized a generation of new student activists to the existential constraints of poverty, as well as helping to develop some of the strongest poor and working-class leaders of the southern movement, like Fannie Lou Hamer of the Mississippi Freedom Democratic Party.

As the civil rights movement in the South focused the nation's attention on white racism and black poverty, its allies in the trade union movement broadened the conversation to include other national economic issues. In late 1962, civil rights activist Bayard Rustin and A. Philip Randolph, head of the Sleeping Car Porters union and the Negro American Labor Council, envisioned bringing the southern tactic of direct action to the North by calling for a March on Washington. The initial call focused on jobs, including investment in public works, and a fair employment practices Act, and whilst the March on Washington for Jobs and Freedom of 28 August 1963 has entered US history as the setting for King's soaring 'I Have a Dream' speech, the labor and civil rights coalition that birthed it is often forgotten.[19]

Attending the march were contingents from the Students for a Democratic Society (SDS). This northern, largely white group was directly funded by the labor movement and directly inspired by their work with SNCC in the South. Two days after the March on Washington, SDS leaders spoke with Stokely Carmichael about SDS's plans for an Economic Rights Action Project (ERAP), aimed at building what Tom Hayden and Carl Wittman called for in a policy paper they wrote later that year, 'an interracial movement of the poor'. In essence, SDS viewed poverty as a sign of the limits of a free market system, one which could not provide sufficient jobs or support for all people. Policy, they thought, should be aimed at redistributing wealth and maximizing democracy, and increasing the participation of citizens through planning and job creation. In their vision, poverty's degrading effects could be overcome through vibrant participatory democracy and creating bottom up solutions for economic problems.[20] This was what they hoped to accomplish in their ERAP programme, even though the project indicated some of the difficulties of such work. For example, the effort in Chicago, Jobs or Income Now (JOIN) initially focused on unemployment and mobilizing community members to push for federal job creation. But the young men they met were frequently sceptical about government jobs, and the older unemployed were both ashamed of their joblessness and hopeful that the private sector might provide, as it had in the recent past. The organizers themselves also confronted the depth of commitment community organizing entailed.[21] Most of the efforts foundered in their first year, but those that survived, like Chicago, Newark and Cleveland, were those where the organizers shifted their attention to local concerns and made the longer-term efforts to become part of the communities they organized within. This shift from 'JOIN' to 'GROIN' (Garbage Removal or Income Now) was met with some scorn by many SDS members who were critical of the limited reformist nature of such efforts; such organizing appeared to mean that SDS was abandoning its broader, more transformative mission of systemic change. This tension, between organizing at local versus national scales, was to recur in all of the economic oriented efforts of the period.

As a project, ERAP was largely concluded by 1968, its SDS organizers moved on to other parts of the movement. Yet the ERAP efforts had other effects, such as helping shift SNCC to economic issues by 1964–5. The ERAP groups also proved to be more radical than the less ideological community organizing practised by groups such as Saul Alinsky's Industrial Area Foundation. In Chicago, for instance, the original JOIN was eventually taken over by local poor and working-class whites in 1967, many of whom formed the Young Patriots Party, which joined economic and anti-racist demands in coalition with groups like the Young Lords and the Black Panthers. All of these groups embraced the idea that 'you start where you're at', but they aspired well beyond garbage removal and new streetlights.

Expanding The Battlefields in Civil Rights and The War on Poverty

By 1965 the Voting Rights Act and the Civil Rights Act had passed. The Equal Employment Opportunity Commission was formed under the latter to enforce Title VII, which barred workplace discrimination on the basis of race, sex, national origin and religion. This part of the law alone had a tremendously galvanizing effect on movements over the coming years, providing legislative ground for expanded inclusion for women and all people of colour. Minimal health care for the elderly and the poor was assured with the passage of Medicare and Medicaid. President Johnson's 'War on Poverty' and the promise of a Great Society were contained in these programmes, and many others that were launched in the central years of this pivotal decade. By some measures, one could argue that the movements had won.

But just as Harrington's book had given the lie to the appearance of hegemonic prosperity, the social movements of the 1960s were quick to realize the limits to the government action they had fought so hard to achieve. At the national level, liberal and civil rights wings of the labor movement continued to press for economic reforms. The United Automobile Workers (UAW) had created a Citizens Crusade Against Poverty, Walter Reuther's multi-year effort that offered leadership training and other kinds of support to the Community Action Programs (CAPs) being funded by Johnson's War on Poverty. The following year, the A. Philip Randolph Institute, under the leadership of Bayard Rustin, and in consultation with economist Leon Keyserling and others, developed a 'Freedom Budget for All Americans: Budgeting our Resources to Achieve Freedom From Want, 1966–1975'. The Freedom Budget included a detailed set of proposals designed to eradicate poverty that covered full employment, sufficient wages, guaranteed income, decent housing, medical care and education, and infrastructure investment such as water and transport. Their intention was to see the budget passed through Congress: it was not, but it served as a blueprint for liberal politicians in the coming years.[22]

The most prominent force to emerge from the local poverty organizing was indigent mothers, who came together in local groups that eventually formed the National Welfare Rights Organization (NWRO). The welfare rights movement represented the convergence of a few movement streams. Leadership came from George Wiley, Richard Cloward and Frances Fox Piven, militant community advocates or veterans of liberal civil rights coalitions: Wiley, for example, was a leader of the Congress on Racial Equality (CORE) and worked on staff of the UAW's Citizens Crusade Against Poverty. Labor unions, like the national United Farm Workers and the Social Services Employee Union in New York City also supported the early work of the welfare rights groups. But the centre of the movement were the women themselves. In 1965–6, various civil rights and labor groups organized demonstrations to keep the pressure on the Johnson administration, while a new tactic was tried out that proved to be more successful than marches in winning funds for the poor: 'minimum standards campaigns'. These campaigns involved direct action by women receiving public assistance, who flooded welfare offices demanding that the state meet minimum standards, including the clothing and furniture that the government had decided met adequate levels of subsistence to the poor.

These welfare activists were able to carry out this campaign because of solidarity between themselves, labor and civil rights activists. Previous support from CORE and other welfare advocates for a union walkout in 1965, for example, yielded a boon for the welfare activists when Social Service Employees Union Local 371 members later provided welfare organizers the complete lists of 'minimum standards'. These organizers were able to leverage the 'wide gap' between what the government said should be in the home and what women actually had and demand significantly higher monthly payments.[23] During 1966, the local and national marches against poverty yielded little by way of expanded funds for the war on poverty, but women were receiving thousands of dollars when they marched on the offices directly. It was this kind of militant direct action that was reproduced in hundreds of smaller groups across the country, which amalgamated in 1967 to form the NWRO.

The demands raised by the women of the NWRO stood in contrast to the economic claims that were coming to be advanced in the middle-class women's movement. Title VII's protection against workplace discrimination resonated with new feminists seeking equal opportunities in the labor market, and these efforts at liberation to work, and to equal salaries, became a central plank of 'second wave' feminism in the years to come. Within a couple of years of the forming of NWRO, class differences between women working for economic empowerment caused some tensions in the movements. The 'mother power' of welfare mothers struck middle-class women as regressive; getting away from limitations associated with the role of mother was a large part of their battle. The equal rights campaign of the feminists, in turn, struck poor women and women of colour as elitist: these groups had always been in the labor market and had long encountered racial dis-crimination, occupational segregation and harassment. They had never had the 'problem' of being stay-at-home mothers; having been systematically denied the opportunity to devote substantial time to their own domestic lives, demanding social supports for doing so was progressive, even radical. These differing demands and viewpoints illustrated the difficulties the movements faced as they grappled with intersectional oppressions.

'Where Do We Go from Here?': The Poor People's Campaign

In early 1968, King invited the NWRO along with dozens of other organizations nationwide to support the Poor People's Campaign. Over the course of 1967, he had been moving in the direction of broader and more systemic critiques of the racial injustice he had spent the previous decade fighting. War and economic inequality became the other targets of his rhetoric and action. King envisioned the Poor People's Campaign as a chance to 'bring to bear all of the power of nonviolence on the economic problem'.[24] Weeks before his death, he convened a Minority Group Conference for organiza-tions and individuals representing the vast scope of the coalition he sought in the Poor People's Campaign. These groups brought competing and potentially divisive demands. NWRO's insistence on support for income maintenance programmes risked labor's support and even more moderate civil rights supporters, who together tended to demand jobs over income. Chicano activists were concerned this was another 'black-white thing', and unsure if they would be full coalition partners; Native Americans spoke of land and fishing rights; Appalachian coal miners pointed to the destruction of the land and environment by all-powerful coal com-panies; and Puerto Ricans emphasized national self-determination. Co-articulating these grievances, making way for diverse leadership, serving multiple politics and cultures – these were the tough reali-ties of class-based organizing in 1968, and it was not clear that King or SCLC would be up to the task.[25]

Nevertheless, King remained committed to an action that would bring both national and systemic focus to the problem of poverty.[26] Finding less support among his closest allies than he had hoped, the sanitation workers strike in Memphis became a central inspiration to King as he struggled to make his Poor People's Campaign a reality. Members of AFSCME Local 1733 had walked off the job in February 1968 when two of their colleagues were crushed to death due to faulty equipment. The local had been fighting for better equipment, sick days and, most of all, a living wage: garbage workers in Memphis earned less than $1.60 an hour, below federal minimums: poverty wages for gruelling work. They faced a paternalistic and intransigent mayor, Henry Loeb, who refused to recognize the union and ceaselessly condescended to the working men. When King visited, he was deeply moved by the righteousness of the fight and the dignity of the workers, and he helped to make the strike national news as he visited three times in his final weeks. It was in Memphis that King was killed, the day he was to lead a nonviolent march in support of the strikers.[27]

The Poor People's Campaign continued in the wake of King's death. That May, over 3000 people moved into plywood A-frame shacks, creating a 'Resurrection City' alongside the reflecting pool on Washington's Mall. Hundreds more travelled across country in caravans, protesting along the way. The mass civil disobedience initially planned by King was abandoned for sit-ins in government offices, lobbying, marching and rallying. One mass rally, dubbed 'Solidarity Day', featured an extraordinarily diverse series of speakers describing economic injustice, and their visions for redress, to a crowd of 50,000. Perhaps most importantly, the participants of the movement lived together for weeks, creating their own mini-society, with communal cooking, a school, music and dancing. For many, the experience itself felt transformative – some reported Resurrection City was the 'only home they'd ever had'. But when reflecting on the political goals of the movement, most participants viewed the experience as a failure, if an educational one. The Economic Bill of Rights had changed, in part reflecting the concerns voiced by Mexican American and Native American coalition partners, among others. More detailed versions of the central demands were elaborated, including at least one version that specified pending legislation for the protesters to support in their lobbying efforts. But the occupation as a whole was burdened by the breadth of its vision. While their disruptive tactics focused attention on poverty, over time it was difficult to understand the strategy of the encampment: the protesters were not going to stay until 'poverty was eradicated', and it was difficult to figure out what 'victory' they could claim to go home.

In the end, circumstances got the better of Resurrection City. The logistics of keeping the camp going overwhelmed the SCLC. Heavy rains made the living conditions unbearable. And the difficulties of realizing an 'interracial movement of the poor' were felt once again. For activists like Corky Gonzales, an emerging leader in the Chicano Rights movement, 'the most important lesson' he drew from the campaign was likely felt, in analogous ways, by other individuals as well: 'that Chicano strength relied on ethnic and racial unity and that, although poverty and oppression were shared by many people, blacks, Mexican Americans, and Indians defined justice differently. Ethnically and racially driven culture . . . resulted in dissimilar and sometimes competing needs.'[28]

Revolutionary Self Help: Panthers Serve The People

In contrast to the movement's more middle-class social base in the South, as the civil rights movement spread northwards it was the urban poor and working class that formed its active core. Joining the movement were also groups that the revolutionaries of the day described as 'lumpenproletariat', the officially unemployed whose means of survival often involved the underground labor market and gang membership. These men and women were purportedly living with political rights, but as second-class citizens nevertheless.

The most violent and direct form of oppression northern blacks experienced was at the hands of the police. Constant harassment and brutality characterized life for blacks in northern cities. The first major riots of the decade occurred in the Harlem and Bedford Stuyvesant neighbourhoods of New York City and Watts, Los Angeles, following police killings of unarmed young men. But these and later uprisings were not the mayhem that contemporary commentators frequently pictured them to be, and they illustrated the deep economic grievances shared among urban blacks. Looting was usually selective and methodical, limited to owners that the communities resented; goods that were typically stolen included basic necessities that poor families could not afford. One man told King at Watts in 1965: 'All we want is jobs. We get jobs, we won't bother nobody. We don't get no jobs, we'll tear up Los Angeles, period.'[29] King described the uprisings as the 'language of the unheard' and his death precipitated the most widespread urban uprisings of the decade. Joining hundreds of thousands in over a hundred cities across the country, 20,000 took to the streets in Washington DC, where writers for the hometown paper pointed out 'at least three out of four had so-called blue-collar jobs. Only one in eight was unemployed', describing it as 'a workingman's riot'.[30]

The 'angry disenchantment' of those rising up in northern cities was organizationally reflected by the Black Panther Party for Self Defense, launched in Oakland in 1966. The Panthers reacted to the scourge of police brutality by asserting their rights to armed self-defence, and it was their visibly militant stand against state violence that first brought the Panthers recognition. But aside from the police, northern racism was often described as more 'subtle' than that which African Americans experienced in the South, though it proved as tenacious.[31] De facto segregation in schools, in neighbourhoods, and on the job created two unequal nations on *both* sides of the Mason–Dixon line. Suffering from poor education, substandard housing, no access to healthcare or good food or adequate transport, northern grievances were transparently economic. Black Panther Party founders Huey Newton and Bobby Seale were both directly familiar with the economic insecurity and violence facing their communities. They were each from poor working families and each had worked for anti-poverty organizations prior to forming the Black Panthers.[32]

In 1968, the emerging Chicano rights movement in Los Angeles burst onto the scene, foregrounding demands that linked economic opportunity and racial exclusion. School walkouts saw high-school students protesting vocational training, faculty and staff racism, and inadequate resources in their schools. The assumption made by these schools was that Mexican Americans would inevitably do low wage service work. Home economics told girls they would cook and clean for others, while boys were sent to shop classes. The students conducted a survey (that was ignored by the school board) which showed they were being pushed out of school and discouraged

Figure 12.1 Black Panther Party members show their support for Huey Newton outside the Alameda County Courthouse, Oakland, California, in summer 1968, after Newton was charged with killing a police officer in October 1967. Courtesy CSU Archives/ Everett Collection. REX/Shutterstock.

from college. In early spring, 10,000 students walked out of sixteen schools with chants of 'Ya Basta' and 'Chicano Power'. The Brown Berets, a Chicano militant group modelled after the Panthers, lent their support to the students. Farmworker organizing had also galvanized the Chicano community in recent years, and 1968 was the year that the Delano grape boycott sponsored by Cesar Chavez and the United Farm Workers went national. The boycott received unusually universal support, uniting feminists, Black Power activists, trade union officials from conservative and liberal traditions as well as the rank and file, and antiwar activists; by its successful conclusion in 1970, 17 million Americans had stopped buying the non-union grapes.

The Panthers themselves began to move in a different direction during 1968. They dropped 'self defense' from their name, and publicly doubted whether a movement could fare well in a firefight against the state. Eldridge Cleaver ran for president in the newly formed Peace and Freedom Party, with JOIN's and the Young Patriot's Peggy Terry as his running mate in some states, and Judy Mage, the former president of SSEU Local 371 in others. The Panthers moved to integrate their race-based focus on the nation's ills with a 'class struggle' perspective, and they launched a Free Breakfast programme in January 1969. By the end of that year upwards of 20,000 children were being served a full breakfast in thirteen cities across the country. It was the first national free breakfast programme in the country, preceding the government-sponsored National School Breakfast programme by six years.

Other programmes, all free, included 'liberation schools' and tutoring, as well as classes in community health, legal matters, drama, preparation for the high school equivalency exams , martial arts; sickle cell anaemia research, drug and alcohol abuse awareness, and community health clinics that included dental, optometry, paediatric and gynaecological care; and distributing free goods and services including clothing, furniture, bussing to prisons, ambulance, pest control, plumbing and maintenance. Community donations from individuals, businesses and churches kept these programmes running, some for months, others for years. Huey Newton reflected upon these programmes in his 1972 book *To Die for the People*: 'all these programs satisfy the deep needs of the community but they are not solutions to our problems. That is why we call them survival programs, meaning survival pending revolution.'33

These programmes pointed up the shortcomings of the federal anti-poverty programmes. Through direct action and direct service, such groups as the Young Lords in New York (who launched a 'garbage offensive' to clean the East Harlem streets) met the people's basic needs and bound together community members who gave their time, energy, expertise and money to keep the programmes running. The Black Panther Party (BPP) and the Young Lords enabled a kind of pre-figurative liberation for poor communities, but most of these programmes were destroyed as part of the brutal repression the Party faced under the vigorous counter-intelligence programme (COINTELPRO) of the Nixon administration after 1968. Describing them as indoctrination programmes for 'impressionable' youth, the Federal Bureau of Investigation focused on the Breakfast for Children Program (BCP) as the most dangerous of the Panther programmes, as noted in this memo from FBI Director

J. Edgar Hoover in May 1969, advocating for the destruction of the Party:

> the BCP represents the best and most influential activity going for the BPP and, as such, is potentially the greatest threat to efforts by authorities to neutralize the BPP and destroy what it stands for.[34]

Nonetheless, such self-help programmes not only survived in some cases, but helped to set the stage for the growth of community-based organizations in urban centres across the country, as well as government aid for community needs.

Rich Man's War, Poor Man's Fight?

The economic critiques offered by these wings of the civil rights and self-determination movements were coming to be mirrored by the Vietnam antiwar movement as well. By 1968, for the first time, majorities polled in the United States identified the war as a mistake, including a majority of trade union members, who from that point on outpaced most groups (save African Americans) in their disagreement with the war. In fact, polls show that working-class and poor people always opposed the war in numbers at least equal to and often greater than their richer and better-educated fellow citizens. The antiwar arguments made by parts of the movement began to emphasize the cost of the war at home, and antiwar groups began to move beyond the campus in their organizing efforts. Beginning in 1967, draft resistance groups in Wisconsin and Boston targeted the working-class youth who comprised 80 per cent of the Vietnam era military. Labor coalitions formed against the war, a remarkable change given anti-communist leadership of the national trade union federation, the AFL-CIO, and the price that union members had paid in recent years for their connections to anything remotely red. Mass marches against the war grew bigger with each passing year, reaching a high point in 1971, when the spring protests in Washington DC and San Francisco were the largest of the era, with over a million marching in DC and close to half that in San Francisco. Among the groups helping to organize and attend these rallies were the NWRO and the Teamsters Union, in addition to hundreds more across the country.[35]

As antiwar sentiment spread, class-based critiques of the military and the war became more prominent. These antiwar platforms were based upon the experience of working-class and poor citizens confronting the draft, service cuts due to war spending, and, relatedly, active governmental neglect and limited job opportunities when they returned as veterans. The Vietnam Veterans Against the War (VVAW), particularly, articulated the reasons why working and poor people should have no part in Vietnam, bringing a highly solidaristic, mutually supportive, and 'bottom up' sensibility to their antiwar organizing. VVAW members visited public high schools and junior colleges in anti-recruitment efforts, describing their experience in and opposition to the war. They organized for better healthcare and housing for veterans.

More than the 25,000 active members of the VVAW came home radicalized by the war. Their defiant attitude came to define the labor relations of the post-1968 period, in the years before boom went bust and the backlash took hold. The labor upsurge began in the newly organized public sector, and the private sector soon followed suit. The numbers tell part of the story: from 1967 to 1975, the Bureau of Labor Statistics counted 47,622 'work stoppages', involving over 23 million workers, in strikes that averaged 24.5 days, an historical strike wave rivalled only by the great postwar work stoppages of 1945–6.[36]

The greatest expansion within the labor movement since the early postwar era took place over the decade of the 1960s and into the 1970s with the growth of unions in the public sector – from 903,000 members in 1960 to almost 6 million in 1976.[37] Through the mid-1970s, public sector organizing and social movements mutually reinforced each other. Women and people of colour comprised majorities in many public sector workplaces, facilitating a consciousness of discrimination and oppression largely absent among their unionized private sector counterparts. New Leftists joined the professions, such as teaching or social work, and linked traditional demands of pay and working conditions to quality of the services they provided the public. By insisting on adequate pay, benefits and pensions, public unions helped to maintain funding to the public sector, becoming a stable ally to those who wished to see increased resources allocated to public goods. For these reasons, public sector (and, similarly, service sector) unions often worked in alliances with the antiwar, civil rights and feminist movements.

Teachers were the first public sector workers to take more militant action to further their goals. Beginning in 1960, strikes among teachers – for union recognition, salary increases, work rules and more – became a prime tactic in their organizing toolbox. Among these was the first Chicago Teachers strike, which began as a wildcat against segregation in the system and the (racist) hiring and promotional practices regarding black teachers. Together, teachers and Memphis sanitation workers inspired a new wave of public sector strikes after 1968, some led by unions and others, like the wildcat Postal Workers strike of 1970, initiated directly by the members. Most of the strikes were illegal, as public worker strikes were outlawed in most states. By the turn of the 1970s, the private sector joined the fight, with 1970 witnessing a 122-day strike of 133,000 workers at General Electric, a twenty-three-day strike of 42,000 coal miners protesting black lung, and a sixty-seven-day national strike among 400,000 autoworkers at General Motors.

The tensions unearthed between labor leadership and the rank-and-file spoke to a set of profound shortcomings in the US labor movement that limited its predilection towards, as well as capacity for, playing a meaningful leadership role during the 'economic moment' of the 1960s movements. The umbrella federation AFL–CIO tended to embrace a liberal anti-communism; they supported President Johnson but contained sufficiently conservative factions that President Nixon found reliable allies during his tenure. Racism within the unions fractured possible urban coalitions, as when building trade unions resisted integration. Even liberal labor leaders, exemplified by the UAW's Walter Reuther, played double roles, supporting the movements from afar, while being less effective or interested in addressing the problems on their home turf, such as consistent racial stratification in the union. For all of its support for national work, including the March on Washington, Citizens Crusade Against Poverty, Freedom Budget or Poor Peoples Campaign, the UAW (and other private sector unions, like the Teamsters and Steelworkers) did not support local organizing work in the cities, and tended to avoid mobilizing their own members for these 'crusades', either as citizen lobbyists or as demonstrators.

Conclusion: Outcomes and Lessons

When we look back on the 1960s we do not frequently dwell on the economic demands that came to the forefront during the decade's later years. The 1960s are typically understood as a period in which a liberal consensus grappled with the question of how a democratic, wealthy society can best extend its rights and riches to previously excluded groups, beyond its more privileged (white, male, working) citizens. Its social movements were the primary catalyst for this reckoning. I have argued here that these movements, facing the limitations of the policy changes they wrought through their struggles, and the ongoing inequities of US society, increasingly adopted class-oriented analyses and demands, and they increasingly inspired and attracted working-class and poor citizens to join the fight. While many of those who joined did so through collective identities shaped by other social experiences – identities of ethnicity, race, gender, veteran status and the like – their class experience importantly shaped the actions they took.

These movements were met with significant repression as redistributive issues were more forcefully waged. And as the positive economic climate that fostered much of the expansive social vision faltered, so the backlash against the movements increased. With the economic crisis of the early 1970s, attacks on the labor movement began in earnest, with workers' economic gains threatened and eroded. Scarcity conditions and a successful neoliberal ideological onslaught helped to foster an already present racial backlash against the expanded welfare state, and many white people turned against taxes and handouts and government largesse and towards a 'law and order' state that tolerated greater repression. The Democratic Party presented similar fractures, with political tensions between different groups in its big tent – more socially conservative unions concerned with jobs; more socially liberal educated groups concerned with rights – undermining solidarity. Ultimately, the 'economic wings' of the movements were not able to withstand such attacks and poor conditions.

Yet, quite a lot was won. Between 1965 and 1972 social welfare spending nearly trebled, and from 1965 to 1970 poverty rates among African Americans dropped by a third. Public unions won a meteoric rise in living standards for their workers: for example, teachers' salaries increased 40 per cent from 1966 to 1973. Millions of economically independent women and much of the extant black middle class can trace their roots to the vast improvement in the terms and conditions of civil service jobs. Various attempts at creating 'an interracial movement of the poor' proved unsuccessful; similarly, groups that had much in common along other political vectors had trouble finding unity across the distances created by class. But the period – and particularly 1968 – represents a moment when progressive movements across a spectrum of issues and touching a vast array of communities came to appreciate that economic justice and racial justice cannot be uncoupled, and that any active critique of US society necessarily involves a critique of its economic system. Their efforts at navigating the difficult challenges they faced are instructive for today's activists, who are arriving at similar conclusions and looking for new solutions.

Notes

1. Taylor Branch, *At Canaan's Edge: America in the King Years 1965–1968* (New York: Simon & Schuster, 2006), 739.
2. Martin Luther King speech at staff retreat for SCLC, 29 November 1967, quoted in the *Martin Luther King Jr., Encyclopedia*, ed. Claybourne Carson (Westport, CT: Greenwood Press, 2008), 268.
3. Rick Perlstein, *Nixonland: The Rise of a President and the Fracturing of America* (New York: Scribner, 2008), 250.
4. Martin Luther King Center, draft of the Economic and Social Bill of Rights (6 February 1968): www.thekingcenter.org/archive/document/economic-and-social-bill-rights
5. King spoke about the 'radical redistribution of economic power' in speeches through summer 1967 and early 1968. For this February 1968 speech see episode 10 of *Eyes on the Prize* (dir. Henry Hampton, 1987) and Nick Kotz, *Judgement Days: Lyndon Baines Johnson, Martin Luther King, Jr., and the Laws that Changed America* (New York: Houghton Mifflin, 2015), 382.
6. See the 'The 11 Point Program of the Young Patriots Organization' on the The Young Patriots and the Original Rainbow Coalition website: www.youngpatriots-rainbowcoalition.org/ypo-resources
7. Felicia Kornbluh, *The Battle For Welfare Rights: Politics and Poverty in Modern America* (Philadelphia: University of Pennsylvania Press, 2007), 88.
8. See Penny W. Lewis, *Hardhats, Hippies and Hawks: The Vietnam Antiwar Movement as Myth and Memory* (Ithaca, NY: Cornell University Press, 2013).
9. See Barbara Ransby, 'The Class Politics of Black Lives Matter', *Dissent* (Fall

2015): www.dissentmagazine.org/article/class-politics-black-lives-matter; Walter J. Nicholls and Tara Fiorito, 'Dreamers Unbound: Immigrant Youth Organizing', *New Labor Forum* 24(1) (January 2015), 86–92.

10. Chad Stone et al., 'A Guide to Statistics on Historical Trends in Income Inequality,' Center on Budget and Policy Priorities: www.cbpp.org/sites/default/files/atoms/files/11-28-11pov.pdf (updated September 2016); Thomas Sugrue, *The Origins of the Urban Crisis: Race and Inequality in Postwar Detroit* (Princeton, NJ: Princeton University Press, 2005), 42–5; William Darity and Samuel Myers, *Persistent Disparity: Race and Economic Inequality in the United States Since 1945* (Cheltenham: Edward Elgar, 1998).

11. Michael Harrington, *The Other America* (New York: Simon & Schuster, [1962] 1997), 183.

12. Ibid. 6.

13. Maurice Isserman, *The Other American: The Life of Michael Harrington* (New York: Public Affairs, 2000), 208.

14. See Robert Collins, 'Growth Liberalism in the Sixties: Great Societies at Home and Grand Designs Abroad', in David Farber (ed.), *The Sixties From Memory to History* (Chapel Hill: University of North Carolina Press, 1994), 11–44.

15. Harrington, quoted in Gordon Mantler, *Power to the Poor: Black-Brown Coalition and the Fight for Economic Justice 1960–1974* (Chapel Hill: University of North Carolina Press, 2013), 15–16.

16. See Dona Cooper Hamilton and Charles V. Hamilton, *The Dual Agenda: The African American Struggle for Civil and Economic Equality* (New York: Columbia University Press, 1997); Nancy MacLean, *Freedom is Not Enough: The Opening of the American Workplace* (Cambridge, MA: Harvard University Press, 2006); Charles Payne, *I've Got the Light of Freedom: The Organizing Tradition and the Mississippi Freedom Struggle* (Berkeley: University of California Press, 1995).

17. Judith Shklar, quoted in MacLean, *Freedom is Not Enough*, 8.

18. Ibid. 29.

19. For the labor side of the coalition see Will Jones, *The March on Washington: Jobs, Freedom, and the Forgotten History of Civil Rights* (New York: Norton, 2013).

20. For a full discussion of ERAP see Jennifer Frost, *'An Interracial Movement of the Poor': Community Organizing and the New Left in the 1960s* (New York: New York University Press, 2001).

21. Amy Sonnie and James Tracy, *Hillbilly Nationalists, Urban Race Rebels and Black Power* (Brooklyn, NY: Melville House, 2011), 30–1.

22. See 'Freedom Budget for All Americans: A Summary' (January 1967): www.prrac.org/pdf/FreedomBudget.pdf

23. Kornbluh, *The Battle for Welfare Rights*, 45; Stanley Aronowitz, *From the Ashes of the Old: American Labor and America's Future* (New York: Basic Books, 2000), 74.

24. Branch, *At Canaan's Edge*, 671.

25. Ibid. 671–4; Mantler, *Power to the Poor*, 104–13.

26. See Michael Honey, *Going Down Jericho Road: The Memphis Strike, Martin Luther King's Last Campaign* (New York: Norton, 2008), 177–9, 365–7.

27. Only in the aftermath of King's death did the white power structure of Memphis accede to the demands of the AFSCME local.
28. Gordon Mantler makes this point in *Power to the Poor*, 198.
29. Branch, *At Canaan's Edge*, 297.
30. Ben W. Gilbert and the staff of the *Washington Post*, *Ten Blocks from the White House: Anatomy of the Washington Riots of 1968* (New York: Frederick A. Praeger, 1968), 151.
31. Hamilton and Hamilton, *The Dual Agenda*, 174.
32. Bobby Seale, *Seize the Time: The Story of the Black Panther Party and Huey P. Newton* (New York: Random House), 3–13, 35–43.
33. Huey P. Newton and David Hilliard, *The Huey P. Newton Reader* (New York: Seven Stories Press, 2002), 229.
34. Quoted in Donna Murch, *Living for the City: Migration, Education and the Rise of the Black Panther Party in Oakland, California* (Chapel Hill: University of North Carolina Press, 2010), 184.
35. Lewis, *Hardhats, Hippies and Hawks*, 137.
36. Edward S. Broderick, 'Understanding Dispute Resolution Techniques: A Key to Effective Federal Service Labor-Management Relations' (Defense Technical Information Center, US Army War College, 1982), 4.
37. Michael Goldfield, 'Public Sector Union Growth and Public Policy', *Policy Studies Journal* 18(2) (Winter 1989–90), 404.

The Memory of 1968

Stephen J. Whitfield

'There is a mysterious cycle in human events', Franklin D. Roosevelt told the delegates to the Democratic Party's convention in Philadelphia, when he accepted the nomination for a second term. 'To some generations much is given. Of other generations much is expected. This generation of Americans', he announced, 'has a rendezvous with destiny'.[1]

That was certainly true in 1936, when the economic and social markers of joblessness, misery and destitution remained widespread, when the end of the Great Depression could not be foreseen, and when the gathering storm abroad was far too ominous to be faced. But if any subsequent single year in American history betokened a rendezvous with destiny, scholars are most likely to move the nomination of 1968. Its signature was protest, but largely bereft of the idealism and hopefulness that characterized the marches at the dawn of that decade. By 1968 the schisms and collisions, fraught with terrors, were dramatic; the frisson that was widely felt could be ascribed to a society breaking down into spasms of violence and outrage; and the citizenry could oscillate in its forebodings between despair and the anxiety of a free-fall. That year of crisis made the satiric songwriter Tom Lehrer's claim (on his 1965 album, *That Was the Year that Was*) even more apt: his fellow Americans must be feeling 'like a Christian Scientist with appendicitis'.

In retrospect the pertinent episodes are easy to summon, starting in January. Perhaps nothing exposed the caesura that was opening up in public life more glaringly than when Dr Benjamin Spock, along with the chaplain of Yale University, William Sloane Coffin, Jr. and three others, were indicted on 5 January. Spock himself exuded respectability and integrity. He had won a gold medal in the Olympics in Paris in 1924, the year he cast his first vote for president – for Calvin Coolidge. The nation's most famous paediatrician, Spock wrote *The Common Sense Book of Baby and Child Care* (first edition, 1946), one of the biggest best-sellers in the history of publishing. That so utterly stalwart a figure, who wore three-piece suits to marches against the Vietnam War, could be indicted for conspiracy to abet draft resistance showed how wildly the time seemed out of joint. So eager was the Department of Justice to discredit the antiwar movement that the prosecution overplayed its hand. The major book devoted to the trial noted that 'when for the first time all five [defendants] met together – after the indictment, in attorney Leonard Boudin's living room, to discuss their common plight – Boudin says the first thing he felt he could do for these conspirators was to introduce them to each other.'[2] No wonder that the US government was losing credibility. Suspicions of its legitimacy were so easily aroused that a play like *MacBird!* could be staged at the Village Gate in New York City. Barbara Garson's parody of the dark Scottish tragedy, in which Shakespeare introduced the word 'assassination' into the English language, floated the implication that John F. Kennedy's successor had plotted to murder him. Performances of *MacBird!* closed on 21 January 1968, but not before raising doubt that so provocative an instance of political theatre could have been imaginable just a few years earlier.

On 30 January the Communists launched the Tet Offensive in Vietnam. Though they were beaten back in the following month and suffered a military defeat (and with a high cost in casualties), the Tet Offensive was a political shock that reverberated all the way to Washington, DC. The Vietcong had demonstrated a capacity to fight their way inside the compound of the US Embassy in Saigon, while also launching simultaneous attacks on over a hundred other South Vietnamese cities without giving US intelligence any inkling of so massive an operation. What 'dragged the United States into Vietnam' had not been motivated by anything palpable, by neither an appetite for territory nor for plunder. What was at stake, as Andrew Preston argues in Chapter 3, was 'excessive concern . . . with credibility'; the US pushed too far the resolve entailed in the doctrine of containment. That policy required revision in the wake of the Tet Offensive, which showed that the war had become a bloody, pointless stalemate. On 27 February, anchorman Walter Cronkite aired a CBS special, 'Report from Vietnam', which concluded that the war was unwinnable. President Lyndon Johnson supposedly reacted to the programme by remarking that, having lost Cronkite, he had lost the mandate necessary to continue the war. Yet no episode that year reveals more blatantly the chasm between collective memory and the historical record. No evidence exists that Johnson ever saw 'Report from Vietnam' (not even on tape), or that he ever made that remark about Cronkite (nor, if the president did so, to whom). After the telecast Johnson's views remained hawkish, and a tectonic shift in public opinion had already been detectable – even if CBS News had never sent Cronkite to visit Indochina for himself.[3]

The most talented and shrewdest occupant of the White House since Roosevelt placed his name on the ballot in New Hampshire. But in this first of the Democratic primaries, held on 12 March, Johnson barely scraped by, with 49 per cent of the vote. Close behind, with 42 per cent, was Eugene McCarthy, a little-known liberal Senator from Minnesota, of scant legislative accomplishment, who promised disengagement from Vietnam. He barely lost to a president seeking vindication for pushing through Congress such landmarks as the Civil Rights Act of 1964; the Voting Rights Act of 1965; an immigration law that ended discrimination on the basis of ancestry; Medicare and Medicaid; a garland of anti-poverty programmes; Head Start; and environmental reform. When Senator Robert F. Kennedy announced his candidacy on 16 March, Johnson realized that a humiliating loss in Wisconsin was imminent; and he bowed out two weeks later, throwing the race into turmoil, as events seemed to spiral out of control.

On April 4th, Martin Luther King, Jr. was assassinated in Memphis; and riots broke out in well over a hundred cities, including the nation's capital, where the fires spread as close as two blocks from the White House. Looting and arson were widespread. The magnitude of the damage to life and property exceeded any comparable episode of civil disturbance since the Civil War. But instead of white mobs rampaging through black neighbourhoods, the night King died, Daniel Matlin claims in Chapter 5, constituted 'the most widespread racial violence in US history'. The acknowledged tribune of the civil rights movement, the most obvious successor to Mohandas Gandhi in the creative application of nonviolent resistance, and the youngest winner in the twentieth century of the Nobel Peace Prize, King has become the most admired of the sixties figures associated with the pursuit of social justice. Streets throughout the nation are named for him, as is a federal holiday (the only one that does not honour a president).

But here collective memory is especially tricky. When alive King was a divisive and even a detested figure. J. Edgar Hoover, the director of the FBI, denounced him 'the most notorious liar in the country', whose campaigns against segregation endangered the peace. Hoover also secretly passed along evidence of communist influences as well as marital infidelity. In Hoover's spat with King, fully 50 per cent of Americans supported the FBI director; and only 16 per cent of the public supported King (of whom, it can be presumed, a considerable portion were black). After Spock in particular persuaded King to condemn the Vietnam War, he even split the civil rights movement itself. President Johnson skipped the funeral in Atlanta; so did the two living ex-presidents, Harry Truman and Dwight Eisenhower.[4] Not only rabid segregationists preferred to keep their distance, even posthumously, from the martyr for racial justice. The reaction to his assassination from a future president was notably devoid of grief. 'This great tragedy . . . began', Governor Ronald Reagan observed, 'when we began compromising with law and order, and people started choosing which laws they'd break'.[5]

The spring of 1968 also exposed generational fault-lines as never before, as though to confirm for the young the sense of disinheritance that troubadour Bob Dylan had lamented three years earlier: 'I got nothing, Ma, to live up to'. No wonder then that Nick Witham, in Chapter 4, detects so little conciliation, so few exercises in empathy across the generational divide, in the 'life writing' of the young rebels of the era. Yet their sense of betrayal should not obscure the importance of the novelty of what Doug Rossinow in Chapter 1 has emphasized, which was the criticism of 'mass consumerism' that the 'young radicals' advanced, as well as the connection that they established between 'political agitation' and the ideals of 'authenticity and direct action'. The interest of the New Left in forging alternative communities also distinguished it from its progressive predecessors. (The decision of Angela Davis to join the Communist Party in 1968 was a rare instance of overtly romantic attachment to the Old Left). Agitation was the hallmark of that year, energized by the deepening conflict in Vietnam. At Columbia University, which Eisenhower had served as president two decades earlier, a student strike lasting six weeks was punctuated by a police bust that netted over 700 arrests, after which traditional commencement exercises that May could barely be conducted. In Chapter 6, Stefan Bradley rightly highlights the iconic significance of the uprising there. Unrest could not be confined to the historically black universities, or to the great state universities, but had spread to the citadels of Ivy League privilege as well.

That spring Hollywood released *Wild in the Streets*, noteworthy for a plot that is feverish and demented. Rock musician Max Frost (Christopher Jones) deceives a US Senator (Hal Holbrook) who is seeking to attract the youth vote, and gets him to endorse a Constitutional amendment to lower the voting age to fourteen. Somehow the amendment passes both two-thirds of the Congress and three-quarters of the states, upon which Frost seizes power. He spikes drinking water with LSD and puts everyone over the age of thirty-five into re-education camps. A stoned member of Frost's entourage, played by Diane Varsi, explains to the US Congress that 'getting old is such a drag'; and at the end of the film, prepubescent kids threaten even teenagers with internment in re-education camps. *Wild in the Streets* hit a nerve, which is why Sharon Monteith sees this film (among others) as symptomatic of 1968. By September the anthem of Frost's band (Max Frost and the Troopers), reached number 22 on the nation's pop charts, as though 'The Shape of Things to Come' were somehow historically determined. Beyond even the evidently porous boundaries of satire, the movie magnified adult anxieties. The polarization based on the actuarial tables – the generation gap – thus piled onto the credibility gap, as the mendacity of the Johnson administration regarding the progress of the Vietnam War came to be known.

Nor was the priesthood immune from the rebellious imperative of 1968. In May, Father Daniel Berrigan, a Jesuit; his brother, Father Philip Berrigan, a member of the Josephite Fathers; and seven others burned 378 stolen draft files in a parking lot in Catonsville, Maryland (to light the fire the Catonsville Nine used napalm). This was 'divine disobedience'. When Daniel Berrigan was sentenced to three years in prison, for the destruction of government property, he fled, and went underground. For the first time in the history of the FBI, an agency heavily staffed with Roman Catholics, a priest made the list of the nation's Ten Most Wanted fugitives from justice. With a haircut that made him resemble an older, fifth Beatle, Berrigan would spend a quarter of his life between 1970 and 1995 in prison denims. Influenced by worker-priests in France and in Latin America, Daniel Berrigan embodied the international ethos of radical protest that constituted the sharpest contrast with a pro-war prelate like Francis Cardinal Spellman. In France itself the Fifth Republic nearly fell that May, a mere decade after the fall of the Fourth Republic. The student demonstrations in Paris probably represented the historic peak of utopian fantasies, recorded in graffiti like 'imagination to power'. In France the secular radical counterparts to the Berrigans were the Cohn-Bendit brothers, Daniel and Gabriel. A book that they published that year, *Obsolete Communism: The Left-Wing Alternative*, argues that 'the real meaning of revolution is not a change in management but a change in man', and that such a transformation should spring from 'joy' rather than 'sacrifice'.[6] Nothing better exemplified the belief that the heavy imperatives of the past could by force of will be busted wide open.

On June 5th, a Jordanian named Sirhan Sirhan fatally shot Robert Kennedy immediately after the celebration of his greatest primary victory, in California. Once again an assassin had altered the flow of events. Dead well before his time, frozen forever in youth, Kennedy has become a hero to posterity. But half a year before his death, pollsters learned that 50 per cent more Americans 'intensely disliked' him than disliked Lyndon Johnson.[7] With the Democratic Party in utter disarray, whoever would be securing the nomination later that summer in Chicago would in effect be drinking from a poisoned chalice. That would be Vice President Hubert H. Humphrey, who had not competed in any of his party's primaries, but enjoyed the support of the delegates-at-large and the bosses, including Mayor Richard J. Daley (who, a biography later revealed, happened to be privately opposed to the Vietnam War as early as 1966, and told Johnson so).[8] The convention held in his city on 26–29 August produced pandemonium, as the protesters intended. 'The spectacle both enacts and denounces', as Martin Halliwell writes in Chapter 7. One result of such political theatre was that the delegates met in the shadow of rampaging violence ('unrestrained and indiscriminate') by the police, according to the official study, *Rights in Conflict*, which was released in December. No one personified political theatre more flamboyantly than Abbie Hoffman or capitalized more adroitly on the publicity that the media could somehow not deny him. No other radical activist seemed as much at home in 1968, when 'the time had come to make outrage contagious'.[9]

That year, 16,889 Americans died in Vietnam – the highest number of any year of the war. It was hard to discern any plausible rationale for such sacrifice of life. The burden of fighting it was borne mostly by draftees; and the antiwar protests were increasingly scathing and unrestrained. 'The war was incredibly unpopular', historian Michael Kazin recalled, 'but the antiwar movement was also unpopular'.[10] The Republican nominee for the presidency, Richard Nixon, capitalized on both sets of attitudes, claiming rather vaguely to have devised a plan to end the war while also promising the restoration of 'law and order'. He won the popular vote by a razor-thin margin of only one-half of one per cent. Had Humphrey not run out of media money at the very end of the campaign that seemed to be gaining traction, Nixon might well have lost in 1968.

Though the antiwar protests make 1968 seem, in popular memory, the perihelion in the influence of the left, the presidential campaign itself revealed the resilience of the right, and thus constituted a harbinger of the succeeding decades of Thermidor. This too, as Elizabeth Tandy Shermer's Chapter 2 makes clear, is a lesson that historians need to draw from 1968 – and not merely because Arizona's Barry Goldwater had proved four years earlier to have been so feckless a messenger of the mantra of small government and of the seething anger at civil rights agitation. With his unabashed dedication to racial supremacy, George Wallace of the American Independence Party exerted special appeal to whites in one region, and indeed carried five Southern states (his own Alabama, plus Arkansas, Georgia, Louisiana and Mississippi), giving him forty-five votes in the Electoral College. Wallace won almost 10 million popular votes (about 13 per cent of the total). He might have done even better had his running mate, General Curtis LeMay, in his first press conference, not blundered into condemning the 'phobia about nuclear weapons . . . I think there are many times when it would be most efficient to use nuclear weapons'.[11] Wallace's effort to attract support from white working-class ethnics in the North and Midwest managed to cut into the constituencies of both of his opponents. A third of the members of the AFL–CIO favoured Wallace, which helps explain why Humphrey became the first Democratic Party nominee in six decades to fail to win over a majority of white voters.[12] (In no subsequent election did whites award most of their votes to Democratic Party candidates for the Presidency.)

Race was the inescapable issue in the public culture of 1968, and could never be far from the surface. How far the white majority was willing to go to eliminate the discrimination practised against the black minority remained an open question, and how bigotry might be reduced offered no obvious solution. On 29 February, the Kerner Commission (officially known as the President's Advisory Commission on Civil Disorders) released its report on race relations, and famously warned that 'our nation is moving toward two societies, one black, one white – separate and unequal'. When journalist Garry Wills discovered that urban police forces were 'arming for Armageddon', and some black militants 'recognize openly the risk of genocide', he feared that the two sides 'are on a collision course'.[13] What was also obvious that year was the deepening fury among black Americans with the persistence of white racism. The conspicuous gap between the promises of equality and the experience of injustice was bound to produce explosions of outrage. Two black psychiatrists, William Grier and Price M. Cobbs, offered their own analysis in a best-seller entitled *Black Rage*. (Grier had trained as a psychiatrist in Topeka, Kansas, at the famed Menninger Clinic, which had declined a request from the NAACP to show the psychic harm of segregation, in the case that would be indelibly known as *Brown vs. Board of Education of Topeka*). The co-authors located among their patients what they called 'cultural paranoia', that is, so profound a suspicion of their environment – the dominant institutions and encounters with white America – that the pressure of such conditions could result in paranoid schizophrenia. Underneath the deference that slaves and their descendants adopted for the sake of survival, Grier and Cobbs claimed, was a seething anger. 'As a sapling bent low stores energy for a violent backswing', they wrote, 'blacks bent double by oppression have stored energy which will be released in the form of rage – black rage, apocalyptic and final.'[14]

This revelation can be contrasted with *The Mark of Oppression*, a major psychoanalytic study that appeared exactly two decades earlier. Its authors, Abram Kardiner and Lionel Ovesey, were both psychiatrists; they were also white. They emphasized the price that their black subjects paid for internalizing their frustration at the white hostility and contempt that limited their lives. Spasmodic release in the form of urban riots had erupted in the 1940s (in Harlem and in Detroit in particular); but *The Mark of Oppression* had shown the effectiveness with which aggression could be inhibited, and a low self-image maintained. A pendant to *Black Rage* that appeared in 1968 and that testified most powerfully to the extremities of the black experience was *Soul on Ice*, which Eldridge Cleaver, a self-confessed rapist and thief, had written behind bars. Along with *The Autobiography of Malcolm X*, which had been posthumously published three years earlier, the eloquent rage that Cleaver recorded led one literary critic, Richard Gilman of the *New Republic*, to conclude that the most authentic voices of black America could not be assessed according to the liberal and universal standards applied to other books. Evaluation of a testament like *Soul on Ice* had to be suspended. That spring Gilman vowed to continue 'judging and elucidating novels and plays and poetry by Negroes according to what general powers I possess, but the kind of *Negro writing* I have been talking about, the act of creation of the self in the face of that self's historic denial by our society, seems to me to be at this point beyond my right to intrude on'. A book like *Soul on Ice*, Gilman explained, comes from such unfathomable depths of alienation and alterity that 'white critics have not the right to make judgments'.[15] But blacks could make judgments as native sons. At the victors' platforms at the Olympics in October in Mexico City, Tommie Smith and John Carlos, both sprinters from San Jose State University, exhibited their own estrangement from the nation they represented on the track by bowing their heads and by raising black-gloved fists. Resistance and repudiation were the indelible signature of the sixties, and especially of 1968, the election year when Cleaver even ran for the presidency on the ticket of the Peace and Freedom Party.

The patriotism that stemmed from a faith in the healing processes of *e pluribus unum* was to be even more severely tested in the succeeding months, however. Still to come, in 1969 and 1970, were the trial of the Chicago Seven (plus Black Panther Bobby Seale) for conspiring to cross state lines to foment rioting at the Democratic National Convention; the revelation of the My Lai massacre, in which about 400 unarmed Vietnamese civilians were slaughtered on 16 March 1968; the free music festival in Altamont, California, which took two lives; the US invasion of Cambodia; the murder at Kent State University by National Guardsmen of four unarmed students protesting the Vietnam War; and the bombing of a research centre in Madison, Wisconsin. These events surely had their antecedents in the chaos of 1968. History does not occur ex nihilo.

What 1968 left unresolved were two simultaneous revolutions that Americans instigated or opposed (or even faced with ambivalence). Both exalted the ideal of equality. One revolution was racial, and Stephen Tuck's thesis in Chapter 9 – that civil rights activism proliferated rather than collapsed in the decade or so after 1968 – can be read as validation of Tocqueville's celebrated discovery of the dynamic power of America's voluntary associations to further egalitarian visions. The fight for racial equality spilled over into other struggles, such as the National Welfare Rights Organization, and served as a model, according to Penny Lewis in Chapter 12, for the grape boycott that the United Farm Workers organized in 1968. Race and class could not be easily or fully disentangled. The other revolution was becoming increasingly urgent and prominent, which was sexual. The 7 September challenge to the Miss America pageant in Atlantic City, Anne Valk demonstrates in Chapter 11, inaugurated as 'guerrilla theatre' the militancy of modern feminism, which has probably transformed more than any other movement operating in 1968 the very texture of American life. The struggle for gay rights did not quite flourish in 1968. The Stonewall riot that is commonly seen as the counterpart to, say, the Montgomery bus boycott occurred in 1969; and Simon Hall shows in Chapter 10 the extent to which for gay men and for lesbians 'the spirit of '68' characterizes the decade of the 1970s. The struggle to realize the vision of equality is integral to the politics of the succeeding half-century, and to the memory of the inauguration of that effort in the sixties. That double revolution – that rendezvous with destiny – can be said with some assurance to continue to haunt the nation.

The assorted shocks of 1968 also threatened to undermine the optimism that has been widely grasped as very deeply in the American grain. After 1968 the traditional faith in a benign and better future could not be so easily sustained. On the contrary, the awareness that obstacles cannot always be overcome, that suffering may have to be endured rather than remedied, and that some conflicts are too perdurable to be resolved are understood to be out of character – the national character.

In the era immediately after the Great Depression and World War II, but before 1968, the can-do spirit of the republic seemed intact. After visiting the United States in 1946, Albert Camus observed that 'in this country . . . *everything* is done to prove that life isn't tragic'.[16] Four years later, when Warner Bros. adapted Tennessee Williams's *The Glass Menagerie* to the screen, the pain of loneliness is overcome at the end because Laura Wingfield, luckily enough, will be welcoming a second 'gentleman caller'. In 1951, Columbia Pictures wanted to add a short documentary to *Death of a Salesman*, immediately after the scene of Willy Loman's funeral, in praise of selling as a career. (Arthur Miller's objection was sustained.) In 1958, shortly before the dawn of the decade of coming apart, the independent producer Dore Schary distorted the ending of Nathanael West's novel *Miss Lonelyhearts* by releasing the protagonist, a newspaper columnist (and Christ figure), from the fate of suffering for others. That revision provoked an acerbic movie critic to note how supremely American was the preference for 'an uncrucified Christ'.[17] The harrowing memory of 1968 would rob many Americans of the sense that their country might be exempt from the irreconcilable conflicts common to the historical experience of others, and would make the shallow belief in inevitably happy endings insulting.

Notes

1. 'Address of Acceptance of the Nomination for a Second Term', in Basil Rauch(ed.), *The Roosevelt Reader: Selected Speeches, Messages, Press Conferences and Letters of Franklin D. Roosevelt* (New York: Rinehart, 1957), 151.
2. Jessica Mitford, *The Trial of Dr. Spock, the Rev. William Sloane Coffin, Jr., Michael Ferber, Mitchell Goodman, and Marcus Raskin* (New York: Random House, 1970), 5.
3. David Halberstam, *The Powers That Be* (New York: Knopf, 1979), 508–10, 511–14; Louis Menand, 'Seeing It Now', *New Yorker* 88 (9 July 2012), 88–92.
4. Beverly Gage, 'The Real J. Edgar', *Nation* 293(25) (19 December 2011), 6.
5. Quoted in Rick Perlstein, *Nixonland: The Rise of a President and the Fracturing of America* (New York: Scribner, 2008), 257.
6. Daniel Cohn-Bendit and Gabriel Cohn-Bendit, *Obsolete Communism: The Left-Wing Alternative*, trans. Arnold Pomerans (New York: McGraw-Hill, 1968), 112.
7. Perlstein, *Nixonland*, 221.
8. Adam Cohen and Elizabeth Taylor, *American Pharaoh: Mayor Richard J. Daley* (Boston: Little, Brown, 2000), 445–6.
9. Abbie Hoffman, *Soon to be a Major Motion Picture* (New York: Putnam, 1980), 99.
10. Quoted in Clara Bingham, *Witness to the Revolution: Radicals, Resisters, Vets, Hippies, and the Year America Lost Its Mind and Found Its Soul* (New York: Random House, 2016), 408.
11. Quoted in Perlstein, *Nixonland*, 348.
12. Perlstein, *Nixonland*, 341.
13. Quoted in Alexander Bloom and Wini Breines (eds), *Takin' It to the Streets: A Sixties Reader* (New York: Oxford University Press, 1995), 426; Garry Wills, *The Second Civil War: Arming for Armageddon* (New York: Signet, 1968), 19.
14. Lawrence J. Friedman, *Menninger: The Family and the Clinic* (New York: Knopf, 1990), 181; William Grier and Price M. Cobbs, *Black Rage* (New York: Basic Books, 1968), 210.
15. Richard Gilman, *The Confusion of Realms* (New York: Random House, 1969), 3–21.
16. Albert Camus, *American Journals*, trans. Hugh Levick (New York: Paragon House, 1987), 42–3.
17. Dwight Macdonald, *Discriminations: Essays and Afterthoughts, 1938–1974* (New York: Viking, 1974), 256–61.

INDEX